D1428890

EMPIRE ON THE ENGLISH STAGE
1660–1714

Contesting the current consensus that Restoration and early eighteenth-century drama referred almost exclusively to domestic social and political issues, *Empire on the English Stage, 1660–1714* shows that the theatre was a crucial location for debates over England's contemporaneous colonial expansion. The book provides a comprehensive account of colonialism, national identity and the representation of race and ethnicity on stage. Joining current historical discussions of the development of British imperial ideology, Bridget Orr argues that dramatic texts and production provide a rich and unexamined archive in which the issues attendant on the emergence of the First Empire figure largely. Her account not only sheds new light on plays by Dryden, Orrery, Behn, Wycherley and Southerne but redirects attention to popular but now marginal texts by Settle, Sedley, Dennis and Charles Shadwell. Attention to the imperial themes of these dramatists decisively redraws the map of Restoration and early eighteenth-century drama.

Bridget Orr is Assistant Professor at the Department of English, Fordham University. She has published numerous articles on Restoration, eighteenth-century and post-colonial literature and culture. She is the editor of a special Pacific issue of *The Eighteenth Century: Theory and Interpretation* (1997) and the co-editor, with Jonathan Lamb and Alex Calder, of *Voyages and Beaches: Pacific Encounters, 1760–1840* (1999).

"A large river with ships" from *The Empress of Morocco*. Reproduced by permission of Cambridge University Library.

EMPIRE ON THE ENGLISH STAGE 1660–1714

BRIDGET ORR

Assistant Professor, Fordham University, New York

PUBLISHED BY THE PRESS SYNDICATE OF THE UNIVERSITY OF CAMBRIDGE
The Pitt Building, Trumpington Street, Cambridge, United Kingdom

CAMBRIDGE UNIVERSITY PRESS
The Edinburgh Building, Cambridge CB2 2RU, UK
40 West 20th Street, New York NY 10011-4211, USA
10 Stamford Road, Oakleigh, VIC 3166, Australia
Ruiz de Alarcón 13, 28014 Madrid, Spain
Dock House, The Waterfront, Cape Town 8001, South Africa

http://www.cambridge.org

© Bridget Orr 2001

This book is in copyright. Subject to statutory exception
and to the provisions of relevant collective licensing agreements,
no reproduction of any part may take place without
the written permission of Cambridge University Press.

First published 2001

Printed in the United Kingdom at the University Press, Cambridge

Typeface Baskerville 11/12.5 pt.   *System* LATEX 2$_\varepsilon$ [TB]

A catalogue record for this book is available from the British Library.

Library of Congress Cataloguing in Publication data
Orr, Bridget.
Empire on the English stage, 1660–1714 / Bridget Orr.
p.   cm.
Includes bibliographical references (p. 323) and index.
ISBN 0 521 77350 4
1. English drama – Restoration, 1660–1700 – History and criticism.   2. English
drama – 18th century – History and criticism.   3. Imperialism in literature.
4. Ethnicity in literature.   5. Colonies in literature.   6. Race in literature.   I. Title.
PR698.145 075   2001
822′.409358 – dc21   00 065091

ISBN 0 521 77350 4 hardback

To Elizabeth and Gordon

Illustrations

Acknowledgments

Numerous institutions provided the resources necessary to complete this project. The University of Auckland granted me a leave of absence and Princeton University provided a Visiting Fellowship in 1995–96. An Old Gold Fellowship from the University of Iowa allowed for further research, and Fordham University supported the final stages of research. The manuscript was completed under the hospitable auspices of the Centre for Cross-Cultural Studies and the Humanities Research Centre at the Australian National University in Canberra, whose respective directors, Professors Nicholas Thomas and Ian McCalman, I would like to thank.

Librarians in the Rare Books Rooms of the Cambridge University Library, in the Devonshire Collections at Chatsworth, in the Firestone Library at Princeton University and in the British Library have all been exceptionally helpful. I would also like to thank the staff of the Alexander Turnbull Library in Wellington, in the National Library of New Zealand.

Josie Dixon, at Cambridge University Press, guided the publication process from its inception. I am most grateful to Victoria Cooper for bringing the book through its last stages.

My teachers at Cornell, notably Laura Brown, Rick Bogel and Harry Shaw, gave me the means to envisage this project. Earl Miner, Nigel Leask, Michael Neill, Bob Markley, Lennie Davis, Simon During, Frank Boyle, Claude Rawson, Claudia Johnson, Richard Eaves, Roger Benjamin, Bridget McPhail, Peter Lake and Helene Furjan offered advice, encouragement and practical help. My readers at Cambridge were both insightful and corrective but most importantly, perhaps, encouraging.

In the most loving way possible, my husband Jonathan Lamb made me write this book. For their aroha I would like to thank Jane

Wild, Phillip Clarke and Frances Walsh; Lynn Enterline and Melissa Deem; Betty Pforzheimer; Helen Weinstein, Hugh Stevens, Louise Gibbs, Paul McHugh and Mel Humphreys.

This book is dedicated to my parents, Gordon and Elizabeth, whose joint passion for social justice and literature has, I hope, informed this work.

Note on the Text

I1 England until 1752 the legal year began on 25 March, so the year 1673 comprised what we would now call 25 March 1673 to 24 March 1674. In this volume, however, years are numbered according to the modern system.

The Gregorian calendar was introduced in 1582, but the Julian calendar remained in use in England until 1752. The Gregorian (New Style) calendar was eleven days ahead of the Julian (Old Style) calendar 1601 to 1699 and twelve days ahead from 1700 to 1752. In this volume, Old Style dates are used.

CHAPTER 1

New Habits on the Stage

REHEARSING CULTURES?

On October 18, 1666, John Evelyn approvingly recorded the adoption of a new fashion at the Carolean court:

18 To Lond: Star-Chamber: thence to Court, it being the first time of his Majesties putting himselfe solemnly into the Eastern fashion of Vest, changing doublet, stiff Collar, bands and Cloake etc: into a comely Vest, after the Persian mode with girdle or shash, and Shoe strings and Garters, into bouckles, of which some were set with precious stones, resolving never to alter it, and to leave the French mode, which had hitherto obtained to our greate expense and reproch: upon which divers Courtiers and Gent: gave his Ma[jesty] gold, by way of Wager, that he would not persist in this resolution: I had some time before indeede presented an Invectique against that unconstancy, and our so much affecting the french fashion, to his Majestie in which [I] tooke occasion to describe the Comelinesse and usefullnesse of the Persian clothing in the very same manner, his Majestie clad himselfe; This Pamphlet I intituled *Tyrannus* or the mode, and gave it his Majestie to reade; I do not impute the change which soone happn'd to this discourse, but it was an identitie, that I could not but take notice of: This night was acted my Lord Brahals Tragedy cal'd *Mustapha* before their Majesties etc: at Court.[1]

The pamphlet to which Evelyn refers was published in 1661 and seems likely to have less to do with Charles II's decision to put on "the Eastern fashion of Vest" than the concurrent staging of the spectacular Oriental drama, Orrery's *Mustapha* (1665), to which he also alludes. Indeed, given the valorization of native costume in "Tyrannus", which signifies political independence, and the stigmatizing of the slavish adoption of foreign fashions, the diarist's self-satisfaction at seeing the King dressed in Persian garb is somewhat surprising: "'Tis not a triviall Remark (which I have somewhere met with) that when a nation is able to impose, and give laws to

1

the habits of another (as the late *Tartars* in China) it has (like
that of Language) prov'd a Fore-runner to the spreading of their
Conquests there."[2] Nathaniel Lee will make the point several years
later in *The Rival Queens* (1677), in a scene in which Alexander's
loyal commander Clytus refuses to give up his Macedonian dress
to wear clothing he sees as emblematic of Eastern decadence:

> Away, I will not wear these Persian robes;
> Nor ought the King be angry for the reverence
> I owe my country. Sacred are her customs,
> Which honest Clytus shall preserve to death.
> O let me rot in *Macedonian* rags
> Rather than shine in fashions of the East.[3]

Although Evelyn's hostility to the assumption of fashions derived
from the absolute, Catholic court of Louis XIV is not surprising,
this enthusiasm for the adoption of costume from the infidel and
despotic Persians seems to require explanation.

Evelyn's response can be accounted for quite simply by tradition; as S. C. Chew demonstrated in *The Crescent and the Rose*, the
courtly practice of wearing Eastern dress both informally, and in
the performance of pageants, processions, masques and even mock
sea-battles, had been in place since the middle of the sixteenth
century.[4] Attempting to interpret other such "rehearsals" of exotic cultures in the early modern period, Steven Mullaney has
suggested that the performance of aspects of alien cultures may
be accounted for by the impulse to establish a stronger sense of
European selfhood against a clearly defined cultural other.[5] In this
schema, rather than comparing and assimilating other "nations"
through the discovery of similitudes, as was the practice in previous periods, the temporary adoption of alien ways on stage or
in masques and pageants underlined the irreducible difference
of exotics. European culture extended its boundaries by first con-
suming and then reforming and/or expelling the other through
representation.

Mullaney's characterization of dramatic performances as refor-
matory projects intended to strengthen national identity is suggestive in the context of Restoration drama. Many of the serious plays
of the last half of the seventeenth century, the heroic drama especially, narrativized episodes from imperial history, whether that
of the Romans, the Ottomans, the Spanish or the Portuguese. The

comedy of the period was much more narrowly focused on London life but even in the comedy, a concern with the definition of a civil, national identity clearly separable from the French in particular, is manifest. Those comic or tragi-comic plays which thematize life abroad in the colonies, in the Indies, among pirates and in utopias satirize the novel social types produced by colonial expansion and settlement.

This pervasive concern with the staging of cultural contact and conflict is unsurprising given the huge expansion of colonial activity in this period but it has only rarely been addressed by literary historians, although the rise of new historicism in Renaissance studies has rendered such interpretations common in the preceding period. Critics have traditionally read through the exoticism of the Restoration heroic drama, to locate a local political meaning allegorized. In the fullest recent study of the Carolean heroic play, Nancy Klein Maguire argues that the tragi-comedies produced by Davenant, Orrery and Dryden between 1658 and 1671 repetitively enacted a drama of rebellion against, usurpation of and restoration of royal power in an attempt to negotiate and perhaps exorcise the traumas of recent political history.[6] As earlier critics have noted, however, these plays are about "empire" as well as sovereignty and subjecthood. Anne Barbeau argued in 1970 that Dryden's heroic plays encoded a theory of history which celebrated the gradual triumph of Christianity, an account developed by John Loftis who suggested that the representations of conflicts between Europeans and American Indians and Moors illustrated "the historical process as conceived to embody a widening territorial expansion of Christendom."[7] More recently, David Kramer has analysed Dryden's construction of an "imperial" literary persona in the context of the Restoration literary and military rivalry with France.[8] None of these critics, however, attempted to relate their analysis of the imperial theme in the heroic drama to Restoration debates over empire, nor extended their account beyond Dryden's texts to encompass the genre as a whole. Yet much of the heroic plays' significance in the two decades of the genre's emergence turns on its role in representing theatrically those processes of imperial expansion and decline, the *translatio imperii* and the clash between Christian European and pagan non-European societies which were central topics in political as well as cultural debate in this period. The genre's utility in negotiating issues of empire is equally apparent in the decades following the Glorious Revolution, when the mode, never fully moribund, was revived. In heroic plays of the 1690s and the early 1700s, female dramatists used the genre to figure the enslavement of women in exotic despotisms, Tory playwrights criticized an overtly mercantilist colonial state and Dennis represented a specifically Whig theory of empire.

It is less surprising that commentary on the comic drama has been unconcerned with questions of national identity and colonialism, given the plays' pervasive focus on local social and sexual conflict. Yet even in the most metropolitan of comedies, such as *The Man of Mode*, the definition of national as well as class-based manners is at stake. The colonies themselves are occasionally the site of comic representation, as in *The Widdow Ranter* (1689); emergent types such as the nabob make their appearance (in *Sir Courtly Nice* [1685]) and emigration and piracy serve as subjects in *Cuckolds-Haven* (1685) and *A Commonwealth of Women* (1686). Wycherley's *The Plain Dealer* has a nautical protagonist whose excoriating analysis of city manners uses the Indies as a benchmark of savagery, in a comparison by which London gains nothing; and in the comic-operatic redaction of Shakespeare's *The Tempest*, serious issues of sovereignty and settlement and the possibility of European degeneration into savagery in new plantations are canvassed.

It is, however, in the serious drama that issues of empire are most evident. Historical scholarship which can help explain this imperial dimension of the plays has emerged only recently. The current literary historical emphasis on the heroic plays' allegorization of domestic politics reflects the dominant trends of historical research, which has stressed that in the years following the Restoration, the political classes of England were preoccupied with local and, at most, national concerns rather than questions of foreign policy.[9] Recent scholarship has begun to modify this view considerably. Developing a theme explored earlier by John Miller,[10] Jonathan Scott has argued that the interconnected anxieties over popery and arbitrary government which fueled the Exclusion Crisis and the Glorious Revolution reflected English awareness that Protestantism was under threat all across Europe during the latter half of the seventeenth century.[11] In his study of London politics from 1688 to 1715, Gary De Krey identifies a split along the emergent Whig/Tory axis within the mercantile community from the late 1670s on, as dissatisfaction grew among those debarred from participation in the lucrative commerce with the Levant, Russia, Africa and the East Indies, by the monopolistic and restrictive companies authorized by the Crown, which jealously guarded its prerogative in regulating trade. In the 1690s, he notes, "the transformation of the City's trading and financial institutions . . . signalled the rise of a new Whig mercantile and financial oligarchy," much resented by City Tories and the landed interest.[12] More generally, Paul Seaward suggests that, although the English were consumed by domestic concerns in 1660, Cromwellian military successes had greatly increased national confidence in foreign affairs and that, over time, European politics were recognized as central to events at home.[13]

The strongest challenge to the previous consensus has come, however, from Steven Pincus, who has argued that the period 1650–68 saw the ideological changes in England which allowed for the transformations in the state necessary for an imperial power after 1688, detailed by John Brewer in *The Sinews of Power* (1989).[14] Arguing that while the first Dutch War was driven by the Rump's disgust at the perceived backsliding of their once idealized republican co-religionists, and a strongly Providentialist conviction of their own rectitude, Pincus suggests the second conflict saw a transformation in the discourse of patriotism, as religious rhetoric was replaced by a more secular conception of the national interest which included, but was certainly not entirely defined by, trade. During these years, Pincus demonstrates, the English came to believe that "they were defending their religious and political liberties against a universal monarch."[15] The usual distinction between foreign and domestic concerns, he argues, has obscured the extent to which the English, both elite and populace, understood their own polity in a European, as much as a local, context. When they went to war with the Dutch or the French, therefore, they were not simply concerned with narrow commercial advantage (as economic and diplomatic historians have suggested) but with their proper and traditional role in preventing universal monarchy. Along with the transformation in notions of the national interest, the concept of universal monarchy was itself undergoing revision in a period which saw maritime and commercial power challenge traditional assumptions about the territorial and institutional bases of imperial authority.

Whether the focus is on the role of internal or external competition over foreign and colonial trade; or on the increasing anxiety over the perceived threat of expansionist Catholic absolutism (to which I would be inclined to add the fears attendant on a resurgent Ottoman empire, finally brought to terms only in 1699[16]), recent historical work placing issues of colonial expansion and empire squarely at the centre of Restoration political discourse has important implications for the literary historical interpretation of this period.[17] With the exception of Michael McKeon's analysis of *Annus Mirabilis* in terms attentive to its imbrication in Anglo-Dutch colonial rivalry, Thale's and Kramer's accounts of the patriotic dimension of Dryden's *Essay of Dramatick Poesie* and the considerable recent literature on Aphra Behn's *Oroonoko* and *The Widdow Ranter*, very little attention has been directed to the nationalist and colonialist dimensions of literary culture in the Restoration.[18] Yet discussion over English poetry from Dryden through Rymer to Dennis is conducted with precisely that competitive and nationalist awareness of a European context which Pincus emphasizes also informed political debate: the concern over the *translatio imperii* was matched by an equally acute interest in the *translatio studii.* Poetic and political power, politeness and greatness, were regarded as interdependent. The most famous example is doubtless what Thale has described as Dryden's "patriotic frame" for the *Essay of Dramatick Poesie* in which an argument over the superiority of French or English drama is conducted on "that memorable day, in the first Summer of the late War, when our Navy ingag'd the *Dutch*: a Day wherein the two most mighty and best-appointed Fleets which any age had ever seen, disputed the command of the greater half of the Globe, the commerce of Nations, and the riches of the Universe."[19] The linkage of poetry and inter-state rivalry is persistent, with Dennis arguing some thirty-five years later in the *Epistle* dedicating his *Advancement and Reformation of Modern Poetry* to the Earl of Mulgrave in 1701, that the cultivation of criticism and the "Poeticall art" in France in the seventeenth century was "very instrumental in . . . raising the esteem of their Nation to that degree, that it naturally prepar'd the Way for their Intrigues of State, and facilitated the Execution of their vast Designs."[20] As an "encourager of Arts, and a great States-man," he suggests that Mulgrave "knows that the bare Endeavour to advance an Art among us, is an Effort to augment the Learning, and consequently the Reputation, and consequently the Power, of a Great People" (1,207). It is no accident that Dryden's invocation in the *Essay* of that peculiarly English form of military power, the navy, recurs in later major discussions of British literary superiority. In Rymer's "Short View of Tragedy" (1692), the critic celebrates Waller's "To the King, on his Navy" (1632) as evidence of his contention that "Since the decay of the Roman Empire this Island, peradventure has been more fortunate in matters of Poetry, than any of our Neighbours."[21] Just as Waller's verses suggest that the "Navy Royal might well give (the King) pre-eminence in power, above *Achilles*" (127), Rymer claims that Waller's "Poetry distinguish'd him from all his contemporaries, both in *England* and in other Nations; And from all before him upwards to *Horace* and *Virgil*" (127). When Dennis picks up the citation of Waller in the third dialogue of *The Impartial Critick,* his 1693 response to Rymer, the choice of poem recalls (in a complimentary fashion) the naval frame of Dryden's *Essay.* It also underlines, however, the importance of Waller's role as celebrant of English naval power, not just in the "Verses on the Fleet" and the "Instructions to a Painter" but in "Of a War with Spain, and a Fight at Sea" and the three poems written to celebrate the defeat of the Turks in the 1680s.

The navy's prominence in literary debate reflects the crucial role of the fleet in Restoration economic, military and political affairs (as well as the dislike for armies documented by Lois Schwoerer).[22] By 1660, Spanish ambitions to be "Masters of the Universe," in the period's resonant phrase, were widely regarded as dead. "The vast increase in power by land and sea which other nations have made upon them since Queen Elizabeth's time," wrote the English Ambassador to Spain Sir Richard Fanshawe in 1662, "hath so altered the balance that Spain must no more pretend to universal monarchy."[23] In English analyses, the defeat of the Armada (significantly, of course, a failure at sea) symbolized the failure of an empire which had neglected to cultivate the population, the commerce, the industry and the agriculture necessary to maintain a powerful state. The control of trade and power at sea was now understood to be crucial to aspirants to imperial power: "To pretend to *Universal Monarchy* without *Fleets* was long looked on as a Political *Chymaera*" argued John Evelyn in his 1674 account of *Navigation and Commerce.*[24] English speculation about the new aspirants to empire centered first on the Dutch, possessors of a formidable navy and colonial power in the East Indies, and, increasingly, on the French. Suspicion of the aggressively Catholic and absolute Louis XIV was fostered by his energy and ambition but assumed particular relevance in England as Charles' predilection for Gallic culture, mistresses, funding and alliance became obvious.

The English were direct rivals of the Dutch in terms of trade and sea-power but the most frequent articulation of their position within the European theatre was a claim that they held the balance of power, rather than a direct expression of ambition for empire. As Charles Davenant put it in 1701, "For many years we have pretended to hold the Ballance of Europe and the Body of the People will neither think it Consistent with our Honour nor our Safety to quit that Post."[25] David Armitage's account of a specifically republican ideology of empire, developed under Cromwell but resurgent at various points through the eighteenth century, is equally emphatic in disavowing claims to the absolute power implied in the term universal monarchy, or "imperium." Armitage argues that the Commonwealth ideologues of empire drew on the Roman notion of *patrocinium*, which implied a federation of autonomous states rather than a single political unit with a centralized government.[26] The notion of confederation was also attractive to Andrew Fletcher, Scottish patriot and neo-Machiavellian whose *Account of a Conversation* of 1703, written in the shadow of Williamite ambition to a universal monarchy of trade, argues for the value of a Europe in which states in geographical proximity and sharing a common language could be grouped together after the fashion of the Achaian League.[27]

The frequent English disavowal of claims to empire reflected the dawning suspicion that imperial states were bound, inexorably, to a process of expansion followed just as inexorably by decline; that they were despotic and, in all previous forms, hostile to commerce, the new engine of social and political change. The disavowal, however, was as factitious, ultimately, as Sir John Seeley's claim that the British Empire was acquired in a fit of absence of mind. The Republican tradition provided an alternative model to universal monarchy through its invocation of *patrocinium* but all the later Stuarts showed considerable enthusiasm in pursuing dominion over the seas. Further, Charles and James showed no signs of wanting to loosen control over their North American plantation colonies or the trading companies and their factories in the Levant, Africa and the East Indies and, however great popular revulsion from France became, Louis XIV's centralized model of national and colonial control was alluring to English monarchs. Assessments of

Charles's and James's foreign policy are disputed but tend to suggest they failed to maintain the authority commanded by Cromwell on the European stage, whether through ineptitude or preoccupation with domestic affairs.[28] It is incontrovertible, however, that, following the passing of the Navigation Acts, foreign and colonial trade grew enormously, with customs revenues contributing substantially to the Crown's relative fiscal well-being in the 1680s and laying the foundations for the extended period of warfare after 1688.[29] James had a particular interest in the navy and was a substantial investor in the Royal African Company and both brothers pursued policies of "royalization and centralization" in the American colonies in the 1680s.[30]

Jealous of their prerogative in foreign and colonial affairs, both Charles and James Stuart maintained a strong grasp over policy in this area.[31] The visions of expansion presented in the heroic plays, in particular, presumably appealed to the monarchy insofar as they focused on precisely those foreign and colonial arenas in which their authority was less open to local dispute.[32] The dramatists whom they patronized are also notable for their involvement in colonial policy: Orrery, for example, who wrote so many of the early, successful examples of the genre at Charles's behest, was "The Man of Munster," the dominant magnate of Northern Ireland. *Altemera* (1661), sometimes described as the first heroic play, had its initial production in Dublin. William Davenant, who was known for his poem *Madagascar*, dedicated to the Lord High Admiral Prince Rupert, later wrote propagandistic celebrations of English expansionism for Cromwell as well as *The Siege of Rhodes*, and was on his way to take up the Governorship of Maryland when he was halted by Parliamentary troops in 1642. Dryden had no personal experience in colonial administration but his Yorkist affiliations informed his poetic as well as dramatic praise of English naval power in *Astraea Redux*, *Annus Mirabilis* and the *Essay of Dramatick Poesie*. Aphra Behn famously claimed the authority of her own experience in Surinam as the basis for her novella *Oroonoko*, successfully dramatized by Southerne.

There was also, as noted above, considerable ambivalence about aspirations to empire, a skepticism more apparent before 1688 in figures like Shadwell than enthusiastic royalists like Orrery. Consistently scornful of colonial adventuring conceived of primarily as commercial, and degenerationist in his assumptions, as the

Stuart regimes ran deeper into crisis, Dryden gradually abandoned the idealized representation of empire as Christian expansionism. After 1688, dramatists with past or continuing Tory affiliations, such as Behn and Southerne, criticized the emergent empire of trade, even as Rowe and Dennis hymned William's achievements as Protestant Liberator. Literary debates play out the contradictions between the appetite for a cultural dominance understood to be the accompaniment of great power and the assertion of liberty as the central political and hence cultural characteristic of the English. As Tim Harris has shown, a concern for "liberty" was claimed by all sides in the political conflicts of Charles's reign and it continued to be a disputed category after the Glorious Revolution.[33] The nature and status of the serious drama, whose traditional role was that of staging and glorifying the nation's past, provided a significant context for this continuing dispute over liberty as well as the increasingly important issue of the relation between liberty and greatness.[34]

My account of relations between empire and the stage in the Restoration thus begins with a discussion of literary debates over the drama, from 1660 to 1714, followed by an account of the imperial ambition encoded in authorial personae, generic assumptions and the thematics of the heroic plays in particular. A crucial aspect of their effect was their spectacular scenic presentation of exotic locales, custom and costume and the tension created between the plays' heroic elevation and the violence and historical "irregularity" they display. In a chapter devoted to representations of Spanish and Portuguese empire, I examine the process by which the English elites witnessed heightened but critical accounts of the foremost European empire, as dramatists presented the Peninsular states in expansion, corruption and decline. In chapters on Levant and Asian plays, I discuss the representation of Oriental, especially Ottoman, empire, the other main contemporary instance of aspiration to universal monarchy. The heroic plays deploy an emergent Orientalist discourse of despotism, irreligion and sexual license, against which England could be defined as civil politically, religiously and sexually. In the utopian and Amazonian plays of the period, the questioning of conventional European assumptions about the ordering of the gender and political order, provoked by the discovery of new societies, is analyzed. In a chapter on comic and tragi-comic representations of metropolitan manners, colonies, colonials and emigration, I examine the establishment of a sense of a specifically English notion of genteel manners, against which foreigners, provincials, creoles and savages are measured and found lacking. The eighth chapter discusses the ways in which the serious drama allowed the English elite to draw on, and distinguish themselves from, the great imperial model of Rome. In a final coda, I discuss Dennis's celebration in *Liberty Asserted* (1704) and Southerne's critique, in *Oroonoko* (1696), of the emergent universal monarchy of trade fashioned by William.

Nevertheless, while empire, national identity and exotic cultures were all demonstrably important in Restoration drama, it would be a mistake to see these subjects as separate from more obviously domestic concerns. Plays with exotic settings contributed to the refashioning of metropolitan selves by providing an implicit or explicit contrast with planters, Indians, Moors, Spaniards and Ottomans but it is clear that they also provided a useful context for the consideration of such urgent topics as usurpation, revolution, succession, tyranny and the ruler's enthrallment by luxury. Although it is the neglected surface of these texts which reveals the fascination with empire, attention to that surface does not displace the importance of their political subtexts, or parallels. Contemporary audiences expected heroic poems to be allegorical, offering several layers of meaning, and could be expected to recognize that such texts had multiple significations. The double-jointedness in the plays' effects, the process by which exotic differences are exploited at the same time that another culture offers a screen for the projection of local anxieties, is also a common feature of what is called colonial discourse. Non-European locales, especially those of the great Asian states which provided the most obvious alternative to Western polities and cultures, offered the opportunity for comparison as well as disguise. Thus the problems of succession which haunted England in the Restoration could be explored through representing the fraternal strife in the Turkish empire, where polygamy and the lack of primogeniture provided a very different but equally uncertain set of conditions for the transfer of power. In a play such as Orrery's *Mustapha*, an English audience could detect parallels between the situations of the Ottomans and the Stuarts but would also be shown that the fratricidal conflicts caused by Oriental practices were crueller and more productive of division than their own.

"DIFFERENCE" IN THE RESTORATION

The intellectual, political and economic history of empire offers one set of frames for understanding the cultural significance of the theatrical representation of colonial expansion in this period and the history of anthropology provides another. Literary historians have generally agreed that Restoration critics such as Dryden, Rymer, Dennis and Temple shared a universalist belief in the uniformity of human nature which was increasingly tempered by awareness of the importance of national and historical circumstances in cultural production.[35] This gradually relativizing "foundationalism" is literalized on the Restoration stage, where widely different polities are shown wracked by conflicts familiar to the English audience, yet also marked in certain crucial ways as different culturally, religiously and politically. The logics which governed the masquerade of ethnic difference, at court and on stage, thus had certain similarities. The Carolean court's assumption of Persian dress can be read as an attempt, of the kind Mullaney describes, to clarify and assert the superiority of English identity, in that adopting the Persians' "fantastical ... apparel" constituted an assertion of sartorial independence from the tyranny of France ("We need no French inventions for the *Stage*, or for the Back"[36]), while borrowing something of the imperial *gloire* of the Shah. The latter ruled over what was described by Chardin, the acknowledged seventeenth-century authority on Persia, as "the most Civilised people of the *East*."[37] They were, Heylyn reported, "addicted to *hospitality*, magnificent in expense, lordly in their compliments, fantastical in their apparel, maintainers of *nobility*, and desirous of peace."[38] These were all characteristics that could serve as welcome signifiers of aristocratic difference from the French, whose aspirations to universal monarchy were reinforced by the authority of their fashions, their letters and their language.

The utility of this costume drama in bolstering English identity is, however, doubtful, given that Louis had the last laugh by putting his footmen in Persian clothing. Further, Mullaney's claim that such performances turned on an increasing sense of an absolute difference between alien and domestic cultures is open to question. Evelyn's account is striking for its ready acceptance of an implicit symbolic equivalence between French and Persian dress, an equivalence rendered explicit in the pamphlet on "Mode," where comparisons between the habits of Chinese, "Negroes," Mexicans and Europeans mingle indiscriminately.[39] This suggests that in some contexts at least, an older series of epistemological assumptions held sway. Outlining a seventeenth-century view of cultural difference which seems akin to the universalism of Dryden, historical anthropologist James Boon argues that:

The Enlightenment fabricated a geographically and "naturally" remote *other* as exotic antithesis to itself. The pre-Enlightenment argued both the best and worst – the perfect and the damned – wherever the sectarian brethren and enemies were perceived, exotically or intimately: Patagonian or pope . . . Moreover, sectarian divisions meant that a clear and exclusivistic dichotomy between the European and the exotic was not formulated until religious reformism had been transformed into nationalism and Enlightenment secularism.[40]

W. D. Jordan puts it more simply: "Until the emergence of nation-states in Europe, by far the most important category of strangers was the non-Christian."[41] Michael Ryan claims that far from presenting a serious threat to European identity, during the Renaissance newly discovered exotics were readily assimilated by classically trained humanists, through the familiar category of paganism.[42] Margaret Hodgen's magisterial survey of the origins of anthropology provides abundant evidence of the tendency to account for the alien in terms of "similarities, similitudes, correspondences, agreements, conformities, parallels" but locates a shift in these practices in the later seventeenth century as skepticism and empiricism gained ground.[43] And the formulation offered by Anthony Pagden in a much more recent study, *The Fall of Natural Man*, is very similar, as he suggests cultural difference in the early modern period was understood (and absorbed) through a principle of assimilation.[44]

Boon accepts Hodgen's empirically argued location of a break between, in Foucauldian terms, an episteme governed by the "element of resemblance" and an order determined by "identity and difference," but he is critical of her endorsement of the truth claims of the disciplines that developed in the Enlightenment.[45] In a provocative reading of Jacobean ethnography, he tries to show that pre-Enlightenment ethnographic procedures provided a less coercive, more avowedly interpretive model of cultural description. Specifically, he suggests that *Purchas His Pilgrimes* (1625) "simultaneously dis-covers from the writings of exploration an Indic

royal symbology, a composite of Sumatran, Javanese and ultimately
Mogul varieties"[46] whose likeness to the Stuart monarchy, and difference from societies stigmatized as vagrant, Purchas's volumes
celebrate. The complementary relations of symbolic reciprocity
Boon discovers in these tomes are, however, doomed to be incomplete and transitory, for in avoiding intermarriage at the top, the
"capstone of any totalised alliance in Jacobean and Maussean
signs,"[47] Purchas's symbology foreshadowed the eventual dominance of an exploitative mercantilism, with an accompanying shift
to taxonomizing representational strategies in East–West relations
and narration.

With Boon's claims in mind, I want to return to another scene of
cultural encounter, Evelyn's account of the reception of Moroccans
at the Carolean court. In January 1682, Charles received an Embassy from Morocco, where the English fort of Tangier, acquired
through the King's Portuguese marriage and surrendered in 1683,
was under constant attack by the Arabs.

[1682. January] 11 To Lond: Saw the *Audience* of the *Morroco Ambassador*:
his retinue not numerous, was receivd in the Banqueting-house both their
Majesties present: he came up to the Throne without making any sort of
Reverence, bowing so much as his head or body: he spake by a *Renegado
English* man, for whose safe returne there was a promise: They were all
Clad in the *Moorish* habite Cassocks of Colourd Cloth or silk with buttons
& loopes, over this an *Alhaga* or white wollan mantle, so large as to wrap
both head & body, a shash or small *Turban*, naked leg'd and arm'd, but
with lether socks like the *Turks*, rich *Symeters*, large Calico sleev'd shirts
etc: The Ambassador had a string of Pearls odly woven in his Turbant; I
fancy the old Roman habite was little different as to the Mantle and naked
limbs: The Ambassador was an handsom person, well featur'd, & of a wise
looke, subtile, and extreamely Civile: Their Presents were *Lions & Estridges*
etc: Their Errant, about a Peace at Tangire etc: But the Concourse and
Tumult of the People was intollerable, so as the Officers could keepe
no order; which they were astonish'd at at first; There being nothing so
regular exact & perform'd with such silence etc, as in all these publique
occasions of their Country, and indeede over all the Turkish dominions.[48]

Two weeks later, he observed the Moors at closer quarters:

[24] This Evening I was at the Entertainement of the *Morrocco [Ambas-
sador]* at the Dut: of *Portsmouths* glorious Appartment at W.hall, where was
a greate banquet of *Sweetemeates*, and *Musique* etc but at which both the
Ambassador & *Retinue* behaved themselves with extraordinary Moderation
& modestie, though placed about a long Table a Lady betweene two

Moores: viz: a Moore, then a Woman, then a Moore etc: and most of these were the Kings natural Children, viz: the Lady Lichfield, Sussex, DD of *Portsmouth, Nelly* etc: Concubines, and catell of that sort, as splendid as Jewells, and Excesse of bravery could make them: The Moores neither admiring or seeming to reguard any thing, furniture or the like with any earnestnesse; and but decently tasting of the banquet: They dranke a little Milk and Water, but not a drop of Wine, also they drank of a sorbett and Jacolatte: did not looke about nor stare on the Ladys, or express the least of surprize, but with a Courtly negligence in pace, Countenance, and whole behaviour, answering onely to such questions as were asked, with a greate deale of Wit and Gallantrie, and so gravely tooke leave, with this Compliment That *God* would blesse the D: of P: and the Prince her sonn, meaning the little Duke of Richmond: The *King* came in at the latter end, just as the Ambassador was going away: In this manner was this Slave (for he was no more at home) entertained by most of the Nobility in Towne;) ... In a word, the *Russian Ambassador* still at Court behaved himselfe like a Clowne, compar'd to this Civil *Heathen.*[49]

Evelyn's account is marked by a series of Orientalist assumptions reversed. Far from being "clownish," the ambassador's only deviation from Court protocol (a matter of considerable complexity and potential conflict) is his failure to make any bodily gesture of "reverence" to the King, an independence of manner Evelyn finds surprising in one who, the diarist is at pains to emphasize, is a "slave" from a culture in which "all these publique occasions" are performed with regular exactitude.[50] More arresting, however, is the account of the Moroccans' behavior at a reception which appears to have been designed to encourage them to display the lustful debauchery with which they were popularly credited. In a scene which at least mimes the possibility of a sexual exchange ("the capstone of any totalised alliance"), the Moroccans are placed between the Kings' mistresses and bastards: "a Moore, then a Woman, then a Moore etc." The tantalizing possibility of erotic interchange is, however, foreclosed by the visitors, who behaved with "extraordinary Moderation & Modestie." The presumably unintended effect of the passage is to emphasize Charles II's rather than the visitors' qualities of sensual autocracy, expressed here by an experiment with the Moroccans' erotic propensities.

In this text, Moors are figures who provoke curiosity, but no unambiguous sense of superiority. The glamorous peculiarities of their clothing remind Evelyn of "the old Roman habite," an implicit ascription of nobility and martial prowess underlined by a later description of their horsemanship. And in the background lies the purpose of the visit: an attempt to come to terms in a military conflict in which the Arabs could not be defeated. Although Evelyn's text is generated by Orientalist tropes either affirmed or displaced, this account does not describe a clash between utterly polarized cultures, but rather represents a ritualized exchange between elite representatives (although "the Tumult of the People was intollerable") of two highly stratified societies, whose different protocols are brought into relation without great difficulty. Tellingly, the Moors' color is never mentioned; their difference is constructed around binary notions quite specifically other than those of black (or even "tawninesse") and white, to wit: clownishness and civility, slavishness and freedom, Christian or "heathnick" religious affiliation. The Moroccan diplomats may be damned but like the pagan Romans, to whom they are compared, they appear civil, and though their polity may be despotic, it is admirably ordered, wealthy and powerful. This seems to exemplify that dis-covery of symbolic reciprocity which Boon locates in Purchas's celebration of royal complementarity.

Such an account of an Indic royal symbology also provides a highly suggestive way of understanding Dryden's presentation of the Mughal court in *Aureng-Zebe* (1675) and Killigrew's, Tate's and Motteux's staging of an East Indian court in their various redactions of Fletcher's *The Island Princess*. These "Indic" courts were easily seen as parallels to the Stuarts' but, like Purchas's representations, they also answered to a pervasive curiosity about the Asian states where the English had significant trade interests. Moreover, just as Boon locates the collapse of visions of symbolic complementarity in the emergence of mercantilism, so too these plays and their sources reflect the way colonial trade will alter interpretive and material relations. The various redactions of *The Island Princess* become more and more focused on the economic advantages gained by successful European intervention in the affairs of "Tedore," and the cultural and religious difference of Indians and Portuguese also becomes much more important to plot and characterization between 1668 and 1699. Dryden's likely source for *Aureng-Zebe*, Bernier's *History of the Late Revolution in the Empire of the Great Mogol* (1671), employs a theatrical rhetoric to shape the narrative, describing the Mughal Princesses, for instance, as "the most considerable Actors in the Tragedy."[51] The tragedy or romance (Bernier uses both terms to describe the political narrative), however, is

followed by an appendix which provided the classic European mercantilist analysis of the economic weakness of despotic states, blaming India's under-development on the lack of safeguards for private
property. The text thus incorporates two modes of discourse: one
which familiarizes the Mughals through their casting as actors in a
tragic romance and another which differentiates India as a polity
and culture by means of a mercantilist analysis which defines the
country negatively against Europe. Just such a conjunction of conflicting elements shapes representations of exotic states on the
stage.

Finally, Boon's description of Purchas's accounts of "Scenicall
History" as "ethnological word drama or rather masque"[52] draws attention to the centrality of performative or theatrical modes, which,
it has been argued, governed both the production and presentation
of the self and communal practices such as diplomatic protocols
in early modern England.[53] The latter occasions, which stage the
confrontation of local and foreign elites with great symbolic elaboration, provide a rich source for the analysis of the terms in which
the nature of nations were perceived. Less ephemeral, because
scripted, are those articulations of an English ideology of empire,
in such performances as the pageants at the Lord Mayors' Shows
(which praised the triumphs of trade) and masques performed for
the Court, as well as the theatre itself. In this context, the heroic
plays' role in the representation of empire seems over-determined;
its generic role as epic *in parvo* was to celebrate national and imperial greatness and its staging drew on the masque, in which the
imperial theme was always central. Davenant and Dryden were producers both of masques and of heroic plays and there was also a
crossover between dramatists and pageant-producers, with Settle
and Crowne both producing popular shows which celebrated England's overseas trade. Courtly, public and popular celebrations of
trade and empire in masque, theatre and pageant were distinct but
there were unifying strands of spectacle and ideology which bound
these different stagings of traffic and ambition together.

ARGUMENTS FROM COMPLEXION

Boon argues that the later seventeenth century saw a shift away from
relations governed by symbolic complementarity to a more marked
sense of cultural difference, identifying intellectual changes such as

the growth of a skeptical empiricism and the effect of mercantilism as the causes of this change. In contrast to Mullaney, for whom the late Renaissance (1550–1650) is the era during which relations of symbolic reciprocity made possible by the dominance of the "element of resemblance" are contested by the emergence of discourses of difference, I agree with Boon's view that such developments are more notable in the later seventeenth century. One of the obvious issues at stake here is the question of "race" in the Restoration theatre. It seems to me difficult to demonstrate that racial difference functions in recognizably modern terms in drama produced during this period, although cultural alterity is of absorbing interest. This claim may seem unconvincing in the light of recent work analyzing Elizabethan and Jacobean literary texts as colonial discourse; my point is not that it is inappropriate to read *Othello, The Tempest* or *The Faerie Queene* as discourses of colonialism but that the way in which "race" figures in such arguments is often over-simplified.[54] In a wide variety of texts including travel accounts, histories, poetic and dramatic narratives about non-Europeans produced in the Restoration, skin color simply does not appear as the crucial marker of identity it is now.

A. G. Barthelemy's wide-ranging study of the representation of Africans in the seventeenth-century English theatre exemplifies the problem created by a static notion of race.[55] Guided by Jordan's *White over Black* Barthelemy's introductory chapter marshals the abundant evidence from classical, patristic and early modern sources which identifies blackness with stereotypical elements such as devilry, concupiscence and disorderliness, and then proceeds to identify instances of this homogeneous image of black villainy in plays "from Shakespeare to Southerne." The analysis is reductive, producing a consolidated stereotype of the "Moor" and then reading the dramatic texts as simple reflections of that image. The problems this produces are illustrated by Barthelemy's discussion of Settle:

A brief mention of one of Dryden's rivals, the successful playwright Elkanah Settle, is warranted here before closing this chapter. In two of his plays, *The Empress of Morocco* and *The Heir of Morocco* (1682), Settle also writes about white Moors. These plays are quite different from any plays I have discussed thus far; they are the only plays I have found in which there are no white Christian Europeans to serve as exemplars of moral and spiritual perfection. What we find instead is a society much like the Italian society in *The White Devil*. In Settle's Morocco plays there are virtuous and evil Moors, forthright and duplicitous Moors. Settle's Morocco plays present the range of humans we generally expect to find in drama.[56]

There are in fact numerous examples of Restoration plays, including such famous texts as *The Indian Queen* (1664), *Aureng-Zebe* and *The Royal Mischief* (1696), which contain no "white Christian Europeans" but do include the usual avatars of heroic virtue. Moreover, Barthelemy's comparison of the "Morocco" plays to *The White Devil* occludes the negative associations of Italian corruption on which Webster's text depends, thus repeating the kind of ethnocentric critical gesture he generally criticizes. Most tellingly, though, he cannot explain why Settle's Moors are "white" at all; his explanatory model is too unremittingly negative. In engravings which accompanied the first publication of the play text, and presumably reflect production practice, the only characters in black-face or black-stockings are the Masquers.[57] As in Orrery's and Dryden's exotic heroic dramas, the aristocratic status of the characters appears here to have overridden an ethnic or racial categorization in both script and performance. The dramatist's invocation of Orientalist tropes notwithstanding, these plays can also plausibly be read as participating in the harmonization of exotic and domestic kingship which Boon locates in Purchas's "masques."

The pressure of England's aggressively mercantilist policies, however, and in particular her growing involvement in the African slave trade and the establishment of the Atlantic triangle, provided conditions in which the assumptions which generated heroicizing representations of Indic and Mughal monarchy were increasingly contested.[58] Ethnographic description, then consisting of geographies, travel accounts, advertising company reports and prospectuses for new territories, was being produced in greater and greater quantities and more frequently by secular writers actively involved in colonial trade. This writing was shot through with inherited assumptions from the usual classical and patristic sources, but tended to base truth claims on original observation rather than the authority of the ancients. Clerics like Purchas who had produced such writing previously operated with theological assumptions such

as the unity of mankind, notions put into question as philological, philosophical and biological speculation produced theories of
Egyptian linguistic primacy, polygenetic human origins and evolu-
tionary models of human development.[59]

The complex inter-relation of the slave trade, the old colonial
system, the development of mercantilism and new modes of ethnographic description rendered in taxonomical terms was remarked
on by contemporaries. In 1680, the Barbadian evangelist Morgan
Godwyn produced a pamphlet entitled *The Negro's and Indians Advocate*, in which he imputed his opponents' denial of human status
to "Negroes" to "the inducement and instigation of our Planters'
chief Deity, *Profit*."[60]

another no less disingenuous and unmanly *Position* hath been formed . . .
which is this, That the *Negro's*, though in their Figure they carry some
resemblances of Manhood, yet are Indeede *No Men*. A conceit like unto
which I have read, was some time since invented by the *Spaniards*, to
justifie *their murthering the Americans*. But for this here, I may say, that if
Atheism and *Irreligion* were the true Parents who gave it Life, surely *Sloth*
and *Avarice* hath been no unhandy Instruments and Assistants to midwife
it into the world . . . The issue whereof is, that as in the *Negro's all pretence to
Religion* is cut off, so their *Owners* are hereby set at Liberty and freed from
those importunate Scruples which conscience and better advice might at
any time happen to inject in to their unsteadie Minds.[61]

Godwyn's traditionalist argument draws on Hale's recently published refutation of polygenetic theories, *The Primitive Origination
of Mankind* (1679), and on evidence of man's barbarity in England
itself to assert the full humanity of the Negro. He contests the
investment of skin pigmentation as a crucial signifier of Negro
brutishness, by drawing on a well-established Christian tradition
that the variety of color in humanity "simply demonstrated the divine patterns of order and accident, of unity and diversity"[62] and
appeals to various historical precedents to suggest the "Ancient
Britons who . . . were clad with skins and did paint their bodies" were
more brutish than Africans.[63] Although G. W. Stocking and A. J.
Barker disagree, the latter contending that throughout the eighteenth century "The predominance of monogenesis and environ-
mentalism effectively undermined the commonest intellectual de-
vice employed by the racialists, the concept of gradation," Hodgen
and Davis concur in arguing that the emergence of progressivist

models of human development did provide a basis for a widely spread nascent "scientific racism."[64] It has been argued that the dependence of these models on the kind of visual evidence demanded by evidentiary protocols of the new science was responsible for the development of the chromatic index of racial difference.[65] Interestingly, Godwyn's attack on the "arguments from complexion" registers his awareness of the importance of engaging not only with the substance of his opponents' arguments but also with their epistemological assumptions: "I shall begin with the first, and that is the complexion, which being most obvious to the sight by which the *Notion* of things doth seem to be most certainly convey'd to the understanding, is apt to make no slight impression upon minds, already prepared to admit anything for *Truth* which shall make for *Interest.*"[66] The identification Godwyn makes here between empiricist assumptions which privilege visible evidence – "the sight by which the *Notion* of things doth seem to be most certainly convey'd to the understanding" – and profit ("minds, already prepared to admit anything for *Truth* which shall make for *Interest*") succinctly anticipates much more recent attempts to show how disciplinary protocols produce a certain knowledge of and power over the objects they define.[67] Godwyn also points to the emergence of a binary logic of alterity, in which older terms of cultural difference such as Englishman/Heathen are supplemented by a new and insidious "homogeneity" between blackness and slavery, amplifying and extending the original division: "These two words, *Negro* and *Slave*, being by custom grown Homogeneous and Convertible; even as *Negro* and *Christian, Englishman* and *Heathen,* are by the like corrupt Custom and Partiality made *Opposites*; Thereby as it were implying, that the one could not be *Christians,* nor the other *Infidels.*"[68]

Godwyn's embattled defence of the Negroes' humanity reflects his own immediate interest in this issue as an evangelist in a plantation colony. The topic also figured significantly in what might seem a very different context: namely, literary critical debate. Thomas Rymer's "A Short View of Tragedy" (1693) is cited by Barthelemy as the most lurid expression of a consistent seventeenth-century prejudice against Moors, as the former's attack on *Othello* returns incessantly to the play's staging of miscegenation, with the protagonist's position and marriage cited as fundamental errors in probability and decorum. Rymer's demolition of *Othello* was part of a more general attack on the failure of English tragedians to respect time, place and persons, in which he complains of Shakespeare that "his Orators had their learning and education in the same school, be they Venetians, Black-amoors, Ottamites, or noble Romans" and that tragedy was set too frequently "in the *Land of Savages,* amongst Blackamoors, Barbarians, and Monsters."[69] Despite his position as Historiographer Royal, however, Rymer's vituperation was hardly exemplary: the attack on Shakespeare (and the related critique of Dryden and Jonson) was addressed and repudiated over the next fifty years by a variety of other critics. Some respondents were silent on the question of the role of "colour" in Shakespeare's fable, but those who did take up the issue were at the least more temperate, and often openly dissented from Rymer's view.[70] Lewis Theobald agreed that Shakespeare's source, Cinthio, designed his tale against disproportionate marriages: "That they should not link themselves to such, against whom, Nature, Providence and a different way of Living have interpos'd a Bar" but goes on to remark "Our Poet inculcates no such moral: but rather, that a Woman may fall in love with the Virtues and shining Qualities of a Man; and therein overlook the Distinction of Complexion and Colour."[71] Theobald also scoffs at Rymer's rabid tone, suggesting a contempt for the prejudice as well as the excess of the latter's views: "Mr *Rymer* has run riot against the Conduct, Manners, Sentiment, and Diction of this Play: but in such a strain that one is mov'd rather to laugh at the Freedom and Coarseness of his Raillery, than provok'd to be downright angry at his Censures."[72]

Theobald's comments are much more muted than the lengthy and spirited denunciation of Rymer which Gildon wrote in an open Letter to Dryden published in 1694.[73] Here, he rewrites Rymer's travesty of the fable (that the play was a warning to maidens not to run away with Blackamoors) "in a Juster light," and defends the probability and propriety of the plot and persons. He argued for the likelihood of the Venetians employing a Christian African to fight for them: "Why therefore an *African* Christian may not be by the *Venetians* suppos'd to be as zealous against the *Turks,* as an *European* Christian, I cannot imagine." Gildon also detects the same prejudice in Rymer that Godwyn locates in the planters: "He [Rymer]... takes it for granted that *Othello* must be rather for the *Turkish* interest than the *Venetian,* because he is a *Moor.*"[74] He justifies Othello's high position with equal directness, claiming that Shakespeare's is an anti-racist text *avant la lettre*:

'Tis granted, a *Negro* here does seldom rise above a Trumpeter, not often perhaps higher at *Venice*. But then that precedes from the Vice of Mankind, which is the Poets Duty as he informs us, to correct, and to represent things as they should be, not as they are. Now 'tis certain, there is no reason in the nature of things, why a *Negro* of equal Birth and Merit, should not be on an equal bottom, with a *German*, *Hollander*, *French-man*, &c. The Poet therefore, ought to do Justice to Nations, as well as Persons, and set them to rights, which the common course of things confounds. The same reason stands in this, as for punishing the Wicked, and making the Virtuous fortunate, which as *Rapin* and all the Critics agree, the Poet, ought to do, though it generally happens otherwise. The Poet has therefore well chosen a polite People to cast off this customary Barbarity, of confining Nations, without regard to their Virtue, and Merit, to slavery, and contempt for the meer Accident of their Complexion.[75]

Gildon parries Rymer's invocation of Horace to prove the bestiality of Africans by attacking such views as vulgar and criminally irresponsible in a man with pretending to learning, citing "the best Travels" or "History of those parts, on the continent of *Africa*" which reveal the Africans to be not only "greater Heroes, nicer observors of Honour, and all the Moral Virtues that distinguish'd the old *Romans*" but "better Christians (where Christianity is profes'd) than we of *Europe* generally are."[76] He emphasizes that Othello is of royal blood and that it was he who condescended in his marriage to Desdemona: a marriage whose difference in color Gildon regards as unimportant:

Experience tells us, that there's nothing more common than Matches of this kind, where the Whites and Blacks cohabit together, as in both the *Indies*: and even here at home, Ladys that have not wanted white adorers have indulg'd their Amorous Dalliances with their Sable Lovers, without any of *Othello's* qualifications, which is proof enough, that Nature and Custom, have not put any such unpassable bar betwixt Creatures of the same kind, because of different colours.[77]

Gildon uses the familiar, traditional arguments from analogy in comparing Africans to Romans, while the praise of African Christians suggests the power of conversion in assimilating non-Europeans, and the justification of intermarriage, dependent on a universalist understanding of humankind, refuses any notion of racial difference or hierarchy.

Gildon's rebuttal of Rymer suggests that even if educated literary opinion was developing along what we call racist lines, such views were by no means uncontested. The awkward implicit admission of the claims about improbability in the fable and persons ("I won't pretend to enquire into the *Justness* of Mr *Rymer's* Remarks on *Othello*; he has certainly pointed out some faults very judiciously; and indeed they are such as most People will agree to be Faults"[78]) need to be set against Gildon's and Theobald's powerful dissent from the notion that Othello's "colour" rendered the plot and characterization unlikely and distasteful. The issue was important to participants in the long-running and competitive critical and editorial struggle over the definition of Shakespeare's achievement and *oeuvre* because the dramatist was being established as the quintessentially English genius: Rymer's critique served as a point of departure for celebrants of the giant's greatness. The issue was not simply to shield Shakespeare from Rymer's intemperance: as Gildon's defence suggests, participants in this discussion realized there were ethical and political questions at stake in the dramatic imperative "to do Justice to Nations, as well as Persons."[79] The notion that the dramatist had such a responsibility is by no means unique to Gildon: in his Preface to *Liberty Asserted* (1704), Dennis rebuts the notion that the play contained "National Reflections which ought not to be made,"[80] claiming that the play contained only "a satyr upon the Government of the French, and not upon their Manners as they proceed from their Climate." The patriotic contempt Dennis pours on the French ("in themselves a brave and gallant Nation; but the Submission which they fondly pay to unlimited Power has plung'd them in Vices which their Natures abhor, and render'd them odious and despicable") is as powerful as the disgust Dryden displayed for the Dutch in *Amboyna* (1672) but the latter's Preface betrays nothing but more contempt for the "mean" persons of his action. A patriotic imperative is common to all the dramatists of the Restoration but it is only with Britain's emergence as a first-rank European and imperial power after the Glorious Revolution that reflections on the moral implications of the representations of other nations emerge as an issue in literary debate. After three decades of expansion in England's colonial trade and empire whereby western plantations worked by slaves, East Indian factories and North

American settlements became increasingly important to the English economy and her European prestige, it is hardly surprising that the issue of "complexion" as well as "nation" appears in such explicit terms.

CONCLUSION

My readings of Restoration plays about empire suggest that they can be seen as a form of colonial discourse insofar as they contribute to shaping perspectives on non-European societies which the English hoped to exploit economically and influence politically, if not annex formally. The plays are also clearly concerned with exploring and defining the history and nature of empire, in order to clarify the imperial possibilities for their own nation. It should be obvious, however, that the drama does not constitute a site for the unambiguous celebration of a putative universal monarchy, nor that the representation of non-European states is predicated on an easy sense of "racial" superiority. Much ink has been spilled in recent years modifying the claims of post-colonial theorists who have assumed that European expansion was facilitated by philosophical and religious assumptions and representational strategies which supported an unproblematic sense of Western superiority.[81] Critics of such positions have included post-structuralists attentive to the internal inconsistencies of colonial discourse;[82] advocates of resistance, who place much more emphasis on the dialectical nature of colonial encounters;[83] and empirically minded historians, who have returned to the subject of empire in order to provide revisionary accounts of the development of Britain and the centrality of colonialism to that process.[84]

The implications for an account such as my own are considerable. It is apparent that many of the texts I examine turn on the kinds of tropes often deployed in early representations of colonial encounter, conquest and settlement by Paul Brown, Louis Montrose and others. Because such figures have a long and mutable existence, although in analysis they often assume a kind of transhistorical fixity, I have attempted at every point to identify the local context as well as the dynamic religious, philosophical and political assumptions and arguments which inflect the invocation of such tropes. My account has thus been shaped not simply by the literary and historical sources on which the dramatists drew, and the immediate political events which shaped their perspective on such materials, but by historical anthropology and the intellectual history of empire.

Equally, it seems to me that Restoration drama is an important and hitherto neglected source for any account of seventeenth- and early eighteenth-century imperial ideology. If, as now seems generally accepted, the drama was an important location for the representation and negotiation of local political issues in the period, it seems perverse to ignore the theatrical interest in questions of empire thematized so frequently in serious plays. Historians such as Steven Pincus, Anthony Pagden, David Armitage and Linda Colley have provided evidence of the proliferation of discourse about colonial and imperial questions in England through this period, with Pincus in particular making it clear that the hitherto rigid division between foreign and domestic politics in the Restoration is misguided. Foreign policy might have been the most jealously guarded royal prerogative but large and increasing numbers of the English were involved in, or affected by, colonial trade, the expansion of the navy, the Dutch Wars and/or emigration to the Western plantations. Interest in such topics, especially among the elites who invested in the trading companies, received or lost grants of land or offices in the Americas, or simply worried about the threat posed by the emergent power of France in the vacuum left by Spain, was intense. Because the exploration of the rewards, dangers and nature of imperial power was frequently mediated by a heroic mode whose representation of non-European states does not conform to our own, post-imperial, highly racialized sense of how cultural difference is likely to be figured, this particular arena of imperial ideology has been neglected. Just as the ideological implications of the love-and-honor nexus can be made legible in terms of class or party competition, the heroic plays' melding of romance and epic forms can be recognized as embodying a vision of Christian empire which answered to the immediate concerns of its audience. Closer examination reveals that the staging of Ottoman or Oriental or Aztec empires was not as fantastic and generalized as it first seems: drawing from travels and histories as well as heroic romance or French examples, the dramatists incorporated and presented a great deal of what was becoming received wisdom about Asian, African and American societies. Such doctrine did not turn on a strong sense of race, which as we have seen was an emergent and

disputed category in this period, but on notions of religious, political and customary difference dictated by history and climate.

Finally, it needs to be emphasized that these plays cannot be understood simply as staged animadversions against Oriental monarchy or the black legend of Spanish conquest: it is their exploitation
of the particular affective and spectacular possibilities offered by
theatricality which enabled them to provide peculiarly pleasurable
and apparently successful ways of processing aspirations to empire
and curiosity about exotic societies. The rhymed heroic play did
not survive the 1670s but the heroic mode continued to be employed in the representation of empire despite the rise of affective
tragedy and bourgeois domestic and sentimental tragedy. The nature of the imperial ideology encoded in the plays changed as the
first empire assumed shape but the genre was a continual resource
in staging imperial contests, celebrating national greatness and, in
some cases, deploring the effects of what Johnson called "European oppression." In comic drama also, one sees a continuity leading from *Sir Courtly Nice* to *The Nabob,* from *The Plain Dealer* to
Cumberland's *The West Indian,* as playwrights satirized the novel
social types of planter, nabob and creole who brought wealth and
a tincture of savagery back to the metropolis. Thus the theatre,
"civilized" by Davenant after 1660, became itself an instrument of
empire.

CHAPTER 2

Enlarging the Poet's Empire: Poetics, Politics and Heroic Plays, 1660–1714

There are three main indices of the heroic drama's imbrication in the Restoration debates over empire. First, as the literary arts were regarded as a site of inter-state rivalry, and the English prided themselves on the superiority of their theatre, dramatic poems with epic pretensions were understood by contemporary critics to bear witness not just to the civility but to the ambition and greatness of the nation. This generic inheritance made the heroic mode, broadly defined, an important vehicle for representing the changing ideologies of empire under all the later Stuarts. Second, many heroic plays produced under Charles and James can be shown either to engage with contemporary arguments over empire or to have plots drawn from doxa about the powerful, non-Western states in which the trading companies were finding economic and military footholds, while those produced under William and Mary and Anne celebrated British military and political conquest in a specifically Whig key, reworking parallels with past figures of imperial greatness but also dramatizing a Republican theory of empire in a North American setting and reappropriating the Roman heritage by focusing on the Roman presence in England. Third, the theatrical presentation of the heroic drama, which drew both on the Caroline masque and on the more popular pageant traditions, not only used exotic costumes, props and dances but also employed sophisticated new "machines" to display scenes of Oriental wealth, sensuality and violence or pagan savagery. The spectacular effects of such machines underlined the technical sophistication of European culture while emphasizing the material spoils available for exploitation in other less civil or more decadent societies. Both texts and productions thus emphasized the religious, political and cultural differences of non-Western states as much as they allowed for "parallels" with English politics.

28

THE EMPIRE OF WIT

Debates over literature in England from 1660 to 1714 all bear the impress of patriotism, a sense of national rivalry which extends backwards to Greece and Rome, in the ancients–moderns disputes, or laterally, in the rivalry with France. Literary historians have noted an "obsession" with the progress of refinement, and an increasingly strong sense of cultural relativism and the importance of national character in discussions of cultural production, which in the case of English literature becomes an emphasis on "liberty."[1] The early controversy over the use of rhyme, the unities and exotic subjects in the heroic drama raised the issue of French influence over English drama, a reaction reinforced by the plays' representations of hungrily expansionist and absolutist Herculean heroes. Later in the 1670s, patriotic pride in the excellence of English drama was challenged by Thomas Rymer, who criticized the formal and moral irregularities of English plays, and in the last decade of the century, by Temple's criticism of modern learning's corruption by avarice, and by Jeremy Collier's attack on dramatic indecency. The responses to these critics were all marked by national as well as party feeling. A consensus emerged which emphasized the importance of a traditional English disregard for dictatorial and constraining rules, eventually identifying "liberty" as the most salient characteristic of political and cultural life (a literary history supplemented by a belief in the effects of the wet and changeable British weather). The process of differentiating English literary excellence from classical and French achievements, however, raised sensitive issues of national identity and history, as critics argued over the Greek and Roman states' relation to the stage, Richelieu's patronage of drama, Elizabeth I's relation to the theatre, the link between restored monarchy and re-opened playhouses, and the perceived decline of metropolitan morals. At stake was not just the literary history of the nation but the future of a people and a state characterized by freedom but also increasingly convinced of a capacity for greatness on a global scale.

One of the most striking symptoms of such cultural confidence is the assumption of a *translatio studii*, in which first the West and then England herself, are figured as the heirs of the empire of wit and learning. Rymer's praise of Waller exemplifies the claims for English poetry as elevated, refined and worthy of comparison with the ancients: Cowley's ode "To Mr. Hobs." (1658) places more emphasis on the translation of learning:

> Long did the mighty *Stagirite* retain,
> The *universal intellectual reign*,
> Saw his own Countreys short-liv'd *Leopard* slain;
> The stronger *Roman Eagle* did out-fly,
> Oftener *renewed* his *Age*, and saw that *Dy*,
> *Mecha* itself, in spite of *Mahumet* possest,
> And chas'd by a wild *Deluge* from the *East*,
> His *Monarchy* new planted in the *West*.[2]

In political discourse the English may have eschewed claims to universal monarchy but in the early years of the Restoration at least, enthusiastically Royalist writers were not shy in making the kinds of claims for national greatness which were regarded as concommittant with a broad political dominion. This link between poetry and empire had ancient origins. The Horatian formulation of the Orphic origins of civil society establishes an identification between the effects of poetry and that of law, claiming that poets were the true founders of the *civitas*, which was itself, the Roman theorists and Machiavelli believed, the source of empire.[3] This doctrine circulated in the Restoration in texts such as Waller's verses "Upon the Earl of Roscommon's Translation of Horace":

> Finding new words, that to the ravish'd ear
> May like the language of the gods appear,
> Such as, of old, wise bards employ'd to make
> Unpolish'd men their wild retreats forsake;
> Law-giving heroes, fam'd for taming brutes,
> And raising cities with their charming lutes;
> For rudest minds with harmony were caught,
> And civil life was by the Muses taught.[4]

This emphasis on poetry's power to rescue men from savagery and usher them into civil society is the first step in a chronology which linked improvements, reformations and restorations in poetry with the growth (or collapse) not just of civility but of national and imperial power. In the *Preface to Gondibert* (1650), Davenant claims poetry's power to inculcate virtue and good order in government is greater than that of divines, commanders, statesmen and lawyers, citing as evidence the close relations of poets and rulers in the ancient world and the institutional support of poetry in Greece and

Rome.[5] This defence of poetry, produced during the Interregnum when Davenant was planning to quit Europe for America, places more emphasis on heroic poetry's ability to give civil shape to the appetite for empire universal in mankind, than on a specifically English achievement of greatness in art and power. In the first decade of the Restoration, however, in *The Essay of Dramatick Poesie*, Dryden rejoins dramatic achievement and patriotism:

Be it spoken to the honour of the English, our Nation can never want in any Age, such who are able to dispute the Empire of Wit with any people in the Universe. And though the fury of a Civil War, and Power, for twenty years together, abandon'd to a barbarous race of men, Enemies of all good Learning, had buried the Muses under the ruins of Monarchy; yet, with the restoration of our happiness, we see reviv'd Poesie lifting up its head, and already shaking off the rubbish which lay so heavy on it. We have seen since his Majesties return, many Dramatick Poems which yield not to those of any forreign Nation.[6]

Dryden celebrates the English possession of an "Empire of Wit" inextricably linked to a triumphant Stuart monarchy: the country's law-giver has also generated new kinds of poetry. This was literally the case in regard to Orrery, who commenced his career as a heroic dramatist at Charles's specific request. Richard Flecknoe's verses memorializing Davenant shift the focus from patron to poet but display a similar sense of the heroic dramatist's role in "civilizing" the theatre after the long period of barbarism:

> Now Davenant's dead the stage will mourn
> And all to barbarism turn
> Since he it was this latter age
> Who chiefly civilized the stage
> Not only Daedalus's arts he knew
> But e'n Prometheus's too
> And *living machines* made of men
> As well as dead ones for the scene.
> . . .
>
> But coming to his *Seige of Rhodes*
> It outdoes all the rest by odds
> And somewhat's in't that does outdo
> Both ancients and the moderns too.[7]

Flecknoe is referring primarily to Davenant's role in introducing those innovations in staging drawn from the masque which greatly enhanced the presentation of the exotic spectacles characteristic of the heroic plays but the celebration of the dramatist's "civiliz-ing" effect also invokes his use of rhymed verse and epic narrative in the *The Siege of Rhodes*. The link between poetry, civility and em-pire informs the transformation of Davenant's role as an English Orpheus into that of poetic discoverer and explorer, with Dryden's celebration of his senior's achievement in "Of Heroic Plays" using more Horatian tropes of navigation:

An Heroic Play, ought to be an imitation, in little, of an Heroic Poem; and, consequently, that Love and Valour ought to be the Subject of it. Both these Sir William Davenant had begun to shadow: but it was so, as first Discoverers draw their Maps, with headlands, and Promontories, and some few out-lines of some-what taken at a distance, and which the Designer saw not clearly.[8]

The epic subject of the heroic plays became identified with the per-sona of their producers, who were satirized as well as celebrated, as imperial tropes of authorial exploration, discovery, plunder and conquest proliferated, especially in relation to Dryden. In the 1673 "Censure of the Rota," he is described as a poetic conquistador, explorer and plunderer, in tropes which literalize Sidney's celebra-tion of the poet as the deliverer of a new golden world:

The honour of the Golden Age (reply'd another) belongs justly to Mr Dryden, who ever return'd home richly fraught from Spain and America: to his Catholique Conquests Poetry ow'd its Indies and its Plate-Fleets; and after such Voiages and Discoveries, he could not but wonder a little at his modest excusing his ignorance in Sea Terms in his Annus Mirabilis. . . . He was the Man Nature seem'd to make choice of to enlarge the Poets Empire and to compleat those Discoverys others had begun to shadow.[9]

The overweening ambition and geographical range of the heroic dramatist was also a subject for mockery in Shadwell's Epilogue to *The Miser* (1672):

> When Seiges now by Poets are prepar'd
> And Love and War 'gainst Nations is declar'd
> When Affrica and Asia are not spar'd
> By some who will in Rhime the World o'errun
> Who in their Conqests will no Country shun
> Not 'scaping the Mogul, nor Prester John
> No American Prince in his throne secure
> Not Totty Potty May himself is sure;

But may the fury of their Rhime endure
Nay in time each Prince in Guinny will be fought
And under these poetic fetters brought:
And we shall see how black rogues lov'd and fought.[10]

Shadwell's vision of the heroic dramatists as poetic Tamberlaines reflects the suspicion with which ambitions for universal monarchy, whether poetic or territorial, were regarded by the less enthusiastically Royalist members of the literary and political community. The emergence of the heroic drama as the most prestigious and popular form in the 1660s and early 1670s troubled critics at the time (and since) for a variety of reasons. At one level, the un-English rant of the "Bedlam Heroes" was regarded as a form of literary overreaching: the fustian excess of the language and characterization were seen as symptomatic of the intolerable arrogance of upstart poetasters.[11] At another, characters like Almanzor, Montezuma and Maximin (who have since been identified by critics as symbolic of such internal threats to political peace as Shaftesbury, the residual Commonwealthmen and even Cromwell) surely embodied that natural if monstrous principle of aggression defined by Davenant in his famous exchange over heroic poetry with Hobbes.[12] Discussing the role of poetry in inspiring military leaders, Davenant emphasized his admiration for leaders of armies, as "the painful Protectors and Enlargers of Empire, by whom it actively moves." He believed that

such active motion of Empire is as necessary as the motion of the Sea, where all things would putrifie and infect one another, if the Element were quiet: so it is with mens minds on shore, when the Element of greatness and honour, *Empire*, stands still, of which the largeness is likewise as needfull as the vastness of the Sea; For God ordain'd not huge Empires as proportionable to the Bodies but to the Mindes of Men, and the Mindes of Men are more monstrous and require more space for agitation and the hunting of others than the Bodies of Whales.[13]

Davenant's enthusiasm for the heroes who shape the enlargement of empire is hardly surprising in a poet who authored imperial masques for Charles's father and wrote a stirring encomium to Prince Rupert's abortive scheme to colonize Madagascar. Dryden's perspective on the Hobbesian itch to power identified here by Davenant has been much more disputed but his fascination with the representation of such restless ambition in his "Herculean heroes" is indisputable.[14] Such fascination is equally marked in the other heroic dramatists, who included in Orrery a man whose own career demonstrated an active lust for power exercised in the colonial theatre of Ireland. Many other Englishmen, however, believed such restless and monstrous ambition could be detected in the threatening activities of Louis, Leopald, the Great Turk and, perhaps worst of all, the Dutch. Even if the courts of Charles and James Stuart found the representations of "the painful Protectors and Enlargers of Empire" attractive, the satiric critique of the "noble savages" of the heroic stage suggests a good part of the political nation was rather more ambivalent about such ambitions.

The satiric commentary on the characterization and language of the heroic protagonists reached its apogee in *The Rehearsal* but also informed Dryden's famous exchanges with Howard over rhyme and the unities. The heat in this debate was engendered partly by questions of status and cultural authority but also focused on modes of theatrical representation regarded as un-English, as the disputes over rhyme and the unities in the heroic plays involved competing claims to be defending English literary honor. Dryden underlined his patriotic motives in playwriting and criticism repeatedly, but so did his opponents: Flecknoe's defence of Howard, critic of rhyme and a strict adherence to the unities, claims the patriotic ground for his hero.[15] Flecknoe closed his *Letter to a Gentleman* (1668) by quoting the Prologue to Orrery's *Henry the Fifth* (1665), in verse which emphasized both the patriotic subject and the English form of the play:

> We have with Forraign Tales so fill'd your Ears,
> As if our Poets were all Foreigners;
> This Author begs you'll lend him but two hours'
> To entertain you with your Ancestours.
> He thinks no stories merit to be known,
> Nor can instruct us better than our own.
> But look not for great Actions in a Play,
> Contracted to the limits of a Day.
> To those strict Rules the French their Poets bind:
> Yet none of them for this a Reason shows,
> But to their Mode of Writing, as of Cloths,
> They think the English ever should agree;
> . . .
> It were not fit, in stories of that Age,
> When we ruled *France*, French Lawes should rule our Stage.

> Nor is it just in Poetry to bind
> Fancy, which is tormented, when confin'd.
> He hopes you will excuse him if he strives,
> To break those Lawes a Forreign Nation gives.[16]

Orrery's patriotic identification of the unities with French oppression, implying the English poetic imagination was less constricted, is appropriated here to supplement the defence of Howard's dismissal of rhyme and the unities as unnatural. This position eventually takes on a much more overtly political hue, pithily expressed in Elkanah Settle's riposte to Collier in his *Farther Defence of Dramatick Poetry* (1698): "For the strict Observation of these *Corneillean* Rules, are as Dissonant to the *English* Constitution of the Stage, as the *French* slavery to our *English* Liberty."[17] The Prologue's emphasis on the specifically English nature of the subject also recurs to Shadwell's complaint about the plethora of exotic themes in serious plays, with Rymer in particular making patriotic complaints about the paucity of heroic plays with English subjects.[18]

In both major literary debates in the two decades following the Glorious Revolution, the ancients–moderns dispute and the controversy over the immorality of the theatre generated by Collier, the relationship between national identity, empire and drama remained central. In the essay which sparked off the English round of the battle of books, "An Essay on the Ancient and Modern Learning" (1690), Sir William Temple incorporated the usual link between political and literary greatness (while famously pushing the origins of knowledge eastward to India) but he also revised the patriotic account of the *translatio studii* negatively, making a swingeing critique of contemporary culture on the basis of avarice. Pursuing a logic developed by Republican commentators on the perceived corruption of Spain through New World wealth, Temple cited the enormous increase in riches provided by the East and West Indian trade as destructive of the pursuit of honor, and hence the arts and learning, in England as well as in the rest of Europe:

May they not have turned more to this pursuit of insatiable gains, since the Discoveries and Plantations of the *West-Indies*, and those vast Treasures that have flowed into these *Western* Parts of *Europe* almost every Year and with such mighty Tides for so long a course of time? Where few are rich, few care for it; when many are so, many desire it; and most in time begin to think it necessary. Where this Opinion grows generally in a Countrey, the Temples of Honour are soon pulled down, and all mens Sacrifices are made to those of Fortune: The Souldier as well as the Merchant, the Scholar as well as the Plough-man.[19]

Temple regarded the compass as the only significant modern invention and navigation and geography as the only spheres of knowledge in which the moderns could claim a significant advantage over the ancients, but he lamented that the ethical poverty of contemporary Europeans rendered them incapable of exploiting their discoveries properly:

> The Vast Continents of *China*, the *East* and *West Indies*, the long Extent and Coasts of *Africa*, with the numberless Islands belonging to them, have been introduced into our Aquaintance and our Maps, but none of Knowledge, brought among us, farther than the Extent and Situacion of Country, the customs and manners of so many original Nations, which we call Barbarous, and I am sure have treated them as if we hardly esteem them to be a part of Mankind. I do not doubt but many Great and more Noble Uses would have been made of such Conquests or Discoveries, if they had fallen to the share of the *Greeks* and *Romans* in those Ages when Knowledge and Fame were in as great Request as endles Gains and Wealth are among us now.[20]

Temple's argument that early modern European empires of trade were corrupting the metropole as mercenary aims drove out "honour" echoes the views detectable in Tory dramatists such as Behn, and foreshadows the preoccupation with luxury so prevalent in the eighteenth century.[21] The assumption central to the Stuart idealization of empire, that wealth followed honor, is summarily dismissed in favor of a perceived opposition between profit and glory which would become a staple in Patriot attacks on the Whig political establishment. Temple was equally prescient in the terms in which he chose to praise English drama in "Of Poetry." Notwithstanding his general preference for the Ancients, Temple singled out modern English drama and the comedy in particular, as superior to that of the Greeks and Romans. Extending and specifying the view that there was a link between English government and literature, Temple produced the much-quoted argument that the peculiarity of English political life (and climate) was responsible for the richness of the nation's comic drama, suggesting that the "greater variety of Humor in the Picture" proceeded from "the Native Plenty of our Soyl, the Unequalness of our Clymat, as well as the Ease of our Government, and the Liberty of Professing Opinions and Factions."[22]

Dennis was more optimistic about the potential of English literature than Temple but his commentaries on the theatre express the ambivalence with which claims to "the empire of wit" came to be seen by some Whigs as well as Tories in the decades of war following the Glorious Revolution. "The Essay on the Opera's" (1706) reiterates the doctrine that in the past, poetry and empire have risen and fallen together: "The Declension of Poetry in *Greece* and antient *Rome* was soon follow'd by that of Liberty and Empire."[23] In "The Usefulness of the Stage" (1698), however, the connection between English drama and imperial sway is much more nuanced:

> To come home to ourselves, Dramatick Poetry began to be brought into form with us, in the time of *Henry VIII* and though since that Time, we cannot boast of such glorious Successes, as we had in the Times of our Fifth *Henry* and our Third *Edward*, when the Conquering Genius of *England*, in triumph seem'd to bestride the Ocean, and to fix an Imperial Foot on the Continent; yet this may be said to the Advantage of the Drama, that since it first began to be cultivated, we have had our Eyes more open, have found that our Constitution is but ill design'd for Conquest; that by being very fortunate, we should run the Risque of becoming very unhappy, and endanger our Liberties, by extending our Empire.[24]

English dramatic success is tied, in Dennis's account, to the growth of a state characterized by Protestantism and Liberty, unambitious for the extended territorial empire likely to bring the corruption which Temple had already detected. His defenses of the stage emphasize that it was during Elizabeth I's reign that Reformed Religion, Liberty and the theatre were all effectively established, thus providing a detailed genealogy for the *idée reçue* that the characteristic form of English literary greatness was identifiable with the nation's most notable political and religious features. He even goes so far, in "The Advancement and Reformation of Poetry," as to set poetic and imperial achievement in contrast, arguing that the English "want only Art, to make ourselves as superior to [the French] in Poetry, as we formerly were in Empire."[25] The conundrum of combining liberty, empire and poetry is finally resolved in *Liberty Asserted*, by the dramatization of a conflict between two different kinds of empire – the tyrannical universal monarchy of the French and the free federation of the English. Here Dennis tunes the imperial thematics of the heroic mode to a specifically Whig key.

THE GLORIES OF THE WORLD

The exploration of empire in the heroic dramas of the 1660s and 1670s is driven by the contemporary fascination with the unresolved questions over Dutch, French and Ottoman aspirations to universal monarchy but also expresses England's global ambition as her marine power and colonies in the Western hemisphere and the East Indies grew. Contemporary political and poetic discourse suggests the incompatibility of an English national identity conceived of as Protestant and free with the pagan or Catholic and despotic character of previous empires; but for Charles and James Stuart, if not for their Protestant subjects, the heroic plays' presentations of monarchs invested with absolute religious and political power were alluring.[26] Further, given the extent to which the new notion of empire, focused on marine power and trade, drew on the old lexicon of universal monarchy, it is hardly surprising that the literary discourse which provided an imaginative critique of empire as previously conceived, inhabited the established forms of national aggrandizement. The heroic drama, generically invested with imperial authority, was the genre best equipped to both display and criticize imperial power.[27]

English ambivalence over the expression of imperial ambition was reflected in the peculiar paucity of serious plays with themes from English history. The heroic drama was conceived of by Dryden as an imitation of a heroic poem, or an "epic in *parvo*," and, as such, it bore the Virgilian burden of epic in representing the nation's glorious past and intimating future greatness.[28] As Thomas Rymer, however, lamented (and a quick count of plays with English subjects confirms), during the Restoration dramatists tended to steer clear of themes from the nation's past. In his "Preface to Rapin" (1674), Rymer censures Davenant for his avoidance of an English subject in his epic *Gondibert* (1650): "One design of the Epick Poets before [Davenant] was to adorn their own Countrey, there finding their Heroes and Patterns of Virtue; whose example (as they thought) would have a greatest influence and power over Posterity; but this Poet steers a different course, his Heroes are all Foreigners: He cultivates a Countrey that is nothing akin to him."[29]

In his "A Short View of Tragedy" (1692), he makes a similar complaint, remarking of the heroic drama that "were a Tragedy after this model to be drawn for our stage, Greece and Peru are too far from us: the scene must be laid nearer home."[30] Rymer believed the most appropriate topics for such plays were episodes which celebrated English triumphs over threats to liberty: "But suppose the memorable Adventure of the Spaniards in '88 against England, may better resemble that of *Xerses*: Suppose then a Tragedy called *The Invincible Armado*."[31] Significantly, this theme is one which demonstrates not so much England's active ambition for empire as her traditional role as check on a Popish and absolutist aspirant to universal monarchy. Rymer's obsession with the traditional form of English power, her marine capacity, led him to include a triumphant navy in his Anglo-Saxon *Edgar* (1677).[32] With the exception, however, of a handful of plays like Orrery's *The Black Prince* (1667), and *The History of Henry the Fifth* (1664), which celebrated England's brief period of territorial rule on the Continent, the heroic dramatists steered clear of local history.[33] In part, this stems from England's pursuit of a "blue-water policy" – as the Marquis of Halifax was to remark in the early 1690s, English greatness was based on sea-power:

Our Scituation hath made Greatnesse abroad by land Conquests unnaturall things to us. It is true, Wee have made excursions, and Glorious ones too, which have made our name great in history, but they did not last; admit the English to be Gyants in Courage, yet they must not hope to succeed in making Warre against Heaven, which seemeth to have enjoyed them, to acquiesce in being happy within their own Circle. In short, it is no Paradox to say that England hath its root in the Sea, and a deep root too, from whence it sendeth its branches into both the Indyes.[34]

Another factor in avoiding English history was, presumably, its contentious nature: the supposed origins of the ancient constitution in Anglo-Saxon England were the subject of fierce legal historical debate, with significant political implications.[35] It is suggestive that a significant number of plays dramatizing the pre-Norman past only appear after 1688. Unsurprisingly, in this context, it is generally assumed that by focusing on the universal monarchies of the past and the great empires of the East, dramatists could get on with shadowing contemporary events more securely – although it seems odd in this case that it was during the Exclusion Crisis, the period of maximum political tension, that so many plays with English subjects actually appeared.[36] The undoubted uses of parallels aside, the heroic dramas used their subjects to explore the nature of imperial power and cultural difference. The plays dramatized the questions central to discussions of empire in contemporary political discourse: the justifications for conquest and settlement and the expansion and preservation of imperial states. As a whole, the genre depicted the rise of Christian empire and carried with it the Providentialist assumption, inherited from the Interregnum, that the *translatio imperii* would pass to the English. It was only after 1688, however, that dramatists started to show what English empire might be.

Two of the interludes revived in *The Playhouse to be Let* (1663), *The Cruelty of the Spaniards in Peru* (1658) and *The History of Sir Francis Drake* (1658) not only represented the black legend of Spanish Conquest in America but predicted the eventual English inheritance of Western empire. Though written under the aegis of Cromwell's Western design, Davenant's prediction of an English triumph in the New World also foreshadows *The Indian Queen* (1665) and *The Indian Emperour* (1667).[37] The Dedication to *The Indian Emperour* figures the power to represent defeated empires as an index of a specifically colonial authority benignly embodied in a beautiful Protestant courtier whose grace stands in contrast to the cruelty of the Spanish:

Under your Patronage Montezuma hopes he is more safe than in his Native *Indies*: and therefore comes to throw himself at your Graces feet; paying that homage to your Beauty, which he refus'd to the violence of his Conquerours. He begs only that when he shall relate his sufferings, you will consider he is an *Indian* Prince, and not expect any other Eloquence from his simplicity, than that, with which his griefs have furnished him.[38]

Settle's Dedication for *Cambyses* (1671) makes a similarly triumphalist claim:

Since the great Characters and Subjects of serious Plays are representations of the past Glories of the World, the arrogance of an Epistle Dedicatory may pretend to some justice, in offering the Heroick Stories of past Ages to their Hands who are the Ornaments of the Present. Once Persia was the Mistress of the Earth, the Royal Seat of the Monarchs of the Universe. Then, as that God the Sun, which they ador'd, lends his kind rays to all lesser lights: so all the Tributary Glories of inferiour Princes shin'd by reflection from the Persian Crown. So now that Sovereignty must cease, and the Eastern monarch Cambyses can pretend to no greatness of his own, but comes to borrow Glories from the Western World, in seeking a Patronage from your favourable goodness. The same Cambyses whom history has represented to be a Blasphemer of the gods, a Prophaner of Religion and a Defacer of Temples, is by your pow'r become a Convert, and humbly payes his Devotion to that Divinity, to whose protection he commits himself and Fortune.[39]

Settle joins the epideictic logic of courtly compliment to the Duchess of Monmouth's beauty to the colonialist topos of savagery soothed by Christian virtue, invoking both the doctrine of the translation of empire and the promise of conversion that justified that transmission of power to Christians. The subject of the play which followed, a conflict between two rival tyrants for control of Persia, depicts precisely the kind of regal criminality and weakness which the ancient historians cited as the reason for the vulnerability of the Persian empire to the rough martial virtue of the Macedonians.[40]

The topics chosen by the heroic dramatists, whether drawn from heroic romances and the French stage or recent travel accounts of Asian and New World nations, frequently focused on a political, military or personal conflict marked by differences in culture and religion. The rash of "Siege, Conquest and Destruction" plays from the mid-1670s emphasizes the popularity of topics which focus on the collapse or consolidation of empires. Plays set in the ancient empires show the state at risk from despotism, as in *Tyrannic Love* (1669), or from aggressors such as Hannibal in *Sophonisba* (1675), while Alexander's weakening and tyranny are analyzed in *The Rival Queens* (1677). The several dozen plays set in Asian states depict the corruption, tyranny and internecine conflict over succession regarded as characteristic of Oriental despotisms, while the numerous plays about Spain and Portugal represented the glories of the *Reconquista*; the black legend of the Conquest in the Americas; Spanish metropolitan corruption through Moorish incursion; and the hubris of imperial ambition.

These texts contributed to contemporary discourses of empire in at least two ways. The implicit narrativization of the gradual triumph of Christian empire aside, the various "stories" offered an opportunity to explore legal and political questions presented by the contemporaneous expansion of English and European colonial power.[41] Some plays show the same concern with justifying conquest through a civilizing mission or conversion central to the inheritance of Roman imperial ideology. *The Indian Emperour* is carefully structured to set the religious and legal grounds for Spanish rule in the Indies against the desire for plunder, pleasure and glory. The virtuous Cortez, arriving in a ship of unprecedented size and armed with guns, overwhelms the Mexicans, aided by their own internal rivalries and weakness. The compulsion evident in the initial meeting with Montezuma, however, where the Emperor is offered a "choice" of surrender or war, and his racking by Pizarro, provide a mordant commentary on the Spanish assumption of their right, as inheritors of the *Imperium Romanum* with a civilizing and Christianizing mission, and a claim, through papal donation, to rule the Indies.

Dramatists were attracted to other episodes in the history of Peninsular conquest and colonization, including the reconquest of Spain, Don Sebastian's hopeless venture in North Africa, and the internal corruption of the Spanish imperial state. The Spanish offered to the English the most compelling example of the attractions and dangers of universal monarchy, against which Charles Davenant warned:

Not only Private Men covet to joyn Mannor to Mannor, with an endless view of Increasing, but Commonwealths also, where one would imagine the Collective Wisdom should think and devise for the best, endeavour to conquer Province after Province, and that if they were always to continue, hoping by good Government to render themselves perpetual; but while Commonwealths thus extend their limits they are working their own Bane, for all big Empires determine in a single Person.[42]

In addition to dramas representing the process of European expansion and corruption, however, there are a large number of plays with Eastern settings which explore what were regarded as the characteristic problems of Oriental, especially Ottoman, empire. The Turks represented a clear and present danger to Europe in the later seventeenth century: Geoffrey Holmes points out that the only reason the English did not fear the imperial aspirations of the Austrian Habsburgs was that they they were known to be preoccupied with fighting against the Ottomans, resurgent after the Austro-Turkish War of 1661–64.[43] People danced in the streets in London on hearing that John Sobieski had lifted the Siege of Buda in 1683 and Waller's anti-Turkish sentiments led the poet to compose no fewer than five poems celebrating the Ottomans' defeat or calling for further holy wars – such sentiments may have contributed to his enormous contemporary popularity. In Settle's Dedication of *Distress'd Innocence* (1691), a narrative of Christian maidenhood endangered by Persian lust, the very recent threat to Christendom represented by the Turks is carefully identified with the equally recent threat to Protestant Britain. The dramatist addresses Lord Cutts of Gowran, well-known as a soldier and enthusiastic Williamite, as a specifically Christian hero:

From your first Honourable Wounds before the Walls of *Buda,* to your last before those of *Limerick,* the no less Favorite of the Great *Lorrain,* than of the Greater *Nassau,* you have been wholly train'd up under the Sacred Gamaliel, Honour. Nor has your Cause been less glorious than your Courage: the common Foes of *Christendom* have been the mark of your Sword; you brought it flusht against the more declining *Turkish,* to Engage it against the more prevailing *Gallick Tyrant.*[44]

The Ottomans were not the only focus of English anxiety during this period. Relations between the East India Company and Aurengzeb were particularly tense in 1674 when the Maratha Sivaji took the title of maharaja in defiance of the emperor's wishes and propelled George Aungier, President of the EIC in Bombay, to establish the Bombay Marine and a force of infantry, cavalry and artillery. Although most criticism of Dryden's 1675 *Aureng-Zebe* has focused on the play's suggestive parallels with English politics, the internal dynamics of India's ruling dynasty were of immediate concern to the English as the EIC was expanding its operations in the sub-continent between 1669 and 1677.

Far more often than has been allowed, the heroic dramatists seem drawn to Oriental subjects because the Levantine and Eastern states depicted were of immediate commercial, military or confessional concern. The Oriental empires were also fascinating because, like the Romans and the Spanish, they presented powerful images of the triumphs and problems besetting universal monarchy. The plays focused on themes familiar from the cogitations of Pufendorf as well as the histories and *relazioni* of Bernier, Chardin, Tavernier, de Thevenot, Rycaut and Knolles: to wit, the ceaseless need for expansion; over-centralized and tyrannical power; problems in succession; the corrupting effects of luxury; the malign effects of harem politics. Although plots and

characterization were constructed in accordance with the imperatives of "love and honour" they were also significantly shaped by
customs and manners materials derived from these travel accounts
and histories. In the operatic *Siege of Rhodes* (1658–62) Solymon's
complaints about the endless need to expand the empire engage
with the arguments expressed by the vizier in Orrery's *Mustapha*
(1665), who speaks the language of the jihad:

> In lazie peace let Christian Monarchs rust,
> Who think no war, but what's defensive, just.
> Our valiant Prophet did by slaughter rise:
> Conquest a part of our religion is.[45]

The influence of both immediate and theoretical interest in the
Ottomans inflects the frequent choice, following Davenant, of a
depiction of the conflict between "the Crescent and the Cross" in
plays such as Dryden's *The Conquest of Granada*, Parts 1 and 2. In several of these dramas, including *The Siege of Rhodes* and *Mustapha*, a
contrast is established between the Oriental viragos who drive their
husbands on to unsustainable conquest and proper, domesticated,
maternal Christian women without ambition, who tame the fierce
Turk and rescue Christendom.[46] *Irena* (1664) is the first of several plays, including Payne's *The Siege of Constantinople* (1674) and
Settle's *Distress'd Innocence* which depict a virtuous Christian woman
at the mercy of a pagan ruler. Other plays showing despotic African,
Asian and near-Eastern states in self-destructive decline, where the
ruler's enclosure within the harem is shown to produce a brutal
sensuality, or the lack of primogeniture is blamed for political instability, include Dryden's *Aureng-Zebe*, and Settle's *The Empress of
Morocco* (1673), *The Heir of Morocco* (1682), *Cambyses*, and, both in
1676, *The Conquest of China* and *Ibrahim the Illustrious Bassa*. Settle
points the moral in his Epilogue to *Cambyses*: "Thus you have seen
the Turkish cruelty / Where Elder brothers reign, the younger
dies." In Orrery's *Mustapha*, Roxalana initiates the action to prevent her own son being killed when his brother ascends the throne:
in Mary Pix's *Ibrahim* (1695–96) the Lucretian narrative is set in motion by the Turkish *droit d'Empereur*. Oriental heroic plays also focus
on the power of "cabals of women" in determining the outcome of
dynastic struggles. "I esteem'd also, that I was not to forget those
two Princesses, as having been the most considerable Actors in
the Tragedy; the Women in the *Indies* taking very often, as well as at

Constantinople and in many other places, the best part of the most important transactions," Bernier remarked in his *History of the Late Revolution of the Empire of the Great Mogol* (1671).[47] The depiction of such demonic figures of lust and ambition as Nourmahal, the Empress of Morocco, the Royal Mischief and the skilful mistress of harem politics, Sheker Para in Pix's *Ibrahim,* illustrate his dictum.

Later heroic plays or dramas with heroic elements by Tories or former Tories, such as *The Widdow Ranter* (1689) and *Oroonoko* (1695), shifted the focus from a critical representation of Spanish or Oriental empire, to the emergent mercantile imperium governed by William and Mary. Here, finally, the new model empire was sometimes itself the subject and in Behn's and Southerne's plays, the colonial societies created by the British were shown to be degraded by the single-minded pursuit of material interest. In these dramas, the heroic values of love and honor are borne by those defeated by the spread of a commercially driven Western empire, with the noble African and American Indian protagonists, victims of a state governed by trade, becoming themselves commodities for exchange. The genre was not simply elegiac, however; as already noted, Dennis used it to praise the new, peculiarly "free" form of British empire in *Liberty Asserted,* while Rowe's 1701 panegyric representation of William as Tamberlane was so successful a celebration of Protestant Empire triumphant, that *Tamerlane* was played regularly on his birthday, until 1815.

The Whig dominance in the early years of the century saw a proliferation of serious plays which celebrated the martial exploits of William and Marlborough and also produced a number of plays representing the Roman invasion of Britain. English history was a vivid site of contestation in the 1690s and 1700s, with Temple writing a hagiographic biography of William the Conqueror in allegorical support of William of Orange, and Blackmore revisiting the Arthurian myth for the same purpose. The return to early British history on the stage provides a suggestive missing link in the narrative of global empire produced from 1660 on. Plays such as *The Destruction of Troy* (1676) had invoked the myth of England's Trojan origins but the early history of the nation – its struggle with Rome especially – had been largely ignored as a theme. As the British Isles became a political unity and assumed an actively expansionist role as a first-rate European and colonial power, dramatists returned to the imperial heritage specific to Britain, focusing on figures of heroic resistance such as Boadicea. The acknowledgment of Roman conquest served as a means of appropriating a complex political, ideological and material inheritance, exploring the dynamics of imperial expansion from both sides of the colonial divide as the English understood themselves to be, simultaneously, liberty-loving resisters of tyranny on the one hand, and order-bearing civilizers on the other.

THE USAGES OF NATIONS

The attractions of heroic plays arose from their spectacular satisfaction of curiosity about exotic cultures, as well as their ability to stage and perhaps exorcise anxieties about domestic and continental politics. Plot and characterization were often shaped by sources in travel books and histories, to provide sketchy but culturally specific images of exotic societies. This last claim may seem rash in view of the general tendency to emphasize the cultural blindness of the heroic drama, a conclusion expressed most eloquently, perhaps, in Scott's own edition of Dryden:

The religion and the state of country where the scene is laid, may be occasionally alluded to as authority for varying a procession, or introducing new dresses and decorations: but in all other respects, an Indian Inca, attired with feathers, must hold the same dignity of deportment, and display the same powers of declamation and ingenuity of argument, with a Roman emperor in his purple, or a feudal warrior in his armour, the rule and decorum of this species of composition is too peremptory to give way either to the currents of human passions or to the usages of nations.[48]

Scott's view has persisted, with those commentators who remark on the exoticism of the heroic plays agreeing that the presentation of different societies produces a generalized sense of "otherness" rather than any very strongly marked evocation of particular cultures.[49] I should emphasize that I am not trying to deny that the heroic plays did contain parallels; rather that the dramas' significance to contemporary audiences cannot be reduced to a single allegorical meaning stemming from domestic politics. This assessment fails to recognize the extent to which Dryden was working with a very different set of assumptions about cultural difference. The assumption of cultural "complementarity" between exotic and Stuart societies identified by James Boon coincides with Dryden's stated conviction in the *Heads of an Answer to Rymer* (1677–8) that "tho' Nature . . . is the same in all Places, and Reason too the same; yet the Climat, the Age and the Dispositions of the People" needed to be respected in dramatic construction.[50] Working within a pre-Enlightenment, universalist framework of belief in the unity of humankind did not mean the heroic dramatists were unaware of, or repressed, cultural differences: rather, they had ways of representing, and indeed of exploiting, cultural alterity which we do not always recognize.

Illustrations of the importance contemporaries attached to respecting customary difference are not hard to find in the critical debates of the period. One such example is the discussion generated by Jeremy Collier's criticism of Dryden's characterization of a corrupt Mufti and a remark denouncing priests in *Don Sebastian* (1689). Collier's attack on the theatre is mostly now remembered for his complaints about indecency but he was also concerned with blasphemy and failures in decorum in regard to rank and manners. His remarks about *Don Sebastian* produced a number of defences which all agreed that Collier had failed to take account of the dramatist's responsibility to represent manners in accordance with climate and custom. As Edward Filmer put it in his *Defence of Plays* (1707): "What shall we say of Sir *John Denham*, Sir *William D'Avenant* and my Lord *Orery*, who when they laid their Scenes amongst the *Turks*, or *Persians*, were oblig'd to make their Persons speak many things unfit for a Christian to utter, as directly contrary to his Faith? Were they then to be look'd upon as *Mahometans*?"[51] Another pamphleteer dismisses Collier's levelling of Mufti and Bishops, mobilizing important indices of difference ("faith" and "complexion") to explicitly reject an allegorical interpretation of Dryden's presentation of the Moor: "[Collier] is furiously provok'd at Mr *Dryden* for saying that *Priests of all Religion are the same* when he himself makes no distinction, but treats the Priests of God Almighty, *Mahomet*, and *Anubis* with the same respect. He is for strengthening his Party, and contracting an Alliance with all Faiths and Complexions; he ransacks *Europe, Asia* and *Africa*, and enters into a religious League offensive and defensive with Sun-burnt *Africans*, and Monsters of the *Nile*. To this end, he labours to find out some relation between the *Mufti* and the Bishops, and very dutifully strains to extend the scandal from *Africa* to *England* that what is said of their Arch-Priest may reflect upon our Prelates."[52] Settle mocks Collier over a different complaint of blasphemy but makes the same point about Collier's blindness to the need for the playwright to represent characters in culturally appropriate terms: "Here *Mustapha*, a Moor of Barbary, for nothing but speaking a word in his own Language, and calling the Month *Abib* in its proper Name, because forsooth that Month is mention'd in Scripture, is therefore Tearing of Bibles, setting up new Prophets equaling *Moses*, and Bantering of Miracles!"[53] Explicitly rejecting a culturally blind or allegorical interpretation of the Moorish characters, Collier's opponents emphasize the dramatic rule that the manners of dramatic persons should follow climate and custom.

The importance of remaining truthful to customary difference and history, as recorded in the sources, is also registered in another of Gildon's attacks on Rowe. In *A Comparison between the Two Stages* (1702), Sullen defends *Tamerlane* on the grounds of Rowe's historical accuracy: "he has describ'd *Bajazet* most exactly as the Histories have left him"; while as to Tamberlane, he continues, "that Hero in all Records, is delivered just such a one as he has made him, allowing something for the shadowing and ornaments of Poetry."[54] It is, however, inaccuracy, both in respect of the historical record in the authoritative source and in regard to customary Ottoman practice and law, with which Critick taxes Rowe. Critick claims that Bajazet's marriage was most improbable, because "the Histories of the *Ottoman* Emperors tell us, that the *Sultan* never marries her who is in his power, till by her Assiduities, Ambition and Cunning, and the Desire of being chief *Sultana*, she infatuates him . . . several Examples might prove this, as we read particularly in the story of *Bajazet's* grandson."[55] Pressed on this claim, Critick replies, "I refer you to the *Turkish* History," a gesture he repeats a page later when expressing incredulity at (Rowe's) Tamberlane offering Bajazet "Liberty and Empire on the condition of his future friendship when the very reason of this War arises from *Bajazet's* perfidy; this Circumstance, I think, makes *Tamerlane's* Generosity little better than frenzy: But the story in *Ricaut* and *Knolles* don't say a word like it."[56]

The importance of accuracy in depicting societies distant from the English in culture and time is succinctly expressed by Edward Phillips in his Preface to *Theatrum Poetarum*:

They likewise err from probability of circumstance who go about to describe antient things after a modern Model, which is an untruth even in

Poetry itself, and so against all *Decorum* that it shows no otherwise then as if a Man should read the Antient History of the *Persians* or *Egyptians* to inform himself of the customs and manners of the modern *Italians* and *Spaniards*; besides that our Author should avoid, as much as might be, the making of any descriptions as should any way betray his ignorance in antient customs, or any other knowledge in which he ought industriously to shew himself accomplish't'.[57]

As we have seen, the industrious display of knowledge about ancient and exotic states Phillips refers to was certainly important to the heroic dramatists. Such exploitation of cultural difference is obvious in the staging of the plays (understood in this period as the Aristotelian category of "scene"), which matched their incorporation of material from sources in voyage literature or history in fable and characterization. Another crucial source of their imperial themes and theatricality was provided by Davenant, inaugurator of the mode in *The Siege of Rhodes*. Davenant's experience in producing masques for the Stuart court has long been recognized as central to his crucial role in the scenic and thematic development of heroic plays.[58] Caroline masques such as Davenant's own *Britannia Triumphans*, which celebrated Charles Stuart's imperium over the sea, overlapped with the early heroic plays not just in their thematic concern with empire but in their scenes and costuming.[59]

The first part of *The Siege of Rhodes* featured elaborate scenery designed by John Webb, Inigo Jones's former assistant. Southerne has suggested that Davenant paid more attention to scenery than any previous dramatist, citing both the playwright's lengthy prefatory discussions of the subject and his unusually full description of the scenes in the text itself.[60] Drama historians have examined this subject carefully, not just because, unusually for the period, designs survive, but also because Davenant's production established theatrical norms. Two notable features of his practice, which became standard in the production of serious plays, were the deployment of backdrops representing location in perspective, flanked by separate screens on grooves, and the situating of the actors in the scene rather than on a jutting apron stage.[61]

The five scenes of *The Siege of Rhodes* which serve as backdrop to the dramatization of a struggle between "the Crescent and the Cross" bring before the viewer the prospect of Rhodes with the Turkish fleet approaching; Rhodes besieged by the Turks at land and sea; Solymon's royal position; Solymon's cattle on Mount

Philermus flanked by his army below; and Rhodes closely besieged. They were not meant to be temporally co-extensive with the action, Holland suggests, but, in line with their derivation from the masque tradition, point to the moment from which events originate and provide a systematic commentary on the action.[62] That commentary, as both the images and Davenant's own remarks suggest, emphasized the binary division between Turks and Christians and, in addition, registered Solymon's power and magnificence. Thus, the "Ornament which encompass'd the Scene" consisted of a frieze decorated by a red curtain on whose right side Western trophies were fixed, and on whose left, Ottoman ensigns. The initial prospect of Rhodes balanced the town "in prosperous estate" against the encroaching Turkish fleet. The perspective recalls the visual and political logic sketched out in one of the most celebrated examples of *ut poesis pictura* of the period, Waller's "Instructions to a Painter":

> First draw the sea, that portion which between
> The greater world and this of ours is seen;
> Here place the British, there the Holland fleet,
> Vast floating armies! Both prepar'd to meet.
> Draw the whole world, expecting who should reign,
> After this combat, o'er the conquer'd main.   (1–6)

In the scene Waller envisages, as in the "ornament" which frames the action of Davenant's opera, the two competing forces are balanced in a struggle for global dominion, presumably reminding the audience of the many marine theatres of conflict in which the English navy was currently engaged.

Davenant's own Prologue emphasizes the importance of the visual dimension of his opera. He was conventionally rueful about the contrast in scale between his production and its subject but he is confident about the illusionistic power of the theatre:

> Who will describe, when any Scene we draw,
> By each of ours, all that they ever Saw.
> Those praising, for extensive breadth and height,
> And inward distance to deceive the sight.   (Prologue, 31–34)

Davenant's scenes can be understood, in fact, as a translation into visual terms of the figure "topographia," the topos of geographical description used in historical or literary narrative.[63] The use of such scenery, characteristic of all the heroic plays, rendered description of the location redundant, while providing the eye with visual excitement and information. Thus Davenant's scenes can be understood as functioning analogously to verbal accounts of exotic or "new" territories, in which the representation of landscape encourages the viewer to take imaginative possession of the prospect.[64] The accuracy of the topographical scenes, their perspectival organization, and their aesthetic enhancement by the frieze, which framed the interior images like paintings, all encouraged the spectator in a pleasurable assimilation of the exoticism represented. While the scenes did reflect masque practice in focusing on marine views and landscapes, it is important to note the novel degree of ethnographic detail incorporated in the images. The initial view of Rhodes, for example, follows topographical convention rather than stage practice, drawing on published views of the town. Solymon's throne, represented in a tent within the Turkish camp, departs from the masque tradition of figuring the monarch in a palatial interior and instead reflects the Ottoman "ancient Law" forbidding the Emperor to "lodg within any walled place not his own."[65] The presence of a stool bearing a sword, recalling the illustration of Solymon enthroned in Artus's *Histoire*, also reflects Turkish practice, which forbad any stranger to enter the Emperor's presence armed.[66]

Davenant's relegation of the actors to the space of the scenes themselves also contributed to the exotic distancing of the action. In comedic production, Peter Holland has suggested, the presence of the actors on a jutting apron stage contributed to the sense of continuity between the audience and performers: both groups seemed to participate in a common social world. In serious plays, however, the action was much more removed from the spectators.[67] Thus, although Davenant believed his proper audience was a refined and aristocratic one, and dedications by later playwrights also stress parallels between royal patrons and the noble characters represented on stage, the action of the plays was kept at a much greater distance from its spectators. The foreign prospects were pleasurable to view but kept at a distance which marked out a crucial difference from the audience, secure in civilized England. When Dryden raised the curtain and had an Indian speak the Prologue to *The Indian Queen* from behind the proscenium arch, he was deliberately underlining the cultural distance of his action.

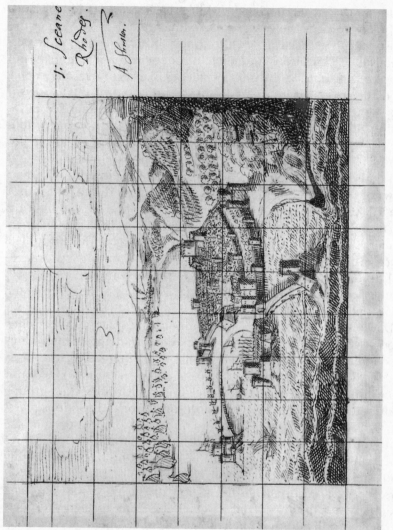

Figure 1. John Webb, "View of Rhodes."

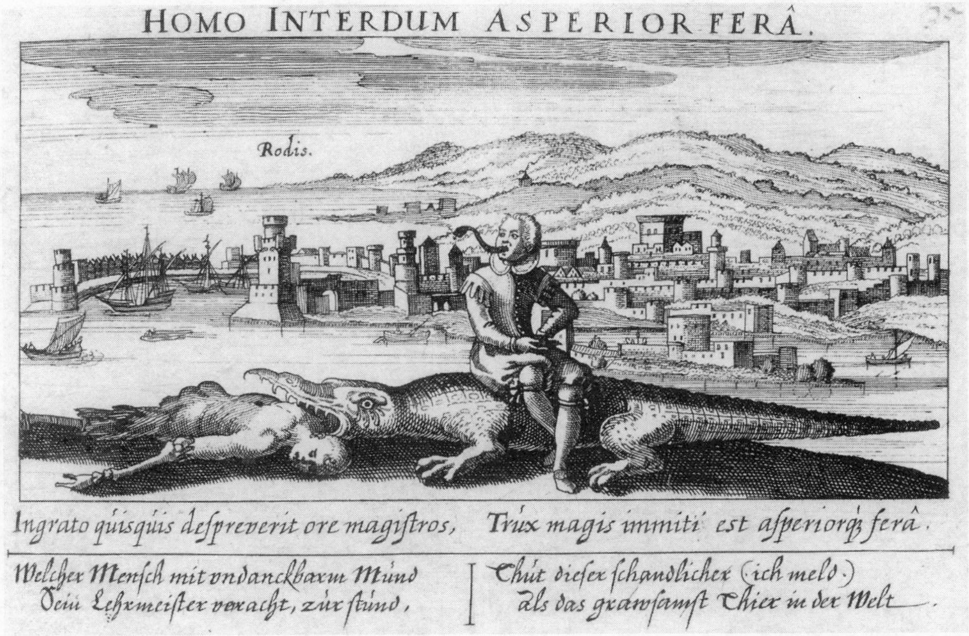

Figure 2. "Homo Interdum Asperior Fera" in Dan. Meisner, *Thesaurus Philo-Politicus* (Frankfurt, 1625) part 3.

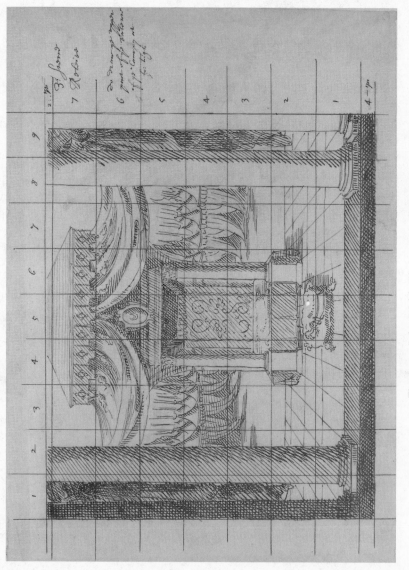

Figure 3. John Webb, "Solymon's Throne."

In the imaginative appropriation of territory enabled by the scenery of the heroic dramas, the locations depicted were not simply pleasurable scenes of contemplation but shown as fertile and improvable pastoral sites and filled with desirable commodities.[68] In *The Indian Emperor*, for instance, Mexico is represented by a charming grotto and a golden altar, images which constitute the country as an exotic "golden world" in literal terms. Colonial acquisition appeared in more than the backdrops. Dryden's and Howard's *The Indian Queen* famously featured a headdress of feathers supposedly brought back from Surinam by Aphra Behn; *The Indian Emperor* established a trend for elaborately decorated altars; *The Empress of Morocco* impressed with a large palm tree. Rather than serving as simple evocations of place or enhancing the dramatic action, the scenes' deliberate aestheticism (framed like paintings or architectural drawings), detailed decoration and color beguiled the eye with an excess of visual "value." The richness of the scenes was aided by costuming which reflected the customs of the locales, in robes and turbans, and enlivened by exhibitions of antic dance. As was the case with the topographical scene in *The Siege of Rhodes*, the costuming drew on engravings from travel books.[69] Audiences were highly appreciative of exotic and exact dress: Pepys was notably impressed with the appearance of the actors in a lost version of *Heraclius*:

The guarments like the Romans very well. The little guirle is come to act very prettily and spoke the epilogue most admirably. But at the beginning, at the drawing up of the Curtaine, there was the finest Scene of the Emperor and his people about him, standing in their fixed and different postures in their Roman habits, above all that I ever yet saw at any of the Theatres.[70]

Although the Royal masque tradition (as well as voyage literature) was an important source of the scenery and costuming so notable in these plays, the heroic dramas also had features in common with an apparently very different kind of production, the annual Lord Mayors' pageants. These were held to inaugurate the new office-holder and featured elaborate *tableaux vivants* with allegorical personages who spoke on moral themes. Those of the Merchant-Taylors Company in particular often included "Indian Emperors," "West Indians," "Tawny moors," "Niggars" and "Negro-Boys" as well as feminine figures named "Africa," "Asia" and "America," "representing merchandize, Traffick and other Dealings."[71] The account of Jordan's 1680 pageant, commissioned by the Merchant-Taylors, heaps up phrase after phrase to evoke a sense of the visual richness of the figures who embodied the possibilities of exotic accumulation:

a large Imperial Pavilion, Guls Fringed and richly garnished and adorned ... bearing the excellent Figures of lively carved camels, which are the supporters of the Said Companies Coat... On the back of each camel, rides a Representator, the one richly adorned with a Golden Robe, a Purple Mantle fringed with Gold, a Black *Indian Face*, Black Curl'd short Hair (a Native *Indian*), an Orient Pendent Pearl in his Ear, a Coronet of Gold decked with Feathers on his Head, Golden Buskins on his feet, laced and furled with Scarlet Silk Ribbon, a Golden Bridle in his Left Hand, and in his Right Hand, a Banner of the Companies, and representeth Treasure. The other is a West *Indian*, invested with a Robe of Silver, with a Silk Scarlet Coloured Mantle, Head, Hair and Face, Black. In his Left Ear and Pendent Diamond, Buskins of Silver, laced with Purple Ribbon, a Crown of Gold Feather'd, in his left hand a Silver Bridle, and in his Right, a Banner of my Lords, representing Traffic.[72]

The verses spoken at the end of the pageant by a "Sea-Captain" provide a concise interpretive coda for the preceding display, in celebrating the various justifications for mercantile activity.

> By Merchants Care and Industry, no doubt
> Many incognita Countries are found out.
> Who between foreign Princes often be
> The Author of a Royal Amity.
> By them many Out-landish brutish Natures
> Have been reduc'd, and become Christian Creatures.
> By Merchants we receive all sorts of Treasure
> Varieties for Profit and for Pleasure.[73]

The mayoral pageants' cultural function was quite distinct from that of the heroic drama but the two modes drew on a similar visual vocabulary to represent the wealth available in a variety of exotic cultures. Further, the pageants' verse and allegorical spectacle articulate an ideology of expansive mercantilism which is implicit in the heroic plays' themes, action and production though rendered opaque in the elevation of the mode. Each of the activities praised by the Sea-Captain is played out in one or other of the rhymed plays. In pleasurable fantasmatic form the drama provides access to unknown countries with splendid stores of wealth. In plays like *The Indian Princess, The Indian Emperor* and *Liberty Asserted* "Royal Amity" and converts are gained, while in dramas such as *The Conquest of Granada*, exotic royalty either discovers its Christian origins or gives way before the power of cross and sword.

Both the mayoral pageants and the heroic drama share a powerful drive to present colonial activity in idealized and nationally unifying terms. Common aims aside, it is hardly surprising that, with the same dramatists writing both pageant and play texts, representational devices should recur. The parallels were limited, however, to the positively valenced evocation of wealth: there is no equivalent in the pageants for the rhymed plays' other notable scenic effects, those of enchantment and especially of horror. Although some theatre historians emphasize the continuity of these effects, linking the executions, rackings, gaunchings and stabbings which abound in the heroic plays to Elizabethan and Jacobean antecedents, there appears to be a substantial increase in their occurrence in serious drama after 1660.[74]

Contemporaries remarked on the development – Settle makes jokes about the tendency in his Prologue and Epilogue to *Ibrahim* ("How many has our Rhimer killed Today?")[75] and:

> How can our author then his doom recall?
> He knows we must under your justice fall;
> Being guilty of so capital a crime
> As shedding so much humane blood in Rhime.[76]

Moreover, the scenes of violence on the Restoration stage were presented with an elaboration of which earlier productions were technically incapable: the manipulation of the wings, of "aerial" effects and of scenery produced new and ever more grotesque impressions.[77] Settle's *The Empress of Morocco* was notorious for its final act, which ends by revealing the villain "cast down upon the Gaunches, being hung on a Wall with Spikes of iron"; engravings in early editions of the play show no fewer than four mutilated bodies.[78] Such images had their origin in contemporary accounts of Barbary which often mention these deadly iron spikes, known as the "Algiers hook." Settle's *The Conquest of China* (1676) exhibits a heap of "murdered women, some with daggers in their Breasts, some thrust through with Swords, some strangled and others Poyson'd."[79]

Finding the blood-letting distasteful, most critical assessments do not pay much attention to the role of violence in the heroic plays. Richard Morton's conclusions are representative: "In *Titus Andronicus*, or in most of the sensational Restoration plays about cruelty and savagery – *Amboyna, The Empress of Morocco, Aureng-Zebe* – there is no significant attempt made to explain the violence or to incorporate it into any theory of behaviour; this is simply how barbarians act."[80]

The African and Oriental empires depicted by the rhymed plays however, were conceived of as despotic, not simply as sites of the generalized savagery implied by the term "barbarian," and the scale and the kind of violence depicted in the drama reproduce such conventional distinctions. Montezuma the Great makes human sacrifices; mutes strangle Sheker Pera in *Ibrahim the Thirteenth Emperor of the Turks* (1695–96). Delariviere Manley's evocation of grotesque Oriental violence in *The Royal Mischief*, whereby the Vizier is shot out of a cannon and his burning remains heaped up in a parodic funeral pyre by his grieving wife begins, however, to verge on satire.

When the *Censure of the Rota* chose to figure Dryden as a dramatic torturer, inhabitant of a grizzly den encumbered with exotic victims, they indicted the producer rather than the consumers of such extraordinary spectacles. Dramatists did strive to overwhelm the audience, not just with the grandeur of their verse, but also by means of the newly effective engines, scenes and machines. Replaying a dispute between scene and rhetoric, visual and verbal power, which had divided Inigo Jones and Ben Jonson, Dryden was habitually straightforward about his desire to establish "absolute dominion" over the spectators through the power of poetry while Davenant, in his Prologue to *The Siege of Rhodes*, placed more stress on purely technical effects:

> O Money! Money! if the WITTS would dress
> With Ornaments, the present face of Peace;
> And to our Poet half that Treasure spare,
> Which faction gets from Fools to nourish Warr;
> Then his contrasted Scenes should wider be,
> And move by greater Engines, till you see
> (Whilst you securely sit) fierce Armies meet,
> And raging Seas disperse a fighting Fleet.   (Prologue, 39–46)

Here Davenant's lament suggests a kind of substitutive relation between theatrical representation and "Warr," figuring the theatre as a space in which fantasies of imperial conquest could be enacted without danger. What is most striking here, though, is his stress on the "Engines" as the primary means by which that paradoxical effect of danger in security could be created. While the images represented on the scenes themselves and the relative distance from the audience contributed to the creation of such sublime effects, they depended on the novel technical capacities of the new theatrical machinery. Contemporary sources reflect an awareness of the engines' splendor. Evelyn commented on the new Dorset Garden Theatre: "I went home steping in at the Theatre, to see the new machines for the intended scenes, which are indeede very costly, and magnificent."[81] Through the first two decades of the Restoration, both dramatists and spectators consistently remark on the pleasure and the power of the effects.[82] As Pepys recorded (August 2, 1664), theatre manager Tom Killigrew boasted that his new theatre was to "have the best Musique, and everything as Magnificent as is in Christendome."[83] Southerne, quoting Pierre Sourel, points out that the etymology of "machine" is the Greek "mechane," attached to the root "medomai," which means "I reflect, I machine something, I govern, I command."[84] This derivation is suggestive of the way in which, not simply for dramatists, but for spectators also, the new machinery of the Restoration stage inaugurated by Davenant figured a novel degree of technical control over theatrical space. The scenic command over the world of the theatre offered to the dramatist by the newly sophisticated engines can be seen as analogous to the power that technological assets such as guns, shipping and cannon provided Europeans in colonial adventuring, dramatized by Dryden in *The Indian Emperor*. The machinery was not simply aesthetically effective: it functioned as an index of political, technological and cultural command in the world beyond Europe so often represented on the stage.

Scenery, costume and action all contributed to render the rewards and the dangers of the mysterious East and the barbaric New World with fantastic vivacity, if not accuracy, beginning a tradition which culminated (in the eighteenth century at least) with the extraordinary pantomimes and visual spectaculars of De Loutherburg, whose subjects included such celebrations of empire as the storming of the Heights of Abraham and the travels of Omai. One might wonder why the heroic dramatists steered clear of direct representations of such messy but exciting aspects of contemporary colonial activity as planting settlements, slaving, buccaneering and trading and focused instead on crucial episodes of the past and present seats of pagan, Catholic and absolute empire. The reasons include the ambivalence felt by many of differing political views within the elite (if not the Stuarts) in aiming at universal monarchy: the theatre provided a space in which previous modes of empire could be explored and criticized as well as celebrated. Then there was the inconsistency between the nature of most colonial activity and the elevated literary means traditionally employed to celebrate European national and imperial power. When Dryden tried to present an episode directly from recent colonial history, in *Amboyna* (1672) which he wrote to consolidate support for the war against the Dutch, the play was a failure. He blamed his material: "the Subject barren, the Persons low."[85] An Indian Princess aside, there was no one of any aristocratic, let alone royal, status who could dignify proceedings, and the play stands as a clumsy record of squalid and violent commercial rivalry.

If Charles and James Stuart had a dream of empire, legible perhaps in their attempts to tighten control in the American colonies and articulated in an idealized form in the heroic drama, it was one informed by the traditional notion of universal monarchy and absolute imperium. The failed and fantastic nature of that imperial dream should not prevent us from seeing the fascinations it held for an English elite becoming aware of new global possibilities. It was no accident that Samuel Pufendorf quoted extensively from Dryden to provide poetic illustrations for his discussions of empire, dominion and trade in the fourth book of his *Law of Nature and of Nations*. The obsessive interest in heroic fantasies of imperial governance gave Tory dramatists considerable acuity in assessing the failures of a colonialism driven primarily by material interest, producing plays which mourned the foul effects of English slaving and settlement in the New World. Shortly thereafter, however, Whig triumphalism takes up the civilizing mission of the form in the name not of Christian glory but of English liberty.

CHAPTER 3

The Great Turks:
The Ottomans on Stage, 1660–1714

Between 1660 and 1714, at least forty plays set in Asia or the Levant appeared on the London stage. They were almost all serious, heroic plays or tragedies, recording turbulent episodes in the empires of Persia, Egypt, India, China and Turkey, showing these states torn by civil war, harem politics, sensual despotism and conflict with European states. Reluctant to recognize these settings as anything more than vestiges of the heroic tradition inherited with the love and honor code from French practice, critics (with two recent exceptions) have been averse to viewing these locations as in any way relevant to the ideological role of the theatre.[1] Close reading of the dramatic incorporation of contemporary assumptions about such Eastern states suggests, however, that the playhouse was an important institution in the development and dissemination of Orientalist views of Europe's predecessors and rivals in empire. This was not a simple exercise in Western condescension; until the early nineteenth century, Europeans had no certainty of military superiority in conflicts with Asian powers; the Ottomans were resurgent during the Restoration and the position of Levant and East Indian traders throughout the period was insecure, and often precarious. The discovery of the New World, mostly populated by peoples whom the early modern English regarded as vagrant and savage, did not displace Asia as the most powerful political, cultural and religious alternative to Europe. Although it seems clear that many educated English assumed the center of power was shifting to the West, the Levant and the Orient provided a contemporary mirror, not simply a historical imaginary, in which local political problems, whether those of succession or the relation between the Crown and private citizens, could be re-imagined, explored and resolved. It is hardly surprising that, having presented alternatives to Western practice such as primogeniture in their productions, dramatists used prefatory material as well as the action itself, to underscore the benefits of European customs. Nonetheless, just as male dramatists were interested in the political effects of polygamy as well as the sensual promise of the harem, female playwrights of the 1690s were interested in the seraglio not just as a site of sexual oppression but as a means of exploring the peculiar power of Oriental "cabals of women." In the early eighteenth century, dramatic representations of alternative gender orders proliferated while Tamberlane, conqueror of Asia, still served as a model for William, ruler of the new-style universal monarchy of trade.

THE GREAT TURKS

The non-Western empire most frequently depicted on stage was the one which embodied the most proximate and pressing threat to Europe, that of the Ottomans. The Koprulu grand viziers, Mehmet, Ahmet and Husein, engaged in major campaigns against the West every decade from the 1650s through the 1710s. The Koprulus had another even more menacing symbolic dimension to English Royalists, in that they had overthrown and executed Ibrahim the Twelfth in 1648. In their ruthless disposal of the hereditary monarch a year before the death of Charles, and their establishment of a highly efficient, reformist military government, the dynasty stood comparison to Cromwell. Although the English, geographically secure from Ottoman attack, were not directly involved in the Austro-Ottoman War which ended in 1664, or the attacks on Poland and Crete in the late 1660s and 1670s, there were Englishmen who fought in the Holy League against the Turks in the 1680s, and the latter conflict was widely reported. The Ottoman defeat at Vienna in 1683 was a prologue to fourteen more years of war, which only ended, owing to help from William III's Ambassador at Constantinople, with the Peace of Karlowitz. The Treaty was a crucial marker in relations between the Ottomans and Europeans because for the first time the Turks accepted the principle of fixed territorial boundaries. There was a Russian–Turkish conflict from 1702 to 1711 in which the Turks were successful but the Ottomans faced defeat once more in 1718. After 1699, the Ottomans were simply much less awesome: suggestively, during the "Tulip Period" of reform which followed Karlowitz, they began to incorporate European customs and technologies.[2]

English attitudes to the Ottomans were obviously affected by their relative insulation from direct attack but there was still plenty of popular fear and hostility directed towards the great Turks, especially during the latters' campaigns. This was significantly mitigated, in the City at least, by the favorable trading arrangements arrived at in 1663, which gave rise to two exceptionally profitable decades for the Levant Company. After 1688, the Turkey traders were the wealthiest in the City *per capita*, a position they had enjoyed for much of the century.[3] Although protected by royal charter, Levant merchants became suspicious of Charles II and James II, believing them to have connived at interloping both by the French and by the old East India Company, and De Krey suggests this gradually tilted the Turkey traders towards Whiggism.[4] Economic interests aside, religious and political convictions inflected attitudes to the Ottomans, and Exclusion Crisis satire alludes to the fact that dissenters and some Whigs claimed to admire the Turkish empire for its toleration, an opinion early expressed by Bodin.[5]

Although, with hindsight, Turkish power can be seen to be in decline at the end of this period, contemporary observers were not nearly so complacent.[6] John Marsh's *New Survey of the Turkish Empire* (1663), the most intemperate and hostile account of the Ottomans in this period, provided a narrative of recent Turkish aggression which preceded an urgent plea that Europeans forget their differences and join in a holy war against the cruel oppressor of Christians.[7] Marsh believed the Ottoman Emperor "is bound by Law at every three years end, to undertake some expedition into Christian territories, for advancing or defending his own territories,"[8] an injunction so effective that already, Asia, Africa, the Levant and parts of Europe itself were "lost" to the Porte. In his Dedication to Sir Andrew Riccard of the Levant Company, he glosses Turkish military success as an effect of sobriety, which had led "this *Asian* People, once the nauseated and basest drags of the World, odious for their Luxury, and infamous for their Slavery" to "become the Mightiest Nation and greatest Lord of the Universe." The author of *Europae Modernae Speculum* (1665) expressed a similar anxiety about the territorial expansionism characteristic of the Ottomans in the introduction to the last chapter of his European survey, itself concerned with "those Parts of Europe That are under the Turk"[9]: "Having surveig'd our own *State*, and what we may *hope*, take we a view of the *Mahumetans*, and what we may *fear*, whose

Dominion is placed most conveniently for the Universal Monarchy he aimed at, being evenly situated between *Europe* and *Asia*, as some think, at the Center of the habitable World; whereby he is ready, on all Occasions, to stretch his Conquests every way."[10]

The theme of Turkish imperial ambition is also central to Paul Rycaut's *The Present State of the Ottoman Empire* (1667), later appended to his continuation of Knolles's *Turkish History*. Rycaut was George Etherege's predecessor as Secretary to the English Ambassador at Constantinople and Consul at Smyrna from 1667 to 1678. *The Present State of the Ottoman Empire* (1667) and his continuation of Richard Knolles's authoritative *The Generall Historie of the Turks* (1603) served as an important source for most plays about the Ottomans. Rycaut's attitudes were considerably more temperate than those of Marsh but he shared the general view that the Turks were expansionist seekers after universal monarchy. His analysis of the Ottoman imperial state followed the model of the Venetian *relazione*, detailing the governmental and military organization and religious practice and beliefs. His account is framed by an address to a general Reader who is told to view the Turks as negative exemplars who should instruct the English in their own good fortune, as free Christian subjects under a ruler who respected private property and the rule of law:

If (Reader), the superstition, vanity and ill-foundation of the Mahometan religion seems fabulous as a Dream, or the fancies of a distracted and wild Brain, thank God that thou wert born a Christian, and within the Pale of an Holy and Orthodox Church. If the Tyranny, Oppression and Cruelty of that State, wherein Reason stands in no competition with the pride and lust of an unreasonable Minister, seem strange to thy Liberty and Happiness, thank God thou wert born in a Country the most free and just in the World; and a Subject to the most indulgent, the most gracious, of all the Princes of the Universe: that thy Wife, thy Children and the fruits of thy labour can be called thine own and protected by the valiant Arm of thy most fortunate King: And thus to know and prize thy own Freedom, by comparison with Forreign Servitude, that thou mayest ever bless God and thy King, and make thy Happiness breed thy Content, without degenerating into Wantonness, or desire of Revolution.[11]

The Turkish Empire, however, does more than define through contrast the virtues of the free Protestant state of Restoration England. No prince, argues Rycaut, can "embrace a large Compass of the Globe, who is pinioned with the bands of his own Laws."[12] It is preferable, though, he claims, to be subject to a king who accepts legal limits on his power, does not punish arbitrarily, and acknowledges "a right of possession and Propriety of Estate as well in his Subjects as himself"[13] even if the consequence of such monarchical restraint is the curtailment of imperial power: "But then they (such subjects) must content themselves with their own borders, or some neighbouring conquest, and this is better, and a greater glory and content, than the honour of being slaves to the lusts of a Monarch, whose Titles comprehend the greatest part of the World."[14]

On the one hand, then, the Ottomans instructed the English in the virtues of their own state, a monarchy limited by law, not absolute and, hence, unimperial: both free and territorially bound. As Tim Harris has stressed, the belief that the King was bound by law was not exclusively a country or Whig conviction but was an important strand of the "conservative legal constitutionalism," which he believes contributed as much to the eventual Tory platform as the early Cavalier–Anglican tendency to absolutism.[15] This suggests Rycaut's account articulated a view of England's peculiar constitutional advantages with wide-ranging appeal. In addition to using the Ottoman state as a positive means of defining the English polity, however, Rycaut invoked the institutions of the Roman empire as a positive contrast to Turkish practice, thus leaving open the possibility of conceiving of an imperial state which was free even though territorially expansive: aggressive but peaceful, just and protective of property. "These two empires being compared," Rycaut remarks:

there will be found a vast difference in the original, foundation, progress, and maximes each of other. For the *Romans* built their City in peace, made Laws by which the arbitrary will of the Prince was corrected; and afterwards, as their Arms succeeded, and their Dominions were extended, they accommodated themselves often to present necessities and humors, and constitutions of the people they had conquered; and accordingly made provision and used proper Arts to keep them in obedience; and next, by their generosity and wisdom won these Nations to admire and imitate their Vertues and be contented in their Subjection. But the *Turks* have but one means to maintain their Countries, which is the same by which they were gained, which is the cruelty of the Sword."[16]

Plays about the Ottomans operated with a similarly doubled, if not trebled, perspective. They did provide a distant context in which local anxieties about the recent revolution, regicide and usurpation of power could be paralleled. It is surely no accident, though, that the most frequently used exotic setting was also the closest, the most threatening and the most familiar – there is after all, only one Restoration play about China, the most distant, exotic nation to the English, and hence presumably the safest location for allegorical representations of domestic conflicts. The late seventeenth-century dramas which used the Turkish empire as a setting generally served, like Rycaut's account, to remind English audiences of the unique advantages of their own free, law-abiding, Protestant polity even if occasionally, as in *The Siege of Constantinople* (1675), they hymned the virtues of arbitrary government. The representation of the problems of Ottoman expansion, preservation and absolutism, however, also provided a template of Oriental despotism which served as a negative exemplar not simply of statehood, but of empire.

Drawing on heroic romance as well as *relazione* as sources and models, serious plays generally had an amatory vehicle for these explicitly political critiques, a plot which staged the conflict of crescent and cross in the terms of love and honor, figuring Christian victory through the topos of a virgin taming a wildman, or using the debauched sensuality of the ruler as a measure of Turkish luxury and corruption. The improper power of women such as the sultana, the 'mother' of the concubines or the Queen-Mother often featured, as did episodes which exploited the glamorous eroticism of the seraglio. The perversions to proper gender relations identified in such characters and institutions was an important element in the plays' pleasurable and instructive exploitation of cultural difference, drawing as they did on material provided by the *relazioni*. Rycaut's *Present State* emphasized the connections between the political and gender order, arguing that the institution of polygamy not only reflected Mahomet's lustful predilections but "next to the satisfaction of his own carnal and effeminate inclinations... his main consideration was the encrease of his people by *Polygamy*, knowing the Greatness of Empires and Princes consists more in the numbers and multitudes of their People, than the large extent of their Dominions."[17] It was also a "Maxim of State" which guided the "disuse of marriage in the Sultan," with Rycaut arguing that the memory of the humiliation of Bajazet's wife Despina by Tamberlane, along with the huge expense likely to be incurred

by a consort, rendered the avoidance of imperial marriage necessary in Turkish eyes. Finally, the vulnerability of any unmarried
woman to the sultan's lust, most graphically displayed in the reign
of Ibrahim XII (dramatized by Mary Pix), served in English eyes
as an index of the absolute and arbitrary nature of Ottoman rule,
and the insecurity of private persons and property in such a state.

"WOND'ROUS TURKISH CHASTITY": SOLYMON THE MAGNIFICENT ON STAGE

Sue Wiseman's recent reassessment of *The Siege of Rhodes* usefully
resituates the text within the context of English domestic politics
and colonial ambition at the point of its initial production during
the Interregnum.[18] Wiseman emphasizes that the opera revised
contemporary, conventional wisdom about the Ottomans in positive terms, a process facilitated by the latters' increasing famili-
arity and diminishing military power. My reading of the text has
a rather different focus. *The Siege of Rhodes* inaugurated the heroic
drama, the genre which encoded English imperial ambition and
anxieties in the Restoration and this role precluded too subversive
a modulation of orientalizing tropes. The opera presents Solymon
with some sympathy but the action as a whole reflects the kinds of
concerns legible in Marsh and Rycaut, by emphasizing the tyrannical power of Oriental despotism, the endless search for conquest
and the fury of the women who urge on the holy war. Davenant's
sources include Richard Knolles's *Historie of the Turks*, and also perhaps Thomas Artus's *Continuation de l'histoires des Turcs* (1612), as
well as various French plays, but the action is shaped by a familiar
topos in representations of cross-cultural encounter, as a virtuous
Christian woman subdues a wild man. Solymon's love for Ianthe
is the sole reason that he is halted in the ceaseless expansion of
his empire. Further, the contrast the text attempts to establish between the modest Christian Ianthe and the fiery Oriental Roxalana
establishes a pattern of oppositions which recurs in a whole series
of heroic plays, and serves as a fundamental index of difference
between the two cultures.

The Siege narrativizes an episode from the on-going epic of
Christian empire, focusing on the conflict between the Turks and
a European colony insecurely perched in the Mediterranean
and garrisoned by a mixed force of Western nations. Somewhat

unsubtly, Davenant underlines the primacy of the English among the allies: "Those desp'rate *English* n'er wil fly! / Their firmness still does hinder others flight" (v.i. 37–38). Alphonso echoes the Turkish praise of English superiority:

> Ianthe cannot be
> In safer company
> For what will not the valiant English do
> When Beauty is distress'd and Vertue too?   (v.i.105–108)

For all its emphasis on English prowess, however, the opera initially suggests some ambivalence about imperial expansion. This may well reflect the highly moralized condemnation of Spanish corruption through empire developed by Commonwealth ideologues under Cromwell but was also an important strand in the more generally held conviction that England's proper role in Europe was holding the balance of power, rather than engaging in aggression. The second act of the first part begins with a discussion between the Rhodian leaders about the weakness imparted to Europe by disunity and the urge to colonize:

> VILLERIUS: By Armies, stow'd in Fleets, exhausted Spain
>   Leaves half her Land unploug'd, to plough the Main;
>   And still would more of the old World subdue,
>   As if unsatisfi'd with all the New.
> ADMIRAL: *France* strives to have her Lilies grow as fair
>   In others Realms as where they Native are.
> VILLERIUS: The English Lyon ever loves to change
>   His Walks, and in remoter Forrests range.
> CHORUS: All gaining vainly from each others loss;
>   While still the Crescent drives away the Cross.   (ii.i.17–26)

The first part of *The Siege* presents the Turkish invasion as a consequence of Christian rivalry and division that stands in contrast to the effective absolute rule of the Ottoman empire, a depiction which prefigures the warnings of Rycaut that "it will evidently appear . . . how formidable their Force; which ought to make the Christian world tremble, to see so great a Part of it subjected to Mahometan Power, and yet no meane thought of to unite our Interests, and compose our Dissensions, which lay us open to the inundation of this flowing Empire."[19] The desperate efforts of the

Rhodians do hold off a final Ottoman victory, but the military initiative is all Solymon's.

In the second part, however, the critique of empire shifts from a condemnation of European ambition and disunity to focus on the Ottomans. Solymon himself questions the wisdom of endless expansion; and the negative representation of the Turkish state's aggression is underscored by the disturbing role taken by the Sultana, Roxalana, in its administration. Her assertion of her public role, and the stress in her relation with Solymon, are contrasted with Ianthe's reluctant adoption of the role of envoy before the adoring Europeans. Gradually the conflict between the two camps is transposed into an erotic contest between two women, who encapsulate the values of their respective nations.

In Act i, scene i of the second part, the Admiral reiterates his condemnation of empire:

> Why should we thus, with Arts great care
> Of Empire, against Nature Warr?
> Nature, with sleep and food, would make Life last;
> But artfull Empire makes us watch and fast.   (i.i.61–64)

However, Alphonso is able to defend continued resistance in the name of freedom and honor, and the Admiral's association of empire, destruction and unnaturalness is taken up by the Turks, who can make no such defense of its ends. Brooding alone after a conference with his generals, Solymon ponders its costs: "Of spacious Empire, what can I enjoy? / Gaining at last what I at first destroy" (ii.ii.53–54). Turkish conquest is here represented as operating in accordance with the logic identified by Rycaut, who claimed that the only means by which the Ottomans could extend and maintain their conquests was "the cruelty of the Sword":

> I was born to govern swarms
> Of Vassals boldy bred to arms:
> For whose accurs'd diversion I must still
> Provide new Towns to Sack, new Foes to Kill.   (ii.ii.57–60)

The emphasis here is on Solymon's potential vulnerability as a despot, driven on by the demands of his vassals and "slaves." Later, however, his quarrel with Roxalana points to another cruelty enjoined by the Ottoman custom, when Roxalana complains of the practice of strangling, or at best imprisoning, the younger sons of

the Sultan: "Because her Son the Empire shall enjoy / Must therefore strangling Mutes my Sons destroy?" (IV.iii.327–28). Solymon
defends the practice, regarded by English commentators as a violation of natural law, without hesitation and without the idealistic
color of Alphonso's response to the Admiral:

> Those are the secret Nerves of
> Empires force; Empire grows often high
> By rules of cruelty,
> But seldome prospers when it feels remorse.   (IV.iii.341–44)

The dispute between Roxalana and Solymon over the death of their
sons not only stands in contrast to the nuptial happiness established
between Ianthe and Alphonso, but turns on an issue which became
emblematic of the cruelty inherent in Ottoman practices. At the
end of the fourth act, Solymon's soliloquy renders the link between
the public and private customs and acts quite explicit:

> With new and painfull Arts
> Of Study'd War I break the Hearts
> Of half the World, and She breaks mine.   (IV.iii.356–58)

Faced with a fierce and rebellious spouse, the Emperor cites domestic disharmony as the primary threat to his hegemony; for the
Rhodians, however, Ianthe's chaste attractions serve as their best
hope of reprieve.

As the Christians' military power declines, the contrast between
the two women becomes more central to the narrative. Ianthe
is cast as a figure of gentle modesty and Roxalana as an ambitious virago. This modifies somewhat Ianthe's presentation in the
first part, where she sold her jewels and braved the seas to join
Alphonso, dressed as a man and fought in battle. In the second
part, she has to be persuaded to act as envoy after the populace
elect her. Roxalana, however, is introduced in the midst of manag-
ing affairs of state, as courtiers and ambassadors solicit her favor.
In the soliloquy which comments on this scene, she explicitly contrasts herself with the passivity of Western queens: "But they shall
find, I'm no *European* Queen, / Who in a Throne does sit but to
be seen" (II.iii.49–50). In two later scenes in Roxalana's "rich pavilion," the contrast is developed further. As the first scene opens,
Roxalana is shown with a "*Turkish* Embroidered Handkerchief in

her left hand, and a naked Poynard in her right" (iv.iii), as she contemplates killing the sleeping Ianthe. The latter's waking beauty, however, subdues her aggression immediately and the two women discuss the virtues of "Christian Ladies." Ianthe not only embodies such modesty but disabuses Roxalana of her conviction that the European liberty of communication between the sexes must produce license, and converts the Empress to a belief in the superiority of Western love relations: "These Christian-Turtles live too happily. / I wish, for breed, they would to *Asia* fly" (iv.iii.129–30). The final scene in Roxalana's pavilion brings the contrast to a climax. Ianthe is discovered weeping over her fear for Alphonso, and Roxalana derides her softness and credulity:

> Soft Fool! bred up in narrow Western Courts;
> Which are by subjects storm'd like Paper-Forts:
> . . .
> Thinkst thou that she, who does wide Empire sway,
> Can breed such storms as Lovers show'rs allay?
> Can half the World be govern'd by a Mind
> That shews Domestick pity, and grows kind?
>
> (v.vi.55–56, 59–62)

Although she eventually relents, the Empress here displays a cruelty comparable to Solymon's obduracy about the necessity to kill his sons. Her unnatural lack of "Domestick pity" and kindness is marked as specifically Asian, as is her apparent willingness to ignore her oaths: "Religion is but publique fashion here; / And Justice is but private interest" (v.vi.73–74), the latter certainly a view shared by Rycaut. Roxalana claims that "Nature our Sex does to revenge incite" (v.iv.75) but her brutality towards Ianthe figures a femininity perverted by corrupt institutions, false religion, despotism and power, won over only by a "wondrous kind" Christian wife.

The Empress's submission to Ianthe's chaste charms mirrors Solymon's. As the latter makes clear, at the end of the play it is Christian womanhood which has subdued the Turk, rather than Christian arms:

> Go back, *Ianthe*; make your own
> Conditions boldly for the Town.
> I am content it should recorded be,
> That, when I vanquist *Rhodes*, you conquer'd me.
>
> (v.vi.208–11)

Solymon's honorable treatment of Ianthe, what Alphonso calls in the first part his "wond'rous Turkish chastity" (Part I, III.ii.127) cannot be read simply as a recuperation of the Great Turk, however. *The Siege of Rhodes* still rehearses a process whereby European subjects conquer a non-Western other; Solymon's seduction by Ianthe, and her clear elevation over Roxalana, uses the love and honor mode to enact a process of psychological colonization in which the norms of Turkish behavior, both domestically and politically, are critiqued and subverted before being abandoned by the Ottomans. It is significant, however, that the text is critical of European as well as Turkish empire; the most powerful template of imperial statehood here is the Ottoman model, depicted with much of the negative doctrine codified by Knolles, but the Christian desire for expansion is also roundly condemned. Davenant produced the opera under the expansionist Cromwellian regime and the ambivalent respect with which Solymon is presented perhaps reflects the dramatist's reluctant admiration for England's Protector. But however fascinated he was by the latter's Western design, Davenant was not capable of providing more than a largely pessimistic depiction of imperial expansion and preservation.

The next dramatization of Solymon's career came in Orrery's *Mustapha*, produced in 1665 and greeted with immediate acclaim. It became a standard feature of the repertoire, and was still being played in the last decade of the century. This play also drew on Knolles's *The Generall Historie of the Turkes*, focusing once more on Roxalana and Solymon, and counterpointing the energetic and intriguing Oriental woman with a virtuous Christian. The action turns on Roxalana's efforts to secure the death of Mustapha, the imperial heir and Solymon's elder son, so that her own son Zanger will not be murdered when Mustapha ascends the throne. Having succeeded in this aim, however, she is denounced by her servants after her own son has committed suicide, and, after being forced to write a confession by Solymon, is divorced and banished. The other main action of the play concerns Mustapha's and Zanger's rivalry in love for the Christian Queen of Buda, whose city has just been taken at the outset of the action. Roxalana is instrumental in rescuing the Queen's infant son from Solymon and in ensuring their continual safety until the end of the play when the Turks and Hungarians join forces against the Spanish King invading from the West.

The play departs markedly from Knolles's interpretation of events in the *Generall Historie*. Knolles is extremely critical of Roxalana, accusing her of excessive ambition in precisely the terms used by Solymon within the play: in his account, she is manipulative, ruthless and power-hungry, first persuading Solymon to break with custom in marrying her and then scheming incessantly with her son-in-law Rustan to displace the popular Mustapha.[20] In Orrery's text, Roxalana is presented as passionate but motivated primarily by maternal love, forced into her schemes by the cruel maxims of the Turkish polity whose rigors the heroic princes also try to modify. Knolles treats the death of Mustapha as an episode demonstrative of the cruelty of particular Ottomans, including Solymon, whom he regards as degraded in age, but Orrery focuses blame on the structures of the Turkish state. In the play, tragedy arises from the collision of natural, maternal feeling and an inhumanly cruel system of succession.

The intrigues in Solymon's camp are again framed by the larger contest between Crescent and Cross, a conflict explicitly represented as the clash of competing religions and political empires:

> RUSTAN: In lazie peace let Christian Monarchs rust,
>   Who think no War, but what's defensive, just
>   Our valiant prophet did by Slaughter rise:
>   Conquest a part of our Religion is
>   . . .
>
> SOLYMON: To Rome I will my dreadful Ensigns lead
>   Rome which was once the universal head
>   Which still the worlds important part controuls:
>   Once she gave Laws to Kingdoms, now to Souls;
>   To that great conquest my designs I bend.
>
> (I.i.23–26, 31–35)

Solymon's triumphal progress is, however, impeded by the intrigues and rebellions set in motion by the ruthlessness of the Turkish laws of inheritance, which specify the death of all younger sons on the succession of the heir: "These fatal Maxims made our Sultans still / As soon as they were Crown'd, their Brothers kill"(I.ii.207–208). In the section on Turcomania in the third edition of his *Cosmographie* (1665) Peter Heylyn provides a summary account of these murderous practices:

Amongst all the jarres and discontents that be, none have been with more unkindness begun, or more eagerness prosecuted, than those of brothers; and that not only in private families but in the stem of Princes: the multitude of Pretendants, being the original of most *civil wars*. To

prevent these publick emotions, the Emperors of *Habassia* use to immure
up all their younger children, in the hill, *Amaza*: the *Persians* do put out
the eyes of their younger brothers, and the *Turks* do murder them: strange
and horrid courses, whereby to avoid the fear of war in the State, they stir
up a war in their own bowels.[21]

It is these "strange and horrid courses" which inspire Roxalana to
bring about Mustapha's death as her maternal care rebels against
the cruel laws of empire. In contrast to her presentation in *The
Siege*, in fact, Roxalana's maternal "nature" is set against the cruelty
of Turkish practice throughout the play; the first act not only sets in
train the plot against Mustapha but shows Roxalana succoring the
Christian infant prince of Buda in defiance of her vizier's advice:

> Fair Empress, when Religion does oppose
> What custom plants, or in our nature grows
> We are incens'd, and yet we then forbear
> T'accuse the Law, but tax th'Interpreter;
> As men refrain to quarrel with the strong,
> But wrongs pretend from those whom they may wrong;
> Our law offends them by their own mistake,
> Whilst what is merciful, they cruel make:
> This infants Blood will quench the flames of War;
> Millions of lives we by his dying spare.   (I.iv.310–19)

Roxalana shows an almost Christian mercy in contrast with the le-
galistic rigor of her advisers but the quality she exhibits is repeatedly
named, specifically, as "Nature":

> ROXALANA: And I, in my perplext condition, must
>   Become unnatural, or else unjust:
>   Must leave a Son to Empires cruelty,
>   Or to a gen'rous Prince inhumane be.
>   My Husband, whom I love, I cruel make,
>   Even against Nature, yet for Natures Sake.   (IV.v.656–61)

Even her opponents agree with this assessment:

> CARDINAL: Think not the Empress will her pow'r employ
>   T'establish him who must her Son destroy.
> QUEEN: Honour has in her Soul the highest place.
> CARDINAL: Nature has greater pow'r than Honour has.
>   (V.iii.135–38)

The dreadful contest between Turkish law and maternal nature is emphasized by the final extraordinary scene of her confession. Orrery added this scene, for which no source exists. Instead of the violent *dénouement* which ends so many of these texts, it produces an effect of elegiac tenderness. Solymon demands that Roxalana "Make haste! Write full your ambition down / In changing the succession of my Crown" (v.ix.697–98) and she counters by reiterating once again that it was her maternal instinct which governed her actions: "I have but little through ambition done / Nature did more, and 'twas to save my son" (v.ix.713–14).

What is at stake in this extended conclusion, which reiterates and publicizes rather than clarifies Roxalana's motivation? Solymon's explanation for his demand is somewhat curious:

> SOLYMON: It is not fit our Priesthood or Divan
>   Should sit to judge the wife of Solymon.
>   But yet the blood by your ambition spilt,
>   Cries out so loud against your audacious guilt
>   That now my People, Armies and the State,
>   Behold your Beauty with malicious hate:
>   And no expedient can satisfie
>   The justice they expect unless you dye.
>   You can to Heav'n alone for mercy trust.
> ROXALANA: Sir, I will dye that they may find you just.
> SOLYMON: But, that your Sex may ever think me so,
>   You must a form of process undergo,
>   Which strict necessity does make me use.
>   You must, under your own hand, your self accuse:
>   Which, as a true Record, may rescue me
>   From false opinions of my crueltie.   (v.ix.652–67)

Solymon's need to get Roxalana's guilt down in writing he attributes to a desire to avoid not the People's, armies' or state's disapprobation, but that of "your Sex." The power of maternal nature, inherent in *all* the "Sex," uniting Roxalana and the Christian queen, is implicitly set in contrast with the "law" which governs the state. Roxalana's situation is one with which her female audience will presumably sympathize. However, the subversive implications of that sympathy are qualified by our knowledge (withheld from Roxalana) that Zanger and Mustapha had made a fraternal contract to override the usual practice of murdering rival claimants to the throne. The brothers, acting rather like civil Christian subjects, attempted to give birth to a new political order, but Roxalana's attempts to save Zanger, governed by her untrammeled nature, brought nothing but disaster to the entire imperial family.

The actions of the Christian Queen provide a counter-example. Equally maternal, the Queen of Buda is prepared to act under the sign of law, honor and policy, at the behest of her advisers risking the life of her son to save her city. In her obedience to the dictates of the Cardinal who advises her, we see a properly governed model of feminine nature, one who submits willingly: "My Lord, your pious reasons make me yield / Nature to Vertue should resign the field" (1.ii.151–52). Her modest Christian virtue also captivates Zanger and Morat, exercising a moderating influence which stands in contrast with Roxalana's disastrous exacerbation of Solymon's jealousy of his son. Roxalana is in many ways an attractive figure, but one whose ungoverned nature, struggling with arbitrary laws, is death-dealing. By contrast, the Hungarian Queen represents a fruitful, submissive and proper maternity, one governed by true religion and capable of reconciling the demands of "Sex" and the "State": capable finally of warding off the Turkish advance and, it seems, of defending Buda successfully against the Catholic aspirant to empire, Ferdinand of Spain.

Mustapha is a play obsessed with maternity and succession, unsurprising given that its production coincided with the growing suspicion that Catherine of Braganza was incapable of bearing Charles an heir. Interest in the Ottomans was high in 1664–65, not just because a new, important trade agreement had been reached the year before, facilitating the activities of the Levant Company, but because the Turks were again at war with the Austrians. Orrery sets his play in the same terrain at stake in the contemporaneous conflict but also uses the very different practices of the Turks to explore problems in monarchical succession visible on the horizon of English politics in the face of the Queen's infertility. The allegorical exploration of such problems is finally foreclosed, however, by the play's insistence on the crucial role of specific Turkish customs in the bloody history of the Empire. The text has little interest in establishing a clear superiority of individual Christians over Muslims in martial or moral terms, with the Protestant Hungarians joining with the Turks to resist Catholic incursion, imperial heirs apparently capable of reform and a heroic presentation of Solymon. Roxalana's dilemma, which sets her "Sex," her very "nature," against the "cruel maxims" of the Ottoman state, is the cause of tragedy, and, ultimately, it is the cruelty of the maxims of Turkish empire which stand condemned, as they destroy the Ottomans themselves.

In *Ibrahim the Illustrious Bassa* (1676) Settle returns to the subject of Solymon's putative infatuation with a Christian beauty and Roxalana's subsequent humiliation. Again, the play's use of a Turkish theme seems responsive to recent campaigns in Poland and Crete, with the action suggesting that the contest between love and honor among the Ottomans always results in erotic failure, for which the resumption of military campaigning is compensation. The play initially presents Solymon as a heroic figure of virtue, one whose glorious martial exploits have been matched by his faultless private conduct; he has broken with Turkish custom to marry Roxalana, giving up the pleasures of the harem and has proved a magnanimous friend to his conquered foes. As in *The Siege of Rhodes*, however, the action shows that virtue tested by Solymon's love for a Christian virgin, Isabella, here betrothed to the virtuous renegado, Ibrahim. Solymon proves incapable of resisting the Ottoman power to put aside a wife and appropriate his subjects' women for himself and only the suicide of Roxalana and her unsuccessful lover, Persian Prince Ulama, forces him to renounce Isabella and allow the happy lovers to return to a Christian kingdom. Although Solymon does finally act properly, three virtuous lives have been lost in his pursuit of an unlawful love. The play thus acknowledges Solymon's greatness but it suggests such glory is always vulnerable to the degradation implicit in the Turkish gender order and the arbitrary nature of Ottoman rule.

Settle's play self-consciously turns away from the political crises usually associated with his mode, turning Shadwell's mockery of the great actions of heroic dramas back on itself in his Epilogue:

> How many has our Rhimer kill'd today?
> What need of *Siege* and *Conquest* in a Play?
> When *Love* can do the Work as well as they?

Although he compares his Dedicatee, the Duchess of Albemarle, to Roxalana, in the Epilogue he emphasizes the distance between the heroic qualities of his characters ("Such Love I'm sure as *English* ground ne'er bore") and the audience. The play presents nobility in both Turks and Christians, with Asteria, Solymon's daughter, attempting to save both Isabella's and Ibrahim's lives despite the latter's rejection of her, and Roxalana refusing the temptations of unlawful love. Both Asteria and Roxalana, though, are not only less alluring than the Christian Isabella, but improperly passionate, killing themselves when their love proves unsuccessful. As in *The Siege of Rhodes* and *Mustapha*, the erotic success of the Christians serves as a synecdoche for a putative cultural superiority rendered dubious by the past and present political and military strength of the Ottomans.

Ibrahim opens with Roxalana glorying in the unique honor conferred upon her through marriage to Solymon:

> By Sacred Rites, I've bound my Royal Slave
> It has been mine, and only my Renown
> T'have joyn'd a Nuptial Wreath t'a Turkish Crown.   (1.i [2])

The connection between power and love so insistent here is underscored by her address to Solymon on his entrance: "Welcome the Worlds great Conqueror & mine" (1.i.[3]). The potential conflict between the terms of love and honor adverted to here is of course absolutely central to this mode but Settle reworks the tension between erotic and political power already ethnicized by Davenant and Orrery to analyze the martial greatness and moral weakness of the Ottoman Empire. In *Ibrahim*, Solymon's virtue is augmented by his apparent capacity to surpass the immoral and corrupting luxury encouraged by Turkish custom, by renouncing the pleasures of the harem to devote himself solely to Roxalana:

> Love, which in Turkish Kings no limits knew,
> But wide and spreading like their Ensigns flew;
> By the new Miracle your Beauty wrought,
> Its first and only constancy was taught.   (II.i, p. 23)

With Isabella's appearance, however, Solymon's "self-subduing" collapses:

> There is a Christian Beauty hither come,
> Who has out-done the Arms of Christendom.
> The Turkish Crescents were Triumphant there,
> But their great Leader is a Captive here.   (II.i, p. 23)

Roxalana's tragedy resides in her gradual realization that Solymon has not renounced the sexual privilege of his position and she upbraids him not just for perfidy but for sliding back into incivility:

> Yes Sir: you rais'd me to a Crown, forsook,
> The rude delights your wilde Fore-fathers took,
> When from the feeble Charms of multitude,
> And change, your heart with one pure flame endu'd
> And all entire to *Roxalana* giv'n:
> As Converts quit Idolatry for Heav'n.   (III.iii, p. 38)

Roxalana's chastisement of Solymon's recurrence to the savagery of "other Turkish Kings" is augmented by Ibrahim's reproaches that the Sultan is improperly encroaching on his subject's right:

> How little does this change appear in You
> When *Solymon*, who lately took delight,
> In Thoughts that soar'd above an Eagle's Flight,
> Now humbly stoops t'invade his Vassals right.   (IV.i, p. 47)

Ibrahim's complaint echoes Rycaut's admonition to the Reader in the *Present State*, reminding the audience that, in the Turkish empire, the Sultan was bound by no laws, that his will was absolute and that there was no security in property or persons. Solymon's conduct towards Isabella represented a return to the exercise of arbitrary power after his apparent renunciation of such customary sway and, despite his final recovery of virtue, the play is scarcely optimistic about the likelihood of the Ottomans reforming themselves from within. Solymon's self-prescribed cure for the personal tragedies he has undergone is to return to those campaigns which Rycaut and the other commentators saw as essential to the Turkish state. Private happiness is reserved for the Christian couple who depart to a Christian nation.

Settle's exploration of the corruption engendered by the absolute sexual power of the Sultans was proleptic: in the most striking later plays about the Ottomans, Mary Pix's *Ibrahim the Thirteenth Emperor of the Turks* (1695–96) and Joseph Trapp's *Abra-mule* (1708), the dramatists return to the theme of despotism tested and corrupted by luxury. In these plays, written in the 1690s and 1700s, the protagonists are notably less heroic. The choice of episodes featuring Emperors who became venal and were destroyed by their sensuality arguably reflects the decreasing anxiety caused by the Ottomans,

who began negotiations for peace in the early 1690s. Earlier playwrights, writing with the threat of successful Turkish aggression to
the fore, either chose Solymon the Magnificent and his consort
Roxalana, or the equally fearsome Mahomet, conqueror of Constantinople and beheader of Irene, as subject.

"JEALOUS OF EMPIRE": MAHOMET AND THE FAIR GREEK

The Irene plays retold the famous episode in which the Sultan
Mahomet, having taken Constantinople, became enamored of a
beautiful Greek captive. His soldiers became rebellious, convinced
that their Emperor had abandoned his valor in a couch of luxury.
Mahomet put down the threatened rising by dressing Irene in the
finest robes and jewels and bringing her before the army and then:

> with one of his hands catching the fair Greek by the hair of her head,
> and drawing his Falchion with the other, at one blow struck off her head,
> to the great terror of them all; and having so done, said unto them; *Now
> by this judge whether your Emperor is able to bridle his affections or not.* And
> within a while after, meaning to bridle the rest of his choler, caused great
> preparation to be made for the *Pelopnessus* and the beseiging of *Belgrade.*[22]

The story was dramatized three times between 1658 and 1675 as
well as of course, most famously by Johnson, a century later. The
episode fascinated because it exemplified so many strands of English doxa about the Turks: Mahomet's ruthless and decisive personal cruelty reflected the absolute power invested in the Emperor,
his freedom from legal constraint, his rights over subject persons,
as well as his paradoxical dependence on the janissaries, utterly
subjugated and yet rebellious. The need for the Emperor to enact cruelty personally, killing his beloved, demonstrated to English
eyes the absolute priority of war over love among the Ottomans,
and served as a vivid emblem of that cruelty which Rycaut identified as the sole means by which they expanded and preserved
their empire. It is also of course a story of Christian womanhood
sacrificed first to Turkish lust, and then violence, in the wake of
the Turkish conquest of a Christian holy place. The story was also
susceptible, however, to more elevated and sympathetic interpretation, in which Mahomet's action served as an emblem of the
self-possession needful in a monarch: the ability to sacrifice desire
in the face of political necessity. While dramatists were never willing

to forgo emphasizing the sensuality and violence inherent in the story and its Turkish setting, they did begin to exploit the allegorical possibilities offered in the context of Charles's licentiousness.

In 1658, Gilbert Swinhoe published *The Tragedy of the Unhappy Fair Irene*, a version which emphasizes Mahomet's treatment of Irene as exemplary of the cruelty necessary to maintain the empire. This play does not focus on the struggles of a heroic Emperor tested by lust but represents the action as a tragedy for Christendom: Irene's fate is not only the result of the measures forced on the Sultan by a bloodthirsty and suspicious soldiery but treated as the fatal outcome of European disunity and weakness. All the Christian characters in Swinhoe's text, including Irene, die: there is no last-minute substitution of a wicked slave or a noble renunciation by Mahomet. Swinhoe includes a Christian hero who tries vainly to rescue Irene and she is herself presented as chaste (unlike the willing paramour of Knolles's account) but otherwise the play follows the action and characterization presented in *The Generall Historie*.

The next version was published by an anonymous author in 1664: Derek Hughes has suggested the text was intended as a mild rebuke to Charles, whose sensual propensities were beginning to cause concern.[23] While this seems plausible enough, it is also important to remember this year saw the final stages of the Austrian Emperor's Turkish War while Marsh's alarmist anti-Ottoman account appeared twelve months earlier. *Irena* presents the heroine as the beloved of Justinianus, the Christian leader aided by a kindly Turk after battle who attempts, with his friend Honorious, to rescue her from the seraglio. After Justinianus saves Mahomet from an attempt on his life by the disloyal Aga, the Sultan, though torn between gratitude and love, allows the Christian lovers to depart together for Italy. The soldiers' fury is allayed by Mahomet killing a slave who much resembled Irene and whom he had fortunately spied the day before being dragged along to her execution for a "notorious crime" (v, p. 82).

This version presents Mahomet much more positively than Swinhoe's: although the Sultan's martial prowess suffers in comparison to the Christians', he does act honorably and his final resolution to resume his conquests underscores his military status. Unlike the earlier play, which presents the action very much from the perspective of the Christians, *Irena* emphasizes the presence of two world-views. The first act consists of an expository scene between two janissaries, followed by rebellious janissaries plotting, while the second act introduces the Christians. The third act shows Mahomet with Irene, followed by Irene and Perinthia with Justinianus and Honorious. The noble characters on both sides then increasingly appear together, and the bravery, honor and integrity displayed by the Christians in such scenes, emphasizing the ungrateful treachery of the Turks, serves as symbolic compensation for the historic scene of European defeat in which the action is located. Although Mahomet is largely exempted from hostile characterization, and indeed reveals himself to be just and law-abiding as well as honorable (by sacrificing a criminal instead of Irene) the text still emphasizes the cruelty of Turks triumphant. Describing his escape in the aftermath of battle, Justinianus reports that when the Turks fell to stripping the dead bodies "'twas my happy fate / To be stript by a Janizary...more charitable than generally / Those kind of people are...I was much pleas'd to find such humanity / In a Barbarian."[24] Although Justinianus benefited from the exception who proves the rule, the Turks are represented as collectively intent on that bloody enlargement of empire which has defined Ottoman greatness: "The Soldiers and People" Mustapha the loyal Bassa pleads, "are / Displeas'd and incens'd to see you lay by / All thoughts of enlarging o' the Empire" (III.iii, p. 47), a plea which is repeated frequently through the play:

> Follow the example of your illustrious
> *Ottoman*-ancestors, And lead 'em again
> Forth, to enlarge your Empire and obtain
> New Conquests.   (III.iii, p. 49)

Mahomet finally relents and resolves, ominously, as in Knolles, "*Peloponesus* I will strait invade / And thence I'le lead 'em to besiege *Belgrade*" (V.iii, p. 86).

Irena is an ambivalent text, drawing on the Turkish setting to emphasize the overweening importance of monarchical responsibility and the iniquity of rebellion but also conscious of the "barbarousness" of the state in which imperial martial virtue was most conspicuous. The successful exit of the Christian lovers to Italy suggests that, however honorable particular Turks might prove, the cruel and restless Ottoman empire could not be a plausible habitation for noble Europeans. In *The Siege of Constantinople*, Henry Neville Payne returned to the Irene story but set the action in the Court of the Christian Emperor, dramatizing the actual siege and fall of the city, as well as its notorious aftermath. Payne's version focuses on the treachery in the Christian camp which led to the Turkish triumph, with false counsellors, disloyal soldiers and grasping citizens all held responsible for the catastrophe. The Chancellor is most guilty: an agent of the Porte, he argues wrongly to engage the Turks, diverts aid from Christian princes and encourages English and Venetian ships to leave harbor. His most egregious act is an attempt to prostitute Irene, which is foiled by his own daughter Calista, when, ambitious to be Sultana, she pretends to be Irene. The army, under Justiniano, refuse to fight without pay, the necessary funds being withheld by the greedy and complacent citizens. The Emperor's brother, Thomaso, alone proffers wise advice and, despite being traduced, fights loyally in the final battle which sees the Christian ruler killed and the Turks triumphant. Befriended by a noble Bassa, having impressed Mahomet with his courage, Thomaso is rewarded with the Kingdom of Morea and Irene's hand, the renegada Calista having been beheaded in her place.

Payne's play invites reading in parallel, as the action seems to celebrate James, excoriate Shaftesbury and damn the City, unwilling to grant Charles more aid in the Third Dutch War. Again, however, an allegorical reading fails to exhaust the play's contemporary significance. The text was produced during the Ottoman war against Crete in 1675–76, and followed persistent Turkish incursions into Poland: England might have been "barricado'd by sea" from direct attack, but other parts of Europe were under direct threat. The play deals with the internal weakness of and among Christian states likely to produce defeat by the Turks by emphasizing the venality of trading nations (including the English and the Venetians) and the suspect motives of the Papacy. The text also, however, depicts the negative effects of a form of government presumed specific to England, where the monarch is bound by law, not arbitrary, consults with his "senate" and cannot (or will not) levy taxes without consent. Although such an analysis clearly adverts to constitutional debates within England about the nature of royal power, the Turkish context complicates what might look like a straightforwardly pro-Stuart position. Rycaut had prefaced his account of the Ottomans by celebrating just such characteristics of English governance, admitting they prevented territorial expansion but arguing their benefit to citizens. In *The Siege of Constantinople*, these characteristics are linked to external defeat, while the ruthless efficiency of the absolute and expansionist Ottomans is highlighted. In the debate with his brother which opens the play, the Emperor defends his practice of consulting with his senate, arguing that "Princes like myself / That circumscribe our actions by our Laws" need to gain approval for their policies from a majority.[25] Having failed to recognize the dangers of such conduct, deploring the imminent fall of his state, the Emperor asks "What can an Emperor, bounded and ty'd / By Laws, Act more than I already have –" (v.i, p. 79), reiterating the plaint a little later:

> My subjects obstinate to all entreaties
> Deny me their supplies; and I'm resolv'd
> Rather to perish with them, than extend
> My Regal pow'r beyond its usual bounds.   (v.i, p. 80)

His brother Thomaso, who advocated ignoring the senate and a policy of appeasement towards the Ottomans, is proved right in his analysis but becomes, in effect, a Turkish vassal. The text excoriates Christian (and specifically English) weakness but it cannot locate an unproblematic virtue in the alternative offered by the Turks. The Ottomans are depicted as effective enlargers of empire and there are noble figures in their ranks but the play's incorporation of such motifs as strangling mutes and poisoned robes, as well as the centrality of the story of Irene's beheading, serves as a constant reminder of the sudden violence with which Ottoman power is gained and maintained. While Thomaso is presented as a figure able to negotiate a successful future under the Turks with honor, the figures of the Chancellor and his renegada daughter Calista tell another story about rapprochement. The Chancellor, who sees himself as "Grand Vizier to this growing Monarchy" (1.i, p. 8) is a figure totally corrupted by ambition while his daughter, who prostituted herself willingly to the Sultan in the same pursuit of power, takes on the hall-marks of Levantine barbarity. Referred to repeatedly as "Medea" (the archetypal Asian villainess), she attempts murder with both poison and the string before being herself decapitated.

With the exception of Swinhoe's text, the representations of Solymon and Mahomet in the plays written between 1658 and 1675 are broadly, if not exclusively, admiring. The depiction of the Ottomans was inflected by local political agendas which sought to admonish various forms of monarchical weakness but collectively the plays also produced – or reproduced – a remarkably consistent image of Ottoman rule, broadly consonant with the views of travel writers and historians. The plays invoked the familiar spectacular tropes of Turkish violence and sensuality, with strangling mutes, stabbings, beheadings, seraglio scenes, eunuchs and the disguise of the veil recurring in most texts. They always used the conflict of Crescent and Cross to structure their action, even when the plot, as in *Ibrahim the Illustrious Bassa*, was primarily concerned with an erotic, rather than martial, competition. When the larger, historic, military victory is Ottoman (as it invariably is, in these texts), the love and honor mode, personalizing the interactions of Turks and Europeans, allows for Christian erotic success which restores a sense of European triumph. Finally, however melodramatic or *précieuse* they might now appear, the plays offered a cogent account of the means by which Turkish empire was expanded and maintained. The ambivalent regard expressed for the great enlargers of empire reflects the fascination and awe inspired by such endeavors, even as the English, led by their supposedly law-abiding and liberal monarchs, actively disavowed such ambitions to universal monarchy.

The next play with a Turkish theme written in the 1680s was Charles Saunders's *Tamerlane the Great*, performed at Oxford before the king in 1681. The play focused on the attempts of a wicked counsellor to ensure the son he had exchanged for a royal sibling was able to take the throne. Saunders emphasized in his Preface that he had no knowledge of Marlowe's play and his version does present the Tartarian hero in a milder light, as Providentially intended to defeat the Turks and honorably intentioned. The play is unusual in having no Christians within either the Ottoman or Tartar courts; and while the text can be read as an attack on Shaftesbury (in the person of the scheming Odmar) and a defense of legitimate succession, it also emphasizes the centrality of Islam and a certain Scythian savagery in the new conquerors of Asia. Tamberlane still "Lock'd in an iron Cage his Rival Slave / While he in barb'rous Triumph mounted on / His shoulders to his Chariot"[26] although the action is reported, rather than shown; and the play begins with a dramatic scene of prayer in the Temple of Mahomet. Muslim belief continues to play an important part in the intrigue, when Tamberlane is deceived by minions prepared to swear falsely on the Koran and murder their enemies with poisoned holy books. The text includes a chorus of praise to Tamberlane as:

> thou to whose high care Heav'n doth intrust
> The Rule of Nations, Monarch of the Earth
> So may you Laurels bear from either Pole
> As you to them shall peaceful Olives joyn
> And in your Conquests God-like Mercy show.   (II, p. 13)

The figure shown in the play, however, is more wrathful than peace-loving.

"SOFTNESS AND EASE": DEPICTING DECLINE

The paucity of plays with Turkish themes in the 1680s presumably reflects the general decline in dramatic production during this decade, a period not only of internal strife in England but one which saw a resounding defeat for the Ottomans when the siege of Vienna was lifted in 1683. Rowe returned to Tamberlane's defeat of the Turks to produce his famous celebration of William III in 1701, and Mary Pix's *Ibrahim the Thirteenth Emperor of the Turks* and Joseph Trapp's *Abra-mule*, produced in 1696 and 1704 respectively, are based on significantly different figures and episodes from Ottoman history from those presented by earlier dramatists. Both the latter chose to depict emperors who were killed precisely because of their inability to overcome their sensual weakness: Ibrahim is never an effective ruler at all, while Selyman is initially a powerful Sultan but collapses into debauchery and is replaced by another lascivious ruler. Charles Goring did produce another version of the Irene story in 1708, but this account stresses Mahomet's vulnerability to Irene's charms rather than his ability to resist sensuality. It is hard not to see this shift to theatricalizing weak Ottomans as a reflection of changing, more confident English views of the Great Turks. These plays provide a riposte to John Marsh's lament that the luxurious Turks had thrown off their debauchery to become the mightiest nation of the world, suggesting that the Ottomans were relapsing into the sensuality from which they emerged.

Like most post-1688 dramas, the later Turkish plays justify revolution, depicting the Sultans deposed in the course of the action as violent invaders of their subjects' persons. There is another kind of political resonance in these texts, also: as Robert Hume points out, "Oriental melodrama" became something of a specialty among women dramatists in the 1690s and 1700s.[27] Moira Ferguson has argued that slavery, including "Eastern" enslavement, became an important location for the projection of Englishwomen's sense of themselves as an oppressed sex.[28] Where the male playwrights of the Restoration exploited the exoticism of the seraglio, celebrated the contrasting purity of Christian womanhood and praised European sexual relations as marked by freedom and ease, Pix and Manley seem fascinated by the overt sensuality of the harem, the license to exploit one's female sexuality and the political authority attached to such covert erotic power.[29] The enclosure of women was also, obviously, a powerful figure of female enslavement, and Manley in particular can be seen as, simultaneously, exploiting and satirizing the contradictory dramatic possibilities of harem politics.

The point at which a putative proto-feminist interest in the position of Turkish women in the Oriental plays of the 1690s and 1700s connects with the on-going preoccupations of the political nation proper is the familiar question of succession. In *Mustapha* and to some extent in *The Siege of Rhodes*, the Turkish practice of polygamy and the resulting proliferation of heirs provided the springs of action as Roxalana attempted to secure the succession for her own son. These Turkish episodes provided both contrasts and parallels to English audiences: Charles was legally limited to one partner by the monogamy enjoined by Christianity but he practiced an unofficial polygamy which would produce an ambitious, rebellious son in the Duke of Monmouth. In the Turkish plays following 1688, when the ruler and heir entitled to the throne by primogeniture were set aside by the Glorious Revolution, polygamy became a less compelling topic and insurrection appears newly legitimate. After 1688, succession was no longer solely determined by maternal bodies and the gender order which organized and legitimated reproduction. In the same period in which England had successive female rulers, their specifically female maternal capacity was becoming much less important in terms of public political life: succession could, and would, be negotiated, without reference to direct heirs.[30] Accompanying this gradual diminution of the political importance of the female body in the national sense, Catherine Belsey has argued that the expectation that women assume a private and domestic identity emerges in the years following the Glorious Revolution.[31] In this new regime, the heroic characteristics of *femmes fortes*, celebrated in heroic romances and heroic plays, will become the objects of satire, and chastity will gradually become the sole measure of female virtue.[32]

In *Ibrahim the Thirteenth Emperor*, *Abra-mule* and Goring's *Irene*, female sexual purity assumes a new importance. These plays are not, however, simply spectacularizations of male sexual violence against chaste victims, exoticized she-tragedies which use the harem to dramatize a heightened sexual dialectic. They provide justification for a change in succession through revolution, depicting the Sultans as improper invaders of their subjects' rights unable (unlike Solymon in *Ibrahim the Illustrious Bassa*) to restrain themselves within proper bounds. While susceptible to a loosely allegorical reading, however, they are also graphic illustrations of the vulnerability of subject persons in the Turkish empire to which Rycaut referred in his Letter to the reader. The actions presented are symptomatic of a corrupt empire increasingly destabilized by luxury, halted in its pursuit of power by the depravity of the single person in whom all power terminates.

Ibrahim opens with a denunciation of the emperor by his own Mufti:

> Now, by our Prophet, what's all this but gaudy Pageantry,
> Ill acted scenes of pomp and show, instead of real greatness:
> O my friend it was not thus of old,
> The great Forefathers of this degenerate Man,
> Instead of treading on the *Persian* Carpets,
> Trod upon the Necks of *Persian* Kings.[33]

The sultan's pursuit of pleasure rather than empire is matched by an equally rapacious and improper appropriation of private property, so "That soon as a Merchant Ship salutes the Port / His Goods are seiz'd, and brought to the *Seraglio* / Without Account, Value, or Justice" (i, p. 2). Ibrahim's rape of the Mufti's daughter, Morena, combines the outrages of effeminate indulgence and the invasion of right outlined in the first scene and justifies his overthrow and the establishment of a regency by the virtuous Amurat. But the promise of reform in the Ottoman state implied by the revolution is ambiguous. The agent of revolution is Amurat, established as a figure of almost Christian probity (promising Morena, for example, that he would never exercise his right to polygamy) but, like his virtuous betrothed, he kills himself. The play finishes with their two deaths, leaving the Mufti distracted with grief and little sense that a new political order has been established on the ruins of the old. The play conveys a sense of the Ottoman empire in crisis, in need of reform but succumbing to its own weakness.

Pix's *Ibrahim* has been remarked on by feminist critics for its peculiarly graphic representation of violence against Morena, who is dragged away by her hair before returning to the stage bedraggled and bloodily violated. The play is fascinated by more than violence, however. While the political analysis the play offers reflects the terms provided by Rycaut, Pix's presentation of the Ottomans, like the account provided a decade later by Mary Wortley Montagu, is markedly feminocentric. The action is set largely in the enclosed spaces of the seraglio, the women's quarters especially. Following the account in Knolles of the brief, unhappy career of Ibrahim (XII) with some precision, she nonetheless erases the role of the Queen-Mother (a crucial player in *The Turkish History*) to emphasize the importance of Sheker Para, the "mother of the harem" and Ibrahim's enthusiastic procuress. By diminishing the part played by the Queen-Mother, who in Knolles–Rycaut joined the conspiracy against her own son, Pix sets Sheker Para's licensed deployment of female erotic power against the outraged patriarchs whose daughters are prey to the sensual Ibrahim. Sheker Para, the Sultan's "little piece of sugar," provides the intrigue, with Ibrahim too indolent and malleable to initiate or control action. The play sees proper masculine rule restored after this feminine challenge but the tragedy has been engineered and largely acted by the putatively unimportant mistress of the harem. It is hard not to identify Sheker Para's illegitimate and spectacular power of intrigue with that of her dramatist, that oxymoronic figure, a female wit. Sheker Para is fascinating not just because her role reflects the eclipse of the traditional source of female authority, maternity (as embodied in the Queen-Mother), and reveals the fissures in masculine identity through her manipulation of Ibrahim, but also because she suggests a capacity for intrigue at Court which would be exemplified, albeit in a chaster key, by female courtiers such as Sarah Churchill.

Joseph Trapp's *Abra-mule* was less feminocentric than Pix's play but also focused on the seraglio rather than the tent or field of battle. In Trapp's play, set in the aftermath of the siege of Buda, Pyrrhus has rescued and loves Russian Abra-mule, enslaved in Mahomet's seraglio and likely victim of his lust. She is also loved by Mahomet's brother Solymon. Mahomet is deposed after a successful revolt, led by the corrupt rebels Haly and Cuprior, is followed by a vote in the divan to replace him with his brother. Pyrrhus and Abra-mule are finally united by a reluctant Solymon when it becomes clear his renunciation of Abra-mule is a test of his virtue as ruler. As in so many of the earlier plays, the improper invasion of the subject's rights in relation to a woman serves as a test or measure of Turkish corruption and despotism.

Like Pix's *Ibrahim,* the play uses the Sultan's erotic violation as a justification for a change in rule, although here the actual conspirators are disparaged. The depiction of emperors who, unlike Solymon and Mahomet, fail the test of honor is matched by a very different formulation of the relationship between empire and arbitrary rule. While *The Siege of Constantinople* emphasized empire could only be won and maintained by absolutism and cruelty, *Abra-mule* makes precisely the opposite claim: "He's the far greater and happier Monarch / Whose pow'r is bounded by coercive Laws / Since while they limit, They preserve his Empire."[34] Rycaut's belief in the bounded security of the English state is here reiterated, in the peculiar context of the Ottoman state, no longer figured as expansionist but attempting internal reform along English lines, for as Solymon himself says: "No Government can e're be safe, that's founded / On Lust, on Murder, and Despotick Pow'r" (v, p. 87). No longer awed by the apparently unstoppable Ottoman expansion, the dramatist proposes the solution to the problems of an empire corrupted by luxury and arbitrary power is a regime bound by the rule of law.

Nicholas Rowe's *Tamerlane* (1701) marks another departure in the depiction of Turkish empire. The play was intended, and read, as a panegyric to William III, described by the author in the Epistle Dedicatory as "the greatest Character of the present Age."[35] The most important characteristics common to both men, Rowe stressed, were a hatred of tyranny and a capacity to give "Peace to the World." This revisionary celebration of William/Tamberlane is joined to a depiction of the defeated Turkish Emperor Bajazet as more personally brutal, religiously fanatic, and heedlessly ambitious than any Ottoman dramatized previously. While Rowe's open acknowledgment of a Parallel Design requires us to recognize Louis XIV in this tyrannical figure, the contemporary meaning of the drama is not exhausted through our recognition of the allegory. *Tamerlane* is a particularly interesting text in the history of British imperial ideology because the parallel allows for a recognition of a specifically expansionist ambition in the English. Such expansionist aggression is presented as peace-making, with conquest as liberation from tyranny but the allegorical vehicle bears too much signification for William to be understood simply as the "ballancer-of-power" and Protestant Liberator supreme. The cultural fantasy at stake here is global domination. England's immediate rival in 1701 was undefeated France but the Ottomans, who had signed peace accords brokered by William's ambassador two years previously, accepting territorial limits for the first time, provided the most powerful image of an empire halted. With the threat of the Porte apparently contained for the first time in centuries, a militarily effective and ambitious ruler and an unprecedentedly wealthy and well-armed state, at least some of the English could imagine themselves as aspirants to empire. As Charles Davenant remarked:

When the Peace of Ryswick was Concluded, we had all the Prospect imaginable of making a greater Figure in the World, than we had done in many Ages: All *Europe* was possessed with a high Opinion of the King's Valour and Conduct. He was acknowledged to be Head of the Protestant Interest, which brought many important Dependencies upon him. He commanded the Two greatest Trading Nations, which gave him a Naval Strength that no other People were able to Face: Our Troops had given such Proofs of their Courage, as did renew our Ancient Glory and Renown in Foreign Parts.[36]

Tamerlane dramatizes such "Prospects."

Commentary on Rowe's text emphasizing the play's role as Whig allegory has been blind to the implications of the shift in its representation of Parthians, Tartars and Turks.[37] *Tamerlane* reintroduces the kind of Christian characters who populated earlier plays about the Ottomans but does not centre the action on a love-and-honor competition between representatives of Cross and Crescent. Instead there is a plot initiated by Bajazet, a compendium of negative Ottoman tropes who has married a betrothed Greek, Arpasia, and is relentlessly ambitious and fiercely hostile to Europeans on religious grounds. His jealousy of his wife's former lover, Moneses, impels him to attempt to make the Muslim Tamerlane equally fanatic, so that his rival will be killed. Moneses also makes an improper request to Tamerlane, begging him to restore Arpasia to him. The test of Tamerlane's character is not, therefore, focused on desire for a Christian woman, as was the case in previous plays but on the much more abstract capacity of the ruler to tolerate, and indeed respect, religious and cultural difference; and to respect the customs and property of a conquered people. (In these matters, Rowe follows Knolles's characterization of Tamberlane in *The Turkish History*.)[38] Removing Tamerlane's dilemma from the personal to the confessional and judicial arena underscores the imagined difference in the nature of English and Turkish imperial rule. For the Sultans depicted in earlier plays, men with absolute power and constrained by no laws, personal temptation was ubiquitous and the ruler's weakness had immediate effects on the polity. Bajazet, who has appropriated another's bride, is guilty of precisely such brutal self-indulgence and his political and military defeat can be seen as the consequence of such ungoverned violence:

> (Love, as 'twas thought, for a fair *Grecian* captive)
> Adds new Horror to his native Fury:
> For five returning Suns, scarce was he seen
> By any the most favour'd of his Court,
> But in lascivious Ease, among his Women,
> Liv'd from the War retir'd.   (I, p. 3)

Tamerlane, by contrast, is depicted as a just ruler whose self-possession is such that he is beyond the kind of private lusts or ambitions which animate the other characters: perfectly self-governed, he is most fit to govern others.

Tamerlane's unambivalent depiction of successful conquest and rule sets it apart from earlier Turkish plays. Tamerlane is Muslim but his difference from the Ottomans is stressed throughout, in a text which foregrounds national and religious diversity to an unprecedented extent, using tolerance of difference as an ethical and political measure. Following Knolles, the Parthian Princes praise Tamerlane for such tolerance and moderation – "No Lust of Rule, the common Vice of Kings / No furious Zeal inspir'd by hot-brain'd Priests" (I.i, p. 2) motivated his conquests they agree, only an impulse "to redress an injur'd People's Wrongs" (I.i, p. 2). Tamerlane's virtues are such they have drawn "all the brave" including "The Christian Prince *Axalla*, nicely bred / In polish'd Arts of *European* Courts" (I.i, p. 2) and we see him befriend Moneses even though "Thy Habit speaks thee Christian" (I.i, p. 6). Bajazet's fanaticism, established in contrast, informs all his conduct: in an action which provides a negative mirror to Tamerlane's protection of his own marriage, he refuses to countenance his daughter Selima's liaison with the Christian Axalla, telling her that should she benefit "From a vile Christian" she dishonored her race, and abusing Axalla, whom he addresses as an "Earth-born Thing / Thou Clod" unworthy even to look at "the Sacred Race of Mighty *Ottoman* / Whom Kings, whom ev'n our Prophet's holy Offspring / At distance have beheld" (III.i, p. 40). In the great exchange with Tamerlane, he echoes the words used by Rustan in Orrery's *Mustapha* and Thomaso in *The Siege of Constantinople* to glorify an absolute, Islamic, Turkish expansionism:

> Prophet, I thank thee. –
> Damnation – Could'st thou rob me of my Glory,
> To dress up this tame King, this preaching *Dervise?*
> Unfit for War, thou shuld'st have liv'd secure
> In lazy Peace, and with debating Senates
> Shar'd a precarious Sceptre, sate tamely still,
> . . .
> Whilst I (curst on the Power that stops my Ardour!)
> Would, like a Tempest, rush amidst the Nations,
> Be greatly terrible, and deal, like Alha,
> My angry thunder on the frighted World.   (I.ii, p. 24)

Bajazet's creed is rearticulated by his instrument, the Dervise (whose name suggests both the frenzy of a "dervish" and the trickery of a "deviser"), in the climactic scene in which the "holy-man" tries to persuade Tamerlane to abandon his Christian friends, cease "fostering the pernicious Christian Sect" (III.ii p. 44) and take up his proper role as scourge of Christians:

> thus says *Mahomet*
> Why have I made thee dreadful to the Nations?
> Why have I giv'n thee Conquest? But to spread
> My sacred law ev'n to the utmost Earth,
> And make my Holy *Mecca* the World's Worship?
> Go on, and wherefoe'er thy Arms shall prosper,
> Plant there the Prophet's Name: with Sword and Fire
> Drive out all other Faiths.   (III.iii, p. 45)

Tamerlane rejects this fiery invocation of the jihad in the name of tolerance, arguing that the "Lord of all . . . blessed the fair Variety" (III.iii p. 45) of faiths by which he was worshipped. The language

Rowe used here to celebrate the variety of human religious practice
not only draws directly on that used by Knolles but echoes that
traditionally employed to defend racial diversity, as an index of
God's creative provision of infinite variety in the human species.[39]
Tamerlane's refusal to figure his conquests as holy war is matched
by a positive emphasis on peace, order and law: both he and others
draw comparisons in these terms between his empire and those of
Greece and Rome. The first example occurs in the first Prologue
to the play, where Betterton remarked:

> In spite of Time, the sacred Story lives
> And *Caesar* and his Empire still survives.
> Like him, (tho' much unequal to his Fame)
> Our Author makes a Pious Prince his Theme.

When the Parthians Princes gather to celebrate their victory over
Bajazet, they measure it by Roman achievement: "Nations unknown
/ Where yet the *Roman* Eagles never flew / Shall pay their Homage
to victorious *Tamerlane*" (II.ii p. 20), as does Tamerlane himself
later, in the scene with the Dervise when he remarks that "*Phillip's*
Son and *Caesar* did as much" to "make the World / Know but one
Lord" (III.ii p. 45). Rowe goes to considerable lengths to identify Tamerlane/William with European rather than Asian models
of empire, not simply by stressing the analogies with Alexander
and Caesar but by emphasizing Tamerlane's Parthian rather than
Tartar affiliations and his Christian alliances. Also crucial is his oft-
expressed anguish over the carnage of war, which stands in contrast to a characterization of Bajazet as a brutal, cruel deformer of
nations who "With Sword and Fire, forc'd his impious Way / To
Lawless Pow'r and Universal Sway" (Prologue). Even the notorious
humiliations which drove the Ottoman to distracted self-mutilation
are here displaced: it is Bajazet who authors the tortures when
telling Tamerlane how he would treat him were their roles reversed.

Rowe's attack on arbitrary power and religious intolerance is
obviously intended to reflect on William's rival, Louis, as well as
casting a retrospective glance at James, but it is important to note
that the warring images of rule in *Tamerlane* refer to imperial states
rather than the government of discrete nations. The defeat of the
Ottoman model of empire, depicted here as despotic jihad, reflects the unprecedented success of European military and diplomatic power in 1699, when the Treaty of Karlowitz was signed. The

rejection of a French model of universal monarchy, drawing on the absolutist and Catholicizing heritage of Roman and Spanish empire, is also implied in the attacks on arbitrary power and religious persecution.[40] The characterization of Tamerlane/William as pious and peace-loving, making war authorized by his Senate and his God, tolerant of the customs and creeds he encounters and respectful of native property, marks him out as heir to the Providentially ordained *translatio imperii.* This hero more resembles the idealized Romans whom Rycaut used to contrast with the Ottomans in his *Letter to the Reader* and, as such, he embodies an emergent dream of British Empire as lawful, tolerant, diverse, peaceful and free. This early Whig vision of a *Pax Britannica* is finely detailed and was enormously successful through the eighteenth century but it is worth noting that the disavowal of imperial ambition, so central to the seventeenth-century English, is not only maintained through the provision of an allegorical action but articulated at a crucial point in the text. As his generals congratulate him on his triumph over Bajazet, Tamerlane disclaims victory:

> It is too much, you dress me
> Like an Usurper in the borrow'd Attributes
> Of injur'd Heaven: Can we call Conquest ours?
> Shall Man, this Pigmy, with a Giant's Pride
> Vaunt of himself, and say, Thus have I done this?
> O! vain Pretence to Greatness!   (iii.ii, p. 210)

Ibrahim, Tamerlane and *Abra-mule* were all successful productions, and regularly revived, unlike Charles Goring's *Irene* which appeared in 1708, had three outings and sank without trace. This seems unfortunate, for Goring's play is much more psychologically detailed than any of the previous versions of the story. His Irene is presented as a guilt-racked mistress, comparable to a figure like Jane Shore, victimized by Mahomet but complicit in her enslaved condition. Even more startlingly, Mahomet is also presented as a figure of pathos, finally driven to destroy Irene with the utmost reluctance, and regretful, rather than heroically vengeful, after the act. The play closes with his sentimental regret:

> Jealous of Empire, and my just Renown,
> I stabb'd a mistress to preserve my Crown.
> But had the Fair return'd my generous Fire,
> I'd slighted Empire, and embrac'd the DAME.[41]

Despite a pathetic, rather than heroic, treatment of the scenario, Goring's use of the Turkish setting is exceptionally detailed, incorporating special black robes of death, Turkish dances, gardens with fountains, scenes before the Divan with the sword of justice displayed and rich feasting on couches. This redaction was clearly responsive to the vogue for she-tragedy, exploring the interior life of the characters with much greater care for the emotional oscillations of guilt and desire in the principals than any previous version of the story. Such a softened characterization of Mahomet was surely also informed by the diminishing awe felt for the heroic figures of Ottoman history.

Johnson's return to the Irene story some forty years later suggests its enduring fascination for dramatists, if not for audiences: the play failed on the stage. By 1710, when Aaron Hill published his *Full and Just Account of the Present State of the Ottoman Empire*, a tolerant and jocular account which incorporated a number of amatory anecdotes, the Great Turks were no longer represented as a military, political and confessional challenge. "The *Ottoman* force has been visibly impaired for more than a century" wrote Charles Davenant in 1701.[42] "The empire of the Turk," wrote Fletcher, "having become utterly corrupt, and now attacked by sea and land, will be easily destroyed."[43] Mary Wortley Montagu's *Letters*, written during her residence in Constantinople in 1713–14, alters the perspective yet again, by offering accounts of social, rather than diplomatic, relations, with individual Turks. Although Levant merchants apparently became more insular during the eighteenth century, leaving off the custom of wearing Turkish dress which had been common previously, Montagu's *Letters* suggest the possibility that sociable commerce as well as "ledger embassadry" might replace military and political conflict.[44] Although the Ottomans continued to wage campaigns against the Russians and the Austrians in the early eighteenth century, it is striking that the Turkish elites in Constantinople began adopting European dress, furniture and manners (along with researching and adapting Western military technologies) during the "Tulip Period" of reform after 1703.[45] This development suggests that the desire to tame the sultanate, fantastically represented in English drama during the period of Ottoman military challenge by the seductive authority of Christian womanhood, was being replaced by a real degree of European influence. The era of heroic confrontation with the Great Turks seemed to be drawing to a close, in the world and on the stage.

CHAPTER 4

The Most Famous Monarchs of the East

English interest in the Ottomans between 1660 and 1714 was generated by economic, military and political concerns of the most immediate nature, producing policies of "ledger embassadry" informed by anxiety over the apparently boundless aims of an aspirant to universal monarchy. The plays which depicted the "Great Turks" largely effaced English mercantile investments in the Porte (although the insecurity of private property was a recurrent trope) focusing instead on a heroic exploration of the rise and potential decline of an empire represented as England's religious, political and sexual antithesis. Collectively, the Turkish plays processed anxieties and fantasies about a newly important trading partner, and a threatening military power, but not through a simple process of negative stereotyping. The heroic mode allowed for the legibility of parallels with English politics but it also placed Turks and Christians in relations of symbolic complementarity, with relations of friendship and love as well as honorable conflict subsisting among the religiously and nationally diverse characters. Within a Providentialist framework, the infidel Ottomans were presumed to face supercession but, for most of the Restoration, that prospect was a distant one. However despotic and cruel they appeared, the Turks were for the most part figured as the subjects of their own history. After the Treaty of Karlowitz was signed, and William's military ambitions appeared more plausible, English awe declined, along with heroic representation.

The other Asian and North African states and empires theatricalized during this period were also of increasing commercial, military and political concern to the English but were more distant and less threatening. In the case of Morocco, India and China, plays set in these states appear to have been produced during the onset of hostilities or with the establishment of new trading arrangements.

Dramatists used historical sources and exploited customs and manners material in their plots, characterization and scenery, providing specific if pithy visions of newly important exotic societies but, until the 1690s, they avoided showing Europeans within these states. Morocco had a substantial population of Christian slaves and successful renegados, while Englishmen were confined to a few small factories in the Moghul Empire and only entered China spasmodically until the 1680s. Such contacts were hardly the stuff of heroic drama, as Dryden discovered in 1672 when writing *Amboyna*, a play set in the East Indies, whose failure he blamed on the fable's "mean persons," almost all of them merchants. The development of an oceanic, universal empire of trade was antipathetic to traditional modes of representation, which valued heroic ambition over the low avarice which was assumed to generate trade.[1] Geographers like Heylyn celebrated global commerce as a divinely ordered means by which different parts of the world were supplied with varied needs, a common sentiment echoed by Pufendorf's citation of Dryden's translation of Virgil – "All sorts of *Goods* their Several Countries know / Ebon's only will in *India* grow / And Frankincense in the Sabaean Bough" – in his *Law of Nature and Nations*,[2] but trade was remarkably resistant to heroic celebration. Tea, coffee, pepper, spices, cottons, silks and slaves became vitally important to the English economy during this period but their acquisition was only rarely the direct subject of dramatic representation.[3] Instead, playwrights worked from travel accounts or recent histories to dramatize national or imperial crises in new trading partners, including spectacular signs of difference in the gender and political order. Such plays not only allowed for more comparative meditation on the processes of imperial expansion, preservation and decline but also provided concise but vivid images of non-Western cultures.

There were also a great many plays with subjects taken from the history of what many thought the most ancient empire still subsisting, that of the Persians. There were trade and diplomatic contacts with Persia under the Safavids but dramatists were drawn to heroic episodes from the pre-Islamic origins of the empire. With a history recorded both in Scripture and in classical sources, it was assumed the Persian Empire was preceded only by the Assyrians. Playwrights thus used the reigns of Cyrus, Cambyses, Darius, Xerses and Alexander to model the process by which empire rose, was expanded and preserved, or weakened into collapse and defeat. The rival motives of conquest, avarice and ambition were canvassed, as were the political and representational strategies by which rulers maintained power; and the role of women in pre-Christian states in the process of becoming civil societies was also examined. The attraction of Persian history as a template for the dramatic exploration of the triumphs and vicissitudes of empire depended not just on its antiquity and the perceived continuity of the Empire into the present but also on its status as a primordial other to the West.[4] Playwrights turned to Alexander's triumph over Darius, and the classical formulation of distinctions between Europeans and Asians embedded in the accounts of the Macedonian conquests, to analyze and reiterate Occidental and Oriental identities and differences.

"WILD AFRICKMEN": SETTLE'S MOROCCO PLAYS

Settle's *The Empress of Morocco* was probably the most spectacular heroic play on the Restoration stage. Critical commentary has focused on the contemporary debate over the play's exotic excess, analyzing its effects in aesthetic terms alone, although the play's initial production, revival and sequel all date from periods of tension over Tangier, a Moroccan port acquired like Bombay on Charles's marriage to Catherine of Braganza. Tangier was a major foreign policy preoccupation throughout the 1670s and '80s.[5] Sari Hornstein has recently reviewed the English ambitions to use the port, acquired like Bombay as a base from which to secure shipping on the South Atlantic coast from the Barbary pirates, and to refit and revictual ships in the Levant trade.[6] Horstein emphasizes that there was such widespread political support for maintaining the port, to which a mole had been added, that, when attempting to gain the King's assent to the Exclusion Bill, the emergent Whigs linked it to a bill of supply for Tangier: "Parliamentarians simply could not imagine that Charles would choose to abandon his Mediterranean outpost rather than abandon his brother."[7] Charles did do so, sending Pepys out with Dartmouth to dismantle the fort and destroy the mole but the policy was highly unpopular because Tangier had become "the symbol of the new-born spirit of imperialism that pervaded the country."[8]

Between 1674 and 1684 (the year in which the port was abandoned) there were three major English naval campaigns in the

Mediterranean, with Sir John Narborough leading the first against the Regency of Tripoli from 1674 to 1676, and the second, against the Regency of Algiers in 1677 to 1679. The third, led by Arthur Herbert, continued the campaign against Algiers until 1683, and, from 1684 until 1688, there was a campaign against the Kingdom of Sally. As negotiations over Tangier proceeded, the Moroccan Ambassador became a regular sight not just at the Court but in the theatre, attending *Circe* or *Psyche, Macbeth, The City Heiress,* and, on Saturday January 14, 1682, "the Morocco ambasador with all his attendants will be treated at the King's playhouse with a play that has relation to that country, viz., Caius Martius with dancing and volting."[9] It is possible, though unrecorded, that Ahmed Hadu attended *The Empress of Morocco,* as the play was performed during his sojourn in London, as was Settle's second play on a North African theme, *The Heir of Morocco* (1682). The Bantam Ambassador, in England in the same year to procure arms in his conflict with the Dutch, did see one of Settle's plays.[10] The date of the first performance of *The Empress of Morocco* is uncertain, but there was definitely a performance in July 1673, not long before the commencement of Narborough's first campaign.

As in so many other heroic dramas set in Islamic courts, the Empress acts as the initiator of action. Morocco is threatened by the vengeful onslaught of the King of Algiers, whose daughter Morena loves Muly Labas, the Moroccan Emperor's son. The lovers have both been imprisoned by the Emperor. The Empress, however, has conspired with her lover Crimalhaz to have the Emperor murdered, and she drives a wedge between Muly Labas and his chief commander Muly Hamet (in love with Marianne) by claiming the latter tried to rape her. Muly Hamet has captured Morena's father and removed the external threat to Morocco but is himself imprisoned after the Queen-Mother's accusation. Marianne releases him but the Empress and Crimalhez plot to kill him on his way to exile, having already killed Muly Labas, the new Emperor. Crimalhaz is executed after he turns on the Empress, who manages to kill the young queen, Morena, before herself being murdered. Muly Hamet returns from exile, is reunited with Marianne and crowned as Emperor.

The source of the play seems to be Lancelot Addison's *West Barbary* (1671), an account of the region's recent tumultuous history, published two years before *The Empress* was staged.[11] Critics mocked Settle's weak grasp of geography and the fustian excess of the language, but the play was remarkably successful. Notwithstanding his defensive remarks justifying the lack of realism in staging a masque in Morocco ("All *Heroick* actions of *Virtue* or *Gallantry* on the *Stage*, being *rated* and valued by the rules of the *place* and *Age* they are presented in, not by the sense or Age or place when and where they were first perform'd"[12]), Settle deploys a plethora of exotic effects specific to the location: stranglings, gaunchings (killing by throwing the victim onto an "Algiers hook") struggles with scimitars, and dances with palm trees. In his dispute with his critics, moreover, Settle defended the customary, geographical and historical accuracy of his representation, while attacking Dryden's *Conquest of Granada* as itself erroneous on such terms.[13] The attack on Settle putatively authored by Dryden, Thomas Shadwell and John Crowne, accuses the former of mistaking Morocco's location in relation to the coast and Mt. Atlas, and of ignorance of the fact that the Spanish held Oran. Parrying these criticisms, Settle responds by claiming Dryden's *Conquest of Granada* shows him to be ignorant of Islamic belief and custom when he "makes a company of *Moores* Dance, and makes adoration of a *Statue* of *Jupiter*. How agreeing *Images* are to *Mahometan* Worship, and what League *Jupiter* and *Mahomet* can have, I leave to the *Judicious* to *Censure*."[14] He also defends his own plot and characterization by invoking historical authority: "prithee, *Old Aquaintance*, read *History*, and understand a little better the *Mahometans* severe rules of honour on their *Womens* score."[15] Although critics since have tended to emphasize the effectiveness of Settle's "critique of literal realism," as Novak puts it, it is important to note that all the parties to this controversy wanted to claim the high ground of historical, geographical and customary accuracy.[16]

The first argument offered in support of the withdrawal from Tangier was the inability to come to a binding agreement with the Moors "through the natural and known perfidiousness of that people."[17] In Heylyn's *Cosmographie*, the inhabitants of Barbary are described as

active of body, well-skilled in Horsemanship, but impatient of Labour; covetous of honour, inconstant, crafty and unfaithfull; studious in matters of their Law and in some of the *Liberal* Sciences, especially Philosophy and *Mathematics*, of which in many parts of the *Mahometan* countrys they are admitted to be Masters: They are also said to be stately of gate, exceedingly distrustfull, in their hate implacable and jealous of their women beyond all.[18]

The serial betrayals and bloodletting in the Moroccan Court reflect the conviction of such jealousy, mistrustfulness, craft and inconstancy, a vision of Barbary Moors equally apparent in Addison's account of the region's recent internecine civil strife.

The Empress of Morocco also bears out Bernier's claim that in Islamic societies "cabals of women" were significant agents in high politics. The Empress Laula exemplifies such manipulative feminine power. She seems to be based on a figure whom Addison calls Laella, the homicidal and unfaithful wife to the fratricidal Muley Hamet Sheck. Like Laula, who is cast as a figure who acts out of blood-lust and desire, revelling in her ability to dominate the action, Laella "plotted with a Feminine Invention" to enjoy "the embraces of her Paramour in a Regal State."[19] Metaphors of theatre and writing are pervasive in her self-representations: she describes herself as "Actor and designer too," and, scorning her daughter-in-law, scoffs: "No Prologues to her Death, let it be done / I could have killed ten Queens while you judge one" (v.i.). Unlike her model, however, whom Addison reports acted to indulge her exorbitant sexual appetites, Laula eventually schemes for no very clear end except the exercise of power itself, for, as contemporary commentators noticed, she seems to embody an Iago-like motiveless malignity: "But what a Character of a Woman was here in his *Queen-Mother*: He designes her Bloody and Cunning, and Ambitious: we will grant she might be unnaturall enough to commit Murthers on her nearest Relation: But no-body was ever wicked for the sake of Wickedness and without design."[20] What we see in Laula is a representation of femininity as a purely destructive force of self-assertion: a woman unconstrained by the bonds of civility who is not afraid to exercise what Hobbes saw as the original power mothers held in the state of nature, the right to kill one's child. She figures the threat of that unlimited feminine desire which is fundamentally subversive of all social order. Settle's play reiterates *Mustapha's* implication that it is only men who can give birth to political stability (when Solymon's two sons privately agree to give up the practice of fratricide) for Laula is dominated by desires which are purely destructive and even senseless in terms of traditional ambition.

Roxalana presented a threat to a social order conceived of as fundamentally unjust and unnatural: the tragedy she unleashes was produced by the clash between maternal nature and the cruel laws of the Turkish empire. Laula is equally the emanation of a despotic and arbitrary polity: like Normahal's, and that of Rowe's ambitious Step-Mother Artemisa, her destructive progress figures the constant struggle waged in such dubiously civilized, antique states against the eruption of chaos.[21] In the Christian states explicitly set in contrast against Solymon's court in *Mustapha* and implicitly in *The Empress of Morocco*, that ravening femininity is putatively controlled. The fascination of the text for Restoration audiences doubtless lay, however, not just in its spectacular exploitation of a specifically Eastern nightmare of maternal power: it spoke powerfully also to an audience aware that their King "like Solymon, was advised by strange women," married to a wife whose barrenness presaged political and social chaos. *The Empress of Morocco* was first produced while the crisis created by the Declarations of Indulgence, the Duke of York's refusal to sign the Test Act, and his second marriage to a Catholic was reaching its height and the possibility of a royal divorce was mooted. Settle's text presents a world similarly threatening to descend into chaos. While the crises of 1671–73 were precipitated by Charles's sympathy for (and James's conversion to) Catholicism, to many observers the root cause of the evil was the Queen and her suspected malign intentions towards the King. Titus Oates was actually to accuse her of attempting to poison Charles. *The Empress of Morocco* presents a Court and state thrown into disorder through the actions of a barren Queen who conspicuously denies all maternal feeling:

> Let single murders, common hands suffice
> I scorn to kill less than whole families.
> In all my Race, I nothing find that's ill
> But that I've barren been; and wanted still
> More monarchs to dethrone, more sons to kill.   (v.i.)

Settle returned to the Moroccan setting, which had proved so successful a decade earlier, in 1682. *The Heir of Morocco*, dedicated to Monmouth's mistress, was produced during the Exclusion Crisis and is concerned with problems of succession. Settle's choice of subject, however, was surely influenced again by the topicality of North African politics: the Moroccan Ambassador was in London in 1682 for negotiations over Tangier, which Charles was preparing to abandon. Although the port was not officially deserted until 1684, when the mole was destroyed, Charles's refusal to sign the

Exclusion Bill, to which the Tangier Bill of Supply was attached, effectively sealed the colony's fate in 1682.

Settle's second depiction of Barbary is as bleak as his first. Albuzeiden, King of Algiers, plans to marry his daughter Artemira, in love with Altomar, a successful admiral, to Gayland, the usurper of Morocco. Altomar kills Gayland, despite his loyalty to the King, and is horribly tortured before his true identity as the heir of Morocco is revealed. On hearing of Altomar's true identity, the King and his daughter kill themselves, while Altomar, or Muly-Mesude, son of Muly-Labas, wills the throne to his brother Cialto. This action is difficult to interpret allegorically; if Settle's sympathies in 1682 were oppositional, it seems odd that his hero Altomar, should be, like James, an admiral as well as Morocco's legitimate heir by succession. On the other hand, the English were engaged in naval conflicts with the Algerines from 1676 through 1683, so Altomar's position as admiral would resonate with an audience conscious of Narborough's and Herbert's campaigns. Viewed in terms of this conflict, Settle's characterization of the Barbary states as violent, unstable and rife with treachery assumes a different significance: the play can be seen as an expansive illustration of the first reason (of Moorish perfidy) which Charles gave to justify abandoning Tangier. Altomar is first introduced in the wake of a naval victory over the Venetians and, in attempting to persuade Albuzeiden to honor his promise to wed him to Artemira, he asks "Have I for this, from all the Ports of Fame / Past all the storms of Fate to make you glorious? / All died your Ocean with the Christian Purple?"[22] Although he is a virtuous infidel, Altomar's service is to a regime which was notorious for aiding the Ottomans against Christian states, enslaving Europeans and preying on Western merchant shipping. Albuzeiden indicts himself for a "savage" cruelty in having "Martyr'd a Monarch on a Gibbet," for:

> In Vengeage to a base Usurper's Blood
> Like an infatuated Savage Indian
> I've built an Altar to a worship't Devil
> And sacrific'd a King t'a Rebell's Ghost.   (v.i)

The Moroccan and Algerian states are not only in internal disarray but threatened by the "wild Africkman" Gayland.[23] However cruel "infatuated Savage" Albuzeiden proves, he is sufficiently honorable to suicide on realizing that he has tortured a prince.

Gayland, whose origins are Numidian, and hence more distinctively African, is figured as an uncontrollable beast, with Altomar responding to his claims of imperial glory contemptuously:

> Mad! How it would please me
> To see the Fierce *Numidian* Lion foam,
> Tear up the Ground, and lash his angry sides,
> Whilst I, like *Hercules*, in State stand by,
> Behold thy Lunatick full tide swell o'er,
> Then smile to hear the Royal Savage roar.   (IV.i)

The Heir of Morocco divides Africa between the cruel and unstable, if spasmodically honorable, Muslims of the Barbary States and the "savage" inhabitants of Numidia and the interior. An English audience presumably found some space for identification with the naval hero Altomar, the mirror-image of their own Narboroughs and Herberts, but the society presented by the play as a whole was an entity which conformed to the largely negative and fearful account in Heylyn and Addison. The play is not a justification for the abandonment of Tangier (hardly a Whig position) but it certainly underlines the difficulty of maintaining a civil polity in a region regarded as unstable and treacherous. Virtue and honor are by no means absent from Settle's vision of Morocco but they are beleaguered.

"GREAT AND RENOWNED MONARCHY": SETTLE'S CHINA PLAY

English interest in the Chinese was generated by curiosity about a vast, apparently stable empire and by the prospect of trade. Like Persia, the Chinese state was understood to be ancient and unchanging, but Jesuit accounts (which provided the primary source of information) tended to suggest the absolutism of the imperial government was less capricious and violent than that of the Ottomans and Persians.[24] While P. J. Marshall and Glyndwr Williams stress the enthusiasm of Sinophile Englishmen in the seventeenth century, accounts of the Chinese were far from uniformly admiring. Heylyn emphasized that the "Government of this Kingdom is meerly *Tyrannical*" and that "the Common People are kept in such awe and fear, that they are rather Slaves than Subjects."[25] The Chinese were dominated militarily and politically by the Tartars but "more of them took up Arms for their Hair and their Habit (when required to conform in those particulars to the Will of the

Conqueror) than had done either for their King or their common Liberty."[26] Commentators tended to distinguish between the
Chinese and the invading Tartars in terms familiar from the accounts of ancient history: China was represented as civilized and
wealthy but vulnerable to the military prowess of her rough northern neighbor, "a base and beggarly Nation" which had begun "to
mount unto the Chair of Empire and Sovereignty, when before
they lived like beasts."[27] For all her antiquity and cultural uniformity, China spent much of the seventeenth century racked by civil
wars and invasions by a more martial neighbor with "a fine dream
of Universal Monarchy."[28]

While some Englishmen, like Sir William Temple, would continue to regard China as a successful model of benevolent despotism, for others the economic possibilities offered by the weakening
of this huge, wealthy and hitherto closed empire were engrossing.
The Sinophile Sir Timothy Tallapoy of Rowe's *The Biter*, an East-
India merchant and "a great affecter of Chinese customs" combined these two interests. Fryer noted that the opening of a sea-
route to the Indies by Europeans had substantially affected Persia's
position as the central Asian market: China goods, like other East
Asian products, were newly accessible, especially after 1685 when
the Manchu Emperor K'ang-hsi opened Chinese ports at the conclusion of the civil wars. Small amounts of tea arrived in London
in the 1660s and regular trade between the East India Company
and China began in the 1670s, with twelve English voyages to Amoy
between 1676 and 1698. Concerted efforts to establish a more extensive trade began in 1683, and culminated in massive imports of
tea in the first decade of the eighteenth century.[29]

Settle's *The Conquest of China* was published the same year the
voyages to Amoy began but focused on issues of empire and culture rather than trade. In one of few serious commentaries on the
play, Derek Hughes analyzes the text in terms of Settle's Hobbesian
treatment of justice as a battle between warring individualists, ungoverned by human or divine authority.[30] The extraordinary se-
quence of events described in the English translation of Martinius's
Bellum Tartaricum (1665), which seems the most likely source for the
play, certainly provided Settle with ample material to "reduce the
various categories of life to inexpertly distinguished categories of
violence."[31] *The Conquest of China* is shaped, however, by more than
confused Hobbesism. Martinius interprets the events he recounts

as an index of Providential wrath or approbation at the treatment of the Catholic missions; the dramatist's reworking of the material is secular. Far from depicting a chaotic world without order, Settle presents the conquest of China (by no means an accomplished fact in 1655 or 1676) as a not unfamiliar process by which the lawful but tyrannical ruler of a softened empire is overcome by the vigor of a youthful prince who has benefitted from a civilizing education among his foes. Settle's reworking of scattered individuals, single actions and episodes, drawn from several decades of recent Chinese history, produces a unified account of imperial conquest which revises the historian's open-ended and weakly Providentialist narrative into a coherent drama of corrupt tyranny overcome first by usurpation, and then by liberating conquest.[32] The play's initial conflict is generated by a highly specific Chinese custom and the action as a whole is framed to be understood as exemplary of Chinese and Tartarian habits and mores. As is the case with other heroic dramas, the play incorporates and recirculates contemporary doctrine about its Asian subjects, while addressing the perennially fascinating questions of imperial decline and expansion.

The play opens and closes with the heir of Tartary and conqueror of China celebrating the rough Tartar vigor which will overcome civil Chinese softness. Zungteus invokes the environmental explanation, originating with Aristotle, revived by Bodin and picked up by Heylyn, for the hardiness of the northerly Tartars in his exhortation to his troops:[33]

> With Mounts of Snow, and Rocks of Ice immur'd.
> Yet these strong Bars have not your Arms withstood;
> The Gods that froze your Climate, warmed your blood.[34]

In his closing speech to his Chinese wife after his successful conquest, Zungteus refers to the fruitful exchange he envisages between the rough Tartars and the "soft" Chinese:

> Your Milder Presence will auspicious be,
> And civilize my rougher *Tartary*
> And whilst the *Chinans* pay allegiance here:
> I'll teach their softer Natures Arms and War.   (v.ii, p. 67)

The action bears out Zungteus's conviction that the Tartars will overcome the "softer" Chinese. His most formidable enemy is a woman, Amavanga, who is his lover disguised as a soldier and whom he wounds in hand-to-hand combat. Amavanga has her historical origin in "one *Heroick* Lady, whom we may well call the *Amazon* or *Penthesilean* of China." Accompanied by 3,000 women "from the remote Province of *Suchuen carrying all*, not only Masculine minds, but mens habits also, and assuming titles more becoming men than women," this "noble and generous Lady gave many rare proofs of her courage and valour, not only against the *Tartars*, but also against the Rebells which afterwards riss against their Lord and Emperour."[35] Her name, however, is a Chinese translation of Zungteus's tutor Amahan, who proved a most effective counsellor and soldier for the Tartars.

In contrast to the Amazonian Amavanga, the Chinese Emperor is a "sluggish King" secure only in peace. His ferocious daughter, abusing her royal prerogative, begins the process of weakening the state by attempting to murder Alcinda, betrothed to Quitazo, whom she herself loves. The second act, which follows the Tartarian preparations for war, shows the Princess engaged in the fatal process of making her choice of a husband. As the King puts it, the "Chinan Laws" require –

> That from the twelve next Princes of the blood
> Our Royal Daughter must two men prefer,
> The most deserving of the Crown and her.
> One of which two, your Father must design,
> The happy Man shall share your Love and mine.   (ii.i, p. 9)

The Chinese Princess herself refers to this practice as an exception to the proper order of gender relations, which would be criminal involving any other less exalted figure. Her insistence on getting her own way erotically when Quitazo proves resistant does prove criminal, suggesting that this imperial custom is a perversion of gender relations, conducive of an effeminizing female tyranny which has contributed to the softening of the empire. Settle did not invent the custom, which is discussed in Semedo's *History of the Great and Renowned Monarchy of China* (1655), although he did alter it slightly by elevating the rank of the suitors: "There are twelve young men sought out of the age of 17 or 18 years, the lustiest and handsomest they can finde; they are brought into the Palace to a place, where the Princesse may see them, and not be seen; and when she hath well considered them, she selecteth two of them: These are presented to the King, who chuseth which of them he liketh best, to be his Sonne-in-law."[36]

Disorder among the Chinese is figured by their rule and defense by women, whether virtuous or vicious. The usurper Lycungus fills the vacuum implied by such effeminacy, successfully claiming the throne while the King still lives. After Lycungus has killed 8 Princes of the blood-Royal, massacred 16,000 students whom he thought might foment rebellion, and the Royal wives have all committed suicide, the Emperor bequeathes his crown to Zungteus in a letter written in his own blood, before falling on his sword. Lycungus is a character based on a low-born thief called Licungzus, whom Martinius suggests lost the Chinese throne after a successful usurpation, through his tyrannical inhumanity. Settle's characterization of his duel with the Emperor follows the source with some specificity: the old Emperor is reported to have written a final letter in his own blood before suiciding and his Court also hanged themselves *en masse*.[37] The massacre of the students is, however, attributed to another low-born usurper, one Changhienchungus, who was reputed to have murdered 18,000 of them. Settle telescopes events and creates one representative villain but his characterizations of the Emperor, Zungteus (described by Martinius as humane, courteous and mild, owing to his Chinese education), Lycungus and Amavanga correspond closely with the descriptions provided by historians.[38] The play reshapes the Jesuit material into a unified action comprehensible as a justified conquest which rescued the soft Chinese from a tyrannical usurper but the heroic scale of events and character, along with a strong emphasis on the positive or deleterious effects of custom and climate, is common to both the historical and the dramatic texts.

THE GREAT MUGHAL

Settle was not the only dramatist interested in the Tartar Conquest: late in his life Dryden wrote to his son and to Tonson remarking he was trying to revise an old play on the subject by Robert Howard, although the play, if it was written, has never emerged.[39] The paucity of dramatic representations of the Chinese is suggestive as the history of civil war, invasion and heroic resistance seems tailored for the heroic mode. Dramatists, however, showed a marked preference for depicting regimes like that of the Ottomans, who were of immediate political, economic and military significance to the English in the Restoration, or the Persians, who figure so centrally in the classical accounts of imperial struggle. This may explain why there is only one serious play about India, Dryden's *Aureng-Zebe*. The play was sufficently compelling, however, to hold the stage well into the eighteenth century.

Vinton A. Dearing, citing James Winn, suggests that *Aureng-Zebe* was inspired by the success of Settle's *The Empress of Morocco* in using a contemporary Islamic milieu for his scene of political treachery.[40] There were other spurs to producing a play about the Mughals, however. Although the beginnings of English rule at Bombay, acquired from the Portugese on Charles's marriage to Catherine of Braganza, were "inglorious," Gerald Aungier, East India Company president in Surat between 1669 and 1677, transformed the tiny community into a flourishing town of 60,000 inhabitants in the early 1670s.[41] Charles II issued five charters to the Company (including one in 1675, the year of *Aureng-Zebe*'s appearance), and they fostered great prosperity: by 1670, their annual proceeds were £1 million a year. Although the English had no "country trade" like the Dutch, selling their commodities on into England and Europe alone, the Restoration saw the framework of the East Indian empire set in place. Elite English interest in the Mughals had a material base which intensified curiosity about a powerful instance of Oriental despotism.

Although verbal echoes from other texts abound, *Aureng-Zebe* is most markedly dependent on Bernier's account of the recent revolution in the Mughal empire. While this is one of the heroic dramas in which discussion of crucial areas of contemporary political life is most obvious and has been most carefully documented, discussion of the political dimensions of *Aureng-Zebe* has been almost exclusively focused on internal English politics.[42] Kirsch's influential reading of the text tends to downplay even that public dimension of the text.[43] Dr. Johnson's remarks in his "Life of Dryden" (1779) are among the few which attend to the play's significance in terms of external relations: "*Aureng-Zebe*, 1676, is a tragedy founded on the actions of a great prince then reigning, but over nations not likely to employ their criticks upon the transactions of the English stage. If he had known and disliked his own character, our trade was not in those times secure from his resentment."[44]

The play's action is generated by internecine political and sexual rivalry. Preoccupied by his lust for the Kashmiri Princess Indamora, the old Emperor retains only a weak hold on the throne as his three ambitious eldest sons, Darah, Sujat and Morat, struggle for power. Aureng-Zebe, the hero, defeats the two older brothers on his father's behalf, but is imprisoned by the Emperor when he refuses to resign his claim to Indamora, whom Morat, now heir-apparent, also covets. The Empress Nourmahal pursues Aureng-Zebe while Morat woos a resistant Indamora; realizing his error the Emperor releases Aureng-Zebe, who defeats Morat's forces, and after a lengthy series of confusions in which Indamora confronts the dying Morat, Melesinda his wife burns herself and Nourmahal takes poison, the hero takes power and the Princess from his father.

Dryden's plotting and characterization depart from Bernier's account significantly, but the play reproduces the latter's Orientalist axioms and romance syntactics. The disorder of the Mughal empire is represented by inversions and ruptures in familial relations of a specifically "Indian" kind. The Emperor's and Morat's invocation of arbitrary power and their abandonment to lust can be accounted for by Bernier's remark that the "decay of the Empires of Asia proceeds from thence, that the Children of the Kings thereof are brought up only by Women and Eunuchs, which often are no other than wretched slaves."[45] So raised, these rulers indulge in "cruelties," "drunkenness," "unreasonable luxury . . . with their concubines" or, "altogether abandoning themselves to the pleasures of Hunting, like some Carnivorous Animals," they "always run into some extreme or another, being altogether irrational and extravagant."[46] The characterization of Morat, favored son of the ambitious Nourmahal, provides a brutal embodiment of Bernier's dicta:

> When Thou wert formed, Heav'n did a Man begin;
> But the brute Soul, by chance, was shuffled in.
> In Woods and Wilds thy Monarchy maintain,
> Where valiant Beasts, by force and rapine, reign;
> In Life's next Scene, if Transmigration be,
> Some Bear or Lion is reserved for thee.[47]

The Hobbesian valence of the passage is modified by the closing allusion to Hindu belief, which gives a cultural specificity to the

general accusation of savagery. A speech by Indamora reframes
the evocation of the state of nature even more suggestively:

> Piety is no more, she sees her place
> Usurped by Monsters and a savage Race.
> From her soft Eastern Climes you drive her forth,
> To the cold Mansions of the utmost North.   (III.i.461–64)

Indamora is herself a Northerner, but the geographical valorization
implicitly extends beyond Kashmir to the "northern climates" of
Europe which Dryden refers to in the Prologue. As in *The Conquest
of China*, the North is associated with a virtue lost to the softened
South.

Nourmahal's conduct and the judgments made by various other
characters, including Aureng-Zebe, reproduce Bernier's dictum
that "the *Women* in the *Indies* as well as at Constantinople and
in many other places, [take] the best part in the most important
Transactions."[48] In the play's third speech, Fazel Chawn blames the
brothers' wives for the internecine war:

> I will remember you foretold the Storm,
> When first the Brothers did their Factions form;
> When each, by cursed Cabals of Women, strove
> To draw th' indulgent King to partial Love.   (I.i.17–20)

Later, Aureng-Zebe excoriates Nourmahal: "The best of Kings by
women is misled / Chained by the witchcraft of a second bed"
(I. i.350–51). The first act also establishes the institutional reason
for the Mughal disturbances, as Arimant points out to his companions that the fatal lack of a law of primogeniture is responsible for
the rebellions:

> When Death's cold hand has closed the Father's eye,
> You know the younger Sons are doomed to die.
> Less ills are chosen greater to avoid,
> And Nature's Laws are by the States destroyed.
> What courage tamely could to death consent,
> And not, by striking first, the blow prevent?   (I.i.40–45)

This echoes Bernier's defense of Aureng-Zebe's behavior:

I doubt not, but most of those, who have read my History, will judge the
ways, taken by *Aureng-Zebe*, for getting the Empire, very violent and horrid.
I pretend not at all to plead for him, but desire only, that before he be

altogether condemned, reflection be made on the unhappy custom of this state, which leaving the succession of the Crown undecided, for want of good Laws, settling, as amongst us, upon the Eldest son, exposeth it to the Conquest of the Strongest.[49]

Disorder in filial and conjugal relations and the wider polity, also evident in the troubles of the English monarchy, could be represented in displaced form in an Oriental drama. The Indianized love and honor action familiarizes the powerful Mughal dynasty, rendering the rulers of the sub-continent comprehensible. The classical tropes Dryden invokes tend also, however, to distance the positively rendered Mughals, suggesting theirs are the virtues of an age superseded both by their own state's decline and by the rise of the West. Thus, certain of the Orientalist figures mark out the beginnings of a sense of radical alterity of a more modern kind. The despotism of the Mughals functioned not only as a negative exemplar of contemporary absolutism but in its specifically Asian form was recognized as posing a threat to the secure ownership of private property, which, as much as Christianity, was coming to be regarded as a peculiarly European characteristic. Bernier's account of the political events and love intrigues of the revolution is followed by an entirely prosaic *Letter* on the circulation of gold in Hindustan. The essay's main burden is to lament the insecurity of individual ownership in the empire, and the deleterious effects on Indian trade, and it became a *locus classicus* for definitions of Oriental despotism, with Pufendorf quoting from the *Letter* in his *Law of Nature and of Nations*:

That *Absolute Propriety* of the *Prince* has been the Reason why that (Kingdom of the Great Mogol) and other Kingdoms of the *East*, otherwise very happy in the Advantages Nature has given them, should lie wild, desolate, and barbarous, and either be always poor and decaying, or at least never arrive at the Splendour and Greatness of the *European* Nations, where the Princes are generally more tender of invading the *Properties* of their Subjects, and where Subjects have the Liberty to defend their own, even against Princes.[50]

But Dryden, less committed to the celebration of Europe in terms of its superior commercial arrangements, ends his representation of Mughal India by focusing on a term of cultural difference which will come to serve as the classic alibi for the English colonial mission in India: namely, sati.

Sati's role in the colonial discourse of late eighteenth-century "British" India has been analyzed by Lata Mani.[51] Valuable as her discussion is, it tends to obscure the extent to which "suttee" already figured as a crucial term in accounts of Indian society in the seventeenth century. Widely read travelers such as Bernier, Tavernier and Fryer discuss the topic at length. Bernier's *The History of the Late Revolution of the Empire of the Great Mogol* includes a dramatic episode in which the traveler himself intervenes to dissuade a widow from burning herself.[52] Bernier's proleptic reforming zeal was unusual but comment on the custom is not. Travelers fell into two camps. Some, like Jean-Baptiste Tavernier, were appalled, regarding the practice as an "execrable custom."[53] Others found it admirable, the women "worthy of no small praise" and hoped to witness an actual burning: "If I can know when it will be I will not fail to go to see her and by my presence honour her funeral with that compassionate affection which so great conjugal fidelity and love seem to me to deserve."[54] Both the stoicism of the women and the spectacular nature of their deaths seem to have appealed to Dryden, to the extent that he ignored the invariable emphasis the travelers and geographers placed on the inveteracy of Muslim antagonism to the practice.[55] Although at least one Mughal Emperor took a Hindu wife, it seems highly unlikely that a Mughal Princess like Melesinda would have participated in this custom.

Aureng-Zebe repeats the oscillation between the two poles of admiration and repulsion detectable both in the travelers' accounts of the practice and in the plays' textualization of the Mughal Court as a whole. Choosing this custom to conclude the action seems emblematic of the way in which Indian society is represented in the drama. *Aureng-Zebe*'s central characters are figured in terms either of Greek or Roman virtue or of savagery; thus one of the two self-immolating widows, Melesinda, is described as an "ancient matron . . . who bore her chains with Roman constancy" and the other, Nourmahal, is, like Morat, a "brute in human form." This figuration fixes Indian society between the familiarizing poles of virtuous paganism and barbarism. For some of Dryden's audience at least, though, the double burnings (in which Melesinda's dignified exit is overwhelmed and contaminated by Nourmahal's "extravagant rhapsody" and onstage writhing) served primarily to underline the sense of cultural distance also implied by the classicizing tropes:

That which was not pleasing to some of the fair ladies in the last acts of it, as I dare not vindicate, so neither can I wholly condemn, till I find more reason for their censures. The procedure of Indamora and Melesinda seems yet, in my judgement, natural, and not unbecoming of their characters. Those Indian wives are loving fools, and may do well to keep themselves in their own country, or at least, to keep company with the Arias and Portias of old Rome: some of our ladies know better things.[56]

Even as Dryden's appeal to Roman precedent underlines his sense that classical analogies could adequately naturalize the burnings, the ambivalence of the first sentence ("I dare not vindicate ... neither can I wholly condemn") reveals a sense of unease in the face of radical difference. The assimilative conviction of knowledge produced by parallels gives way to a recognition of otherness, a difference marked here by a scene of violence against women which would be canonized as an index of Indian inferiority and occidental superiority.

SUN-KINGS: THE PRINCES OF PERSIA

English relations with Persia, whose rulers still bore an aura of solar divinity appropriated by Louis XIV, were governed by trade and diplomatic considerations, buttressed by theological and historical interest in the state's pre-Islamic Emperors. Sentiments towards the Persians appear to have been generally positive, with John Ogilby, Cosmographer and Geographick Printer Royal, critical of their supposed excesses in "Wantonness and venereal Exercises," not least their addiction to "the horrid sin of sodomy," but otherwise panegyric:

The *Persians* are naturally endu'd with Prudence and Understanding, quick-witted, and Learned, wherefore there are many excellent Poets among them, and they highly esteem Moral Philosophers, are not inclin'd to any disdainful Behaviour, but are affable and courteous, not only to one another, but especially to Strangers, to whom, (as we said before) they are also very hospitable.[57]

Their civility aside, not only were the Safavids inheritors of an ancient and wealthy empire but they were known to be potential allies against the Ottomans. Throughout the sixteenth and seventeenth centuries, various European powers attempted to establish such an alliance with Persia against the Turks but a treaty was never reached: more, it seems, because of difficulties in communication than for lack of willingness on either side. The English became much more involved in Persian trade after they aided the Shah in taking the strategic island of Hurmuz from the Portugese in 1622 but, during the Restoration, their position was gradually undermined by the Dutch, while the French began a concerted effort to enter the Persian market in 1664. Trade improved again in the last two decades of the century but remained hampered by the Dutch and the rampant piracy of the Persian Gulf.[58]

While the dramatic representation of other Asian and near-Eastern states focused on fairly recent, well-documented historical episodes reported by historians or contemporary travelers, the presentation of the Persians leant much more heavily on ancient history. Mary Delariviere Manley's dramatization of recent events in Colchis recorded in Chardin's *Travels into Persia* (1686) was exceptional: virtually all the other plays about Persia which appear from the 1670s on drew on classical sources such as Plutarch's *Lives* and Quintus Curtius's *History of Alexander* or La Calprenade's and De Scudery's romances. Dramatists concentrated on members of the first great Persian dynasty: Cyrus, founder of the Persian empire; Cambyses, his son; Darius, who was defeated in his long duel with Alexander; and Alexander himself, the first European conqueror of Asia. Lee's *The Rival Queens* was the most successful and frequently revived of these plays, inspiring dramas on similar themes such as *The Rival Kings* (1677) and *The Siege of Babylon* (1677), although its literary historical importance has turned on its unrhymed representation of sentiment, pathos and interior life. The cultural centrality of Lee's play, however, depended on its theme as well as its treatment. The ancient Persians were attractive subjects to dramatists because they provided the pre-history of Western empire: their early history was recorded in Scripture, and thus, along with the Assyrians, they figured as Europe's origin, as well as, Edward Said has suggested in relation to *The Persians*, her primordial Other. Civil society arose in the East and the Persians' long engagement with the Greeks preceded, and thus in a sense modelled, the struggle between Rome and Carthage, as well as the contemporary European conflict with the Ottomans.

Pufendorf's *Introduction to the History of the Principal Kingdoms and States of Europe* (1699) includes a pithy record of the rise of the earliest empires: Assyrian, Persian and Greek. His account of the Assyrians provides a template of imperial rise and fall – after recording the empire's expansion through conquest and the effective means of its preservation, he describes its collapse:

The Ruin of this Empire under *Sardanapalus* is not so much to be ascrib'd to his Effeminacy, as to this, That the Kings allow'd too much Power to the Governours of Provinces, of so vast an extent. These grew at last too powerful for the Kings themselves, who being lull'd asleep by Voluptuousness (the Effects of Peace and Plenty) did not, as they used to do formerly by great Actions, endeavour to maintain their Authority among the people.[59]

The historical narrative quickens when Phillip and Alexander appear, individuated, legible and dynamic. This sense of the Eastern empires as historically bound and static (by no means unadmirable to seventeenth-century eyes) was reinforced by the remarks of contemporary travellers like Chardin, who commented in the Preface to his *Travels*: "it is not in *Asia* as in our *Europe*, where there are frequent Changes more or less, in the Forms of Things, as in the Habits, Buildings, Gardenings, and the like. In the *East* they are constant in all Things: the Habits are at this Day in the Same Manner, as in the Precedent Ages; So that one may reasonably believe, That in that part of the World, the Exteriour Forms of Things (as their Manners and Customs) are the same now, as they were Two Thousand Years since."[60] The dramatic representation of the Persians exploited this sense of antiquity along with the great wealth and sensuality noted by the ancient historians. In play after play, Persian riches and luxury are displayed and moralized: they serve as signs of greatness and of corruption, motivating conquest by rough and more valorous nations, including the Greeks, who in turn succumb to Oriental excess. The whole process of imperial greatness and decay was encapsulated in the spectacular career of Alexander, who gained and lost an Asian empire in a single lifetime.

The first Persian play to appear in the Restoration was Settle's *Cambyses*, produced in 1671 and a considerable success. Derek Hughes has recently analyzed the confused and anxious treatment of authority in this heroic drama as an early symptom of the process by which joy over the defeat of usurpation was being replaced by concern over succession.[61] The play presents political and judicial processes as fluid, ambiguous and arbitrary, with crucial questions of power and justice decided by subversive hypocrites, bloody tyrants, absurd punctilio and arbitrary laws. Settle's Prologue, which refers to the *"Turkish* cruelty / When Elder Brothers reign, the Younger dye," suggests an analogy between the Persian world of fratricidal violence he is presenting and the Ottoman Empire but the two environments are in fact quite distinct. While Islamic belief does figure in the action of plays about the Turks, primarily as a motivation for conquest, Allah, the invention of the "Great Imposter" Mahomet but uncomfortably close to the Hebraic and Christian God, is never presented as an agent. In *Cambyses*, however, supernatural forces hover over the scene, shaping events through prophetic dreams and magical appearances. Divine retribution is the organizing principle in the chaotic world depicted here. Cambyses is excoriated in the first scene by the Egyptian Princess Mandana as a "defacer of temples" (I.i, p. 4); he dreams his own death at the hands of a woman with a dagger in a spectacular scene of spirits in a cloud and, dying, he proclaims "Heaven itself is a Confederate" (IV.i, p. 54). Mandana's dagger, which kills him, was supposedly of divine origin, suggesting that the Egyptian deities revenged themselves upon a blasphemous invader. Smerdis's imposture and usurpation is revealed in another spectacular scene in the Temple of the Sun, when a discussion over the divinity of Kings is interrupted by the interposition of a "bloody cloud" which parts to reveal the truth-telling ghosts of Cambyses and the real Smerdis.

Settle's deployment of such extraordinary supernatural effects, presumably a major factor in the play's success, was licensed by the Scriptural accounts which saw the Persians, their conquests and their prophecies, as instruments of Providence. As Samuel Clarke wrote in 1664, Cyrus the Great was "an Instrument of Gods Power used for the chastising of many Nations, and the establishing of a Government in those parts of the world, which yet was not to continue long."[62] Although he suggests that Cyrus "received the knowledge of the true God from *Daniel*, whilst he governed *Susa* in *Persia*, and that *Cyrus* himself had read the Prophesie of *Isay*, wherein he was expressly named," Clarke also reports a dream, interpreted by the Persian Magi, recorded by the Persian Dionysius and quoted by Cicero, in which the Sun appeared to Cyrus to foretell the length of his rule.[63] Settle's dramatic representation of the early Persian Emperors not only used their chronological and cultural distance to facilitate the depiction of contemporary anxieties over just rule and succession but exploited their imbrication in a pre-Christian realm where divine intervention was continually manifest in prophecies, dreams and magical appearances. Such recourse to the supernatural was not only spectacular visual entertainment but served to remind audiences of the final, Providential frame within which all human history was unfolding, providing reassurance that order would prevail in both the short and the longer term. Settle also framed the written version of the play with explicit reference to that Providential design, drawing particular attention to its manifestation in the *translatio imperii* from the ancient, pagan East to the modern, Christian West, in his Dedication. The promise of imperial greatness embodied in the Martial Dance which Cambyses presents to Mandana, when a masque of Captive Princes advanced "Adorn'd with Chains, and Coronets of gold" bearing a triumphant conqueror (II.v, p. 26), can thus be seen as a vision of future wealth and power intended to pleasure the English elite as much as the Egyptian Princess.

In *The Rival Queens*, produced some six years later, Lee focused on Alexander, the Persian Nemesis. Although, recently, critics have tended to see the conflict in this play as erotic, with public issues displaced by affective concerns, P. F. Vernon's introduction to the text rightly emphasizes the way Lee's selection from the source material stresses Alexander's slide into tyranny and debauchery.[64] While the play does place a new emphasis on intensities of feeling in flawed characters, internal struggle is by no means exclusively concerned with amatory relations. The corrupting effects of Alexander's success, his adoption of a foreign mode of life and his alienation from his Greek followers are the engines of Lee's action. Alexander's accelerating brutality and loss of self-control is primarily legible in the conflicts between Macedonians which rend his Court, in his violence towards Lysimachus and in his killing of Clytus, rather than in the erotic contest between Statira and Roxana. Clytus in fact regards Alexander's preoccupation with Statira as yet another symptom of his corruption.

Lee's Dedication to the Earl of Mulgrave suggests he saw a parallel in the Babylonian excess associated with Alexander's last days and his own times, remarking that the age was "wild, unthinking, dissolute" (l. 44), one whose "business is senseless riot, Neronian gambols, and ridiculous debauchery" (ll. 45–46). Both Dryden and Sir Car Scroope pick up this topic in their prefatory verses, distinguishing between effeminate courtiers, "the *Persians* of the Pit," and the valor of active military men like Admiral Sir Edward Spragge, whose "heroic worth struck envy dumb / Who took the Dutchman and who cut the boom" in a successful strike against Algiers pirates (31–32). Lee's depiction of Alexander offered a rebuke to a Court notorious for its license which had also, some years previously, adopted Persian vest. Costume is an important signifier in many of the serious plays with exotic settings but nowhere more than in this text, where it figures Alexander's "unmanning" in the most graphic visual terms. For Clytus, the voice of Greek values, the signs of Alexander's corruption are his entanglement with Persian women, the tyrannical Eastern cruelty with which he treats loyal soldiers and his delusions of divinity. In the first act, after Clytus has complained of Alexander's abandonment of war for love of the Persian Princesses, Cassander and Thessalus complain of Philotas's and Parmenio's unjustified deaths and Polyperchon describes Craterus and Hephestion worshipping Alexander "in Persian robes" (I.i.249). In the second act, Alexander appears preceded by Chaldean Priests and his commanders Nearchus and Eumenes, "With their white wands and dressed in eastern robes / To soothe the king, who loves the Persian mode" (II.94). In this scene, Clytus's solitary refusal to kneel to Alexander, who exhibits both his enthrallment by Statira and his tyrannical violence to Lysimachus, provides a powerful visual image of Greek loyalty to Macedon values. The next act, which sees Alexander and Statira reconciled, closes with Alexander asking Clytus to bear him off before a celebratory banquet in which "Gay as the Persian god ourself will stand" (III.435), an event from which Clytus begs to be excused. The fourth act opens with Clytus in his Macedonian robes, flanked by the other Greek commanders all dressed in Persian costume, angrily refusing to give up his "old habit" for the "fashions of the East." Clytus identifies his clothing with "the reverence / I owe my country" and her sacred customs (IV.i.3–4) just as he regards his refusal to kneel to Alexander as manly:

> And while you blushing bow your head to earth
> And hide 'em in the dust, I'll stand upright
> Straight as a spear, the pillar of my country
> And be by so much nearer to the gods.　　　　(IV.i.36–40)

Clytus refuses Persian clothing three times in this act, before taunt-
ing Alexander that his father, in conquering Greeks rather than
Persians, was truly manly: "Phillip fought men, but Alexander
women" (iv.ii.142). When Alexander runs the old man through,
an action he himself describes as bestial, he reaches the nadir of
alienation from his Macedonian identity. The clothing motif recurs
in the final act, when Alexander, reeling in poisoned frenzy, has a
last vision which recapitulates his own career and the cultural logic
which sustained it:

> Parmenio, Clytus, dost thou see yon fellow?
> That ragged soldier, that poor tattered Greek?
> See how he puts to flight the gaudy Persians,
> With nothing but a rusty helmet on, through which
> The grizzly bristles of his pushing beard
> Drive 'em like pikes.   (v.ii.23–28)

The difference between the plainly dressed but martial Greeks and
the effeminate and "gaudy Persians" occurs in Curtius but Lee's deployment of the clothing motif puts it to highly theatrical use, as
a visual means of figuring Alexander's corruption. Lee's was a deliberately negative interpretation of Alexander's actions: in a 1661
translation of *The Life and Death of Alexander the Great*, the conqueror, who has replaced his personal guard of Macedonians with
Persians, justifies his sexual liaisons and his deliberate intermingling of customs as a matter of imperial policy:

I have joyned to my self in marriage the Daughter of *Oxatres*, who is a
Persian, not disdaining to get Children upon a Captive. And afterwards
desiring abountantly to encrease the issue of my Body, I took to Wife
the Daughter of *Darius*, and was the Author that near friends should
beget their Children upon Captives, minding by this Holy Covenant
to exclude the difference between the Conqueror and the Conquered:
Wherefore you must now think that you are not Soldiers by me adopted,
but more Natural, and that Asia and Europe is one Kingdom without
any difference: I have given unto you Armour after the manner of the
Macedons; I have brought all strangeness and novelty into a custome, and
now therefore you are both my Soldiers and Countrey-Men, in all things
receiving one constant form and fashion. I have not thought it unseemly
in the least for the Persians to shadow the customes of the Macedons,
nor the Macedons to counterfeit the Persians, seeing they all ought to be
under one Law and Custome, who should live under one King.[65]

Here Alexander emphasizes that the creation of his Eurasian state requires not just a carnal mingling of peoples but a single, unified set of customs and manners to be shared by all his subjects. In *The Rival Queens* Lee rejects this policy, by presenting Alexander's Persianization as personally and politically disastrous, thus dramatizing Evelyn's assertion in his pamphlet on "the Mode" that the adoption of foreign costume prefigured military and political domination. Stigmatizing the kind of cultural hybridity Alexander proclaimed, Lee's Orientalizing vision of the East, also legible as a critique of the effect of a Francophile Court's adoption of Gallic fashion and effeminacy, actively championed xenophobia.

The Persian plays which followed *The Rival Queens* continued to reflect on the British polity, in dramas which hymned the noble but defeated Darius (James) or celebrated William as a new Cyrus or Alexander. The plays also continued to explore the motivations, processes and effects of imperial conquest in more general terms. In his *Law of Nature and Nations*, Pufendorf quotes Grotius on the unjust causes of war: "Under the first Rank is to be placed Avarice and all extravagant Desire of increasing Wealth, as also Ambition, and the Hopes of enlarging Rule and Dominion, of growing Great, and purchasing a False Fame and Glory by the Oppression of others." Pufendorf glosses this to the effect that "*Avarice* is a cause of War usually conceal'd and dissembled with great Care because it supposes a base and sordid spirit. But *Ambition* is generally favour'd in the World, under the name of Gallantry and Fortitude. And it is commonly thought Greatness and Bravery of Mind, to grasp after, and fight for what belongs to other Men."[66] John Crowne's *Darius, King of Persia* (1688) serves as a mordant commentary on imperial ambition in the terms established by Grotius and Pufendorf. Darius's Persian forces, under attack by Alexander, are consistently ridiculed by his Bractian auxiliaries for their irrationality, their slavish subjugation and their extravagant dress. The most abusive is Bessus, aspirant to imperial power and one of Darius's murderers:

> Nay, I have ever thought a *Persian* King
> Was at the most, but Master of a Mint.
> Persia has Gold and Jewels but no Men;
> It has been long depopulated, all
> By Slavery and Vice; by Women, too.[67]

While Bessus and his fellow conspirators are punished for their treachery to Darius, however, their very European critique of the

Persian state seems to be underwritten by events, staging and the words of the loyal Greek Patron, who remarks that

> the true Soldier does Mankinde create
> By forcing Reason on a brutal State.
> When Oaths are Wind, and Laws but childish Rods
> The Soldier comes, like Thunder, from the Gods.
>
> (II.ii, p. 28)

Patron's argument that European conquest will bring order to a lawless state appears to bear out the view of the treacherous Nabarzanes, who argued "Europeans are Men, for they enjoy / Their Reason, wisely gathered into Laws. / Here they are Brutes, for only strength commands" (I.i, p. 6).

The constant European sniping at Persian dress ("The Men cannot be seen for Plumes and Gold / Nor can the Gold for Diamonds be seen" (I.i, p. 6), symbolizes Persian effeminacy and military ineffectualness but the displays of wealth also suggest the European justifications for treachery and conquest in Persia in terms of lawgiving and civilization are specious: that Avarice, as much as Ambition, is the motivation. In a great set-piece scene which recalls the second act of *The Rival Queens*, Crowne (following Curtius closely) describes Darius's procession before battle. Priests bearing fire on silver altars appear first, followed by a train of Officers in Golden Robes and Collars, then Darius himself attended by his generals, all of whom – except the Greek Patron – prostrate themselves on the ground. This scene of fantastic wealth and absolute, semi-divine power, is matched at the end of the play by Darius's appearance, wounded and bloody, on a humble wagon. In a translation of Curtius's *Life of Alexander* published in 1690 and clearly intended as a compliment to William, these scenes are moralized in the Hellenophile terms invoked by Lee at the end of *The Rival Queens*: "This was the splendid and solemn Procession of *Darius*. But how different was the appearance of the Macedonian Army! Here was no glittering Golden Armour, but bright and serviceable steel; an Army fit for Expedition."[68] In a speech to Darius by Eudemus, an Athenian exiled by Alexander, the Greek draws the moral:

Here indeed is so much Purple and rich Armour, that its value will be incredible to those whose Eyes have not been dazzled by its Splendour. But in the *Macedonian* Army, you'll find that rough and manly fierceness, instead of all this effeminate Bravery . . . your Golden Armour and rich

Furniture could hire better Soldiers out of the Enemies Countrey, than those who so proudly wear them.[69]

The avaricious motivation which has led Patron and the Bactrians to Darius's service is here succinctly laid bare.

In the plays about Persia dramatists regularly include the scenes and costumes of glittering splendor so prominent in the sources, so evocative of a despised Oriental luxury and yet so filled with promise to the avaricious. As England's own Alexander went to his warlike work, however, the drama reflects more of the human cost, as well as the material gains and glory, associated with military conquest. In John Banks's *Cyrus the Great* (1696) the play begins and ends with dreadful battle scenes: Act 1, scene i opens on "a wide spacious Land, ruinous and almost cover'd with dead Bodies, suppos'd to be after a great Battel" as Cyrus's kinsmen and officers discuss the terrible effects of war on "the poor and plunder'd Peasants"[70] and a "bloody mangl'd Coarse" [I.i, p. 6] rises from the carnage to warn Cyaxares, Cyrus's uncle, of his nephew's future triumphs. The last act is also set in a battlefield covered in dead bodies, closing with a scene of unparalleled grotesquerie, when Panthea, daughter of the Amazonian Thomyris, is shown weeping over the mangled body of her husband Abradates, who has been torn apart by the hooked wheels of his own war-chariot. She has attempted to reattach the limbs, one of which comes off again when a sorrowing Cyrus attempts to kiss the corpse's hand. Although the play closes with Cyrus about to enter Babylon in triumph to marry the Egyptian Princess Mandana and dispose of his new territories, the prevailing mood is one of mourning, rather than triumph, as the very last action shows Thomyris removing the bodies of her daughter and son-in-law for burial.

Banks claimed to have written *Cyrus the Great* in the 1680s, so the play's depiction of a fierce dynastic rivalry between uncle (Cyaxares/James) and nephew (Cyrus/William) is presumably fortuitous. Despite the play's complimentary reference in the Prologue to "conquering *William*," the emphasis falls on the cost of war rather than its rewards in terms of glory or wealth, modifying the claim that Cyrus makes to be liberating Asia from Assyrian tyranny, restoring "The World to its dear antient Liberty" (II.i, p. 11) rather than actively seeking "the Empire of the World." Skepticism about rulers with aims to be "Universal Master of the Earth and Seas"

recurs in Cibber's *Xerses* (1699), a play which attacked the tyrannical ambition of Louis XIV but also, more unusually, the literary
means by which the powerful publicized and celebrated their triumphs. *Xerses* satirizes a hack who composes panegyrics for the
Emperor's non-existent victories, orchestrating a Triumph for a
battle which was in fact, lost.

> – Poor Slaves and vagabonds are hir'd
> To personate the seeming Captives of
> A real Victory: vast empty Coffers,
> Suppos'd of Treasure taken from the Enemy,
> High-castl'd Elephants, rich gilded Trophies,
> Spoils, and Armour, Trumpets and Songs prepare his Way.
> The People stare upon the gaudy Show,
> And rend the Skies with echoed Welcomes;
> While he in solemn Pace stalks proudly on,
> And e'en swells out the Hero of a Theatre.[71]

The collapse of Xerses's valor, figured by the hollow celebrations,
is matched by his turn to a rapacious sensuality, leading him to
torture Tamira, wife of the virtuous Artabanus. In the last act of
the play, the false pageantry of a faked victory is replaced by emblems of Xerses's tyranny, as a rack bloody with Tamira's blood,
three dead ravished virgins and, finally, a handkerchief stained with
Tamira's blood are displayed to the enraged populace. The play is
not only highly critical of the effects of ambition perverted, as an
"Aweful Man" turns from conquest to tyranny, from "mustering half
the world" to raping his subjects – less conventionally, Cibber also
looks skeptically at the mechanisms by which the effects of imperial
greatness are created. Heroes are here the creatures of creatures,
as poetasters design spectacles in which defeated leaders pretend
to an epic virtue which they lack. Even the embodied sufferings of
Xerses's victims, emblems of his arbitrary will, are transmuted into
signs of martyrdom, becoming tokens in the struggle for "liberty."
Cibber's mordant vision of the imbrication of imperial pretension
in theatricality, where Emperors imitate player-Kings, suggests a
skepticism about the mechanisms of ambition which reflected on
his own newly expansionist culture, as well as more obvious past
and present seekers after universal monarchy. The Poet's Chorus
in praise of Xerses may have reminded viewers of the contemporary proliferation of poetic and dramatic works which paralleled

William with Cyrus, Alexander, Tamberlane, Arthur, William the Conqueror, and the Plantagenets, despite the fact, as Rowe remarked in his Epistle Dedicatory, that his Majesty still wanted "such a deciding Victory, as that by which *Tamerlane* gave Peace to the World" (A [4]).

Along with the depiction of world-historical figures whose careers epitomized the processes by which empires rose and fell, plays about the Persians reiterated and recirculated important assumptions about what constituted the broad differences as well as similarities between Europe and Asia. As Restoration character lists suggest, the most salient term of collective identity for Europeans through the seventeenth century was "Christian," specified by nation. In Crowne's *Darius*, however, the Greek Patron distinguishes between "Europeans" and Persians, amplifying the distinction to claim reason, law and manliness for the West, with the Persians named bestial, slavish and effeminate. In a period of burgeoning contact with near-Eastern states, plays set in the pre-Christian world of the Persian empires allowed dramatists to revisit and explore classical Greek and Roman formulations of Eurasian differences in terms of culture, politics and economics rather than assuming religion was the only salient factor. While many of the plays focused on periods of crisis, identified with Oriental corruption, other episodes allowed dramatists to explore the processes by which civil society (the prelude to empire) was constituted.

The role of women was a significant element in such explorations. In his Prologue to *The Ambitious Step-Mother* (1700), Rowe argues that the dramatists of the present age were superior even to Shakespeare in their treatment of women, for by ransacking the "Ancients Store" of "antient Heroines" they copied women "in every Height of Nature."[72] One such ancient heroine, Thomyris, the famous Amazon, figured in an eponymous text in 1707 as well as appearing as an important character in other plays. While Anne's presence on the throne was clearly important in stimulating such productions, earlier plays about the Persians also include female figures of considerable power and complexity, demonstrating qualities which an emergent, domestic model of femininity eschewed. In Settle's *The Ambitious Slave*, the Indian Princess Herminia, a mild and virtuous figure who is properly Queen of Persia, is rejected by her husband in favor of the mysterious, ambitious slave of the title, the low-born Scythian Celestina. Celestina is figured as a kind of amatory Amazon, who wants to "Tell the vain babling World I raign by Conquest."[73] In a scene which distinguishes between the two women in terms of womanliness and aggression, Celestina instructs the infatuated King to show Herminia the "Civilityes of a Wife," while the Indian Queen helplessly bemoans her own lack of spirit:

O for the spirit of the great *Semiramis*
To meet my wrongs, and stemm the storm that sinks me.
No, I've too much the Mother's Milk within me,
Weep like a Girle, and bend beneath my sufferings.

(ii.ii, p. 25)

Herminia's invocation of the great Assyrian Empress underlines her own very different passivity, while Celestina's Scythian nationality links her to the Amazons, thus suggesting a possible origin for her unnatural ambition. Her overreaching is paralleled by the resentful perfidy of the eunuch Mirvan, who complains bitterly of his enforced unmanning. The play's depiction of disorder in gender and political relations, never properly resolved, invokes mythic figures (of Amazons) and exotic practices (such as castration) in a gesture towards explaining subversion but the confounding of order and justice is never fully accounted for. Here the exotic setting itself, ungoverned by a divine presence of the kind legible in other Persian plays, provides the only explanation for a criminalized state.

Nicholas Rowe returns to the issue of improper female ambition in *The Ambitious Stepmother* (1700). Here, the old Persian King's enthrallment by Artemisa, the eponymous step-mother, who had her first husband murdered to enable her to become Queen, is emblematic of the weakness in the Persian state. In conversation with the old soldier Memnon, Artabanes, second son to the King by Artemisa, claims that once the discord fomented by his brother and mother has been quieted, "Rough *Greece*, alike in Arts and Arms severe / No more shall brand the *Persian* Name with Softness"[74] but will instead "pay their Homage to the throne of *Cyrus*" (iii.ii, p. 47). Although Artabanes's bombastic older brother Artaxerses threatens fiercely, in the final scene he kills himself when he discovers his wife dead, and the boyish but determined Artabanes takes the throne. Artabanes's most serious duel is not with his self-destructive sibling but with his mother, who uses sacrilegious treachery (by having her enemies taken captive during worship in the Temple of the

Sun) to gain her ends. Artabanes proves himself a fitter heir than
Artaxerses not just because, unlike his brother, he overcomes his
disappointment in love to take up his duties but because he rele-
gates his mother to her proper place. Refusing her bloody advice to
kill his brother, Artabanes tells her roundly that as a woman, she is
"form'd to obey," and "Desire of Government is monstrous in you"
(IV.i, p. 61) and in the closing scene he restricts her to the women's
quarters, where she will rule only among "maids and Eunuchs."
The final exchange between Artemisa and her son reiterates the
argument that the weakness and discord in the Persian state had
its origins in an effeminacy caused by the unnatural usurpation of
power by the Queen-Mother. "Look on that scene of blood" says
Artabanes, "the dire Effects / Of cruel Female Arts ... / By our
bright Gods I swear I will assert / The Majesty on Manly Government" (v.ii, pp. 89–90). Artemisa defends herself vigorously, reminding her son that his father "Was proud to be the Subject of my
Sway / The Warrior to the Woman's Wit gave way" (v.ii, p. 90), but is
forced finally to accept his authority. Her banishment to her proper
realm opens up the possibility of a new scene of Persian greatness.

Rowe's meditation on the dangers of female rule provides a
"back-story" to the more public dramas of imperial consolidation
and disintegration in earlier plays like *Cyrus*, *Darius* and *Xerses*
while working with similar assumptions about the effeminacy of the
Persians under their later rulers. Delariviere Manley's *The Royal
Mischief*, which was unusual in using Chardin's account of contemporary Persia, rather than a classical or romance source, has been
described as a feminist satire on the conventional representation
of near-Eastern states as scenes of excessive sensuality and violence.
Certainly Manley's description of a Vizier being stuffed alive into
a cannon, blown out and then reassembled by his grieving widow,
who stretches herself out on the smoking fragments, seems sufficiently grotesque to be understood as a counter-phallic parody
of exotic violence and excessive devotion. The scene recalls both
Aureng-Zebe, in whose last scene real and parodic satis occur, and
Banks's *Cyrus*, in which a distraught widow attempts to re-unify her
husband's scattered remains. The incident has its origin, however,
in Chardin's narrative of the involved and melodramatic affairs of
the kingdom of Libardian. In Chardin's account, the young prince
of Libardian, Levan Dadian, took his aunt by marriage to wife,
after sending his own spouse back to her father with her nose,

ears and hands cut off, and her purported lover, his Vizier, was "stopp'd into the Mouth of a *Cannon*" at the same time she was maimed.[75] In Chardin's view, the episode was "perhaps not unworthy to the Remembrance of History" for "certainly 'tis a thing equally to be observ'd and wonder'd at, That such small and inconsiderable Kingdoms should continually produce such Tragick Revolutions."[76] The episode has another virtue, however, as an exemplary instance of Oriental barbarousness: "Nor shall I be accus'd to have injur'd the People of these Countries, while I tell ye how wicked they are, when you have read this part of my Story; Since the bare Relation which I shall make in representing 'em such, will justifie me perhaps in the Judgement of my Readers."[77]

Chardin, concerned to be seen to be doing "justice to nations" as Gildon would put it, prepares the reader for a "bare Relation" which is nonetheless already flagged as a "Tragick" demonstration of Oriental wickedness and political instability. The people of Colchis, the scene of the action, were dismissed by Heylyn as "very rude and barbarous; so inhumane and void of natural affection, that they sell their children to the Turks."[78] Manley's adaptation of the story of Levan Dadian and Darejan (Homais) is currently read without regard for their status as emblematic Circassians but as a tragic demonstration of the wickedness of a patriarchal gender order. Recent feminist readings of *The Royal Mischief* thus emphasize that Manley's play celebrated her eponymous heroine as an embodiment of "sexual and political prowess" who resists being the means by which patriarchal culture violently attempts to unify itself.[79] While Manley's alterations of the source bear out claims that she wishes to underline the violence enacted upon and produced by women confined (of whom supposedly secluded Eastern women were prototypical) the play cannot be regarded simply as feminist rather than party allegory. Sharing Chardin's assumption that in the East one observes an unchanging and ancient social order, *The Royal Mischief* elides chronological and cultural distance, using its setting to explore and criticize the gender repression conceived of as crucial to civil society. The setting, however, also establishes a critical distance between the English audience, putatively members of a civil Christian polity which regarded freedom of conversation between the sexes as a distinguishing characteristic of their own society, and a wild, unstable and oppressive Asian nation. Homais is a familiar type from heroic drama, a *femme forte* with generic antecedents in Indian Queens Zempoalla and Nourmahal, as well as the ancient heroines of Greek, Roman and Eastern imperial history and, as such, she personified a kind of energetic, appetent and ambitious feminine identity against which a domestic, modest model of Christian womanhood was continually compared. Her complaints about her enclosure do provide a novel, feminist etiology for these Oriental viragos but her characterization is consonant with that of figures like Roxana in *The Siege of Rhodes*, a text which also attempted to articulate the effects of the different gender orders of Asia and Europe. In Davenant's opera, Roxana is persuaded that the European freedom of intercourse between the sexes brought happiness rather than license but derided Christian women as "soft fools" unfit for governance. Manley reworks the figure of the Oriental virago with sympathy and admiration but fails to deconstruct the antithesis between such heroic women, denizens of ancient history or the East, and modern English ladies implicit in this mode. In *The Royal Mischief*, Homais embodies the violence produced by rebellion against sexual tyranny while Selima demonstrates the destructive self-abnegation of such tyranny internalized. Understanding their own position in terms of difference from, as much as parallel to, the putative sexual despotism of Asia, Englishwomen could not view this play simply as a negative reflection of their own gender order but also as a reminder of their own civil, Christian privilege.

Manley's is the only play which uses recent Persian history as a source: Lewis Theobald's *The Persian Princess* (1708) returns to romance, showing a pair of Armenian Princes, one virtuous and one vicious, assuming the Persian throne when the King is poisoned. The play included scenes set in the Temple of the Sun and a wicked Priest urging the mild King on to human sacrifice, and drew the usual moral that "Our *Persia*, that for Discipline and Rule / Stood Candidate with *Sparta*, rough in War / Patient in Labour and disdaining Ease" had become licentious and ripe for conquest by a more martial nation.[80] Although contemporary commentators regarded the Persians as more cultivated than the Turks and their tyranny less despotic, John Fryer at least continued the tradition of viewing Persian monarchs as licentious and their people slavish. In his *A New Account of East-India and Persia* (1698), he remarked that "their natural Ingenuity . . . exceeds all the *Eastern* people, both for facetiousness of Wit, Civil Behaviour, and Gallantry in Appearance" but reported also on the custom which forced men to "bring their own proper Wives to Court, to remaine there all that time prostitute to [the Emperor's] lust."[81] Bearing out Chardin's contention as to the continuity of things in the East, Fryer argued that the seventeenth-century Emperors were in important respects continuous with their pre-Islamic forebears:

They esteem their Emperors not only as Lords Paramount, but reverence them as Sons of Prophets whose Dominion is grounded more on Hierarchy than mere Monarchy. For as of old the Persians adored the Sun as a Deity, and celebrated his rising with many Hymnes, and were daily employed in Sacred Anthems for its Praise; so now the Idolators become Infidels, they still espouse the Divine Right as well as the Lineage of their Sovreigns.[82]

Brought up in the seraglio with "Toothless Old Women, Ignorant and Effeminate Eunuchs, a Tutor more versed in Books than the Affairs of the World," it was hardly surprising the Emperors were themselves licentious, unable to lead their troops and manipulated by their chief ministers.[83] The account provided by the Ancients of a luxurious, absolute, cultivated but corrupt and effeminate Persia was thus borne out by current observers and reiterated endlessly on the stage. At the same time this vision had licensed aggressive intervention in Persian affairs, it also facilitated the development of Whig Hellenophile opinion which cast France as Persia and Britain as the Greek defenders of liberty.[84]

ORIENTALISM

In 1707, Delariviere Manley returned to an exotic subject in her *Almyna: or, The Arabian Vow.* The play's actual location is vague, although the hero is Almanzor, Conqueror of Spain, but the atmosphere is markedly Oriental, inspired by Antoine Galland's recently translated *Arabian Nights Entertainments.* Norman Daniel has argued that Galland's publication marks a shift from the simple incorporation of Arabian, Persian and other near-Eastern materials into European literature legible from Chaucer and Boccaccio on, to a much more self-conscious literary "Orientalism."[85] My own view is that those English plays using Asian and North African locales during the Restoration and into the early years of the eighteenth century were inflected by a newly urgent sense of cultural and political difference from Oriental and Islamic societies, as the English entered into unprecedented relations with such states through trade, war and diplomacy. Plays were often produced in the context of a new trade or military initiative, drew on current geographies, histories and *relazione* and thus helped circulate received wisdom about various Asian and African states. These dramas, however, were not fully "Orientalist" in the sense invoked by Daniel or Said, although they can be construed as an emergent form of such discourse. The actors in the Asian dramas of the later seventeenth century are the subjects of their own histories sharing the stage of global history with Western Christians. Their differences in religion, in social and political structure and in gender relations disturb and fascinate Europeans but such differences are explored with some seriousness, not yet having solidified into signifiers of inferiority.

At first reading, Manley's play might seem to depart from earlier Oriental dramas, precisely because it draws self-consciously on Galland's creation of a fixed, static, objectified and generalized "Orient." In fact, though, her text explores precisely those aspects of the religious, political and gender order which are encapsulated in the generating frame of Galland's *Tales*, to wit, erroneous religion, despotism and the enslavement of women. Galland assumes that his audience can take such "Oriental" characteristics for granted: tropes of Eastern difference, they no longer require articulation or analysis, while serving as the ground for his narration. In *Almyna*, however, Manley inverts the relation established by Galland and, instead of deploying the frame-story of Scheherezade to conjure up further exotic fantasies, she explores and criticizes the religious, cultural and political axioms encapsulated in the frame-tale. As was the case in *The Royal Mischief*, the critique of Oriental custom glances at the English audience also: while beliefs regarded as specific to Islam are criticized, the text invokes misogynist assumptions prevalent in Europe.[86] Thus the play interrogates, while it exploits, Galland's invention of a new Orientalism, by emphasizing the specific cultural and political grounds in which literary discourse, as much as gender and political relations, is imbricated.

Almyna is a radical revision of Galland's *Entertainments*. Instead of the hapless heroine keeping herself alive through the endless provision of stories, she actively takes up the challenge of dissuading the Sultan from his barbarous views through logical and historical argument, not narrative prowess. She persuades him of the correctness of her views of female rationality and courage by persisting in them to the point of death. Almyna is a deliberate and positive variant on the Oriental virago: she is as ambitious as the Empress of Morocco and Rowe's ambitious Queen Artemisa, announcing that "I feel the Sacred Glowings in my Bosom / And am devoted all, to Death or Empire"[87] but is virtuous, learned and chaste. Manley revises the Sultan's character in an equally striking manner by emphasizing his fraternal love for his brother Abdalla, so that, breaking with custom, Almanzor names his brother as his heir, rather than killing him. In one sense, the play rehabilitates ambitious Oriental women and cruel Turks, showing them capable of revising despotic practices in gender and political relations both.

Almyna is emphatically not a satire on Orientalism *per se*, however. The play opens with the groans of the Sultan's most recent victim echoing in the audience's ears: we hardly need reminding that "So absolute, Alas! Our Caliphes are / Tis Death to all, who dare to cross their Wills!" (II.i, p.11). The spectacular but entirely factitious scene in which Abdalla, the Sultan's brother, is invested as heir, makes repeated reference to the Moorish triumphs over Europeans – "All Spain submits to great *Almanzor's* Arms!" (II.i, pp. 4–5) – and emphasizes the religious nature of the conquests. The characters rehearse supposedly Islamic beliefs about women, framed by references to the Koran, with the Sultan claiming females are "Born to no other end, but propagation / Instinct to them, as to their fellow Brutes / Goads on, to Multiply" (I.i, p. 9), while Abdelezar calls the learned Almyna "A contradiction to her very nature" (I.i, p. 9). Almyna convinces the Sultan that women do have souls first by telling him about a series of biblical and Roman women worthies, who include Semiramis, Judith, Virginia, Lucretia and Cleopatra, and then by the fortitude with which she faces death, dressed in the customary fatal black robe which Charles Goring would also employ in his *Irene*. As was the case in the first important Oriental drama, Davenant's *The Siege of Rhodes*, the infidel despot undergoes a conversion, abandoning the religious and political precepts regarded as most characteristic of his culture, to adopt Western-style family values and companionate marriage.

Like earlier critiques of tyranny and rebellion, the lust for conquest and the softening which accompanies the consolidation of empire, Manley's critique of misogyny in *Almyna* cuts both ways, East and West. To allegorize the Oriental tropes in this play risks

effacing the extent to which the text not only recirculates Orientalist political dicta but participates in the construction of feminist
Islamaphobia. Manley's articulation of misogynist beliefs did not
preclude their being read as a satire on contemporary elite British
attitudes to women but they are too embedded in a thoroughly
familiar context to be seen as bearing on domestic practices alone.
As the Bey of Tunis was reported by John Morgan to have said to the
English Court: "All you *Frank-Christians* are ever ready to upbraid us
with the Ignorance and Incapacity of our Women; boasting, that, as
our Wives are bought like Slaves, kept like Nuns, and fit for nothing
to be maintained in Idleness at our Expence, yours bring you Fortunes, assist you in all your Affairs and are capable of everything."
Europeans, however, he pointed out, are themselves purchased by
their wives' dowries and "As to Liberty, they [Turkish women] have
as much as Decency and Custom admit of; For Estate, if they bring
any, it is for themselves and their Children."[88]

The Bey's remarks are a useful reminder that plays about Asia
and Africa share with travel accounts the appearance of coherence,
in which the narrative can obscure the extent to which knowledge
of strange places, things and people is produced not just by singular
impressions, but by exchanges with strangers. Many of the heroic
dramas set in the near-East, in the Empire most proximate to Europe, play out the drama of contact between Europeans and Asians
in terms which efface pressing English commercial "interests" in
the Levant by focusing on the military and erotic exchanges encoded in the tales of love and honor. Their epic elevation notwithstanding, such dramas demonstrably played a significant role in
the codification of elite English views of the nature of non-Western
societies and provided a context in which different models of empire could be explored, analyzed, appropriated or dismissed. The
knowledge produced by the symbolic complementarity of Boon's
Indo-Sumatran monarchies, an epistemology recognizable in many
of the heroic dramas, depended on relationships of exchange
which recognized and cultivated likeness rather than difference
or identity. Now that the identification of differences has consolidated into negative occidentalist doxa, habitually deployed for
the purposes of what Pufendorf and other early modern commentators called avarice, it is worth noting that the past from which
Orientalism emerged offered other, less purely negative models of
knowledge and relationship between Europeans and Asians.

CHAPTER 5

Spain's Grand Project of a Universal Empire

In 1660, Spain was still a puissant power in Europe and beyond but educated opinion held that the Spaniards had failed in their most ambitious project: "they have effected great and noble things, *viz.* their Conquest over the *Moors,* and the *New World,* together with *Philip* the Second's Conquest or Possession of *Portugal:* and they have failed of as great, *viz.* their Design upon *England* in 88 and in their Grand Project of an Universal Empire, which had almost broke the Heart of this Monarchy."[1] From 1660 to 1714, speculation centered on whether the Dutch, or later the French, were replacing the Spanish as the new aspirants to Western empire. The conventional wisdom was that the Spanish empire was too weak, depopulated, unskillful in governance, and widely dispersed to function as an effective entity and late seventeenth-century geographers, historians and political analysts treated the Peninsular power as exemplary of the failure of an imperial state apparently blessed by many advantages but brought down by ambition and intolerance.[2] Spanish empire was nonetheless an absorbing topic for dramatists. John Loftis pointed out in *The Politics of Drama in Augustan England* (1963) that the War of the Spanish Succession seemed to provoke an outburst of comedies with Peninsula settings,[3] while in *The Spanish Plays of Neo-Classical England* he analyzes the widespread borrowing from Spanish literature throughout this period, arguing that Spain and Portugal offered Dryden and his fellow authors an attractive reservoir of exotic literary materials and heroic themes.[4] More recently, David Kramer has suggested that Dryden's interest in the "heterocultural" and imperial themes of Spanish history enabled him to assert his own poetic authority, as a great English poet, against the weighty claims of the Ancients and, in particular, the French.[5] A more mundane but still important factor in focusing dramatic attention on Spain is surely the fact that, in the

first decades of the Restoration at least, English trade was heavily weighted towards the Peninsular, influencing popular opinion
favorably.[6]

More powerful reasons for the obsession with Spanish empire
in Dryden, Behn, Pix and Congreve are suggested by Richard
Helgerson's recent account of the development of English national
identity in the Elizabethan period. Helgerson argues that, like
Portugal which fell to the dynastic claims of Spain, and Holland,
which emerged as a nation in opposition to Spanish dominion,
Elizabethan "England necessarily defined itself and the character
of its overseas expansion in terms of its relation to Spain."[7] That
relation was an awkward mixture of similarity and difference, because, like the Spanish (and the Portuguese), England prized itself
on its nobility but, like the Republican Dutch, it was a Protestant
nation which depended on trade. Helgerson's account stresses that
early modern national self-representations based claims to cultural
legitimacy on an alignment with those other cosmopolitan and elite
states which embodied order and stability,[8] an idea perfectly embodied in the doctrine of the *translatio imperii*. He also analyzes
the tensions between mercantilist and aristocratic notions of empire, suggesting Hakluyt's collections of voyages should be seen as
the prose epic of the English nation, providing a legitimation for
colonial trade generally despised by the nobility as a sordid and
avaricious pursuit. The success of such legitimation was reflected
in Raleigh's "heady talk of commanding the world through trade,
an aristocratic idea of universal conquest [which] piggybacks on a
mercantile idea of universal commerce."[9]

The ideological differences between such positions is never really satisfactorily resolved in English epic, the literary form traditionally devoted to the celebration of national greatness. Curiously,
although Helgerson discusses Milton's attempt to function as his
nation's "imperial law-giver," he shows no interest in the heroic
plays produced contemporaneously with *Paradise Lost* which are
conditioned by the same tensions and conflicts which he identifies
in epic poetry. As a genre, the heroic plays attempted a reconciliation between the aristocratic mode of heroic romance and the
epic celebration of kingship and empire associated with absolutist
monarchy.[10] Their capacity to reveal as much as harmonize the tensions subsisting between the King and the political nation, which
included merchants but consisted largely of the aristocracy and

gentry, has been well documented but their imbrication in the national and colonial issues canvassed by Helgerson, has not. Yet the extended depiction of Peninsular empire on the stage under the later Stuarts is clearly playing out that dialectic of identification and difference by which free, Protestant England defined herself against absolutist, Catholic Spain. Davenant's Cromwellian operas, *The Cruelty of the Spaniards in Peru* and *The History of Sir Francis Drake*, along with that *locus classicus* of the black legend of Spanish Conquest, *The Indian Emperor*, and the two parts of *The Conquest of Granada* all established a model of Spanish empire as great but cruel, serving as an instrument of Providence in freeing Spain from the Moors and conquering and converting the Americas. These early plays do also suggest the Spaniards were intolerant, hypocritical and more interested in, and corrupted by, avarice than their claims of glory and piety suggested but the heroic plays were written in a mode which almost, if not entirely, occludes mercantilist avarice as a motive for colonial conquest. This allowed Dryden to bracket the low and squalid business of trade, slaving and settlement by which English colonial expansion was actually effected, to focus instead on the noble actions of Europe's great imperial model, while disavowing her crimes.

By the time he wrote the elegiac *Don Sebastian*, a mournful tribute to Portugal's quixotic Crusader, Dryden had abandoned the possibility that the English might pursue overseas empire as a project of civilization and conversion rather than trade and settlement. Later dramatists, whether Tories like Behn, or Whigs like Pix, reflected a more generalized skepticism of and contempt for the Spanish, and in plays like *Abdelezar, The Conquest of Spain* and *The Fatal Friendship*, depicted them as corrupted by their long engagement with the Moors and their unjust American conquests. The Portuguese, however, traditional allies of the English, and victims of Spanish ambition as well as early practitioners of oceanic empire, were celebrated in the popular redactions of Fletcher's *The Indian Princess* by Tate and Motteux. These productions, whether dramatic or operatic, effected an unprecedented harmonization of mercantile and aristocratic modes of colonial action. Celebrating the expansion of informal Portugese power in the Moluccas through conversion, intermarriage and military prowess, these texts suggested that European avarice and ambition might both be satisfied in the process of Christianizing and civilizing the wealthy pagan nations of the East.

As was the case with dramatic representations of the Turks and other non-European nations, plays about the Spanish implicitly or explicitly invited comparisons between their gender order and that of the English. The institutions which organized sexual identities and relations were again treated as symptomatic of other political, religious and cultural distinctions, with Spanish men characterized as lusty but sterile, "more hot than virile in his lust," and their wives relatively infertile: "the Women are Mothers so young and early, that Nature is decayed in them before the half of their teeming."[11] This putative reproductive feebleness was cited as a cause of the empire's weakness through depopulation. Spanish women were also reputed to be enclosed by jealous husbands whose familial tyranny reflected that of their absolutist monarch. Heylyn attributed this jealousy to Moorish influence – "this humour of jealousie might be derived on them from the *Moores*, who in the strict guarding of their women were the *Spaniards* Tutors: it being death in *Barbarie*, to this very day, for any man to see one of the *Xerrife's* Concubines" – and also to climate, regarding jealousy as "A frenzie which much rageth in most *Southern* People, but not predominant in the *Northern*."[12] The sexual success of Englishmen like Behn's Rover or Pix's English Colonel Peregrine in *The Spanish Wives*, who rescue women immured by oppressive guardians or spouses, did not reflect so much a feminine openness to ethnic difference, as a growing English sense of the superiority of their own more liberal and civil gender order along with a chauvinist conviction of English virility which increased with her military successes abroad.[13]

Spain's complex ethnic inheritance was also an important factor in the representation of Spanish empire and functioned as an important index of shifting conceptions of inter-ethnic contact. While the *Reconquista* was recognized as a great triumph, geographers and political analysts concurred in viewing the Spanish expulsion of the Jews and Moors as an instance of the religious and cultural intolerance which weakened the empire, by depriving it of skill, wealth and human resources. By banishing 170,000 families, Pufendorf remarks, "the Kingdom nevertheless was despoil'd of vast Riches, and of a great Number of Inhabitants."[14] Despite the expulsion, however, slurs against the purity of Iberian blood reflected suspicion of the effects of intermarriage between the Moors, the Jews and the Peninsular Christians. Thus Pufendorf remarks: "Some also will have them to be very Malicious, which they say is the remnant of that *Jewish* Blood, which is intermingled with that of the *Portuguese* Nation."[15] This proto-racist suspicion, also legible in Behn's *Abdelezar*, was accompanied by a more liberal hostility to the religious intolerance and cruelty of the Spanish, whose "Court of Inquisition is esteemed an inhuman and execrable Tribunal among other Nations."[16] The other great triumph of Spanish empire, the conquest of America, generated equally ambivalent responses in terms of national and ethnic characterization. The conquest was notorious among Protestant nations for its cruelty, and under Cromwell the doctrine that the English were destined to rescue the victimized Indians from their Hispanic enslavement was given theatrical form in Davenant's two operas.[17] Its recent republican articulation notwithstanding, the conviction that Spanish dominion was fundamentally unjust, and that the English had a responsibility to avenge the injured Indians, became axiomatic. Mary Pix recurs to the black legend of Spanish guilt in *The Fatal Friendship* in which the villainess possesses many American plantations and an Indian slave of royal descent, who abhors being made accomplice in her mistress's crimes. Accompanying her mistress at all times, the royal slave Zelaide serves as a visible emblem of a specifically Spanish history of, and propensity to, ruthless cruelty, exemplified by their treatment of the Indians. The conquest of America, the play implies, has corrupted not just an individual but a whole European society.

THE BLACK LEGEND

Davenant's two operas, *The Cruelty of the Spaniards in Peru* and *The History of Sir Francis Drake*, provide the starting point for theatrical representations of Spanish empire in this period. Davenant had a history of producing masque and poetic texts supportive of Stuart imperial ventures and pretensions and he lent his talents to the Protector's Western design with vigor. The first piece included a scene in which an Indian Prince was roasted on a spit:

A dolefull pavin is pla'd to prepare the change of the Scene, which represents a dark prison at a great distance; and farther to the view are discern'd Racks, and other engins of torment, with which the Spaniards are tormenting the natives and English Marriners, which may be suppos'd to be lately landed there to discover the Coast; two Spaniards are likewise discover'd, sitting in their Cloaks, and appearing more solemn in Ruffs, with Rapiers and Daggers by their sides; the one turning a spit, whilst the other is basting an *Indian* Prince, which is roasted by an artificiall fire.[18]

This scene provided the most graphic possible emblem of Spanish atrocities and the justification for the violation of their territorial claims in the New World. The other interlude, *The History of Sir Francis Drake*, presented another motivation, that of avarice. In this action, Drake and his fellow Englishmen steal a train of silver-laden mules from the Spanish, earning the gratitude of the Indians released in the skirmish as well as appropriating the booty. This succinct rehearsal of the moral and material justifications for attempts to diminish Spain's American hegemony is articulated by a grateful Indian.

Davenant's pithy version of the black legend was crude but effective and its patriotic appeal survived the change of regimes: the interludes were revived as acts in *The Playhouse to be Let* several times during the 1660s. Dryden's engagement with Spanish history was much more complex: his ventriloquism of ethnic slurs in *Amboyna* was not characteristic of his depiction of the Spanish in his major plays. In the 1660s, the evidence of *Annus Mirabilis* suggests that Dryden was an enthusiastic proponent of England's future as an imperial power, one which gained its stature from the nobility of its monarchs and aristocracy but was also enriched and supported by the successful activities of her merchants and seamen. Nonetheless, even in this text, his suspicion of mercantile activity expressed itself in the characterization of the Dutch as luxurious consumers, "perfum'd prey" whose Carthaginian voluptuousness stands in contrast with the rough (Roman) valor of the English.[19] Steven Pincus has demonstrated that many Englishmen believed that the United Provinces were seeking a new kind of universal monarchy, that they had "an immoderate desire to engross the whole traffic of the universe"[20] and make themselves "masters of the commerce of the universe."[21] As one sees most clearly in *Amboyna*, Dryden was not only antagonistic to such monopolistic pretensions in the Dutch but was and remained hostile to such a purely mercantile vision of empire. In *The Hind and the Panther* he attacked the lack of apostolic zeal which informed the commercial priority of English expansionism:

Here let my sorrow give my satyr place,
To raise new blushes on my *British* race;
Our sayling ships like common shoars we use,
And through our distant colonies diffuse
The draughts of Dungeons and the stench of stews;
Whom, when their home-bred honesty is lost,
We disembogue on some far *Indian* Coast:
Thieves, Pandars, Palliards, sins of ev'ry sort,
These are the manufactures we export.
And these the Missionaries our zeal has made:
For, with my country's pardon, be it said,
Religion is the least of all our Trade.   (*Works* vol. iii: 2, 556–67)

Throughout his career, he preferred to represent Christian expansionism in the epic terms offered by Spanish history, as a flawed but noble narrative of aristocratic and royal military prowess aimed at civilization and conversion.[22]

Dryden's first essay at the imperial history of Spain was *The Indian Queen*, co-authored by Robert Howard. The play, often referred to as the first fully fledged heroic drama, preceded *The Indian Emperor* and depicted Montezuma's successful recovery of Mexico, after his aunt Zempoalla, with the help of the General Traxalla, has usurped the throne. The play's sources included both heroic romances and historical accounts which were shaped to present a powerful representation of a semi-civil society, wealthy, monarchical and warlike but tainted with superstition, human sacrifice and improper female power. Although the love and honor mode familiarized the Peruvians and Mexicans, the Prologue and Epilogue, characterization, props and scenery are all used to emphasize the cultural distance of the action, hinting at the Indians' fate as European prey. The Prologue is presented as an echo of the discovery of America; after the curtain has risen, music awakens a pair of Indian children, who speak a dialog from the stage which celebrates their Edenic happiness but repeats prophecies that "Our World shall be subdu'd by one more old" (*Works* vol. viii, Prologue, 12) and detects the arrival of that world in the audience. It was highly unusual to have the Prologue spoken from behind the proscenium arch, rather than from the apron stage, so that the physical distance of audience and actors underlined the cultural difference referred to in the speeches. The graceful theatrical conceit by which the spectators are identified as denizens of the old world was problematic, however: the Indians' apprehension of the violent quarrelling and

"Doom" consequent on the Spanish Conquest had to be refigured as supplication to merciful and forgiving (English) "Deities." This more optimistic framing of the Indians' fate signals the conviction that the cruel Spanish will be superseded by the English.

The Indian Queen uses the pre-Columbian setting to explore the urge to conquest and empire presumed ubiquitous but more easily observable in nations less polite than those of Europe. This America does not present a war of all against all but its inhabitants are noticeably free of the ties imposed by Christianity and law. The play pits two uncivil figures of untrammeled ambition against each other, as Zempoalla's *realpolitik* cunning, sexual opportunism and bloody superstition clash with Montezuma's hunt for glory. Like the other Herculean heroes of this genre, Montezuma is a "noble savage" of whom the civil, honorable Acacis remarks, *pace* Davenant's remarks on ambition to Hobbes, "Like the vast Seas, your Mind no Limits knows."[23] Montezuma's restless intolerance of authority is eventually legitimated by the discovery of his royal birth but his characterization remains that of a figure impatient of rule, order and civility. The gods, he tells the Ynca, "Gave me not Scepters, nor such gilded things / But whilst I wanted Crowns, inlarg'd my minde, / To despise Scepters, and dispose of Kings" (II.i.26–28), an account of an anarchic greed for power partially accounted for by the belated account of his upbringing in a cave, trained by Garruca to spend his days hunting after "savage spoils" (v.i.247).

Although Zempoalla's ambition receives no overt explanation other than her sex, its manifestations suggest that, like Montezuma's, her semi-savagery derives from, and is fed by, her less than fully civil environment. As a woman, she is debarred from fighting *per se* (although her daughter will express Amazonian intentions in *The Indian Emperor*), but her aggression is repeatedly expressed in her thirst for human sacrifice. This is an important aspect of her characterization, licensed by Purchas's mention of the sacrifice of "Captives: to get which, they made their warres, rather than seeking in their victories to take them to kill."[24] Zempoalla threatens to make sacrifices in every act, first promising the gods "Princes," and then the Ynca, Orazia, and Montezuma. The final act takes place in a Temple of the Sun, made all of gold but centered on a "bloody Altar" attended by four priests in habits of red and white feathers "as ready for sacrifice" (v. i.). The dramatists use this ritual violence as an index not only of Zempoalla's cruelty but of the measured savagery of her state, in thrall to false gods. The Indian Queen's arrogance is also figured by another ethnographic detail drawn from Purchas; her appearance on the shoulders of her slaves, creating a highly effective tableau, was presumably inspired by the knowledge that Montezuma "never set his foot on the Ground, but was alwaies carried on the shoulders of Noble-men."[25] Commentators have remarked on Behn's claim that Zempoalla's headdress was her own Surinam souvenir, reflecting that its appearance was suggestive of the exotic commodities to be gained through colonial trade but the blood-red feathered costumes of the temple-priests were surely as striking, underlining the Mexicans' sanguinary paganism.[26]

The world presented in *The Indian Queen* was not without nobility but the ambiguities in its depiction of the re-establishment of kingly power reflect more than contemporary doubts about the Restoration.[27] The play's enormously popular spectacularity enabled the audience to envisage a new world, not just of scenic effects but exotic territory, ripe for conquest and plunder. The Epilogue makes its own connection between theatrical novelty and colonial trade – "You have seen all this old World cou'd do, / We therefore hope to try the fortunes of the new" – going on to remark:

> 'Tis true, y'have marks enough, the Plot, the Show,
> The Poets Scenes, nay, more, the Painters too:
> If all this fail, considering the cost,
> 'Tis a true Voyage to the *Indies* lost:
> (*Works* vol. XII, Epilogue, 5–6, 11–14)

The Indian inhabitants of that world, whether a half-savage stranger like Montezuma, or a bloodthirsty female tyrant, presented images of pagan greatness and wealth implicitly in need of the Christian conversion and civility which had served as justification for Spanish conquest. The depiction of Indian pathos, in the victims of such conquest, which framed the action in Prologue and Epilogue, however, addressed and invoked the contemporary English justification for intervention in, and appropriation of, Spanish colonial possessions and profits.

In *The Indian Emperor* Dryden returned to the black legend, dramatizing the conquest itself. The historical and romance sources for the play, whose first and last acts are particularly close to their likely origins in Purchas, Montaigne and Gomara, have been thoroughly canvassed, as this is a play whose action is perhaps more resistant to allegorization than any other heroic drama.[28] Dryden's

Montezuma had a long after-life as a pre-eminent version of the "rational primitive," providing the inspiration for Voltaire's *Alzire* and Henry Brooke's *Montezuma*. Although the play's dramatization of cultural conflict remained popular, the imminence of the Second Dutch War rendered the topic of imperial conquest especially apposite at the moment of its production. While dissenters and Commonwealthmen might disagree, the Dutch were widely represented not just as England's rival in colonial trade but as aspirants to a universal monarchy of commerce. *The Indian Emperor* provided a vehicle for exploring the heroic model of empire, aristocratic, Christianizing and civilizing, to which the Dutch trading empire, based on profit and without a concern for conversion, was seen as antithetical. Dryden's representation of the Conquest was, however, sufficiently critical of the religious bigotry, greed and violence of the Spanish to satisfy the expansionist Protestant assumptions of his audience. The longstanding conviction of a Providentialist English mission in the Indies shadows the play, which also takes explicit issue with the justification of conquest in the Spanish claim to universal monarchy. As Pagden puts it, the latter depended on a historiography which asserted that the empire Jupiter founded was recreated by Augustus, passed through a succession of political translations to Constantine the Great, who bequeathed it to the Papacy, from which, as a "quasi-hereditary property" it passes to a series of Germanic rulers, including Charles V, Spain's ruler during the Conquest. His claim, as Holy Roman Emperor, was underwritten both by the Bulls granted by Alexander VI to Ferdinand and Isabella to occupy a vaguely described area of newly discovered lands and by Montezuma's fictionalized "donation" of his "empire" to the Spanish. Charles's responsibility, as lord of all the world, involved converting pagans who became incorporated in the empire and, if necessary, preparing them for conversion by rendering them civil.[29] In Montezuma's speeches, Dryden includes the reported rebuttals of such claims by several Amerindian rulers to provide a detailed and specific critique of the validity of the various "donations" and their legitimation of Spanish rule in the New World, although he retains a vague sense of the conquest as part of a Providentially ordered *translatio imperii*, prophesied by the Indians themselves and capable of renovation by the English. His treatment of the cruelty by which conversion is attempted assaults the religious justification, attacking as hypocritical the Spanish conviction that the natural resources of the Indies were a reward for the process of evangelization. The belief that the Spanish metropolis, as well as her colonists was corrupted by the wealth of the Indies had been a crucial element in the Cromwellian critique of Peninsular hegemony but there was plenty of evidence for such a view in Purchas, and the black legend was probably widespread by the time Dryden dramatized it. He acknowledged the greatness of Spanish achievement but his critique of the cross-and-booty mode of Peninsular empire implicitly invited the audience to ponder the potentialities of their own liberal, Protestant, oceanic expansionism.

Dryden's exploration of Europe's most significant modern colonial conquest was informed by the tension between his apprehension of the event as a heroic action bringing Christianity and civility to a pagan, half-civil society and his recognition of the dubious legality, avarice and intolerance of the Spanish record – tensions rendered particularly acute in a Yorkist with an interest in the definition of an imperial fate for the English which disavowed both the Peninsular model and the Dutch. The formal index of these tensions can be identified in the paradox critical both to this text and to the heroic drama in general, noted in John Loftis's remark that *The Indian Emperor* suffered from an "incomplete reconciliation of [Dryden's] philosophic argument with his dramatic form. An arraignment of Spanish atrocity in America provides a principal theme of the play, yet that theme is conveyed by way of dramatic action turning on a series of formalized love intrigues conducted within literary conventions shared by the French romances."[30] Loftis's objection summarizes the almost ubiquitous inability to recognize either that, in the process of representing imperial conquests and crises, the heroic dramas characteristically incorporated a great deal of what we think of as "ethnographic" and historical material, or that the romance mode embodied a perception of non-Western cultures (other than vagrant or savage societies) as like or similar to European nations. Nations distant from England in time and space like Persia, China or Mexico could serve as locations for the depiction of local political problems as well as alternative models of empire not just because they were safely far-off but because such societies were still seen as variants on a universal pattern. At the same time, however, as we saw in *Aureng-Zebe*, the heroic mode was incorporating customs and manners material such as sati, which was increasingly difficult to assimilate and functioned instead as a sign of radical difference and even inferiority. As English colonial expansion quickened, the heroic plays include more such signs of difference, and the epistemological assumptions of the mode, which imply a broad human equivalence between the noble representatives of civil nations, were increasingly challenged by a more powerful sense of ethnic difference.

The Indian Emperor is a particularly interesting text in terms of this tension between an ethnographic, historic and imperial perspective concerned with expediting and justifying colonial expansion and a generic mode which, like Boon's "symbolic complementarity," narrativized cultural exchange, including marriage, on broadly equal terms.[31] A certain ambiguity is manifest from the outset, as we note in the Dedication to the Duchess of Monmouth:

> Under your Patronage *Montezuma* hopes he is more safe than in his Native *Indies*: and therefore comes to throw himself at your Graces feet; paying that homage to your Beauty, which he refus'd to the violence of his Conquerours. He begs only that when he shall relate his sufferings, you will consider he is an *Indian* Prince, and not expect any other Eloquence from his simplicity, than that, with which his griefs have furnished him. His story is, perhaps the greatest, which was ever represented in a Poem of this nature; (the action of it including the Discovery and Conquest of a New World.) In it I have neither wholly follow'd the truth of the History, nor altogether left it. (25)

Montezuma is figured here both as Dryden's child and as a lover from heroic romance, a puppet whose story the poet ventriloquizes and a princely hero. He serves as a pathetic emblem of Spanish cruelty, whose best hope lies in the superior civility of the English, whose charity includes speaking for the Indians, by mingling native "simplicity" with heroic "eloquence" in their rehearsal of his story. This passage, however, also highlights the means by which the process of dramatic representation might be seen to repeat the violent conquest of the "Native Indies," in its enactment of Montezuma's triple subjection: by the Spanish, by Dryden's representation and by his obeisance to the Duchess. The violently imperial pretensions of the heroic mode as a genre, the frequent subject of satire by contemporaries, are here laid bare by the poet himself.

Dryden's own emphasis on the "irregular" nature of the text, marked more by "Flame" and "Zeal" (26) than "Art," is an unusual acknowledgment of the difficulty of harmonizing heroic action and historical record faced by other dramatists. His remarks in the "Connexion of the *Indian Emperor* and the *Indian Queen*" place a strong emphasis on his attempt to present a specific episode of cultural confrontation with at least a certain historical veracity:

> So that you are to imagine about twenty years elapsed since the conquest of Montezuma; who, in the truth of history, was a great and glorious prince; and in whose time happened the discovery and invasion of Mexico, by the Spaniards, under the conduct of Hernando Cortez, who, joining with the Traxallan Indians, the inveterate enemies of Montezuma, wholly subverted that flourishing empire ... the conquest of which is the subject of this dramatic poem.
>
> I have neither wholly followed the story, nor varied from it; and, as near as I could, have traced the native simplicity of the Indians, in relation to European customs; ... the shipping, armour, horses, swords, and guns of the Spaniards being as new to them, as their habits and their language were to the Christians.
>
> The difference of their religion from ours, I have taken from the story itself; and that which you find of it in the first and fifth acts, touching the sufferings and constance of Montezuma in his opinions, I have only illustrated, not altered, from those who have written of it. (27–28)

The tensions inherent in the story's at best ambiguous record of European conquest are legible in the characterization as well as the structure of the action. *The Indian Emperor* conspicuously lacks a Herculean hero: Montezuma is a markedly passive figure, who resists torture with an admirable stoicism but completely lacks initiative. Although later celebrated as a "rational savage" he is presented throughout the play as priest-ridden, notably by a figure whom Dryden first named "Calliban." In actions which mirror Zempoalla's, the Emperor and the rest of the Indian characters are introduced in a temple in the aftermath of a human sacrifice and, prior to the first battle with the Spanish, Montezuma retreats to a "Magitians Cave" (II.i.14) to consult "the Infernal race" (14). Despite the courage he shows in resisting the Spaniards' torture, he has to be rescued by Cortez. His actions, moreover, are governed not primarily by a desire to save his empire but by a senescent lust for Almeria. As in *Aureng-Zebe*, the monarch's superstition and his senile infatuation seem to figure a fatal decadence in the state, which breeds internal strife and opens the way to external conquest.

Cortez can be construed as the protagonist but does not really dominate the play. He is the representative rather than the embodiment of imperial power, and acts towards Montezuma with the deference of an envoy rather than the arrogance of a conqueror. This produces a curious sense of a power vacuum – in a play about conquest: "*Charles* the Fifth, the Worlds most Potent King" (I.ii.253) is conspicuous by his absence, as Cortez struggles not simply to fulfill the mandate from his sovereign but to keep his subordinates in order. The vacuum perhaps stems ultimately from the implicit premise that the Spanish, no less than the Indians, are destined to be displaced by another "race," the English. From the beginning, however, Cortez functions as the locus for positive identification with the colonial mission, announcing to Montezuma in the first act that: "Like you a man, and hither led by fame / Not by constraint but by my choice I came" (I.ii.248–49). The emphasis on "choice" suggests that Montezuma is equally free to "chuse" peace or war but the unlovely Vasquez makes the unconditional nature of the Spanish demands explicit:

> *Spain*'s mighty Monarch, to whom Heaven thinks fit
> That all the Nations of the Earth submit,
> In gracious clemency, does condescend
> On these conditions to become your Friend.
> First, that of him you shall your Scepter hold,
> Next, you present him with your useless Gold:
> Last, that you leave those Idols you adore,
> And one true Deity with prayers implore.   (I.ii.266–73)

Unlike Cortez's heroic bluster, Vasquez's demands are a pithy recapitulation of Spanish imperial doctrine. He invokes the Emperor's claim by Papal Donation to universal monarchy, and in recognition of the Spanish juridical consensus that the only way "the Castilian monarchy might claim sovereignty *and* property rights in America was if the Native Americans themselves could be said to have surrendered their natural legislative authority to the empire voluntarily,"[32] he attempts to establish a relationship of vassalage. Montezuma's angry rejection of the proffered terms is a direct rebuttal of his notorious supposed "donation" of his *imperium* to Charles V, an official Spanish fiction of whose veracity the English, among others, were unsurprisingly skeptical.[33] Dryden ensures that the corrupt and violent Vasquez, rather than Cortez, articulates the demands. At the very moment the contentious claims are made, Cortez is distracted by the ladies, "entertaining *Cydaria* with courtship in dumb show." The management of this scene is characteristic of Dryden's overall negotiation of his contradictory vision of the Conquest as heroic and venal. Nominally the fame-seeking head of the Spanish enterprise, Cortez enters into an amatory exchange with the Indians while Vasquez and Pizarro articulate contentious Spanish doctrine. After initiating the encounter, the distracted Cortez is left unblemished by the rhetorical bluster of his companions and cements his claims to humanity and to local power by seeking an alliance with Montezuma's daughter, Cydaria. His gallant courtship of the Indian Princess adds to our sense of his superiority to Vasquez and Pizarro by the contrast it forms with their sensual debauch in a grotto in Act IV, scene ii, which leaves the Spanish militarily vulnerable. This initial scene of contact between the two nations is structured by a clear verbal and visual disjunction between the two modes of interaction which mingle discordantly throughout the play. In the center of the stage Vasquez and Pizarro speak with the violent "zeal" of what we might join with Dryden in calling "historical truth," a zeal which later issues in war and torture, while Cortez, the hero of love and honor, silently begins his courtship on the margins. As the play unfolds, the kind of amatory intrigue Cortez has begun appears to dominate the development of the action, as the Indians in particular seem motivated primarily by the passions and codes governing love and honor. Thus Alibech's and Odmar's crucial betrayals of their nation are represented as motivated by a repudiation of loyalty and a surrender to an overwhelming passion:

> I by Revenge and Love are wholly led:
> Yet Conscience would against my rage Rebel –
> – Conscience, the foolish pride of doing well!
> Sink Empire, Father Perish, Brother Fall,
> Revenge does more than recompense you all.   (IV.iii.58–62)

Odmar decides to betray his dynasty and his state to revenge himself on the triumphant Guyomar, just as Almeria earlier, intending to kill Cortez, falls in love with him instead and attempts to barter his life and love for her betrayal:

> – Suppose one lov'd you, whom even Kings adore:
> Who with your Life, your Freedom would restore,
> And adde to that the Crown of *Mexico*   (IV.i.61–63)

The love and honor code, however, works to enhance our sense
of the Indians' nobility also, as Guyomar and Alibech function as
models of integrity in affairs of state and of the heart, although,
tellingly, their adherence to the code is of absolutely no use in
maintaining the Indian state. At the end of the play, there is no
place for the characters who have most completely fulfilled the
requirements of "honour," as the couple are dispatched to the
limbo of exile in a barren and resourceless wasteland:

> Northward, beyond the Mountains we will go,
> Where Rocks lye cover'd with Eternal Snow;
> Thin Herbage in the Plains, and Fruitless Fields,
> The Sand no Gold, the Mine no Silver yields:
> There Love and Freedom we'l in Peace enjoy;
> No *Spaniards* will that colony destroy.   (v.ii.368–73)

There is a disjunction here between the characters' moral worth
and their destiny which reflects the tension between the text's formal strategies and its historical materials. For while Indian betrayals
of the code of honor, along with Montezuma's sensual and spiritual
weakness, do contribute to the downfall of the empire, the action
cannot be contained, or fully represented, in the terms of heroic
romance alone. The heroic mode is supplemented and interrupted
by pastoral elements on the one hand, and the historical record on
the other. The invocation of hard and soft pastoral tropes which
define the new world as both Edenic and wild, artlessly seductive
and savage, complicates the symbolic equivalence established between the noble Indians and heroic Cortez. Their characterization
in terms of a shared acceptance of the honor code and a pattern
of amatory interaction which culminates in the betrothal of Cortez
and Cydaria – the latter an instance of what Boon regards as "the
capstone of any totalised exchange" – seems to operate in accordance with the logic of resemblances or similitude, diminishing
if not negating cultural difference. That difference returns with
a vengeance, however, in the two registers of pastoralism and his-
toricity referred to above. The characterization of the Indians is
given a cultural specificity by their naivety or savagery and the representation of the Spanish is inflected by Dryden's repetition of
Purchas's and Montaigne's accusations of cruelty. The action is
focused and organized not just by the turns of the love intrigue
but by the very particular historical narrative which emphasizes

the Indians' fear and bewilderment in the face of guns, armor, ships, siege and torture. Dryden's invocation of the last, in the scene in which Montezuma is racked, marks the point at which the text's inability to present an artfully heroicized version of history becomes most glaring. The Spanish mode of expansion is here deconstructed by its ugliest exponents, as the naked lust for gold and conversion is not only articulated but motivates, with the help of a peculiarly European technology of torture, a gross violation of both the Emperor's body and the heroic mode of representation. Montezuma's suffering marks a fracture of decorum symptomatic of more than Dryden's difficulty in wedding matter and form. In this scene, the most brutal realities of history, such as the role played by Western technologies of violence in colonial encounters, break into and disrupt the formal harmony of a text whose representational strategies are intended precisely to displace and idealize such processes.

Although Montezuma's racking, arguably the rhetorical and affective climax of the play, marks the point at which conflicts within imperial doctrine and with its modes of representation become most obvious, other such tensions are legible in the text. In the very first scene, the discussion between Cortez, Vasquez and Pizarro invokes differing tropes of discovery: Cortez celebrates the "new happy Climat" (I. i) in Edenic terms: "Here Nature spreads her fruitful sweetness round, / Breathes on the Air and Broods upon the ground" (i.i.21–22), while Vasquez, by contrast, invokes the language of savagery, desert and dearth:

> Corn, Wine and Oyl are wanting to this ground,
> In which our Countries fruitfully abound:
> . . .
> No useful Arts have yet found footing here;
> But all untaught and Salvage does appear.   (i.i.5–6, 9–10)

Cortez defends the country against Vasquez's claims using both cultural relativism and a rather different ascription of noble savagery:

> Wild and untaught are Terms which we alone
> Invent, for fashions differing from our own:
> For all their Customs are by Nature wrought,
> But we, by Art, unteach what Nature taught.   (i.ii.11–14)

His defence of the natural simplicity of the New World nothwith-standing, however, his words later in the scene reveal the most orthodox Spanish conviction of a Christian right of conquest and exploitation:

> Heaven from all ages wisely did provide
> This wealth, and for the bravest Nation hide,
> Who with four hundred foot and forty horse,
> Dare boldly go a New found World to force.   (I.i.31–34)

The "forcing" of the New World genders it female and the explicitly sexual narrative of European masculine possession implied here is played out in the action, in Cortez's properly chivalric courtship of and betrothal to Cydaria, in Vasquez's and Pizarro's degraded seduction and detention by Indian women in the grotto, and in Vasquez's attempted rape of Alibech. The economic exploitation implied by Vasquez's fantasies of a willing nature which excretes and urinates floods of gold and silver showers – "Each downfal of a flood the Mountains pour, / From their rich bowels rolls a silver shower" (I.i.29–30) – is also enacted in the text which follows. Both sets of tropes invoked by the conquistadors, the pastoral metaphors which elevate and the savage which degrade, foreshadow the play's naturalization of possession and domination, whether heroicized in Cortez or excoriated in Vasquez and Pizarro. Like the New World itself, the Indian characters are divided between the poles of a posi-tively valenced pastoralism and a negative savagery. Cydaria figures as an artless child of nature but Almeria and Alibech are both quite Amazonian in their willingness to fight the Spanish. The latter cel-ebrates the fact that "Our Women in the foremost ranks appear" (II.ii.587) and the former announces her own determination to resist:

> Go lie like Dogs, beneath your Masters Feet.
> Go and beget them Slaves to dig their Mines,
> And groan for Gold which now in Temples shines;
> Your shameful story shall record of me,
> The Men all crouch'd, and left a Woman free.   (III.i.66–70)

Although Alibech is a virtuous character, the firmness she shows and shares with the vicious Almeria suggests that both women have something of the Indian Queen's savagery, just as Montezuma's appearance after a human sacrifice of 500 souls darkens his characterization. The pastoral or savage inflection of the Indians' characterization disturbs the culturally levelling effect of the heroic romance mode, implicitly differentiating them from the Spaniards and reducing their status as agents by mobilizing an implicit narrative of conquest made explicit in the play's action. The characterization of the Spaniards, however, also departs from heroic norms, in terms provided by the historical sources. Cortez, as we have seen, is a hero on a decidedly modest scale, whose honorable dealings with the Indians depend on the dramaturgical sleight-of-hand which leaves Vasquez and Pizarro bearing the burden of guilt for the sexual, economic and political exploitation involved in the Conquest. Vasquez's failing is sensual lust; Pizarro figures the conquistadors' greed and cruelty. Both are taken prisoner by Guyomar after succumbing to the temptations of Indian women, but Vasquez eventually dies in a quarrel with Odmar and Guyomar over Alibech. The exchange which precedes the fatal encounter reveals that neither Odmar nor Vasquez is honorable, but the latter's words not only point to the Hobbesian manoeuvring and assumptions that consistently undercut the play's heroic posturing, but lay bare the brutal libidinal economy which accompanies military victory: "I Love too deeply to mistake the Face," Vasquez says, "The Vanquish'd must receive the Victors Laws" (v.i.94–95). He simply asserts the absolute right of conquest, a conquest he desires because it will give him the (unwilling) object of his sensual desire. Moreover, although the language of love and honor is invoked by both parties, the primary metaphors used here are those of commercial exchange: Odmar claims he wanted to "buy" Alibech, who was to be "conveyed" to him as a special property "reserv'd" from the reduction of all other Indian women to "common prey." The idealized claims of "Love and Honour" are impugned by their replacement here by lust, might and commerce. Vasquez's penultimate speech does suggest that Cortez's virtue is capable of redeeming the honor code which has been not simply violated but deconstructed by the preceding exchange:

> He never will protect a Ravisher:
> His generous Heart will soon decide our strife;
> He to your Brother will restore his Wife.   (v.i.102–104)

Cortez is figured here as the Indians' protector, again displacing a wholesale condemnation of the conquistadors' sexual exploitativeness in a process completed by Vasquez's death.

The other main sources of Spanish guilt are the greed and cruelty figured by Pizarro, who joins a Christian priest in racking Montezuma. Loftis remarked that "As the victim of Inquisitional zeal and the lust for the gold of the Conquistadores, he is tortured on the rack; and he bears his sufferings with exemplary fortitude. To be sure, *the fact that he is portrayed as a defenceless sufferer of persecution represents an infringement of neo-classical decorum as it was conceived by the stricter theorists who would have royal dignity maintained.* His sufferings, however, are a necessity of Dryden's plot" (my emphasis).[34] Not simply an isolated instance of the indecorous pressure produced by plot clashing with form, however, Montezuma's sufferings mark the climactic point of strain between the heroic mode and its attempt to produce a heroic representation of empire. The scene provides a blistering riposte to the Spanish conviction that the precious metals of the Americas were a reward for their efforts at conversion as Cortez himself predicts the corrupting effects of greed:

> If this go free, farewel that discipline
> Which did in Spanish Camps severely shine:
> Accursed Gold, 'tis thou hast caus'd these crimes;
> Thou turns't our Steel against thy Parent Climes!
> And into *Spain* wilt fatally be brought,
> Since with the price of Blood thou here art bought.
>
> (v.ii.132–37)

His horror at the insult to Montezuma's royal dignity points directly to the "poisoned chalice" of Indies gold that will bring Hispanic decline. By this point, Cortez's attempts to distance himself from his reprobate fellow conquerors seem futile: addressing Montezuma as "Father" rings hollow in a scene interrupted by on-going reports of the battle in progress between Mexicans and Spanish. Montezuma remains supremely unconvinced by offers of a possible restoration of his power by Charles V so that Cortez ends as a figure peculiarly reprobated in these years, a destroyer of monarchy. The Spanish extinction of native sovereignty presented here was not only couched in terms of an imperial dominion Englishmen of all political shades would reject but served as a negative exemplar for their own early colonial policies, which depended not on conquest but on the Roman law doctrine of *res nullius*, notoriously expounded by Locke. Locke argued that property rights in new territories could be established by settlers who "planted" the land, as opposed to the indigenous "occupants" who had neglected, if hunters and gatherers, to mix their labor with the soil. This emphasis on agriculture, as opposed to conquest, also reflected a strong element in traditional conceptions of English national identity.[35]

Dryden's evident ambivalence about the conquistadors' triumph, which he naturalized through the invocation of savage and pastoral tropes, celebrated in Cortez's virtue and excoriated in his inclusion of vicious episodes from the historical record, is nowhere more evident than in his treatment of technology. Guyomar's report of his first view of the Spanish ships is a paradigmatic moment in the play's enactment of the colonial encounter. In verse understandably celebrated as some of the most beautiful in Dryden's oeuvre, the Indian Prince recounts the extraordinary sight of European arrival:

> MONTEZUMA: What forms did these new wonders
>   represent?
> GUYOMAR: More strange than what your wonder can invent.
>   The object I could first distinctly view
>   Was tall straight trees which on the waters flew,
>   Wings on their sides instead of leaves did grow,
>   Which gathered all the breath the winds could blow.
>   And at their roots grew floating Palaces,
>   Whose out-bow'd bellies cut the yielding Seas.
> MONTEZUMA: What Divine Monsters, O ye gods, are these
>   That float in air and flye upon the seas!
>   Came they alive or dead upon the shore?
> GUYOMAR: Alas, they liv'd too sure, I heard them roar:
>   All turn'd their sides, and to each other spoke,
>   I saw their words break out in fire and smoke. (I.ii.105–18)

The passage figures the Spanish arrival in sublime terms: their ships and cannon are "wonders" which overwhelm the imaginative capacity of the wondering spectators. This ascription of divine power to European technology pastoralizes the Indians in the terms of innocent simplicity Dryden invoked in his dedication, as Guyomar draws on a series of natural metaphors to describe the "wonders." Both sublime and pastoral modes emphasize Indian naivety and their cognitive and material vulnerability. Comparable moments of wonder recur, with Guyomar remarking during the first battle:

> I fell'd along a Man of Bearded face,
> His Limbs all cover'd with a Shining case:
> So wondrous hard, and so secure of wound,
> It made my Sword, though edg'd with Flint, rebound.
>
> (ii.iii.25–28)

Later in the same scene Montezuma refers to gunfire: "For deaths Invisible come wing'd with Fire" (ii.iii.33). By Act ii, however, the sublime associations of Western technology have disappeared as completely as the Edenic figuration of Mexico. The final instance of machinery we see is, after all, the rack, as Montezuma's torture renders the ideological and material violence, which make the Conquest possible, appallingly visible.

Dryden himself drew attention to the difficulty of representing this "greatest" of all stories with harmonious regularity but the sardonic commentary generated by *The Conquest of Granada* provides a suggestive contemporary gloss on precisely the tension generated between indecorous and horrible "Historical truth" and "Artifice" in the dramatization of colonial conquest in the heroic plays generally. One of the pamphlets leads the reader into a nest of book-torturing virtuosi:

But a little further we beheld many engins of torture; here indeed was the scene of death, here was one book suspended, another torn upon a tenterhook, a third dead from a stab receiv'd from a cruel Penknife; drawing nearer I found 'em all belonging to Mr. *Dryden*. Here lay *Almanzor* stretch upon the rack, that pain might force out words far distant from his thoughts; here the *Maiden Queen* lay deflour'd, and there the Indian *Emperor* was defac'd with the scratches of a barb'rous stile.[36]

The pamphlet's figuration of the Indian King precisely reiterates the repeated subjection, to Spanish torture and to poetic representation, which characterized Montezuma's representation in Dryden's Dedication.

AVARICE AND AMBITION

The violence of word and deed in heroic plays was a frequent subject for such mockery, which in retrospect seems acute in its recognition of an imperial aggression inherent in the very mode of representation. Scenes of torture *per se* were rare, however, particularly when perpetrated by Europeans, but another episode of such deliberate judicial violence occurs in *Amboyna*, a play set in the East Indies and written to shore up support for the Third Dutch War. Steven Pincus has argued that, during the course of the previous conflict, hostility to the Dutch was replaced by Francophobia, as a broad swathe of Englishmen began viewing France, rather than Holland, as the true seeker after universal monarchy. Dryden's dislike for the republican and commercial Dutch remains unambivalent, however. Rehearsing a notorious "massacre" of English merchants by Dutch East India Company officials first publicized in 1624 (with the relevant pamphlets being reprinted in 1672), the play provides what one character describes as "a pretty emblem of the two nations which cuckold his Catholick majesty in the Indies." By 1665, the Spanish and Portuguese had been largely displaced in the East Indies by the Dutch and the English, whose seventeenth-century wars were primarily concerned with issues of colonial trade. Dryden was critical of the Spanish Conquest but he recognized the greatness of the achievement. Mercantile rivalry was hardly comparable.

Dissatisfied with the play, although it succeeded on the stage, the dramatist complained the subject was "barren, the Persons low, and the Writing not heightened with many laboured Scenes."[37] The play's failure is precisely a function of the difficulty Dryden faced in attempting to dramatize a sordid and brutal story of colonial commercial competition: the actors in this tragedy were merchants, not soldiers, and as such inappropriate for heroic representation. The formal index of this problem is the play's tragi-comic structure, oscillating between farce and the blank-verse seriousness of the scenes between Captain Towerson, the English East India Company "general," and his Indian Princess, Ysabinda. As a company servant, Towerson is forced into an unheroic passivity, explaining to his Dutch rival for Ysabinda that "Here I am a Publick Person, intrusted by my King and my Employers, and should I kill you . . . I shou'd betray my Countreymen to suffer" (II.i.111–15). He is characterized as a pacific spokesman for free trade, taking implicit issue with the Dutch ambition at a global dominion over commerce, as well as the bellicose mercantilism of some of his own countrymen:

What mean these endless jars of Trading Nations? 'tis true, the World was never large enough for Avarice or Ambition: but those who can be pleas'd with Moderate Gain may have the ends of Nature, not to want:

nay, even its Luxuries may be supply'd from her o'erflowing bounties in these parts: from whence she yearly sends Spices, and Gums, the Food of Heaven in Sacrifice. And besides these, her Gems of richest value, for Ornament more than necessity.   (1.i.220–27)

With this figure at its center, the primary love plot is a degraded version of a heroic amour, for, while the Anglo-Dutch competition for the Indian Princess, a synecdoche for the possession of Amboyna, reflects the link of territorial and amatory conquest recurrent in the heroic plays, the mercantile Towerson and Harmon are capable only of ignoble inaction and brutal rape. In the absence of any military conflict, Dryden's representation of European–Amboynese relations is conducted almost entirely in terms of sexual competition and exploitation. Apart from Ysabinda, and a few dancers, the Amboyners themselves are almost entirely absent from the action: the island itself exists solely as an example of luxuriantly feminized natural bounty, in which "Luxuries" and "the Food of Heaven in Sacrifice" are produced without any apparent human labor. In the quarrel over Ysabinda, Towerson attempts to deny the synecdochical relation Harman Jr. identifies between Ysabinda and the island ("You've the Indies in your arms" [II.i.325]) by disclaiming any pecuniary motivations for his marriage: "Hold, you mistake me Harman, I never gave you just occasion to think I would make merchandise of love; Ysabinda, you know, is mine, contracted to me ere I went for England and must be so till death" (II.i.89–92). Nevertheless, the language he employs ("contracted," "make merchandise") underlines the linkage between love and acquisition, love and location: after the rape he reassures Ysabinda that she is still "Paradise," "still as fragrant as your Eastern groves," while Harman Jr. rages that "the plenteous Harvest is his."

   In the subplot, the displacement of inter-European commercial rivalry into a sexual competition becomes even more obvious as Julia, the wife of the fiery-tempered but ineffectual Spanish gallant Perez, cuckolds her husband with both an Englishman and a Hollander. Julia turns her intrigues into an economic-political joke: "If my English lover Beaumont, my Dutch lover Fiscal, and my Spanish husband, were painted in a piece, with me amongst them, they would make a pretty emblem of the two nations which cuckold his Catholic majesty in the Indies" (II.i.255–58). She develops the conceit further:

JUL: My husband's plantation is like to thrive well betwixt
you.

BEAU: Horn him: he deserves not so much happiness as he
enjoys with you; he's jealous.

JUL: Tis no wonder if a Spaniard looks yellow.

BEAU: Betwixt you and me, 'tis a little kind of venture that
we make, in doing this Don's drudgery for him; for the
whole nation of them is generally so pocky, that 'tis no
longer a disease, but a second nature to them.

FISC: I have heard indeed, that 'tis incorporated among
them, as deeply as the Moors and Jews are, there's scarce a
family, but 'tis crept into their blood, like the new
Christians.   (II.i.337–46)

Julia pursues the metaphorical identification of sexual enjoyment
and husbandry, casting herself as a "plantation," but Beaumont
and Fiscal develop the analogy misogynistically, turning the (colonial) "venture" into "drudgery," as Julia's account of cuckoldry as
cross-cultural cultivation becomes diseased miscegeny, and Spain's
ethnic intermingling, the result of Arab colonization of the Iberian
peninsula, is recast as sexual infection. This contempt for miscegenation, repressed in the Towerson–Ysabinda alliance (in which
the heroine, though an Amboyner, is emphatically aristocratic, and
hence superior to the boorish Dutch), resurfaces in the casual
bonding of the North European rivals over a Spanish woman whose
"easy virtue" they read as a function of her tainted blood. Trade and
planting assume a depraved hue as colonial expansion is figured
not as profit for, but as infection of, the metropolitan population.

Amboyna's sordid world of sexual and commercial intrigue on the
fringes of the Indies might seem far removed from what Mrs. Evelyn
famously called the "utopia" of *The Conquest of Granada* but the
plays are linked by more than their production during the Third
Dutch War. The plays represent two sides, or modes, of empire:
Amboyna depicts overseas expansion in the form of colonial trade,
as a degraded activity of Avarice, while *The Conquest of Granada*
presents the inaugural moment of Spanish imperialism as a heroic
action of Ambition. For Dryden, the Dutch Wars could be figured
in comparable terms, as a struggle against rebellious, ungrateful,
would-be engrossers of trade, against whom the English might display a truly heroic virtue. As he thundered in his Dedication to
James:

When the *Hollanders*, not contented to withdraw themselves from that obedience which they ow'd their lawful Sovereign, affronted those by whose Charity they were first protected: and, (being swell'd up by a pre-heminence of Trade, by a supine negligence on our side, and a sordid parsimony on their own,) dar'd to dispute the Soveraignty of the Seas; the eyes of three Nations were then cast on you: and, by the joynt suffrage of King and People, you were chosen to revenge their common injuries; to which, though you had an undoubted title by your birth, you had yet a greater by your courage.[38]

Critics have often argued that the Dedication refutes the claim that Dryden was parodying heroic virtue in *The Conquest* and, cer-tainly, it seems implausible that we, or more importantly, the Duke of York, were not meant to take seriously the continuity between the whole "series of Heroique Actions" (Dedication, 26–27) which made up the latter's career, and Almanzor's triumphant progress. If the Dutch dramatized in *Amboyna* provided the most glaring in-stance of colonial expansion as sordid parsimony, *The Conquest of Granada* was surely intended to explore the alternative pre-eminent moment and model of Christian empire, as yet unsullied by the tears of the Indians. The Dedication not only celebrates James's role as soldier and Admiral but cites a heroic literary genealogy from which Eugene Waith, among others, has drawn to explain the peculiarities of the "Herculean hero."[39] Waith's definition of this figure, in *Ideas of Greatness* and elsewhere, provides the liter-ary historical antecedents of these characters but little sense of their cultural function in specific texts or genres. James Thompson has recently argued that, instead of allegorizing threats to politi-cal stability in England, or civil society generally, as other critics have done, we should see the hero of *The Conquest of Granada* as an emergent type of colonial administrator, acting with uncon-strained force on the boundaries of European empire.[40] The prob-lem with this suggestion lies in the difficulty of reconciling the very limited activities of such figures, who might include George Aungier in Bombay, or Bacon, the Virginian rebel dramatized by Behn, with Almanzor's greatness of achievement. James's success as an Admiral made him a prototypical English hero, one whose triumphs lay in asserting England's peculiar right to "Soveraignty of the Seas." He heralded the future greatness of English oceanic empire, combining in his royal person both the nobility of ambi-tion and the national affinity with marine power which Purchas had celebrated as the defining characteristic of modern European empire:

And our Age which God hath blessed before many former, produced as Twinnes Navigation and Learning, which had beene buried together in the same Grave with the Roman Greatnesse, and now are as it were raysed againe from the dead.

Hence it is that barbarous Empires have never growne to such glory, though of more Giant-like stature, and large Land-extension, because Learning had not fitted them for Sea attempts, nor wisdome furnished them with Navigation. Thus the Persian, the Mogoll, the Abissine, the Chinois, the Tartarian, the Turke, are called Great, but their greatnesse is like Polyphemus, with one eye, they see at home like purblind men neere to them, not farre off with those eyes of Heaven, and lights of the World, the Learned knowledge, whereof is requisite to Navigation. The Chinois at home, is hereby stronger, and so is the Turke: but the other are braved by every petty Pirat on their owne shores: the rest like Ostriches spread faire plumes, but are unable to rayse themselves from the Land: yea, their Lands also (as hath happened with the Abissine) and Sea-townes taken from them to the downfall of their estate.[41]

The English had defined themselves in terms of their insularity and their marine power from the late sixteenth century but, by the middle of the seventeenth century, the importance of sea-power for any seeker after universal monarchy was becoming apparent. The wealth of the Indies could allow any such aspirant, even a Republic like the United Provinces, which lacked a standing army and a monarch, to seek domination by bribing politicians and bringing other states to their knees by means of economic warfare.[42] During the Second Dutch War, for many Anglican Royalists, as Steven Pincus points out, this identified Holland as the enemy to the balance of power, while for radicals, it was Louis XIV who figured as the potential tyrant. By the end of the Third Dutch War, many more than radicals were suspicious of the French King's ambitions. Less obviously, however, the English, who already figured themselves as Neptune's chosen, were themselves preparing to take up a role as an imperial power, as the Stuarts oversaw the expansion of trading operations, funded campaigns against the Barbary pirates, tightened their grip on their Western colonies and fought to prevent Dutch global commercial hegemony. Dryden would later salute James's capacity to prosecute such policies in *Threnodia Augustalis*, when he closes the poem with a vision of maritime imperium:

Behold, ev'n to remoter Shores
A Conquering Navy proudly spread;
The *British* Canon formidably roars,
While starting from his Oozy Bed,
Th'asserted Ocean rears his reverend Head;
To View and Recognize his ancient Lord again:
And, with a willing hand, restores,
The *Fasces* of the Main.   (*Works*, vol. III: 510–17)

Dryden's dramatization of the *Reconquista* celebrates the ambition and the valor of the military heroes who secure the nation and lay the basis for its expansion, thus modeling the role in which the admiring monarchist casts James Stuart: "You are still meditating on new labours for your self, and new triumphs for the Nation; and when our former enemies again provoke us, you will solicite fate to provide you with another Navy to overcome, and another Admiral to be slain. You will, then, lead forth a Nation eager to revenge their past injuries; and, like the *Romans*, inexorable to Peace, till they have fully vanquish'd" (Dedication, 25–31). Though not without criticism of the Castilian monarchs, *The Conquest of Granada* presents a considerably more positive view of the Spanish empire than *The Indian Emperor*, as the episode dramatized is much less ideologically freighted with English ambition and Protestant revulsion, with the reconquest of European territory from the infidel Moors representing an unproblematic good for Christendom. Dryden was clearly aware of the Spanish tradition of contiguity between the expulsion of the Moors and the Conquest of America, which cast Cortes and Pizarro as the heirs not only of Caesar but of El Cid, the eleventh-century hero of the *Reconquista*, and a celebrated Corneillean hero.[43] In *The Conquest*, however, he focuses on the restless mind and valorous action of the hero who purifies and consolidates the nation and, in so doing, learns how to enter civil society.

Indeed, Almanzor's marginal, if not hostile, relation to civil society for much of the play might seem to problematize identifying James with the self-described "noble savage": pursuing the parallel, however, we might view Dryden's revelation of Almanzor's Christian birth and his incorporation by the Spanish monarchy as reassurance that the headstrong Catholic who refused to temporize over his alien beliefs in the Succession Crisis was nonetheless a true native son.[44] The continuing dispute over Almanzor's role, however, reflects the difficulty of identifying him with a single figure or ideological intention, particularly given the contradictory attitudes to imperial greatness which informed Dryden's own views.[45] *The Indian Emperor* arguably dramatizes not simply the corrupting effects of the sudden acquisition of colonial wealth but also the dangers of degeneracy which attend journeys away from the metropolis, the source of civility: as Pagden points out, in European thought, the Thomist *ius peregrinandi* is always at odds with the Horatian injunction that it is unlawful to breach the natural boundary of Oceanus.[46] In *The Conquest*, by contrast, we witness the historical means by which the originally civil Christian city and state is secured from the usurping infidel, while Almanzor's own transformation, from Moorish, pagan, noble savage to Christian Arcos, figures the process of conversion by which the Roman and Christian empires traditionally incorporated the *barbaroi*. From this perspective, Almanzor's turbulent and contingent assumption of Christian identity suggests his affinity with the New Christians, Spanish Moors or Jews whose motives for conversion were always suspect, and who serve as exemplary instances of those perpetual strangers whose inclusion in civil society was dubious, insecure and threatening.

Like the heroic plays which depicted significant episodes from the history of Ottoman empire, *The Conquest of Granada* shapes its analysis of the mind which "grasps at universal monarchy" (Part 2: iii.ii.116) by establishing both implicit and explicit contrasts between law-abiding and merciful Christian monarchy and a cruel Islamic despotism. Unlike the partially pastoralized and savagified Mexicans of *The Indian Emperor*, the Moors are sophisticated infidels, to whom Almanzor, raised in the woods of Africa, stands in savage contrast. Almanzor himself is another type of Davenant's "painful Protectors and enlargers of Empire," animated by the monstrous ambition native to "the Mindes of Men."[47] His doubled origin as Christian/Spanish and African as well as his movement between the two sides confirms the ubiquity of this human quality but his final attachment to Ferdinand and Isabella signals the inevitable triumph of a specifically Christian form of empire, naturally entitled, and better able, to attach and domesticate his restless ambition. Although Almanzor initially seems in every sense an affiliate of the Moors, the play's depiction of Boabdelin's rule problematizes the identification. In the first part, Boabdelin acts like a weakened Ottoman despot: despite the imminence of Spanish

invasion and the factional conflict wracking Granada, he celebrates
his love "With pomp and Sports" (i.i.3). His tyranny is demonstrated in both a judicial and an amatory register, when he ungrate-
fully insists on Almanzor's death and forces himself on Almahide,
while his refusal to acknowledge his vassalage to Ferdinand reflects
the inability to honor contracts with Christian powers regarded as
characteristically Moorish perfidy.

The second Part reframes the action from the Spanish perspective, beginning with Ferdinand's confident assertion of the
Castilian claim to European and Indian empire. Although Derek
Hughes has argued Ferdinand's is a thoroughly materialist account
of imperial rise and decline, lacking the Providentialist certainty
of Dryden's source,[48] the King does preface his description of the
process by a reference to divine will: "All causes seem to second our
design; / And Heav'n and Earth in their destruction join" (Part 2:
i.i.3–4). His understanding of empire seems entirely conventional.
Isabella's speech draws attention to the contemporaneous discovery of the Americas, with its poisoned chalice of gold, but her words
seem designed to suggest that her priority is, rightly, the recovery
of Castilian territory from the occupying infidels, rather than the
expansion of the empire into the Indies:

> Not all that shining Ore could give my heart
> The joy, this Conquer'd Kingdom will impart:
> Which, rescu'd from these Misbelievers hands;
> Shall now, shake off its double bands:
> At once to freedom and true faith restor'd:
> Its old Religion and its antient Lord.   (i.i.22–27)

The Spanish claims to political dominion, supported by the first
part's characterization of Boabdelin's divided, sanguinary and
tyrannical rule, are underwritten by the depiction of the superior gender relations of the Christian Court. The happiness of
Ferdinand and Isabella's relationship, predicated on mutual love
and respect, in which the husband asserts that "Whatever *Isabella*
shall command / Shall always be a Law to *Ferdinand*" (ii.i.137–38),
stands in stark contrast to the domestic unhappiness of the infidel
couple. Boabdelin's marriage is a microcosmic version of his regal
tyranny, governed by such suspicion and rage that he is prepared
to condemn his wife to death without any legal process whatsoever.
The marital relations of the two royal pairs bear out the familiar

European conviction that their monogamous relationships, in which the wife enjoyed greater freedom than Islamic women, produced more harmonious partnerships, modifying masculine authority by a diffusion of womanly grace through the Court. Where Moorish Granada is dominated by Boabdelin's ungoverned fury and the unforgiving cruelty of the Zegrys and Abencerrages continually threatens to spill blood, the Spanish camp and Court, having overcome such internecine conflicts between Castilians and Arragonese, is characterized by the mercy Isabella displays towards Benzayda, Ozmyn and Almahide. Lyndaraxa's ruthless exploitation of her sexuality for selfish political ends, a clear perversion of the proper female role as gentling influence, amplifies the contrast with the two figures of Christian womanhood celebrated in the commanding but merciful matron Isabella and the maidenly Almahide/Isabella. Almanzor's near-corruption by Lyndaraxa, manifest in his attempted seduction of Almahide, marks the climax of his imbrication in the cruel and lawless Moorish Court.

Dryden's characteristically schematic use of contrasts, which drew from and influenced other such comparisons of Christian and Islamic states, was not simply a panegyric to Castille, however. Ferdinand's readiness to accept Lyndaraxa as his vassal suggests an amoral opportunism at odds with a sense of Providential mission, and the Spanish victory depends, in the end, on Moorish weakness rather than Spanish strength. Unlike later dramatists, moreover, Dryden's presentation of the two groups struggling for domination of the Iberian peninsula here eschews, or rather criticizes, distinctions of "blood" or "race" which intensify and reify difference. In the opening scene of the play, the rancorous Zegry Zulema attacks the rival Abencerrages for their "villain blood." Boabdelin replies that "From equal Stems their blood both houses draw, / They from *Morocco*, you from *Cordova*" to which Hamet replies "Their mungril race is mixt with Christian breed, / Hence 'tis that they those Dogs in prisons feed." Abencerrage charity is then defended by Abdelemech, who invokes a tenet of Islamic law well known to Europeans:

> Our holy Prophet wills, that Charity,
> Shoud, ev'n to birds and beasts extended be:
> None knows what fate is for himself design'd;
> The thought of humane Chance should make us kind.
>
> (I.i.172–79)

Such uncharitable attempts to dehumanize on the basis of religion or "breed" are here clearly condemned. The play's structure as a whole depends, in fact, on an assumption of fundamental equivalence between Moors and Christians, so that Almanzor's African origin is unquestioned and the discovery of his Christian parentage turns not on any visible or "natural" distinction of "race" or "blood" but instead, the most traditional of romance topoi, jewels and a mark. The only point at which the text verges on invoking tropes of race with seriousness is in Boabdelin's characterization towards the end of the play. In the first part, Almahide's relations with Almanzor were mediated by her veil, itself a signifier of Eastern enclosure, which she opened and closed to signal the possibility of mutuality. In the second half, her erotic relations are figured by a scarf, a token which recalls the handkerchief in *Othello* (as Elkanah Settle was probably the first to note).[49] The extremity and murderous intent of Boabdelin's jealousy also recalls the Shakespearean text, *locus classicus* of the effects of suspicion in a miscegenous marriage. Dryden's parallel with *Othello* complicates the otherwise schematic presentation of the Moorish King, by suggesting his attachment and anguish was riven with an unspoken element of self-hatred.

PLUNG'D IN RUIN

The Conquest of Granada represents the crucial moment in the consolidation of Christian empire by means of a comprehensive contrast between the two main religious and political cultures striving for dominance on the borders of Europe. The text includes some references to the dubious future development of Spanish empire but the play is generally celebratory of Christendom's, and implicitly England's, capacity to absorb and transform incivility and infidelity. When Dryden returned to a serious consideration of the Peninsular project in *Don Sebastian*, his perspective was very different. The Jacobite lament for James/Sebastian, a noble sexual criminal depicted in defeat and exile, is not only an elegy for a lost monarch deserted by his perfidious people but a despairing vision of the failure of the project of universal monarchy conceived of as Christian greatness. Dryden's conversion presumably strengthened his admiration for such ambitions, whose best English hope resided in "*Albanius* Lord of Land and Main" (iii.i.219), whom he apotheosized in terms recalling the masques which celebrated his father's marine dominion, in *Albion and Albanius* (1685). Although historians of foreign policy have emphasized James's concentration on internal conflicts, he continued and intensified his brother's attempts at "royalizing and centralizing" control in the American and Caribbean colonies. For Dryden, the Revolution of '88 not only exiled the King but destroyed a potential expander of English, and Christian, greatness.[50]

In choosing to dramatize the story of Sebastian, Dryden chose a figure memorialized enthusiastically in literature but less kindly assessed by historians. In Pufendorf's words:

Through the over-forwardness of this young Prince, *Portugal* receiv'd such a blow, that it fell from the Pinnacle of its Greatness: For some of his Court Favorites did put this magnanimous and ambitious Prince, upon such Enterprizes as were surpassing both his Age and Power, and were in no way suitable to the present junction of Affairs, so that his whole Mind was bent upon Warlike Exploits, and how by Martial Exercises to revive the ancient Valour of his Subjects, which by Peace and Plenty, was of late much decay'd.[51]

Sebastian's desire to turn his subjects from their preoccupation with colonial trade towards a pursuit of honor was a project of heroic glory at odds with avarice sufficently consonant with Stuart mythologizing to attract Dryden's sympathy, however doomed it proved in the event. In choosing a figure whose crusade was eventually judged quixotic, however, the dramatist rings the death-knell not just on Stuart monarchy *per se*, but the heroic conception of Christian empire, certainly as it related to the English. The sole mention of global mastery by Sebastian emphasizes its status as fantasy:

> If *Portugall* and *Spain* were joyn'd to *Affrica*,
> And the main Ocean crusted into Land,
> If Universall Monarchy were mine,
> Here should the gift be plac'd.[52]

The play's reworking of the familiar struggle between the Crescent and the Cross is highly unusual and not simply because of its pessimism about Christian expansionism at a point at which other dramatists were expressing more confidence about Europe's capacity to defeat the Ottomans, the primary source of an Islamic threat. Like Payne in *The Siege of Constantinople*, Dryden analyzes

Christian failure in terms of the weakness of the Europeans, whose disloyalty and errors render them vulnerable to a formidable, if sanguinary and venal enemy. Sebastian's heroic aspirations in love and war, however, not only fail hopelessly but appear misguided: in a judgment unrefuted by the action, Muley-Moluch reminds him "In what a ruine has thy head-strong pride, / And boundlesse thirst of Empire plung'd thy People" (1.i.382–83). Even more tellingly, he is utterly marginal to the main political maneuverings which see Muley-Moluch replaced by his ductile brother, Muley-Zedan, under Dorax's tutelage. Sebastian's failures might be considered partially redeemed by Dorax/Alonzo and Antonio, who are both signally successful in their respective appropriations of power in the one case, and sexuality and wealth in the other. Theirs, however, are much more modest successes – which turn on adopting the mores and habits of the Africans, working with the grain of the culture, and in one case quitting it – than any fantasy of transforming Barbary into a civil, Christian state.

Although the discovery of Sebastian's and Almeyda's relationship finishes the play, much more of the action depends on the Renegado, the European who has "crossed over" to Islam, depicted here seriously in Dorax's slow and painful resumption of Christian identity, and comically in Antonio's deft manipulations of Affrick costume and custom. The renegade is perfidy personified, "more than Traytor" as Sebastian says, embodying a complete repudiation of religion and nation, God and Sovereign, which is morally worse than the ignorance of the savage. Dryden's focus on this type obviously figures his contempt for his countrymen's abjuration of their loyalty to James but the significance of the category exceeds this metaphorization. The internal division which created the renegade was as unavoidable a fact of human nature as the existence of modes of human life external to Christianity and European civility. Even Dorax's redemption has its ambiguities: although he recovers his integrity, it appears he is to remain in Barbary as Muley-Zedan's chief counsellor, living out his life as "Dorax" rather than Alonzo.

Renegades were a common feature of Barbary, whose several nations were vividly present in the minds of late seventeenth-century audiences familiar with the predations of pirates against whom the Stuarts fought four campaigns.[53] Although the ballads and popular narratives which recorded tales of the Sally pirates emphasized the horrors endured by Christians enslaved, Norman Daniel emphasizes that the repudiation of Christianity by such captives could produce the kind of success enjoyed by Dorax (and also by Ibrahim the Illustrious Bassa).[54] Dryden combined the Regencies of Algiers and Tunis and the Kingdom of Morocco but this unified Barbary does not figure simply as an allegorical backdrop: it is presented as a dense web of highly specific locations, institutions and practices. The emphasis on slavery certainly reflects popular views of the region but it is also possible that Dryden was underscoring his vision of Whiggish treachery by literalizing the trope most often used to decry Stuart absolutism. As Dorax asserts to Benducar, "Slaves are the growth of Affrick, not of Europe" (II.i.255). A society with "real" enslavement and tyranny looked very different and much worse than English autocracy, the latter now replaced by a regime consisting of those who, in Dryden's view, had commodified themselves, being willing to barter the most sacred loyalties.

As in *The Conquest*, Dryden eschews slurs against "complexion" but few others: the play is noticeably more concerned with emphasizing the religious, cultural and political differences of Africans and Portugese as grounds of identity than his earlier heroic plays. Muley-Zedan's opening remarks underscore the hostility of the two groups and identify Islam with tyranny and slavery, the most distinctive signifiers of Barbary, whose amplification structures the action which follows:

> Now *Affrick*'s long Wars are at an end,
> And our parch'd earth is drenched in Christian Blood
> My conquering Brother will have Slaves enow,
> To pay his cruel Vows for Victory.   (I.i.1–4)

The following scene in the slave market, which initially threatens to dispose of a King by lot, takes a comic turn as the gallant Antonio throws himself into attracting "postures" (a term with erotic overtones), for the benefit of potential purchasers. The scene retains a frightening edge, however, as sellers and buyers haggle over the bridled Antonio as if he were a piece of horse-flesh. One merchant asks to see him stript, and Mustapha responds "He's the best piece of Man's flesh in the Market, not an Eye-Sore in his whole body: Feel his Legs, Master, neither Splint, Spavin, nor Wind-gall" (I.i.532–34): not a "Bauble" as the merchant puts it but "a substantial true-bred Beast; bravely fore-handed; mark but the cleanness of his shapes, too; his Dam may be a Spanish Gennet, but a true

Barb by the Sire, or I have no skill in Horse-flesh" (I.i.543–44).
Antonio's enslavement mimes the comic narrative of one "T. S.,"
who claimed to have enjoyed a series of liaisons with his female owners, and ends with his triumph, as he escapes with Morayma and
half her father's wealth. For all its comic triumphalism, however,
Antonio's career provides an infinitely more graphic view of the
process and circumstances of slavery than previous dramas, suggesting that Southerne turned not just to Don Sebastian himself, but
also to Antonio, in creating Oroonoko. The slavery of *Don Sebastian*
is not an Eastern abstraction or a political trope but an institution
taking on ever more reality, both in its traditionally threatening piratical form, and as a new means of profit to the English audience.

Another critical index of cultural difference is the more familiar
display of sanguinary tyranny (described by Almeyda as "salvage
greatness") which precedes Muley-Moluch's overthrow by the rab-
ble, aided by the treachery of his favorite Bendacur. For all the
Lockean parody in the rebellion scene, the Emperor's demise reflects the prevailing view of the instability of such Islamic despotisms. Dryden also places a novel emphasis on the role of Islam,
however, creating in the Mufti a figure of unparalleled hypocrisy
and venality. Although the satire on this "Churchman" attracted
Collier's wrath, Dryden's abuse of Islam in this play is pervasive,
extending well beyond the Mufti's characterization. The opening suggestion that a human sacrifice was required by an angry
God is followed by references to the Prophet's venery (IV.i.177–
84), women lacking souls (V.i.109), prophecies received in the ear
from a pigeon, the infinite flexibility of Islamic law – which the
Mufti claims would prefer the rape of, over marriage to, a Christian
(III.i.94–95) – and circumcision (II.ii.65). This amount of detail is
unprecedented in other plays about Islamic societies and, along
with the depiction of slavery and the pervasive iteration of the
trope of African monstrosity, creates a much more detailed and
negative depiction of Barbary than earlier, heroic representations
of Ottoman empire or, indeed, of Morocco itself.[55]

Dryden's representation of Barbary still relied more on differences of political and gender order, customs, manners, costume
and religion than "race," despite Sebastian's vaunt to the Emperor
that "*Affrick* is stor'd with Monsters; Man's a Prodigy" (I.i.372). The
purported "monstrosity" of Africans does not prevent Antonio's
marriage to his "pretty infidel," or Dorax's passing as a Moor until

he has "taken off his Turbant, and put on a Perruque, Hat and Crevat" (IV.iii) in a scene which recalls Clytus's stubborn loyalty to his national dress. An ambivalence about the issue of intermarriage novel in Dryden's work may, however, be legible in the irony that it is Almeyda who most frequently invokes a horror of African monstrosity when resisting what she sees as an improper marriage to Muley-Moluch, although she is herself the child of European and African parentage and, like Sebastian himself, has become monstrous by her marriage (V.i.551). Although Antonio and Morayda's cheerful alliance suggests otherwise, the pervasive association of monstrosity with Christian–Moorish intermarriage, whether Almeyda's with Muley-Moluch, Zayda's with Juan or the incestuous union between their children tends to suggest the unnaturalness, if not the criminality, of such bonds. The horror of incest, endogamy imploding, is here recast as an effect of improper exogamy, when Zayda's voyage to Portugal brings her into criminal contact with Juan. The public failure of Sebastian's imperial venture, a hopeless attempt to bring the monstrous Africans within the pale, is matched by the affective disasters attendant on miscegenation.

Dryden's problematization of marital alliance between representatives of different nations a quarter-century after his celebration of such a relation in *The Indian Emperor* suggests a radical shift not simply in an individual perspective but in a culture.[56] There were earlier instances in which the heroic mode incorporated much more evidently "racial" tropes but they are decidedly the exception. The most conspicuous example is *Abdelazer* (1676), a depiction of the havoc wreaked in the Spanish Court by the son of Abdela, a King of Barbary defeated by the Spanish. There is little greatness in Behn's representation of the on-going conflict between the Moors and the Spaniards. Like a janissary in reverse, her protagonist has been incorporated within the Spanish Court, converted, married a noblewoman and proved himself a valiant fighter, although his refusal to give up his Moorish costume is a sign of alienation which attracts suspicion. Like Almanzor, he is a barbarian whose integration in Christian society is fraught, both for himself and for his "hosts": like Dorax, his crossing over to another set of religious and political loyalties, here cemented by marital and erotic relations, suggests to the other characters an inner instability and capacity for treachery. Unlike Dryden, however, Behn was not at all reluctant to inflect her depiction of the disastrous effects of a failed attempt at cultural integration with the traditional slurs of devilry, magic, concupiscence, bestiality and blackness associated with Moors, whether "Tawnie" or "Negroe," which she found in her source, *Lust's Dominion: or, The Lascivious Queen* (1599–1600?). This hardly suggests Behn felt a particular affinity for the racially "Other," as feminist critics have suggested in relation to *Oroonoko*.[57] The protagonist is superlatively wicked, and the epithets hurled at him by the unlikeably rancorous Phillip were presumably regarded as no less than just by contemporary audiences.

The play's incorporation of ethnic insults is more complex than it appears. *Abdelezar* is highly unusual among heroic plays of the 1660s and 1670s in its foregrounding of ethnic difference by means of skin color rather than emphasizing religion and custom. The protagonist's consciousness of the distinctions of "person" rather than creed, which render him a spectacle and an object of sexual fascination or revulsion, show Behn reviving tropes from early seventeenth-century texts to fashion novel characterizations of racialized identity which proved proleptic. Abdelezar's motivation for his machinations is an (heroically) understandable desire to revenge himself on the dynasty and nation which has conquered his father and removed his own hopes of rule. His vengefulness is equally motivated by a specifically racial *ressentiment*, however, rendered explicit in his first exchange with his brother-in-law Alonzo:

> Because, Sir, I am married to your Sister,
> You, like your Sister must be jealous too:
> The Queen with me! With me! A Moor! A Devil!
> A slave of Barbary! For so
> Your gay young Courtiers christen me: – but Don,
> Although my skin be black, within my veins
> Runs bloud as red, and Royal as the best. –
> My Father, Great Abdela, with his Life
> Lost too his Crown: both most unjustly ravisht
> By Tyrant Phillip: your old King I mean.
> . . .
> I was but young, yet old enough to grieve,
> Though not revenge, or to defie my Fetters;
> For then began my Slavery.[58]

Abdelezar's speeches reveal a private wound in excess of his resentment at military defeat and political subordination which ambiguates his characterization by Phillip, his successful opponent, as a "Hell-begotten Fiend" (i.i, p. 8). Confident of his valor, it is in his erotic relations that Abdelezar's anger turns to reveal the wounds to self-esteem inflicted by his suspicion of the Spanish disgust for his "Person": "what is there here –" he asks Alonzo, "Or in my soul, or Person, may not be belov'd?" (v.i, p. 61). His affair with the "easie Spanish dame," the Queen, satisfies his desire to revenge himself on her husband, his father's conqueror, but also allows him to return contempt for contempt. In his unsuccessful attempt to woo Leonora, however, her rejection brings his internal struggle with self-loathing to the surface:

> Aye! There's your cause of hate! Curst be my Birth,
> And curst be Nature, that has dy'd my skin
> With this ungrateful colour!   (v.i, p. 63)

He as quickly reminds himself – and her – that "Beauties as great as thine have languish'd for me," although this depends, it seems, on "The Lights put out!" (v.i, p. 63).

If Abdelezar's complaints echoed those of a variety of Renaissance "aliens" like the bastard Edmund, Shylock and Othello, all driven to murderous rage by their social exclusion, his location within the Spanish Court underlined the peculiar dangers to a colonizing power which sought to expand empire by the traditional means of integration, by an insistence on conversion. Behn's vision of Spain reanimates the ancient suspicion that her conquests had brought not just poisoned gold but an adulterate population, spasmodically rebellious communally but, even worse, hypocritically lurking as a resentful cancer within a body politic too intolerant to accommodate difference. The rehearsal of racial slurs in *Abdelezar*, and the protagonist's anguished awareness of, and angry resistance to, such definitions, provides an ugly but prophetic documentation of the psychological effects of European colonization, as the hitherto insignificant category of "complexion" becomes central to a depiction of cross-cultural relations in the Spanish empire.

FAILURES GREAT

Plays with Spanish settings proliferated in the early eighteenth century, presumably as a result of England's involvement in the War of Spanish Succession (1702–13). Serious plays by Whig dramatists approached Iberian history very differently to Dryden, focusing less on the great moments of imperial triumph and more on the periods of decline and crisis in Peninsular affairs. The critique of tyranny in such plays obviously had local reference but plays by Congreve and Pix amplified the judgment of political analysts that Spanish imperialism was not only in irreversible decline but morally and politically repugnant.[59] The dissolution of the Spanish empire was in fact the cause of the war, as Britain, along with the other members of the Grand Alliance, sought to prevent the consolidation of Iberian continental and overseas possessions in French hands. The fearful consequences of such imperial dissolution, as well as the dire effects of expansion, were doubtless in Charles Davenant's mind when he warned, in his *Essay upon Universal Monarchy*, that "when these great Empires arrive to their old and declining Age, the Diseases contracted for want of Action affect and interrupt the Peace and Felicity of Mankind, as much as the furious Excursions of their Youth and Manhood."[60] While his father had accepted such ambition as natural in man, Davenant *fils* regarded the pursuit of empire as immoral: "The Ambitious Part of Mankind have hunted after this Game for near four thousand years, with Short Intermissions and breathing whiles, and commonly without any Regard whither or no in the Pursuit they follow'd the Rules of Honesty, Common Justice or Virtue."[61] Like Andrew Fletcher, Davenant takes issue with economic arguments for universal monarchy ("all great Monarchies degenerate into Tyranny, with which Trade is incompatible"),[62] along with Mexia's claims that imperial states promote virtue, learning, peace and justice, arguing that instead the latter produce "War, Thraldom, Poverty and Persecution," but determines that the *fons et origo* of such evils is the imperial tendency to despotism, for "all big Empires determine in a single person."[63]

The most prominent late seventeenth-century representation of Spain, Congreve's *The Mourning Bride*, is suffused with skepticism about Spanish expansionism. The play's Granadian setting and African characterization have been elided both in readings which view its detailed condemnation of Peninsular tyranny solely as a vehicle for Whig revolutionary myth and in feminist analysis of the way "the female characters function as the cause and locus of patrilineal strife."[64] The first kind of account finds it difficult to incorporate Zara, who appears extraneous to the defense of revolution and the allegorized treatment of Stuart succession, while the second fails to recognize the cultural specificity of her characterization as a passionate African Queen. Congreve's choice of Spain for a critique of absolute power in family and state was overdetermined: the Peninsula was by 1697 a by-word for both. More specifically, however, *The Mourning Bride* addresses the problems of empire, traditionally conceived, for which Spain was model. Manuel, engaged in civil war with his Valentian neighbors and first presented as the triumphant conqueror of the Moors, figures the restless hunting after power criticized by Davenant: Almeria's disdain for "The gilded Trophies of exterior Honours" (1.iii.27) signals the empty amorality of the King's victory. The depiction of Spain focuses on the "bondage" both of mind and of body which accompanied the enlargement of empire, as Manuel attempts to impress his will in the most violent terms, not just on rival Spaniards and suspected rebels but on his daughter. His unsuspected competitor for control of sexual relations, and hence power more generally, is Zara, wife of the defeated Moorish King whose passion for Osmyn/Anselmo has already provoked the unsuccessful Moorish invasion which returns Osmyn to Spain. Zara is the wild card hindering Manuel's furious and eventually futile attempts to control events, another "hellish Moor," whose willingness to deploy her mutes and her poisons introduces an alien mode of violent intrigue to the Court.

Congreve's depiction of Zara is far from monstrous, however: although a foil for Almeria's passively resistant virtue, she is a figure of heroic and pathetic proportions. The play was indebted to *Love Triumphant* but Drydenic also in its eschewal of overtly racializing tropes in its presentation of doomed African–Spanish romance. Along with her queenliness, admired by the King and productive of unshakeable loyalty in Selim and her mutes, Zara deliberately recalls Dido, another African Queen seduced, abandoned and ruined by a European Prince *en route* to empire. As such, she embodies the human cost not just of masculine sexual exploitation but that implicit in the European's appropriation of undeserved goods and honors. In her great speech upbraiding Osmyn/Alonzo her language recalls Virgil:[65]

> Thou hast a Heart, though 'tis a Savage one;
> Give it me as it is; I ask no more
> For all I've done, and all I have endur'd:
> For saving thee, when I beheld thee first,

Driven by the Tide upon my Country's Coast,
Pale and expiring, drench'd in Briny Waves,
Thou and thy Friend, 'till my Compassion found thee;
Compassion! Scarce will't own that Name, so soon,
So quickly was it Love; for thou wert God-like
Ev'n then.   (II.ix.38–47)

Zara is not Dido; she is a self-confessed adulteress who provokes a war disastrous for her country, but her passion, unlike that of earlier African and Oriental viragos, is figured as heroic and womanly rather than simply monstrous. On the one hand, as Osmyn admits, "This Woman has a Soul / Of God-like Mould, intrepid and commanding" (III.vi.71–72); on the other, the pathetic rhetoric of her complaints prefigures the widespread eighteenth-century use of heroic elegy to naturalize exploitative relations between European colonizers and indigenous peoples from the Caribbean to the Pacific brilliantly analyzed by Marty Wechselblatt.[66] The pathos modifies and softens her characterization as an African *femme forte*, hell-bent on vengeance, implicating Osmyn.

Zara's accusation that Osmyn is "savage" and culpable has substance. Having pretended to be the Prince of Fez to Albucacim, he accepted honors and hospitality while committing adultery with the latter's wife. Osmyn's Moorish disguise, which continues his unhappy exile from his identity and affiliations, is a just punishment for his earlier exploitative appropriation of an African identity. His alienation can only be redeemed by the sufferings he endures when realizing his deception threatens the stability of his own marriage as well as the extended Spanish state initiated by the alliance between Valentia and Granada. The murder of the King, effected by his taking Osmyn's place in his "Turbant, and his Robe array'd," reiterates the danger of succumbing to a passion for an African Queen: identity goes first and then life itself. In Manuel's case, however, his despotic conduct has already suggested his infection by the savagery consequent on absolute power, so that his assumption of a Moorish disguise confirms, rather than initiates, his corruption. By accepting Zara's proffered stranglers and disguising his minions as Moors, Manuel blurs the distinction between his supposedly civil, Christian Court and an Islamic despotism in the most graphic way possible. Instead of being Albucacim's conqueror, he is his mimic, deceived and manipulated by Zara into needless violence which costs his life.

The Mourning Bride reiterates the dangers of straying from one's native shore for love or power: as in *Don Sebastian*, strong statehood here depends on avoiding foreign women, adventures and ambitions. The play also suggests, however, that the consolidation or defense of the state may well lead inexorably to such entanglements and temptations, with potentially disastrous consequences. As England came to the end of the Nine Years War, even a Williamite might be counting costs. The consolation offered by *The Mourning Bride* is that the nation is saved from invasion and tyranny and Christian marriage survives exotic adultery, while the violence of those identified with threats to political and familial order, the play's African and Spanish "Moors," turns on its instigators.

Mary Pix's *The False Friend* revises *The Mourning Bride* by recasting Zara as a Spanish noblewoman driven to murderous jealousy by her unrequited passion for Emilius, son of the Sardinian Vice-Roy. The dangers attendant on exogamous relationships are adverted to early in the play, when Lovisa, Emilius's French beloved, expresses her remorse for breaking "the strongest Ties / Ties which even *Barbarians* hold most Sacred," namely those of "Parents, Family" and "Native Land"; and the dangers of such relations seem confirmed by the death of the unfortunate lovers.[67] The play suggests, however, that the cause of their demise is more complex and specific than the folly of trying to defy the well-known hostility of France and Spain. The lovers are killed by Appamia, of whom we learn immediately that "Large are her Possessions in both the *Indies* and in *Spain*" (i.i, p. 4) and who is accompanied at all times by a royal slave, Zelaide, a converted Indian Princess. Rather than figuring Appamia's black heart, as recently suggested by Jaqueline Pearson, it seems much more likely that Zelaide's continual presence and unwilling involvement in her mistress's crimes were an emblem of the corruption in the Spanish caused by their conquests in America. Far from embodying evil, the noble and virtuous Zelaide is a living reminder of the black legend, thus suggesting that Appamia's corruption is somehow caused by her vast Indian inheritance. The embodiment of loyalty, Zelaide nevertheless resists doing evil, asking her mistress whether "the only Service" she must do her "Generous Mistress" is to "Leave her Name Accurst" (iv.i, p. 46). Zelaide has not only been the subject of violence but is forced into acting violently herself, by a mistress acting in defiance of her own Christian teaching by preaching suicide and murder:

Why dost tremble? You said you were a
Princess born; and that thy Swarthy Veins
Carry'd the Royal Blood of those, who heretofore,
Were Lords of *Mexico*! It must be false;
Thou hast a *Plebian* Soul; else, thou hadst
Used that skill, which I implore: and died,
E're been my slave.   (ii.i, p. 28)

When Lovisa is lamenting the exile imposed by her Clarissa-like
disobedience, Zelaide's sympathetic identification invokes her
nation's self-alienation under the Spanish yoke:

Oh! Who can here words like these, and keep their
Temper! Not Conquer'd *India*, Groaning under
Her Tyrannic Masters, shows a greater Wretch!   (ii.ii, p. 32)

The contrast between Appamia's exploitation of Zelaide and the
latter's conviction that her closeness to her mistress has dissolved
her formal slavery into friendship is emblematic of Spanish perfidy and Indian generosity: "O Faithful Slave!" exclaims Appamia,
"*India* alone can breed thy Fellow!" To which Zelaide replies "I was a
slave till your goodness rais'd me / To your Bosom" (i.i, p. 12). The
self-destructiveness inherent in Zelaide's complete identification
with Appamia's interests reaches its climax in the last few moments
of the play, when in words which recall Montezuma's defiance of
his torturers, she says she will "offer up my Limbs" but "not all the
Agonies, *Spain*, or hell / Can invent shall force Confession from
me" (v.ii, p. 58).

Appamia's crimes are most obviously attributable to her excessive passion, while her victims are blamed for their departure
from filial obedience. The play's Spanish setting, however, inflects
these doxa with special significance. Towards the end of the play,
Bucarius designs "To fly to the *Indies*: and there revel / In Love and
Pleasure; too great for Laws" (v.i, p. 53). Conquered America is not
simply a source of wealth and the site of Indian suffering but an
incitement to exactly the kind of murderous lawlessness enacted by
Appamia. The carefully crafted relationship between Zelaide and
her mistress provides an intimate emblem of precisely the kind of
violence and corruption bred by the poisoned chalice of American
gold and glory, as Appamia, in hypocritical disregard for Christian
sanctions, exploits and sacrifices her royal slave's natural nobility
in a lawless pursuit of amatory conquest. The disaster fashioned

by Appamia's corruption threatens to engulf all of Sardinia, as the Vice-Roy, who had used her American revenues to secure order in a Spanish possession filled with unpaid and mutinous soldiers, retires to a cloister with his family extinct.

The False Friend reworks both the black legend and Congreve's critique of exogamy and despotism to figure the corruption consequent on Spanish expansion in America and Africa under the aegis of their past ambitions of "universal monarchy," an aspiration in 1700 most distinctly identified with an expansionist France in alliance with her southern neighbor. In *The Conquest of Spain*, Pix returned to a Peninsular setting, dramatizing the ignominious process by which the last Gothic King Rhoderique is driven from the throne and replaced by the Moors. Choosing to represent one of the most humiliating episodes of defeat in Spanish history, Pix reverses Dryden's heroic perspective by depicting the defeat of Christian Europe. This reversal is an effect both of the strong Whig hostility to Spanish expansionism on theoretical grounds and of the concrete circumstances of war: the play was produced just after the capture of Gibraltar and the victory at Blenheim. Pix's vision of Spain emphasizes the internal disorder and external weakness produced by a tyranny with which her own newly triumphant nation is presumed to stand in contrast. The premise inherent in this recounting of Spanish defeat is that the mighty empire which flourished after the *Reconquista* also became tyrannously cruel and was again vulnerable, albeit this time to liberal Christians.

Pix's Prologue emphasizes the difference between Britain's ruler Anna, beloved by her people, who are ably led against France and Spain by Marlborough, and the "unhappy Monarch" who loses his throne. The depiction of Spain in the play itself amplifies the implicit contrast between the two warring states by focusing on Rhoderique's tyrannous ingratitude: he rapes Jacinta, daughter of his "prop of empire" the loyal General Julianus, thus provoking her betrothed, Theomantius, to ally himself with the Moorish General Mullymumen.[68] The play is full of familiar tropes: the rape of Lucrece is invoked but the parallel is hardly sustained by developments, as the Spanish nation is comprehensively ruined, rather than consolidated, by the ravisher's actions. Pix's characterization of Rhoderique figures him as a sensual tyrant more interested in debauchery than war but one who, oddly, seems already to have access to the corrupting colonial booty, as Jacinta is invited into apartments "Rich with the wealthy spoil of ransack'd Nations" where "The *Tyrian* Purple and the *Indian* Gold" await her.[69] Here the rather generalized portrayal of rapacious despotism is given a specifically Spanish edge.

The play is resistant to allegorical reading because Pix makes no bones about the tragedy of a Christian state being overrun by a "barbarous infernal Race" (ii.ii, p. 18). The contradiction between the desire to celebrate a well-deserved Spanish defeat and profound hostility towards the invading force of Moors is never really resolved, either in the characterization of the Moorish General Mullymumen or in the conclusion of the action. The play is equalled only by *Abdelazer* in its invocation of the traditional tropes of Moorish devilry eschewed by Dryden in his depiction of Spanish–Moorish conflict. In one such instance, Julianus exhorts his troops with a nightmare vision of the catastrophic effects of Moorish victory:

> What Coward wou'd not arm in such Defence?
> The invaders from the cursed brood of Hell,
> Distinguish't from the rest of Human kind
> By horrid Black, the emblem of their Souls.
> O! Friends, can ye have Patience to imagin
> Your Wives and Daughters made a Prey to these,
> And not boil o'er with manly Indignation?
> Our Women fear to look upon these Monsters,
> Yet must become their Slaves if we are Vanquish'd;
> Slaves to their Pride and to their Brutal Pleasure.
> Our guilded Pallaces, and pleasant Gardens,
> Will then be made a Kennel for these Dogs;
> Whilst we with fruitless Rage, and idle grief,
> Behold our Temples Sack'd and Rites Prophan'd.
>
> (iii.i, p. 26)

The emphasis on rape, followed by threats to property and religion, may reflect the dramatist's gender: the change of regimes is here presented in terms more of the implications for the population and culture at large, than of Dryden's focus on broad historical process and dynastic succession. The racialized revulsion from the Moors expressed here, however, marks a negative shift in heroic representation, in making "national reflections which ought not to be made" in crudely dehumanizing terms. Julianus's speech is not an isolated expression of sentiment: the emphasis on the cruelty and incivility associated with Moorish blackness is sustained throughout. Horrified by Mulleymumen's interest in Jacinta, Theomantius upbraids him to his face as "Monster" and "perfidious Fiend, Hell's gloomy Agent" (IV.i, p. 57), although, ironically, it is only Rhoderique and not the Moorish General who proves a "Tyrant, and a Ravisher." Mulleymumen appears capable of mercy, allowing Margaretta and Antonio to leave peacefully but there is no full recuperation: Jacinta is mortally wounded as she is being returned to her father, from whom the invader intends removing her, once the kingdom is quiet. Spanish weakness and treachery lead "the black Sons of rapine" to complete political triumph untempered in this text by the usual counter-balancing Christian amatory success.

Pix's demonized vision of Moorish invasion closes the cycle of plays about Spain in a racialized register of Whig triumphalism. As was the case with late plays about the Ottomans, Britain's ancient bogeys are presented here not in their moments of triumph but, as Thomas Rymer would have had it, in defeat, under weak and corrupt leaders. Empire is defined negatively, as an immoral pursuit of wealth and power productive of tyranny, instability and guilt, without any shading of Stuart admiration for the achievements of Catholic expansionism. As commentators had realized decades earlier, however, new forms of imperial power, dependent on the maritime control of colonial trade and territory, were evolving. While many royalists might recoil from identification with the Dutch practitioners of such commercial imperialism, the Portugese, allied to the English through Catherine of Braganza, and historic defiers of Spain, offered a more generally acceptable model of oceanic empire, combining honor and profit. The great success of Tate's and Motteux's redactions of Fletcher's *The Island Princess* suggests that for a couple of decades these texts managed the difficult task of reconciling the contradictory demands that European colonial adventures be seen to be honorable but not too Ambitious, and profitable without Avarice.

Portuguese gallantry and colonial success is a recurring note of Restoration accounts of the nation:

This Crown hath had wonderful Success, both in the *East* and the *West-Indies*, where they have wrested *Brasile* from the *Hollanders*; and at Home also; for though they be but a Handfull of People, yet by immuring themselves in very strong Places, as they took by Shipping and Naval Sieges from the *Indians*; adventuring in all weathers to relieve one another, to the disappointment of their Enemies, who thought by Sieges at Land to recover the Places they had lost by the opportunity of such tempestuous seasons, they have fixed themselves so in those *Indies*, that they command a great part thereof, and the best also.[70]

In the reworkings of Fletcher's play, Tate and Motteux drew directly on this history of colonial "adventuring," eschewing the more usual struggles of Crescent and Cross or American atrocities. Tate was presumably drawn to the text because the 1680s saw considerable conflict in the Indonesian archipelago. Although Tidore and her traditional enemy Ternate were not directly involved, in Bantam the old Sultan was usurped by his son with Dutch aid. The Sultan had purchased guns from Charles in 1682 to help see off this challenge but to no avail, and the English factory was closed in 1684, with a new fort (York) being built at Benkulen on the west coast of Sumatra.[71] The Spice Islands' usurpation in Fletcher's text presumably suggested a parallel with recent events in the East Indies, although Tate and Motteux recycle Fletcher's account of one of the on-going sixteenth-century conflicts between Tidore, Ternate and the Portuguese, a brief narrative of which was available in Purchas. The Moluccans were mostly Muslim but, as a result of Portuguese missionary efforts, some had converted to Catholicism, a situation which disturbed the Dutch, who tried to Calvinize the islanders after they gained power in the seventeenth century. Such efforts at conversion had incensed local rulers and a Muslim confederation, headed by the Sultan of Ternate, was formed to drive out the Portuguese and their religion. After Governor Diego De Mesquita had Sultan Hairun of Ternate "treacherously" murdered in 1570, the Portugese were almost constantly at war with the confederation.[72]

The play uses a complex love-plot to initiate the political and military action which reshapes the historical record of implacable Moluccan resistance to conversion and Portuguese perfidy as a myth of Christian gallantry and evangelical triumph. Although the enormous wealth produced by the nutmeg and mace grown in these particular Spice Islands is adverted to, the economic reasons for the desire to dominate these territories is largely effaced by the emphasis on the Portuguese role in re-establishing political order and converting the local Princess, if not her brother the King. The Portuguese rivals are not merchants but soldiers of noble birth, who win their way to influence through alliance, conversion and military success. These dramas thus solve the dilemma Dryden found so problematic in *Amboyna*: an essentially commercial venture is rewritten to demonstrate the code of love and honor bringing civility and Christianity to a disorderly, pagan polity.[73]

The first act establishes a five-way rivalry for the hand of Quisara, Tidore Princess, among three Moluccans – the feeble Kings Bakam and Syana, and the wicked Ternatean Governor – and two noble Portuguese, Armusia and Ruidias. The amatory competition justifies Portuguese intervention in local affairs, as the Princess Quisara promises her hand to anyone who succeeds in rescuing her brother from the Governor of Ternate, who is holding the King hostage in the hope she will marry him. Armusia rescues the King by disguising himself as a merchant (thereby underlining his gentle birth) and using explosives to blow up the Ternatean castle, the first of two instances of European fire-power which draw attention to the Christians' technological prowess. Quisara is then in a quandary because she has already received Ruidias's addresses in an encouraging manner but is now inclining to Armusia. The Governor, meanwhile, has not abandoned hope and, disguising himself as an Indian Priest or, in Motteux's opera, as a Brahmin, he persuades the Tidore King that the Portuguese not only intend to gain influence and possible hereditary rights through alliance with Quisara but are planning conversions. Secretly overheard by the King and Governor, the latter's claims are confirmed when Quisara tests Armusia's (Christian) faith by asking him to renounce his beliefs to prove his love. Naturally he refuses and she reveals she has herself been converted by his conviction. The King, egged on by the Governor, pronounces Armusia's and Quisara's deaths but they are rescued by the disappointed but selfless Ruidias, who shells the town from the Portuguese fort. The Governor is exposed, the King expresses his admiration for the conviction and gallantry of the Christians and order is restored.

The rewriting of the historical record involved here is thorough. All three versions of the play record but reverse the culpability of the Moluccans and Portuguese in regard to the death of the Sultan of Tidore: whereas in fact he was murdered by the Portuguese Governor, in the dramatic retelling the Portuguese rescue him twice from the Governor of Ternate. The Princess's successful conversion is central to the plot and implies a more general process of

Christianization has been embraced by Tidore's indigenous rulers, despite their organized resistance to Catholicism. The brief alliance between the King and Governor refigures the very effective Muslim confederation led by the Sultan of Ternate as a wicked and unsuccessful manipulation of pagan bigotry. As in *The Indian Emperor*, however, an indigenous critique is legible despite the attempt to represent colonial expansion as a heroicized action of love and honor. These dramas do not share Dryden's interest in rehearsing the black legend but an equally effective analysis of Portuguese motivation is provided in *The Indian Princess* by the Ternate Governor. In his first attempt to persuade the King to his side, he argues:

> These men came hither, as my Vision tells me,
> Poor, weather-beaten, almost starv'd, feebled,
> Their Vessels like themselves, most miserable,
> Made long sute for Trafique, and for comfort,
> To vend their childrens toys, cure their diseases:
> They had their sute, they landed and to the rate,
> Grew rich and powerful, suck'd the Fat and Freedom
> Of thy most noble Isle, taught her to tremble,
> Witness the Castel here, the Citadel,
> They have clapt up the neck of your Tidore.[74]

The Governor's account is in defiance of the action as represented but not unconvincing in itself: while the dramatists' all mobilize a revulsion against usurpation to cast the Governor as villain, his speeches do draw attention to the more informal means by which the Portuguese were attempting to establish themselves, not just through commerce and military power but by conversion. Articulating a position one imagines not dissimilar to that of the Muslim confederation, he attempts to make the same points to Quisara:

> The Portugals, like sharp thorns (mark me, Lady,)
> Stick in our sides like Razors, wound Religion,
> Draw deep, they wound till all the life-blood follows,
> Our Gods they spurn at, and their worship scorn,
> A mighty hand they bear upon our Government.
>
> (IV.ii, p. 35)

While the primary concern is with the conversion of the Tidore royalty, Tate (though not Motteux) suggests that force rather than reason is the best persuasive to Christianization:

1. Well, for my part, I'll to the Temple and pray for you all: I
tell you Neighbours, I trouble Heaven so seldom, that sure
I may be heard, when I come. For I begins to like this
Portugals Person Religion: What can these Worm-eaten
Gods of ours do for us?

4. Worm-eaten Gods! I tell you, Neighbour, you do our Gods
wrong, and me wrong: I made 'em of the best season'd
Timber the Island would afford.

3. But do the Cannon Bullets think there is no Law?

4. No, nor Gospel neither; Law, prithee run to a Granado,
when it comes piping hot out of a Mortar-piece into the
Town, and tell it there's Law; 'twill scratch thy face for
thee, worse than e'er thy Wife did.   (v.i, p. 50)

Motteux, later to become an East India merchant, used his operatic
version to smooth Fletcher's/Tate's verse but the most noticeable
alterations to the content, the musical additions excepted, are a
novel emphasis in the opening of the play on Spice Islands' wealth,
his "white-washing" Quisara and his reworking of the allusions to
Moluccan belief in more credible terms, as Hindu. The opera thus
begins with Armusia's panegyric to "delicious Eastern climes" in
which "The very Rivers as we float along / Throw up their Pearls"
and "The Earth, still cloth'd in Flow'rs / Teems with the Birth
of Gemms and dazzling Riches."[75] The connection between the
possession of such resources and the Tidore Princess, implicit in
Fletcher and Tate, is made explicit in his next few lines:

> We *Portuguese* now travel thro' the Globe,
> New Worlds disclose their Beauties and their Prides to our
>   embraces,
> And we the first of Nations find these wonders.
> But of 'em all, this Island boasts the greatest;
> A Princess whom all Nature's Blessings grace,
> The very Sun, I think, respects her Charms;
> Nor dares affect 'em with the common gloom.   (i.i, p. 1)

The synechdochical relationship of "Indies" wealth and femininity
central to *Amboyna*'s depiction of colonial competition in the neighboring island of Amboyna reappears but inflected now with a novel
degree of racial awareness: Quisara, Armusia implies, is not
black. A more distinct awareness of "difference" is also legible in
Motteux's eradication of the Fletcher/Tate altars to Thor and the
Governor's generalized disguise as a "Moor Prince": instead the

latter appears as a Brahmin. This is still in defiance of the Islamic adherence of most Moluccans but suggests a desire to underscore the confessional, as well as the ethnic, divide, more convincingly and distinctly.

These particular celebrations of European colonial activity were markedly successful on the stage. Although political and religious affiliations inflected all English depictions of Iberian empire, it is not difficult to see the attractions this particular text held for diverse audiences over a long period of time. The model of empire here brings wealth and civility and enlarges the Christian community but avoids the illegal usurpation of indigenous rights and the cruelty of Spanish exploitation. "Remember w'are I'th' Palace of the Island, / Not our own Fort" (i.i. [pp. 2–3]) says Chrystophero at the opening of Tate's play: local sovereignty, unlike in Mexico, is to be respected and, indeed, reinforced by the Europeans. This fantasy of informal empire resolved the conflicts inherent in both commercial and heroic visions of expansion.

The shifts in the depiction of Iberian history in serious drama from 1658 to 1714 play out the anxieties and aspirations of the English elites as they contemplated the accelerating decline of the greatest model of Christian empire. For Dryden, strong supporter of the Stuarts, and Catholic convert, there was as much to admire as to criticize in the Spanish model, which could be understood as preparing the way for the westward progress of British power. Increasingly hostile to the prospect of an empire driven solely by the avaricious imperatives of trade and settlement, having seen his last hopes for a more heroic, evangelical expansionism collapse after '88, Dryden unsurprisingly focused finally on Peninsular failure, rather than success. After 1688, with Spanish instability emerging as a real and present danger to the balance of power, Whig playwrights as well as ideologues turned to episodes of Iberian crisis and decline. In these later plays the critique of Spanish tyranny, the hunger for power which built the empire and created the black legend, is imbricated in Christian Spain's long struggle with the Moors. Just as England is becoming "Britain," attempting a novel, bloody and self-conscious consolidation of its Celtic fringe, and increasing her possessions abroad, dramatists focus not just on the dangers of external aggression but on the risks of incorporating religious and ethnic aliens. However distinctly the English sought to differentiate themselves from their predecessors in empire, resolutely disavowing claims to universal monarchy, unflattering parallels would emerge as Britain was "pacified" and unified and the country took its Western spoils. One of the gains Britain made in the Treaty of Utrecht, along with Gibraltar, Minorca, Nova Scotia, Newfoundland and Hudson's Bay, was the *asiento*, the right to trade slaves to the Spanish New World. Thus the British supped at the poisoned chalice.

CHAPTER 6

Brave New Worlds: Utopian Plays
of the Restoration

One of the most frequently performed plays in the Restoration theatre was the adaptation of *The Tempest* which Dryden and Davenant produced in 1668.[1] Among the other plays of the period which drew on utopian and voyage traditions were John Weston's *The Amazon Queen: or, the Amours of Thalestris to Alexander the Great* (1667); Edward Howard's *The Six Days Adventure or the New Utopia* (1671) and his *The Women's Conquest* (1670); Thomas Durfey's *A Commonwealth of Women* (1686); Charles Hopkins's *Friendship Improv'd: or, the Female Warriour* (1700); and Peter Motteux's *Thomyris, Queen of Scythia* (1707). These plays are mostly tragi-comedies by minor male writers, spread widely over the period, and have attracted little attention from literary historians preoccupied with generic issues, high political interpretation or women-authored texts.[2] There is a rich literature dealing with the masculine prose utopias of the seventeenth century and feminist work has begun on the utopian writing of Margaret Cavendish and Mary Astell but the utopian dramatists of the Restoration have been ignored.[3]

The dramatic utopias produced before 1688 transcribe an elite, royalist and masculine exploration of alternatives to a gender and political order newly perceived to be particular, local and problematic: with the notable exception of Charles Johnson's *The Successful Pyrate*, an idealized depiction of a pirate colony on Madagascar, those published after '88 tend to use Amazonian analogies to celebrate the female rule of Anne. In a context in which voyage literature was proliferating as colonial expansion accelerated, and in which political philosophers like Locke not only speculated on the primitive origins of government but were drawing up constitutional plans for New World territories, it is hardly surprising a plethora of utopian texts should appear. Authorities such as Davis and Faussett agree that seventeenth-century utopian writing was produced in response to the increasing knowledge of other societies and cultures produced through trade and colonization; by the circulation of tales of shipwreck and social inversion on far-distant islands; by the desire to create new societies in the New World; and by the perception of domestic moral and political corruption. This account has been supplemented recently by feminist critic Kate Lilley who has pointed to the emergence of feminist utopias which, she argues, can be differentiated from masculinist examples of the form. As Lilley puts it: "Men's utopias have focused on political systems and laws; utopian writing by women has tended to focus strategically on the possibilities and problems of gendered social life and the weight of custom – micropolitical questions of sexuality, maternity, domesticity and self-government – while declining the burden of representing a fully articulated model of a new political order."[4]

Lilley's account of early feminist utopian writing is a valuable one but her distinction between the male- and female-authored forms is not sustainable theoretically or empirically. To make the theoretical point first, as Faussett has expressed it: archaic bodily metaphors idealize the world as feminine, maternal and universal, although in reality it was, and is, riven by social differences and practices that have been the masculine domain. Faussett argues that the Same–Other split postulated in Lacan's account of the mirror-stage, which is based on bodily identities, was in early myth telescoped into a duality of man and earth, and that utopian notions of nation and nation, or Old World and New World, depended on and played out a dichotomy of known (masculine) and unknown (feminine) worlds.[5] To make the point empirically, one frequently finds in masculinist utopian writing fantasies of sexual plenitude or pornotopias, and also, in accounts of Amazonian societies, visions of an inverted gender order. Far from being uninterested in questions of gender and maternity, a significant number of male authors of utopias use the mode to articulate dreams of a sexualized world in which the original separation from the maternal body and the channelling of desire into socially approved behaviors are annulled.[6] Examples of such writing in the Restoration include Henry Neville's *Isle of Pines* (1668) and erotic cartographies such as Cotton's *Erotopolis* (1684). Utopian texts which present an inverted gender order include Hall's *Mundus alter et idem*, republished in a plagiarized form in 1669 as *The Land of Parrots: Or, the She-Lands*. Although there are significant differences in male- and

female-authored utopias, questions of sexuality and gender are in-
trinsic to the mode. Further, those Restoration dramatic texts I have
cited indicate that male members of the Royalist culture in which
Cavendish, Behn and Astell participated were also interested in
exploring "the problems of gendered social life and the weight of
custom" by constructing fictional alternatives.[7] Barker-Benfield's
recent account of the cult of sensibility claims that the licentiousness of rakish behavior exemplified by Rochester not only established a boundary of aggressive hyper-masculinity against which the
movement to reform manners would define itself in the following
century but that Rochester's conduct and writings are informed
by a measure of principled commitment to female sexual, social
and economic equality.[8] In this account, the carnivalesque excesses
of rakish conduct could be seen as attempts to live out the erotic
utopianism legible in contemporary libertine discourse. In a somewhat different register, what Ros Ballaster has called the "seductive
forms" of Behn and Manley also employed eroticized utopian and
voyage forms to license the feminine production of political discourse which not only commented on contemporary affairs but
postulated an alternative polity more sympathetic to women.[9]

Largely ignored to date in the accounts of both the utopian
proto-feminist and libertine refashionings of Restoration subjec-
tivities is the question of cultural identity. In the dramatic utopias,
however, this issue is foregrounded. England's expansion into the
Caribbean, North America and the East Indies brought wealth but
also a host of constitutional and cultural problems. New territories
often duplicated metropolitan economic and political tensions as
well as demanding that accommodation be made with very different societies.[10] The external threat presented by exotic or savage
cultures to English colonies insecure both legally and materially
was matched in metropolitan eyes by the colonial's tendency to
degenerate, far from the centres of civility and in dangerous proximity to unbridled savagery.[11] On the other hand, the discovery
of previously unknown societies also generated reflection on the
peculiarities of European manners and speculation about alternatives to European practice. The Cartesian rationalism that played
such a crucial role in the development of feminism also encouraged the cultural relativism that was such a marked feature of the
Enlightenment.[12] As we have seen, a striking feature of Restoration
serious drama is the use both male and female dramatists made of

Oriental settings to explore questions of sovereignty, subjection and sexuality in their own society by invoking the institutions of "Asiatick" despotism, polygamy and the seraglio.

Among the utopian and Amazonian plays produced in the Restoration, *The Tempest, The Six Days Adventure, The Women's Conquest* and *A Commonwealth of Women* are striking examples of speculative reflections about lands where not just custom but the laws of nature can be tested and even suspended. To some extent they are theatrical analogues of those Hobbesian and Lockean philosophical myths about the state of nature and the origins of society which the patriarchalist theorist Filmer called "poetical fictions."[13] As was becoming traditional, they are set on desert islands or the land of the Amazons, places where proper order has not yet been established or where its violation is legend.[14] In each of these plays, the foundation of stable political society is shown to be inseparable from the establishment of a gender order which denies women power. Further, the texts narrativize the usurpation of maternal authority and the institutionalization of female subordination as a passage from savagery to civility. That narrativization does not simply rehearse philosophical myths of origin but identifies patriarchal domination as constitutive of any civilized society, marking out colonial and exotic locales where such domination is threatened as barbarously in need of reform.[15]

At the same time, however, all the plays register an awareness of the cost involved in the establishment of patriarchal civility. Although Weston's *The Amazon Queen* shows Thalestris frustrated in her attempt to procreate with Alexander, the play does allow a forceful articulation of the virtues of female rule and the oppressions of marriage. In Dryden and Davenant's *Tempest*, symbolic castration ends the masculine fantasies of a new world of untrammeled libidinality and political freedom. In Howard's and Durfey's plays, the emphasis lies on the negative effects of female oppression. Despite an inevitable reinscription of traditional forms of goverment and family, these texts focus quite obsessively on the injustices of the contemporary gender order.

RESTORATION PLAYS

The Preface to Weston's *Amazon Queen* introduces the first of a series of negative comparisons, suggesting that the "Language of this barbarous Queen" may be much below that of "the great *Pompey, Mustapha, Montezuma,* and our reviv'd *English* heroes."[16] In fact, however, Thalestris and the other Amazons are effective disputants, arguing female government ensures legitimate succession: "We think it fitter we should rule than you / 'Cause women's heirs must always needs be true" (i.iv, p. 7). She also articulates powerful female objections to marriage:

> I'll have no Master for Companion,
> If I would take the air, I first must know
> If 't be fair weather in my husband's brow:
> And all my dearest friends I must forswear,
> Lest he should think they are to me too dear:
> My fortune too is his, and I must be
> Stinted in point of generosity.   (i.iv, p. 8)

Her critique of marriage is not entirely feminocentric but includes a scorn for the imprisonment enjoined on both parties:

> For with a kind and sprightly liberty,
> They meet by natures choice who both are free:
> Whilst marri'd fools, like Curs in Couples ti'd,
> Would fain be running where they are deni'd.   (ii.vi, p. 21)

The Amazonian celebration of liberty is carefully distinguished from license, with Amalthea insisting, in her amatory debates with Eumenes, on the women's adherence to annual, serial monogamy (i.vi, p.12). For all the cogency of their arguments, however, the Amazons are defeated by the masculine refusal to co-operate with their practices. Thalestris's erotic defeat in the competition for Alexander by Roxana and Statira, both utterly conventional, if antithetical kinds of women, suggests the Amazon project has no future: that the Amazon Queen will be, as Almathea puts it, "famous for destruction" but "Fail in more god-like generation" (ii.i, p. 16). The inherent unnaturalness of the Amazonian political and gender order is implicit in their failure to reproduce their own socius through "generation."

Dryden's and Davenant's *Tempest* has no interest in a feminist theory or praxis but does address, in a comic key, the sexual and political foundations of civil society. The Restoration text alters the original quite markedly. The play begins with a storm and shipwreck but the island is now populated with extra characters: Miranda has a sister, Dorinda, and a foster-brother Hippolito, rightful Duke of Mantua. The children have been brought up in ignorance of each other and sexuality but, when Dorinda and Hippolito meet, they fall in love. Ferdinand falls in love with Miranda and is sequestered in a cave with Hippolito and the two youths fight a duel because Hippolito, in utter ignorance of sexual convention, claims all women for himself. Ariel finesses a reconciliation between Prospero and Alonzo, Antonio and Ferdinand, while Hippolito is "cured" of his all-engrossing desire by the loss of blood he sustained in the duel. The low characters, Stephano, Mustacho, Ventuso and Trincalo, all quarrel over who is to rule the new territory. Stephano proclaims himself Duke, and Mustacho and Ventoso, Viceroys. Trincalo rejects their pretensions and tries to gain a title himself by marrying Caliban's sister, Sycorax. Stephano then attempts to seduce Sycorax, in a scene which ends in uproar. The low characters disappear until, much subdued, they join the rest of the company to watch Ariel dance a saraband with his lover, Milcha.

The revised *Tempest* has generated two significant essays since the 1970s. Earl Miner, in a ground-breaking article, emphasized the origins of the play's redaction of libidinal fantasies in Fletcher's *Sea-Voyage* as well as *The Isle of Pines*, and noted its references to contemporary theories of government.[17] Katherine Eisaman Maus focused on the latter topic, pointing up the ways in which the text rehearses, in a largely comic key, the divine right and contractarian theories of sovereignty then in keen contention.[18] Neither of these accounts attends, however, to the importance of the island's status as a "new plantation" in the text's treatment of political dispute. Arguments over sovereignty in the 1660s had a specifically colonial dimension, as Stuart claims over North America were being extended and the colonial inhabitants of the Caribbean and Atlantic colonies attempted to resist the control of royal appointees.[19] Dryden and Davenant give voice to these rebellious inclinations through the sailors, who attempt to establish a new political order without reference to their previous subjection. Resisting Stephano's pretensions, Ventuso asserts that "When you are Duke you may chuse your Vice-roy; but I am a free subject in a new plantation and will have no Duke without my voice" (ii.iv, p. 3).

Another crucial issue in colonial territories, that of "aboriginal title," or the claim to sovereignty by the indigenous inhabitants, is also played out in a comic key in the play, as first Trinculo and then Stephano attempt to gain power through a marriage with Sycorax: "From this worshipful Monster, and Mistress Monster, his Sister, I'le lay claim to this Island by alliance" (II.iv.220–22) Trinculo says. The principle enshrined here is Vattel's famous insistence that a "dwarf is as much a man as a giant is; a small Republic is no less a sovereign state than the most powerful Kingdom."[20] The Glorious Revolution's interruption of succession would make it much easier for the English to pursue settlement in the Americas and Australia under the legal color of *res nullius*, a Roman law doctrine notoriously amplified by Locke to claim property in land depended on the proprietor mingling labor with the soil. Drawing on the ancient European antipathy to vagrants, this axiom denied the property claims of nomadic or non-agricultural indigenous owners. Before 1688, however, as Paul McHugh points out, the Stuarts were careful to avoid explicit denials of native sovereignty: to do so would problematize their own position as hereditary proprietors. By the beginning of the seventeenth century, rather than claiming the acquisition of new territories was justified through conquest or unilateral assertion, the emphasis had shifted to establishing consensual relations with the indigenous communities of America: "The Stuarts might have conceived their government over Englishmen as a divine gift, but there is no evidence they felt God had given them a similar right over the native societies of America. The charters in which the Crown erected systems of government for the New World consistently defined the *imperium* therein constituted in personal terms, which necessarily excluded the Indian tribes."[21] The treaty-making process of the mid seventeenth-century to pre-Revolutionary period embodied the Crown's recognition of the survival of Indian sovereignty until ceded by the tribe, notwithstanding the broad territorial claims made in the charters.[22] *The Tempest* dramatizes these issues in a comic key, attempting to resolve them through the invocation of a discourse of savagery which effectively displaces the rights of indigenous and creole peoples under natural or common law by denying their humanity.[23]

Sexuality and gender are critical to that discourse of native and colonial savagery. The play rehearses three passages from savagery to civility, of which the first is the awakening and curing of

Hippolito's untrammeled libidinality. His appetite can be understood as an effect of his barbarous upbringing, symptomatic of
the degeneration widely regarded as consequent on removal from
the centers of refinement, a regression or savagification which also
points to our primitive origins. The sailors' acceptance of monarchical authority after their violent and competitive failure to establish an alternative order rehearses a Hobbesian passage from
the state of nature to political society naturalized as hierarchical.
Most interesting, however, is another hitherto unnoticed redaction of the Hobbesian schema. In *The Philosophical Rudiments of
Government*, Hobbes argues that the original form of sovereignty
was maternal, based on the power the mother had over her off-
spring, and claims also that that sovereignty was lost only by men's
violent usurpation.[24] In Dryden and Davenant's *Tempest*, the specifically maternal nature of aboriginal sovereignty is emphasized by
the addition of Caliban's sister Sycorax, whose claim to the island
provides one of the crucial means by which the sailors attempt to
gain primacy. We can see Prospero's establishment of patriarchal
governance as a re-enactment of the original masculine usurpation which removes the island from the state of nature. The play
shows that civilizing patriarchal usurpation threatened by a re-
crudescence of original maternal authority, marked most distinctly
as savage, as Sycorax promiscuously confers sexual favors and political pretensions on one plebian after another, until returning to
an incestuous union with her brother.

Apart from the multiplication of characters, Dryden and
Davenant's most striking alteration of the Shakespearian text is
the increased separation of high and low plots. One effect of this is
the provision of two different versions of the colony. In the first, a
pleasurable royalist projection of unproblematic sway, Prospero's
absolute gubernatorial rule is disturbed only by the unruly desires of the colonizer himself. In the second, dystopian version
of settler society, the only authority resides in the savage hands of
Sycorax's barely human off-spring, producing a squalid competition for power among those constitutionally unfit for its exercise.
The lack of integration between the two plots and the eventual
departure of all the Europeans from the island suggest the impossibility of resolving the tensions invoked by the rehearsal of
constitutional argument in a colonial setting.

However fanciful in conception and gorgeous in production, the revised *Tempest* engaged the serious questions of sovereignty and civil identity arising from colonization. In his Preface to *The Six Days Adventure or the New Utopia*, Edward Howard argues his play also engages with a fundamental issue of "natural law" and government – the exclusion of women from political power.

What can be objected against my introducing the several commonwealths of men, and women, grounded on supposed custome, by affirming it to be novel, and consequently unallowable, the objection is not at all solid, because it is not more impossible that such a manner of rule might be practis'd, than that there were *Amazons* in one or more parts of the world, (if we will believe Authors) who had a supremacy over men, obtain'd by force of law or power, or at some time or other conferr'd on their ambition by a prevalent indulgence to that sex; or that some Countreys at this day admit of Queens as well as Kings, and perhaps it is more the authority of usage and manners, than the law of nature, which does generally incapacitate the Rule of women, there being not seldome to be found as great abilities in them (allowing for the disadvantage they have in not being suitably educated to letters,) as are to be observ'd in men of greatest comprehensions. But this is suggested not disputed here: the characters in this Play being rather made use of to confirm the judgement and practice of the world in rendering them more properly the weaker Sex, than to authorize their government; though the ambition of that Sex, as likewise the value they are apt to allow themselves, may call it a severe policy.

Howard backs away from a fully fledged rationalist critique of the "authority of usage and manners" which prevent women from assuming political power but, as he acknowledges, his play does *suggest* that it is the "judgement and practice of the world" rather than "the law of nature" that renders them the weaker sex. Perhaps it is that "suggestiveness" that led Aphra Behn to contribute a panegyric to Howard, in which she compares him favorably to Thomas More:

> This *New Utopia* rais'd by thee
> Shall stand a structure to be wonder'd at,
> And men shall say this! this is he
> Who that Poetick City did create,
> Of which *Moor* only did the Model draw
> You did compleat that little world, and gave it Law;[26]

Howard's play presents a Commonwealth in which, according to ancient law, men and women rule by turns. No-one can remember when women last reigned but all acknowledge – the men most reluctantly – that it is the female hour and a group of genteel women claim the magistracy. The female magistrates are initially divided on whether to establish monarchy, anarchy or to retain a "Republick" but settle for the last. They are petitioned by male citizens who want to retain a husbandly mastery; the ladies decide the institution of marriage will be maintained only where men are obedient, and refer all petitions for separation to the courts. The next act of the female politicians is to reform the laws of courtship, giving women the initiative, drawing up a catalogue of men fit to make love, marry or continue Platonick and referring all points of amatory difficulty to a High Court of love. If a particularly attractive man is located by the female Commissioners he will be named a "Publick lover." However, the new regime comes to a rapid end when the men present a petition proclaiming their withdrawal of amatory services and start fleeing the country. The female council disbands and, by public acclamation, the Commonwealth is replaced by a monarchy.

The representation of female government in the play reinforces the thoroughly traditional assumption that even elite women are overwhelmingly preoccupied by private – not to say sexual – concerns, and thus constitutionally unfit for public life. Far from being militantly Amazonian, their concerns are presented as exclusively erotic and domestic. Despite this profoundly conservative characterization of female nature, however, the play does suggest that all is not well in the gender order it eventually recuperates. A few virile wits aside, the utopian Commonwealth is "manned" by a series of grotesque failures in masculinity, ranging from Sir Grave Solymour, a familiar senex of Puritanical hypocrisy who has disowned his son and pursues an ingenue; to Peacock, a Narcissus who desires a wife only to beat her; Foppering, who is himself beaten by his spouse; and Orlando Curioso, who provides the ladies with beauty aids. All the domestic relations in the play are characterized in terms of control and domination, and the women's attempt to seize command, though doomed, reflects their prior experience of enforced subordination. The ladies' attempt to alter the power balance between the sexes in favor of their own gender highlights the degree to which, both informally and legally, in public and private, Englishmen had the advantage of women. Not just the reform of legal codes but the reversal of the terms of erotic encounter – which involves, for example, parading the men in a circle to assess them in a parody of the trope of beauties being displayed to the Sultan – emphasizes the conventionality of women's position as objects of the male gaze. So does the paradox with which the play concludes, whereby the wits persuade the female magistrates that they can only regain the idealized position of the courted lady – a position whose lack of real authority has been made plain – by giving up all pretensions to power.

The eventual replacement of both male and female magistracies by a monarchy is meant, I think, to signal the unnaturalness of Commonwealths and female rule both. As the nobly born Polidor puts it in the lines which close the play:

> Nature has made for men her Salique-Law
> Given Women to continue men, not govern,
> And though both Sexes here have held Republicks
> (A Usage different from all other Countreys)
> In each example we may wisely see
> No rules so good as lawful Monarchy.   (v, p. 84)

The utopian magistracy, exemplified by Sir Solymour, is presented as unfit for public office by virtue of cruelty, hypocrisy and lust, and very properly replaced by Polidor. This is hardly a surprising conclusion from a loyal royalist such as Howard and neither is the play's failure to make an "argument" for an inversion of the usual custom of the world in regard to the female exclusion from power. Nonetheless, Howard's speculation about the reforms in the gender order likely to be effected by female government reflect a high degree of awareness about the inequities women suffer and their anger at their subordination. There is nothing in the characterization or the action to suggest a yawning chasm of intelligence or judgment between the best of each sex – the women's dominance is ended because they are shown to be less willing than the men to abandon heterosexual love. Heterosexual love is only available on masculine terms: as Crispina reports to the other ladies, every "considerable person in the Commonwealth" has resolved "Not [to] receive, or make love, except we part with our power!" She is initially staunch in her rejection of this ultimatum, arguing that "for my part I should rather / Be content to starve my affection a while, than not / Maintain our rule" (v, p. 79) but the report that the men are leaving *en masse* produces a rapid change of heart. In a context in which, it has been made clear, erotic and domestic relations are the only sphere in which women have hitherto had any sense of agency or identity the coercion is successful, psychologically credible but hardly poetically just. The play's "argument" and conclusion coincide in upholding the general practice of female subordination but the text's action and characterization "suggest" the claim for equality is not without merit.

Howard was clearly interested in the topic of female domination and, in particular, the way in which the structure of heterosexual love problematized women's capacity to assume public roles. In a slightly earlier play, *The Women's Conquest,* set in Scythia, a state bordering the land of the Amazons, he presents a female ruler, Parisatis, who has absolute command as Queen but voluntarily accepts the extreme subordination to her consort enjoined by her country's law.[27] The plot counterpoints Parisatis's individual and tragic experience of marital oppression with the attempts by the Scythian women to have their lot improved and the intervention by the neighboring Amazons on Parisatis's behalf. Adopting a patient Grizel position, Parisatis protests her husband Tysmanes's cruelty but refuses to resist him:

> I dare believe
> The Law that first here gave this liberty to man
> Did tacitely imply the Husband should
> Not be a lawless Tyrant to the Wife.   (III.i, p. 40)

She flees the Court and joins the Amazons but takes no part in their conquest over Tysmanes and the Scythians. Mandana, the Amazon Queen, is merciful, and reunites a repentant Tysmanes and forgiving Parisatis and then, announcing that she too will "hold my sceptre from obedience," decides to marry Bassanes, a brave and loyal Scythian. The conclusion, which has been brought about by the successful Amazonian military action, shows the Amazons volunteering to give up their political and soldierly roles. Mandana orders her subjects to take husbands and be obedient wives:

> My Warriors, you will all take Husbands now?
> Here are men fit to match your spirits.
> . . .

And let your Conquests henceforth be to love
And give man sole supremacy
I hope our kingdoms shall unite in making
Laws may fit each Sexes duty.   (v.i, p. 79)

Parisatis's notable example of willingness to endure abuse aside,
there is little in the play's action up to this point which prepares us
for Mandana's decision. The specific law under which the Scythian
women suffer – their husband's right to divorce them instantly at
any moment – is a synecdoche for the generalized male tyranny in
domestic relations exemplified by Tysmanes. Rousing her troops
before battle, Mandana does refer to the customary assumption
that women's inferiority is "natural":

I see
You are all resolv'd, as does become
This cause I fight, by which we'll fight even Nature
To confess she was a partial Mother
To our Sex, when she made Man
First heir of Glory.   (iv.i, p. 62)

Her troops, however, are inspired by a profound sense of injustice:

Did but the Women
Of this World besides hear this, they'd be asham'd
To think they had not broke the yoke of Men.   (iv.i, p. 62)

Howard's conclusion in this play is similar – if even more arbitrary –
to that in *The Six Days Adventure*. In a contest between heterosexual
love and political power, his plays suggest, women always choose
love, despite the fact that – or in fact, perhaps, because – they
are so manifestly disadvantaged by the institutionalization of love
in courtship and marriage. The consistent emphasis in Howard's
texts on the unjust legal or conventional means by which the gender order is regulated, along with his depictions of women effective in political and military roles, among which one could include his characterization of a Boadicea-like figure in his heroic
poem *The British Princess*, suggest that, notwithstanding the conventional containment of female rebellion in his plays, it is the
rebellion which compels. The use of fantastic locales – utopian
and mythical – licensed an exploration of very local resentments
but also reflects the increasing awareness that law encodes not
the law of nature but particular customs and particular judgments.

However superior monarchy may be to Common-wealths, and men to women, it is the apparently inevitable revolutions in political and sexual institutions which emerge as the constant in these plays.

The last Restoration play of this type invokes both the desert island and the land of Amazons for a much more satiric depiction of gendered and colonial identities. Durfey's title, *A Commonwealth of Women*, might lead one to expect a heroic play about the Amazons similar to Howard's but in fact, generically, the text is an odd *mélange*, drawing on intrigue comedy as well as the voyage and utopian traditions deployed by *The Tempest*.[28] The action is divided between London and a barren island that borders the luxuriant Amazonian Country. The play begins with the hero, Captain Marine, eloping with Aminta, the daughter of Don Sebastian, former Governor of several Portuguese islands. Aminta has been brought up by the villainous French pirate La Mure, who stole all Don Sebastian's Indian treasure and forced him, his wife Roselia, and their other children Nicusa and Clarinda to take refuge on the desert island. The family is separated and while Don Sebastian and Nicusa eke out a miserable existence on the desert side of the island for sixteen years, on the other, Roselia has become protectress of the Amazonian Country. Marine and Aminta, accompanied by three wild fellows of the town who have rambled to sea to desert their wives, are also shipwrecked on the island – pursued by the villainous LeMur. Don Sebastian and Nicusa, Marine's party and LeMur all end up in the Amazons' power: the runaway husbands are put to domestic labor, Don Sebastian's family is reunited, Marine is pledged to Aminta and Roselia gives up her power as Protectress to her husband.

Like Howard's, Durfey's play explores the possibility of female government only to reject it in the end in favor of a reconstitution of traditional domestic and political arrangements. While *A Commonwealth of Women* satirizes any dream or project of sexual separatism, male or female, however, the masculine domestic irresponsibility which gives rise to specifically colonial dreams of wealth and sexual freedom is Durfey's primary target. The play divides the "salvage" island into two spaces, one a site of hard, the other soft, pastoral. The desert side, initially inhabited by Don Sebastian and Nicusa and then by Marine's confederates, is barren, a "barren island," marked by "Nothing" but "Rocks and Barrenness; Hunger and Cold" (II, p. 14). It is also, clearly, a masculine space, potentially deadly to women, for there Aminta very nearly gets eaten by the starving crew. Across the ravine is the female realm of the Amazons, lush and fruitful, a "Heavenly Place", "Elizium" as Marine puts it. It is only in the maternal space of Roselia's Protectorate that the manifold sins and mischances of the male world can be rectified. The process of reformation is completed by Roselia's voluntary resignation of power but, as with Mandana's in *The Women's Conquest*, this surrender cannot erase the effect of the preceding depiction of masculine cruelty and weakness and feminine resentment and resistance.

In the third act Roselia makes a powerful speech in defense of her sex:

> They that say Women are not fit to Govern
> Betray their weakness and their want of knowledge
> For what perfection is there in the male
> That is not in the Female; Grant, their Compound stronger,
> Their bodies coarser, and more fit for Wars
> Which some of us, do haply contradict:
> I cannot yet conceive, why this should bind us
> To be their Slaves; our Souls are made as theirs;
> And that we have hitherto forebore t'assume
> And manage thrones; I say altho' we have not
> Challeng'd a Sovereignty in Art and Arms;
> And writ ourselves Imperial, hath bin
> Mens Tyranny, and our Modesty—not defects,
> Or want of Judgement.   (III.i, pp. 23–24)

This analysis is never really challenged in the play, nor does Roselia recant. The creation of the Amazon state is presented as a rational and defensive response to the masculine selfishness which characterizes all Marine's fellow-travellers, the three wild fellows of the town. They also seek a "new world" but their dreams are grossly materialist and misogynist. In the play's second scene, Franville, Frugal and Hazard meet in a tavern and find they are all "fixt, and of one mind," resolved to "forget and despise [the] Vexatious and Impertinent Sex" (I.ii, p. 7). Franville, a peacock, resents his wife's preoccupation with her own dress, and so has "prepar'd a Wardrobe, that shall outshine the Sun in the new World, where we are going" (I.i, p. 6). Frugal claims to be deserting his spouse because he believes he is a cuckold and his wife is a scold and extravagant. In revenge, he has "put all my Plate, Money and Jewels into two Chests, and intend to seek some other Countrey; where I will live, grow rich and plant a Colony" (I.ii, p. 7). Hazard simply expresses "an Antipathy to Woman-kind" (I.ii, p. 7). When this unlovely group are deposited on the desert island, having had to throw all their prized possessions overboard, their misogyny reaches its nadir in their agreement to cannibalize Aminta. Their punishment in Amazonia aptly enough takes the form of being forced to wash, sew and spin, as they lament ever having left their wives.

All these plays conclude their explorations of alternative worlds by confirming the rectitude of extant gender and political institutions. As Tories, the dramatists share a certain suspicion of utopian dreams, whose most powerful contemporary political form theoretically was the Republican fantasy of Harrington and whose material instantiation, now that the experimentation of the mid-century was over, were the pirate commonwealths of the Caribbean and the South Seas. It is noticeable, though, that where Dryden and Davenant used a "new plantation" as a locale in which the origins of sexual and political order could be poetically rehearsed and confirmed, the utopic fancies of Howard and Durfey are nothing like so confident of the justice of the customs and practices they interrogate. It is not perhaps a coincidence that such masculine doubt coincided with the emergence of English feminism among Tory women.

AUGUSTAN AMAZONS

Carol Barash has shown recently that Anne's accession to the throne provided a fruitful context for women poets, who linked her accession to political power to their own legitimacy as authors. Unsurprisingly, these writers often invoked Amazonian imagery. These developments are not strikingly apparent in the theatre.[29] Although feisty heroines in breeches parts recur in these years, and Boadicea, the very embodiment of the British woman warrior, appeared in eponymous plays in the late 1690s, those few dramas with explicitly Amazonian heroines show little interest in exploring alternative gender and political arrangements. Amazon parallels serve instead to suggest historical precedents for a female reign marked by an extended and expensive war against a tyrannous empire: thus the fulsome Prologue to Motteux's *Thomyris* (1707) emphasizes, though disavowing, the parallel between the struggle of "a Warlike Northern Race: / Who, bless'd and free, contented with their own, / For Glory fought, and the World's Good alone" and Anna's "Genius" quelling "the World's ambitious Foe."[30] *Thomyris* is more concerned with representing the difference between the brave and liberal Scythian Court, in which royal prisoners are freely paroled, and the treacherous and oppressive Persians, who rely on fraud to gain military advantages their cowardice precludes. The opera develops a contrast between Thomyris/Anne, "Queen of the Northern World" (I, p. 3) who fights not for "greater Empire" (I, p. 3) but "for Liberty," and Cyrus the Grand / Louis XIV, "Who, luxurious, ev'n in Arms" clogs "Armies with a Female Train" (I, p. 2) and, having resigned his camp to the Scythians, leaves "Lethargic Drugs, mix'd with the gen'rous Juice" (III, p. 42) to gain victory by trickery. The opera retains a few elements of the traditional depiction of the Persians as soft and decadent but the main emphasis falls on the contrast between the liberty-loving Scythians and the slavishness of their foes. Thomyris herself is a figurehead, brokering amatory relations but in no sense serving as an emblem of specifically female power. In this text the patriotic allegory overwhelms the Amazonian vehicle.

Charles Hopkins also invokes female military leadership in *Friendship Improv'd: or, The Female Warriour*. Although Hopkins's sympathies are antithetical to Motteux's, gender reversals serve again primarily to affirm normative arrangements and to echo the high political perspective. The play is set in a Sicily usurped by Zoilus from the true heir Maherbal, Zoilus's General and ignorant of his true identity. Maherbal's bosom friend Locris is a woman educated as a man, in love with and loved by Maherbal, who understands his passion only as friendship. The play is critical of tyranny, usurpation and expansionism with proper regal and sexual identities assumed only at the close, when Zoilus's defeat is effected with Roman help and Locris resumes her female role and marries Maherbal. Hopkins had Jacobite sympathies and the play is certainly legible as a critique of the warlike William, whose particular friendship with his favorite William Bentinck was rumoured to be erotic. This potential libel is of course contained by Locris's return to femininity, as well as shadowing the royal marriage between a legitimate heir and a usurper. The play's willingness to criticize military ambition was daring but its depiction of gender relations was not.[31]

It might seem paradoxical that the periods of female rule were less productive of Amazonian and utopian dramatic fantasies than those of the rakish Stuart brothers. Arguably, it was precisely the latitude in sexual conduct fostered by the Restoration Court, along with the increasing awareness of customary differences which allowed and even provoked dramatists like Howard, Behn and Durfey to explore alternatives to extant gender arrangements. Further, the Glorious Revolution has been understood recently as a watershed in gender as well as political institutions and identities, displacing a system of succession which depended on real female bodies with a contract brokered by (masculine) political subjects.[32] William and Mary's reign, in which her greater right through inheritance was rendered subordinate to her conjugal relation to her husband, exemplified the new dispensation: Mary was wife first, and Queen second. Anne, whose husband was happy to function as consort, had considerable difficulty in mobilizing an effective iconography of Queenship, a problem not simply of ineptitude but cultural and political change.[33] If, as Catherine Belsey suggests, following Lawrence Stone, women were being redefined in terms of privacy, domesticity and maternity, the Amazon becomes a much more disturbing and alien figure than she was in the later seventeenth century, when an inherited right to female rule and power, embodied for instance in the revered Elizabeth, was assumed. In an argument later developed by Nancy Armstrong, Susan Staves goes even further, arguing that traditional forms of heroic identity, the military mode of selfhood embodied by the warrior, was being replaced by a peaceable subject, the civil, private gentleman for whom the lady was the original model.[34]

The revision of political and gender roles following '88 was further complicated by the increasing awareness of England's, shortly "Britain's," new role as an imperial power. Traditionally understanding themselves as liberty-loving defiers of tyranny, and without the quasi-hereditary claims of the Spanish or Austrian imperial houses, as we have seen the British found it difficult to articulate a coherent ideology of empire. In the last decade of the seventeenth century, however, their litotic depictions of universal monarchy, whether Ottoman, Hispanic, Persian or Macedonian, began to be supplemented by representations of the founding of the British nation in the early duel with Rome. In addition to the pamphlet wars in which England's role in a unified Britain, and Britain's global role, were debated, dramatists began structuring their plays with one of the most persistent literary tropes figuring the establishment of empire, namely, the rape of a modest woman which, revenged, consolidates the *civis*.[35] The heroines of late seventeenth-century she-tragedies were legible not only as victims of a specifically Stuart tyranny but as Lucretian sacrifices to the greater good of the emergent nation.[36] Following ancient precedent, early eighteenth-century British drama suggested that the mortal confirmation of female virtue could secure national purity and potential greatness.

SUCCESSFUL PIRATES?

A single, remarkable return to the masculinist version of a colonial utopia is identifiable in Charles Johnson's *The Successful Pyrate* published in 1713. This tragi-comedy dramatizes the extraordinary story of Captain John Avery, celebrated for having taken the Great Mogul's ship, the *Ganj-i-sawai*, in 1695, and then establishing a kingdom on Madagascar with which various European Courts established diplomatic relations.[37] As Joel Baer has remarked, there was widespread interest in such pirate commonwealths in the early eighteenth century, as commentators pondered the paradox that men (and women) who had so deliberately flouted the law of civil society should nonetheless generate their own apparently successful regulatory "economy" or "System of Government."[38] Both Defoe's *General History of the Pyrates* (1724) and the retellings of the Avery legend suggest pirates were believed to have adopted a variety of forms of government, ranging from the quasi-monarchical to the egalitarian. The Avery story, especially as dramatized by Johnson, implies that a hereditary monarchy is the natural solution to the power vacuum created by pirate rebellion against extant authority but, as Marcus Rediker makes clear, the dream of a fully democratic "Libertalia" was a much more potent aspiration among the rovers themselves.[39] The pirate utopia recorded in Defoe's *General History* was supposedly located on Madagascar, although, like its founder Captain Misson, it appears to have been fictional. Rediker argues, however, that the fully egalitarian community, devoid of religious, racial, property or class distinctions embodied in Libertalia "was a literary expression of the living traditions, practices, and dreams of an Atlantic working class."[40] While this does seem plausible, it is hardly surprising that the representation of pirate life which reached the stage reflected rather more conventionally hierarchical assumptions about the likely development of a new political society.

The Successful Pyrate depicts the possible later adventures of a Plain Dealer who has actually made good on his determination to quit London for the Indies. Like Manly, the hero Arviragus, King of the Island of St. Laurence, Laurentia or Madagascar, was a hero who "commanded a Fire-ship in the *Dutch* Wars" (1, p. 2). On his return from battle, however, he was drummed out of the Service for caning a superior officer and, again like Manly, he found "his Friend had entirely deny'd his Trust, had cheated him of his Estate, and was marry'd to his Mistress –" (1, p. 3). After these embittering experiences, Arviragus "declared War on Mankind" and "renounc'd the Rights he was born to as a Member of Society," pausing only in India when shipwrecked to marry Zelmane, an Omrah's daughter, and father a son, before proceeding to establish himself as sole monarch of Madagascar. The play interrogates the claim made early by the loyal Admiral Boreal that greatness like Arviragus's is comparable to that of other "Royal Out-laws" like Romulus who "leapt the Pale of Custom" to create a throne and empire (1, p. 3). Arviragus's claim to imperial legitimacy, always problematic by virtue of his frequently proclaimed status as a Briton, is tested and found wanting by his own weakness in the face of sexual temptation, and by the external threat posed by a group of disloyal conspirators who manipulate the pirate population's antipathy to marriage. The play closes in an interesting compromise: with the rebellion defeated and his own temptations overcome, Arviragus returns to Britain to resume his former identity. He leaves his throne, however, to his half-Indian son Aranes who is betrothed to Zaida, Aureng-Zebe's grand-daughter. Thus the renegade re-enters European, civil society, renouncing his own rebellious claims to sovereignty, but the colony he has planted is to endure, by virtue of his alliances with the most powerful local dynasties.

Like earlier masculinist utopias, *The Successful Pyrate* dramatizes questions about self-government and its relation to the origin and nature of political power. While the play's action, like that of *The Tempest* or *The Six Days Adventure*, defends legitimately constituted monarchical power, however, its particular fantasy of the colony has to incorporate much more aggressive and sophisticated indigenous and planter populations than are visible in earlier texts, and, in so doing, highlights the conflict between the drive for colonial conquest and a reverence for traditional authority. The Laurentian conspirators are not the plebian buffoons of *The Tempest* but genuinely sinister malcontents able to manipulate the crowd whose mutable loyalties first gave Arviragus power. The plebs themselves are greedy and licentious fools rather like the low characters in *The Six Days Adventure* or *The Widow Ranter*, but they are also distinctly resistant to government, both domestic and political: it is Arviragus's order that all must marry which gives the ringleaders their chance to foment rebellion.[41] While the piratical origin of the mob explains the extremity of their rebelliousness, the presentation of a restless local elite surely also adverts to the planter populations of the Caribbean islands, notorious for their verbal and physical conflict with the representatives of metropolitan power.[42]

The indigenous, here Indian, characters, are also quite distinct from the generalized figures of savagery or inversion in *The Tempest* and Amazonian plays, and in the end they, rather than any of the interloping Europeans, resume power. Aranes and Zaida are the most honorable and well-born characters in the play, with the latter boasting a truly imperial origin, as Aureng-Zebe's granddaughter. This virtue and breeding underwrites the rectitude of the hero's decision to resign his throne to Aranes. Arviragus's abdication not only suggests the impossibility of a virtuous European subject throwing off the inherited obligations (and rights) which constitute his identity as a "private Man" but also implies that sovereignty in a non-European nation properly belongs with the native rulers:

> Here I resign all Power and earthly Rule:
> The gaudy Tinsel of Ambition,
> First tempted me to leap at once the Pale
> Of all Laws Human and Divine, to reign,
> But here I lay it down– Take it, *Aranes*;
> Thou may'st without a Crime enjoy my Throne,
> That was not the foul Purchase of my Guilt,
> Altho' the Means that fixt me here were bad. (v, p. 61)

The play's conclusion, which refers to a plan to retrieve the pirates (and a good proportion of their great wealth) unsuccessfully mooted by the Marquis of Carmarthen, draws a crucial distinction between Arviragus's illegitimate power, based on outlawry and thievery, and Queen Anne's properly imperial sway, unmoved by avarice:

> BOR: With what contempt the *Brittish* Heroine view'd
> That vast Temptation, Wealth; but in *Britannia*
> Strict Justice sways alone.
> ARV: Ay, there the Goddess *Themis* rules in Person,
> She holds the equal Balance of the Globe,
> And trembling Guilt dares not approach her Throne.
>
> (v, p. 62)

Unsurprisingly, Johnson's play serves to contain the most radical political implications of pirate social organization by depicting the most famous buccaneer colony as a debased replica of metropolitan society, where the double usurpation of British and native sovereignty is finally curtailed. Much of the play's interest derives in fact from its acuity about the extent to which pirate society (and by extension plantation colonies) were of necessity imitative of European cultures but in partial, often transgressive and subversive, form. Arviragus's career raises the question of whether he is a mime of Romulus or simply an ambitious thief but *The Successful Pyrate* also focuses on pirate "justice." The "Articles" that served as the equivalent of a legal code were the mimetic dimension of pirate culture that most fascinated observers, who recognized these regulations as a version of the social contract. Johnson includes a courtroom scene which mocks what the conspirator De Sale condemns as "these silly Forms of Justice" (v, p. 55), and stands in striking contrast to the panegyric to Anne's semi-divine establishment of order over the whole "jarring World" (v, p. 62) which closes the play.[43]

Johnson's sensitivity to the peculiar importance of imitation and pretence in pirate commonwealths obviously addresses a more general curiosity visible in Defoe's collection but it has a reflexive dimension also. The Prologue suggests a dramatist as ambitious as William Davenant to transport the viewer to an exotic land, drawing attention to the illusory means by which the distant is brought near:

> Without the Toil the distant World you see,
> And view all Nature in Epitome –
> . . .
> While young remov'd to *Africk's* warmest Bed
> Transplanted Slips of the true *English* Breed.

Then – When our Musick bids the Curtain rise,
And shows the shadow'd Landskip to your Eyes,
Let powerful Fancy your weak Faith beguile,
Believe your selves in *Madagascar's* Isle.
Behold the Men and Manners of the Place,
We'll make your Passage easie cross the Seas.

The potential dangers which connected the transporting delusion of theatrical performances and the degraded pretence of pirate society are most graphically illustrated by a bizarre story from Defoe's *General History of the Pyrates*. In his account of Captain Bellamy and his crew, Defoe recounts the adventures of "a Stroler, a Fellow who had pass'd thro' a great many real as well as fictitious Scenes of Life." But "the stroling Business not answering the Greatness of his Soul (as he expressed it) he thought it more profitable to turn Collector."[44] After being captured and transported to Jamaica, he became a pirate, one of "these Marine Heroes, the Scourge of Tyrants and Avarice, and the brave Asserters of Liberty" (588). While on board, he wrote a play called *The Royal Pyrate* which was performed to great applause until a scene in which Alexander the Great, examining a pirate, declaimed "Know'st thou that Death attends thy mighty Crimes / And thou shall'st hang to Morrow Morn betimes" (588). At this point a drunken gunner, convinced his friend Jack Spinckes needed to be rescued, roused his friends and led an attack on the performers in which "Alexander" lost an arm, and a number of others were wounded. At a Court-Martial the next day, Alexander and his audience were reconciled but the play was forbidden further production.

This anecdote connects the potentially subversive activities of acting and piracy in two ways. The stroller's career argues for a continuum between performing and piracy, as each activity is shown to be motivated by a baseless and delusionary ambition; unsatisfied in the theatre, the purported "greatness of soul" segues into the more dramatic forms of criminality. The scene of performance makes the point a different way, by suggesting that the collapse into chaotic violence is an inevitable corollary of the crew's shared immersion in fantasy, whether caused by psychological disturbance (delusions of greatness), intemperance (pirates were notorious drunkards) or sheer ignorance and stupidity. Unaware of *The Royal Pyrate*'s status as an imitation (and entirely unconscious that heroic plays might even be regarded by skeptical viewers as satiric), the gunner and his comrades figure here as creatures driven not simply by unleashed appetite but by the abject irrationality which has led them to mistake their own parody of society for a utopia.

For all the condescending comedy in Defoe's recounting of this episode, the fear that theatrical representations of "Successful Pyrates" might lead to criminal careers and scenes of carnage appears to have been real. Dennis himself, horrified by what he took to be the glorification of Avery's career in Johnson's play, wrote to the Master of the Revels to protest the text's licensing, complaining it would lead "Gentlemen of the Galleries . . . to turn Robbers upon the high Seas, to plunder our Ships, and to fill our Jayls with our Merchants, and our Hospitals with their Wives and Children."[45] It seems self-evident, as Baer suggests, that Dennis mistook the play's "Moral" but the latter's angry denunciation of the fascination exerted by the representation of piratic mimicry expresses an unsurprising fear of legitimating the buccaneers' subversion of every norm of public and private life. Perhaps Dennis's fears were prescient, for the piratical ideals of race, gender and class equality, their desire to distribute property equitably and their refusal to accept a normative heterosexuality are no longer generally regarded as entirely fantastic.

CHAPTER 7

The Customs of the Country: Colonialism and Comedy

Four months before the first production of *An Evening's Love* (1668), the *London Gazette* carried news of the final ratification of a treaty between England and Spain to protect both parties from French ambitions to universal monarchy. As a consequence, Maximillian Novak suggests in his Commentary, the "general atmosphere of the play ... is coloured by foreign relations" and the processes of courtship and marriage echo the establishment of treaty arrangements between the two nations.[1] Responding to Dryden's obvious interest in developing cultural contrasts between England and Spain in this play, both Bruce Kramer and Derek Hughes have recently analyzed *An Evening's Love*'s comic depiction of the determining effects of national custom.[2] Such responsiveness to the importance of location, or what Aurelia calls "chorography," in understanding the customs and manners, institutions and practices which gave shape to human identity and conduct, in love as in empire, has not been much attended to by modern critics of Restoration comedy but was a given for Dryden's contemporaries. The shaping effects of climate and history on national manners and temperaments, not least in questions of sexuality, had been proposed by Aristotle, demonstrated by Bodin and was endlessly reiterated by popular "chorographers" such as Blome and Heylyn.[3] As manners manualist Peacham put it, "the wit, disposition, yea, devotion and strength of man followeth the qualitie and temperature of the Climate."[4] The development of literature itself was increasingly understood to be inflected by environment, so that, however much English writers borrowed from their predecessors or their foreign rivals, the end result would be transmuted into a truly English form.[5] National sensitivities, as we have seen, also enflamed rejections of what were regarded as slavish importations of alien practices such as the use of rhyme in serious drama.[6] By the last decade of the century, however, the hostility of the puritanical aside, a critical conviction of a peculiarly English national greatness in comedy had arisen, based on the climatic argument that the range of oddities in temperament observable in English plays, presumed to reflect the culture at large, arose from the unevenness of the weather, as well as the unparalleled personal liberty of English subjects.[7]

More recent critical insensitivity to the importance of location and national identity in Restoration comedy is not universal: primarily concerned with "influence," early twentieth-century critical debate was preoccupied with disentangling English drama from the debt to Molière, and John Loftis's more recent account of the "Spanish Drama" of Restoration England was concerned to demonstrate the Peninsular settings of such plays were "functional" in terms of theme and plot.[8] Peter Stallybrass's and Allon White's Bakhtinian account of literary attempts to discipline unruly zones of the London metropolis has alerted critics to the importance of place in early modern depictions of England, so that dramatic distinctions between the fashionable districts occupied by gentry and nobility, the mercantile city, the criminal haunt of Alsatia, the suburbs, the country haunts of rustic boobys and the wild Celtic peripheries might be taken more into account, not just as signifiers of status for individual characters but as a means of mapping the civil heart of the nation and its barbarous fringes.[9] Feminist critics have been sensitive to female playwrights' interest in the way foreign settings facilitated the depiction of the internal alienation of women within patriarchal culture, while Derek Hughes identifies a shift from a preoccupation with the "stranger" within, during the years 1660–88, to a concern with distinguishing external difference after '88 as a development of fundamental importance in the drama of this period as a whole.[10] Nonetheless, following attempts to define the role of "wit" in the comedy of manners (the genre of choice for most critics), the dominant critical trends in the comic drama have been a concern with sexual politics *per se*, or the refraction of class conflicts through courtship and sexual intrigue.[11]

Sexual, economic and status competition were obviously central concerns in Restoration comedy and it is not my intention to dispute their importance. Rather, I hope to broaden the extant account of the dramatic creation of identity by demonstrating the extent to which comic characterization and conflict was informed by national and colonial interests and anxieties. At the simplest level, this is a question of documenting the number of new social types appearing on stage: East Indies merchants, planters and colonial prostitutes begin to figure within comic depictions of the metropolis as resolvers of plots, providers of wealth and eccentric adopters of exotic custom. Generally benign in their effect, such characters also carried the threat of degeneration or even a collapse into savagery to which all travelers away from the centers of civility were presumed prone. Also striking is the national anxiety of Gallic influence we noted in Evelyn's *Tyrannus*, as genteel Englishmen attempted to find a style of self-presentation both cosmopolitan and not slavishly imitative, their fear being that, as Jacinta puts it in *An Evening's Love*, "your wild *English*" were "a kind of Northern Bear, that is taught its feats of activity in *Monsieurland*, and for doing 'em too lubberly, is laugh'd at all the world over" (1.ii.101–104). The delighted excoriation of the Frenchified fop allowed the English dependence on "Monsieurland" in dress, literature and manners to be acknowledged and disavowed, and the true English gentleman distinguished from affected dandies characterized by their subordination to the style of a despotic and expansionist neighbor.

A final novel comic type symptomatic of England's own expansionism was the sea-captain. Such figures, from the Plain Dealer through Captain Porpus of *Sir Barnaby Whigg* to the astoundingly successful Ben of *Love for Love*, reflect the increasing importance of the navy in English national self-definition and power, economically and militarily.[12] If, however, as many have argued, the later seventeenth century saw the replacement of the warrior as a cultural ideal by the polite, private gentleman, it is unsurprising that navy commanders were satiric butts.[13] The navy was the senior service, led by a Prince of the blood, but its ranks were divided between "gentlemen and tarpaulins." The occupation always threatened to taint, for although it was military and hence potentially glorious, the constant, often disciplinary contact with rough plebians, along with the absence of women, was also likely to degrade. As the victor of Lowestoft, James Stuart might be celebrated as a national hero, but Manly, who wielded his plain-dealing contempt for the social niceties like Indies savagery, was hardly a genteel model of masculinity, and most Restoration "Captain Porpuses" were also less than fully civil, speaking a vile sea-argot and entirely inept in their relations with women. To that extent, the comic satire on the navy seems to exemplify the recent belief that the late seventeenth century rejected the military model of virtue.

Claims that the "warrior" model of masculinity was replaced in this period by a cultural ideal of gentlemanly politeness, however, sit oddly with the evident eagerness of well-born royalists, in the years between 1660 and 1688, to gain naval commissions by demonstrations of courtliness, and the massive militarization of the nation after 1688 vital to the Irish, Scottish, continental and American campaigns which consolidated the United Kingdom and extended imperial power in the years 1689–1715. In fact, of course, one model of "social personality" did not simply replace another. J. G. A. Pocock suggests that, rather than "virtue" simply disappearing after 1700, the Harringtonian ideal of the independent patriot, with sufficient landed property to enable him to engage in public affairs and bear arms in defense of his nation, served as a longstanding challenge to the emergent vision of a commercial society, in which, *pace* Defoe, private citizens could hire mercenaries to defend the state and control government through the purse-strings.[14] Further, while political writers and moralists detected and articulated new social ideals, the theatre provided an important arena in which such ideals could be challenged, tested and ridiculed. Lawrence Klein has argued persuasively that, during the Restoration, the dominant definitions of English civility were provided both by the established Church and, more especially, by the Stuart Court, so that Shaftesbury's crucial contribution to Whiggism was to fashion a cultural politics and history which allowed politeness to supplant, or at least challenge, the older, Stuart-authorized Tory courtliness which included claims to literary and cultural authority.[15] In the comic drama before 1688, however, courtliness itself is as much a satiric butt as excessive politeness was after 1700: Dorimant mocked such manners as Mr. *Court*age, and Sir *Court*ley Nice is one of the most famous Restoration fops. As well as pitting "Honour" against "courtliness," and "politeness" against "virtue," comedies from 1660 to 1714 used forms of masculinity which signified valor to highlight the limitations of the dominant modes of civility. Thus *The Plain Dealer* plays out a tension between the rough heroic virtue of the sailor and the courtly hypocrisy required by the fashionable Town, and Shadwell's, Dennis's and Centlivre's early eighteenth-century depictions of military life all celebrate the sexual, social and military gallantry of the officers and gentlemen of William's and Anne's reformed services and mock the effeminacy of the self-consciously "polite."

Many post-'88 comedies focusing on military life do explore the differences in patriot and commercial values: the triumph of the genteel ideal of a life without occupation, supported by a good estate which specifically obviates the need for personal military service, is nowhere more acutely depicted than in Farquhar's *The Recruiting Officer*, where Plume willingly resigns his commission to settle down to a well-funded rustic affluence as a private gentleman. As is hardly surprising, however, in a nation almost continually at war over decades, the "warrior" model of virtue, however modified, is never simply replaced or satirized. A central focus of early eighteenth-century comedy is in fact the complex process by which the services themselves were reformed. Professionalization was ambiguous – it allowed the "warrior" figure to be modernized and revalorized but the incongruity in polishing those often seen as mercenaries rather than citizen-patriots, remained – thus the sea-fop's aim to create a "polite" navy in Shadwell Junior's *The Fair Quaker of Deal* (1704) is treated as more ludicrous than the drunken fraternization with his men by the fop's antithesis, the old-style "illiterate Wapineer" Commander Flipp. Shadwell also presents various new-style captains both competent and polite, patriotic and polished but, as Geoffrey Holmes points out, the very success of such new aspirants to gentility caused considerable resentment.[16] While a comedy like his later *The Humours of the Army* is satiric at the expense of the new professionalism fueled primarily by careerism and greed, the play makes it clear that the military campaigns offered a powerful means of defining the new British identity which incorporated the disparate Celtic nationalities now joining England in the United Kingdom. The comic harmonization of the internal dissension which still wracked the nation is vital to *The Humours of the Army*, while other plays like Centlivre's *The Wonder: A Woman Keeps a Secret* began to heroicize valiant North Britons. Austen's ambivalent representations of military figures a century later suggest that the conflict between admiration for successful men of war, even when conceived of as professionals, and the idealization of polite civilians who could depute the responsibilities of defense, was a constant feature of an expansionist eighteenth-century British society.

In Restoration and Augustan comic drama we see not only that (masculine) social personality but sexual relations and identities in this period were shaped to a significant and obvious degree by England's colonial expansion. East Indies merchants, fops and tarpaulins could all be understood to be uncivil by virtue of their imbrication in, or orientation towards, locations and cultures beyond fashionable London, whether Oriental, French or Oceanic, thus providing a variety of antithetical means by which a truly polite English gentleman could be defined. Along with dramatizing the highly charged contests over what constituted masculine civility, however, the comedy produced both before '88 and after also mobilized cultural distinctions to point towards a specifically English ideal of liberality and civility in conjugal and familial relations. The well-documented parallels between arbitrary power in the family and the political sphere (whether the tyranny involved was absolutist or puritanical) were regularly amplified in the comedy by reference to the even greater despotism presumed to oppress women in southern Roman Catholic countries such as Italy and Spain, and in the Islamic nations of the East, notably Turkey. Charles Sedley's *Bellamira* literalized the common analogy of female oppression and slavery, by centering the plot on the adventures of a Devonshire gentlewoman sold into West Indian slavery. The comic emphasis on the peculiar sexual and social freedom of English women became an important element in British imperial ideology, initially by confirming a sense of cultural superiority, and later, in a process which has been well documented, by linking the political and religious dimensions of the civilizing mission of empire to the reform of gender relations.[17]

RAMBLING

Presiding over the re-establishment of a refined culture of courtliness in the years after 1660 was a rambling man, or, more heroically, an Odysseus, whose vicissitudes in evading capture by Parliamentary forces sound like the stuff of intrigue comedy and whose continental peregrinations were extensive. Charles's lengthy exile, however, and the refinement it lent him, was a cultural sword that cut both ways. He had acquired polish and his modish tastes in the theatre and the visual arts provided a crucial stimulus for what Dryden famously saw as a general improvement in polite "conversation" but the notorious license of the Carolean Court saw it rapidly denounced for luxury and debauchery. Charles had been "finished" abroad but also it seemed, corrupted, thus symbolizing in the most graphic terms the danger inherent in the travel recommended as necessary for the creation of a "compleat gentleman." The courtesy books such as Peacham's which advised travel also warned against its dangers, whether of over-indulgence corporeally or by mental pollution in error or atheism.[18] Such warnings were informed in the broadest sense by the deep ambivalence in European tradition about departures from one's native land, identifiable, Anthony Pagden suggests, in the tension between the ancient antipathy to voyaging most famously voiced by Horace and the Thomist articulation of a *ius peregrinandi*.[19] Many in the English elite were aware of their own and their nation's need for refinement in the wake of the Interregnum's repression of the arts but, insofar as it involved the adoption of foreign modes most evident in travel, the process was threatening to national identity.

The ambiguous effects of travel are variously legible in Restoration comedy. A significant number of plays, especially those by Dryden, Behn and, later, Pix, use Spanish settings to explore conflicting mores, particularly those pertaining to courtship and sexual relations. Here the erotic and social mobility and aggression of the rake assumes a national cast, with the Englishmen's frank and at times forceful pursuit of women figuring a bluff manliness which stands in contrast to the tyrannical or finicky Dons. Plays like *An Evening's Love, The Rover* and *Gibraltar* literalize familiar metaphors of amorous pursuit as military conflict, piracy and treaty-making, and do so not simply to explore the aggressivity of love relations but to make a virtue of the specifically English style of frank directness. The broad erotic success of Englishmen in Spain for diplomatic or military purposes serves in contrast, however, to the effeminacy of the fop corrupted by Gallic fashion. Through the Restoration and beyond, the fop figures the deleterious effects of travel, as a fashion victim seduced and enslaved by the enchantments of French style. It is not hard to see that these different responses were expressive of the relative cultural and political confidence with which the English faced the two nations, one in alliance and decline and the other frighteningly powerful and ambitious.

An Evening's Love depicts the amatory adventures of Wildblood and Bellamy, two gentlemen in the English Ambassador's retinue presumably present in Madrid to assist in the Treaty negotiations. The action as a whole celebrates the alliance of the two nations by figuring the marriage of Wildblood and Jacinta as a treaty, with Jacinta remarking on their engagement that "The prime Articles between *Spain* and *England* are sealed" (IV.i.780–81). The play not only (notoriously) drew on Calderon's *Mock-Astrologer* but draws attention to itself as a Spanish action: as Bellamy says to Wildblood in the first scene, "we must submit to the Custom of the Country for courtship" (I.i.84), and later, when the women's foolish father is threatening them with a nunnery, he is answered by Don Lopez, who points out "the Custome of the Country, in this case Sir; 'tis either death or marriage" (v.i.429–30).[20] The text includes a good deal of apparently more incidental customary material. Wildblood's complaint about his meat links gustation to geo-politics: Spanish taste has been despoiled by their superabundance of the Indies spice:

I had a mind to eat of a Pheasant, and as soon as I got it into my mouth, I found I was chawing a limb of Cinnamon; then I went to cut a piece of Kid, and no sooner it had touch'd my lips, but it turn'd to red Pepper: at last I began to think myself another kind of *Midas*, that everything I touch'd should be turn'd to Spice. (I.i.38–43)

Bellamy's response, that "for my part, I imagin'd his Catholick Majesty had invited us to eat his *Indies*" (I.i.44), develops Wildblood's comic play on the corrupting effect of Spain's colonial wealth, hinting at the familiar metaphor of the poisoned chalice. None of these tropes is purely occasional, however: the references to Indies' wealth prefigure the Englishmen's success in grasping the sexual and monetary prizes at Spanish expense, so that Don Melchor is dismissed at the end of the play by being told that his "plate-fleet is divided; half for *Spain* and half for *England*" (v.i.559–60). The eroticizing effects of Spain's heat is predictive of the speed of the courtships, bearing out Beatrix's remark that "long tedious Courtship may be proper for cold Countries, where their Frosts are long a thawing; but Heaven be praised we live in a warm Climate" (I.ii.14–17). The Peninsula's history of ethnic intermingling enables Jacinta's testing of Wildblood, a man entranced by the exotic.

Jacinta's successful seductions in the guise of progressively more "alien" women, a Moor and then a Mulatta, seems to argue for the text's investment in notions of alliance and connection rather than the impermeability of difference. In the initial contests of wit between the cavaliers and their ladies, the Englishmen invoke both religious and ethnic slurs: unable to distinguish the dark-veiled Jacinta and Theodosia in a chapel full of other genteel worshippers, Wildblood complains "There's no knowing them, they are all Children of darkness" (1.ii.7–8), while the spurned Bellamy tells his friend that "their beautie 'tis much as the *Moores* left it; not altogether so deep a black as the true *AEthiopian*: A kind of beautie that is too civil to the onlookers to do them any mischief" (1.ii.87–90). The women fight back effectively, insulting the graceless Gallic mimicry of the English but Jacinta's disguises keep the trope of Spanish miscegenation alive, when she courts Wildblood, first as the Lady Fatyma, and then as a Mulatta. Wildblood excuses his attraction to the latter by claiming "there's something more of sin in thy colour than in ours" (IV.i.96–97), a conviction entirely belied by his own serial infidelity.

When disguised as the Mulatta, Jacinta tells Wildblood he behaves "as if you meant to o'er-run all Woman-kind: sure you aim at Universal-Monarchy" (IV.i.89–91). The pervasive language of conquest and booty, underwritten by the Englishmen's local and overall victories (beating Don Lopez for example, in a scuffle, as well as comprehensively besting Don Melchor and Don Alonzo), reframes the apparently equal-handed representation of negotiation between different nationals as an English triumph. The acquisition of Spanish women serves not only as material but cultural enrichment for the "lubbardly" Englishmen. In an early exchange, Wildblood admits as much to Jacinta: "Faith, we live in a good honest Country, where we are content with our old vices, partly because we want wit to invent more new. A Colonie of *Spaniards*, or of spiritual *Italians*, planted among us would make us much more racy" (II.i.90–93). In response, she has the politeness to make a witty acknowledgment of the prime cultural superiority the British can claim: "I hear your women live most blessedly; there's no such thing as jealousie among the Husbands; if any man has horns, he bears 'em as loftily as a Stag, and as inoffensively" (II.i.97–99). The slur on English manhood is contained, however, by the play's overall celebration of Wildblood's and Bellamy's amatory success.

Dryden's play is unusual in the dense inclusion of details of custom but the overall scenario of Englishmen engaging in triumphant sexual campaigns to appropriate Spanish women recurs, suggesting an amatory equivalent to the pervasive English piracy against Iberian shipping and possessions in the New World, a relationship hinted at by the title of Behn's *Rover.* The latter adaptation of *Thomaso* reframes the cultural contrasts dramatized by Dryden for feminist ends, strengthening the portrayal of patriarchal power notorious to Spain by framing the action as the women's last-ditch attempt to evade the nunnery and unwanted matrimony. The play emphasizes, though, the vulnerability of women to the free-booting Englishmen, coarse and appetant, as much as to the tyrannical masculine authority of Helena's brother.[21] Behn does include one proper English gallant in the form of Belmont but his practical inefficacy, compared with Wilmore's clumsy but successful forcefulness, suggests the weakness of the truly civil. Blunt, the grossest and most violent of the English milords, exemplifies Jacinta's charge of lubbardliness, being too unsophisticated to recognize a prostitute and sufficiently ungoverned to try to revenge himself on a lady. The Spanish men in this play are notably less nuanced and visible than in Dryden's: the rivals for the women's hands are almost indistinguishable, whereas Dryden's three Dons were highly individuated. These changes suggest that Behn found the Neapolitan–Spanish setting and plot useful primarily to argue the pervasiveness of masculine oppression in gender relations: in Spanish territory, the tyranny was institutional, but the impulse to dominate was as prevalent among the supposedly more liberal English.

John Dennis's *Gibraltar: or, the Spanish Adventure*, written some twenty years later during the War of the Spanish Succession, sets the amatory adventures of two English Colonels, Wilmot and Vincent, in the vicinity of the Spanish fort being attacked by the British. Preoccupied with "the Love of my dear Countrey, and the Desire of Glory,"[22] Wilmot (whose name recalls that of Behn's "Wilmore") conceives of Leonora's and Jaquelinda's seduction as a raiding party, with the women to be ravished and abandoned before the men return to the fleet. The play shows this aggressive ambition transformed into marital alliance. In keeping with their masculinist perspective, the two Colonels imagine that the greatest obstacle to their plans is the implacable tyranny of the women's uncle, Don Diego, whose Spanish jealousy they give a thoroughly Whiggish spin, with Wilmot announcing "I have observ'd in most Countreys, that the baser the Men are, and the more Slaves to one another, the more they Confine and Tyranize over the Women; whereas we, who have ourselves a due and noble Sense of Liberty, give freedom

to our Wives and our Mistresses" (i, p. 3). Vincent suggests that in
Spain women are not to be trusted with liberty, to which Witmore
replies "what signifies a Woman's being Chaste in the Flesh, if she
is a Whore in Spirit?" (i, p. 3). The action suggests that, while the
Colonels' suspicions of Spanish men as jealous and venal affecters
of honor are well founded, the women are spirited and chaste,
wanting only to find suitors capable of appreciating such virtues.

While *An Evening's Love* figured the harmonization of cultural
difference as negotiation, *Gibraltar* suffuses the sexual intrigue
with martial and political imagery. Rather like Behn's Rovers, the
Englishmen are described as "Lusty, Vigorous, Rampant Dogs"
(ii, p. 15); as "Brutal Dogs" expecting "Plunder and Petticoats"
(ii, p. 14); and as "Bloody-minded Colonels" (iii, p. 23) with plans,
Jacquelinda suggests accurately enough, "to Plunder us, Dismantle
us, and leave us to be seized on by the first Comer" (iii, p. 24). The
first exchange between the lovers rapidly exposes the mutual national suspicions but in a considerably uglier key than in Dryden's
text. Stung by the suggestion that the English displayed cowardice
at Calais, Wilmot excoriates the Spaniards, "so long inur'd to Slavery ... that Custom has made it Nature to them. And like Beasts
that are by Nature Wild, but that are brought up in Chains, they
wou'd Starve and Perish, if they were turn'd but loose, to enjoy
the Liberty of the rest of their kind" (iii, p. 25). In the verbal
sparring which follows, however, the women propose their suitors
remain with them in Spain, under their amatory sway, despite the
Englishmen's protests that their matrimonial subjection would be
coupled with the other tyrannies incident to a country with "an Inquisition and Absolute Power" (iii, p. 26). Persuaded by the ladies'
wit and beauty, however, the latter incomparably greater than that
of their "cold, Flegmatick, Dow-bake'd" countrywomen, Vincent
prepares to surrender, although Wilmot remains resolute. The
dilemma is not resolved by the intrigue which manages to dispatch
the women's uncle (the latter entirely managed by the panders
Guzman and Fourbe, a Spaniard and a Frenchman, Leonora and
Jacquelinda) but by the unexpected incursion of a victorious party
of English soldiers who presage the final conquest of Gibraltar.
The British military victory, and the swamping of Spanish territory by a rapacious English soldiery, is balanced by Vincent's and
Wilmot's both agreeing to stay in Spain as a condition of marriage,
although the apparent surrender of patriotism to love is negated

when Wilmot reveals he will be remaining with the garrison at Gibraltar.

Gibraltar represents a high-tide of triumphalism in comic depictions of Anglo-Spanish relations, with Spain figured as an "Enchanting Place" full of literal and metaphorical fruits ripe for the plucking. Wilmot and Vincent do scarcely anything to forward the plot: not only is the intrigue undertaken on their behalf by other less manly French and Spanish men, prepared to disguise themselves as women, but the main blocking agent is Wilmot himself, unwilling to settle outside England. In a "Western World" witnessing increasing British military success, the external challenges to adventuring English lovers, even those as unwitty and unresourceful as Wilmot and Vincent, melt away. When main force fails, those well-equipped with "the sinews of war" by a universal monarchy of trade can purchase amatory mercenaries to ensure their success over enemies depicted as venal, slavish, avaricious and effeminate.

The figure antithetical to the successful English rovers and men of war is the wealthy fool who has traveled for pleasure in the hopes of acquiring a distinction in taste which has eluded him at home. These Francophile fops of whom the Man of Mode, Sir Fopling Flutter, is the most famous example, are amusing but contemptible Englishmen whose complete subordination by French manners suggests a loss of self-possession whose political equivalent is slavery. The flourishing foppery of the 1670s is in fact inflected by the mounting anxiety over the King's relations with Louis and the fear of French expansionism becoming widespread in these years. Evelyn's *Tyrannus: or, The Mode* provides the most effective gloss on the anxieties generated by the English adoption of foreign costume, commenting that "when a nation is able to impose, and give laws to the habits of another ... it has (like that of Language) prov'd a Fore-runner to the spreading of their Conquests there."[23] Fops resemble Frenchmen not simply in their mimicry of costume, language and social practice but in their lack of liberty and, hence, manliness. In James Howard's *The English Mounsieur* (1674), an early version of the type called Frenchlove displays his lack of gallantry to various women of quality, his cowardice to the men, and falls into the clutches of the courtesan Mrs. Crafty, who uses his Francophilia to trap him into marriage. He is also shamed by an English tailor, who, along with a milliner, has been supplanted by French artisans. This commercial rivalry provides for a subplot in which the English craftsman establishes his superiority by brute strength, before forcing the Frenchman to sell his domestically manufactured garments to Frenchlove. The play is unusual in emphasizing the economic as well as cultural consequences of adopting Gallic modes but this mercantile rivalry, repressed in the more sophisticated examples of the type, underlies the consistent practice of demonstrating the Francophile's appetite for Parisian commodities.[24] In *The Man of Mode*, for example, Sir Fopling's intoxication with France is crisply demonstrated in his exhibition of designer goods, when, in illustration of Emilia's remark that "He wears nothing but what are originals of the most famous hands in Paris," Flutter admits with mounting excitement that his gloves are Barrot, the garniture, Le Gras, the shoes, Piccar, the periwig, Chedreux and the gloves, Orangerie.[25]

Evelyn's belief that "we need no French inventions for the Stage, or for the Back" was not universally accepted by dramatists or men of fashion but, just as Dryden believed he could appropriate and improve through Englishing foreign plays, so too the fashionable heroes of the comedy incorporate French style without being its victims. Thus on first meeting Dorimant, Fopling claims to recognize him, not as another Gallic simulacrum but as the real thing: "Dorimant, let me embrace thee, without lying I have not met with any of my acquaintance, who retain so much of Paris as thou dost, the very air thou hadst when the marquise mistook thee i' th' Tuilleries, and cried 'Hey chevalier,' and then begged thy pardon" (III.ii.170–75). Dorimant's response, both measured and caustic at the impervious Flutter's expense, suggests his own understanding of the limited if necessary role of fashion allows him to use taste to augment, rather than degrade, his manliness: "I would fain wear in fashion as long as I can, sir, 'tis a thing to be valu'd in men as well as baubles" (III.ii.176–78). Sir Fopling, on the other hand, is reduced to a "bauble" by his servitude to modishness. The fop's commodification is caused by an obsession with personal adornment which is later cast as peculiarly feminine, and certainly, for all his gallantry, Sir Fopling is an effeminate figure. It is interesting, however, that the earliest critique of the effects of luxurious consumption, characteristically figured by female dress, which accompanied the great expansion of mercantile and commercial capitalism in the late seventeenth and early eighteenth centuries, is focused on masculine rather than feminine consumption of foreign apparel.[26]

INDIES VOYAGERS

Travel to the Continent was an important component in polite education although, as we have seen, it had its dangers as well as its rewards. Voyages to the Indies, almost always undertaken for profit, were not only downright dangerous but threatening to sanity as well as civility. Dryden's contempt for those actively engaged in colonial ventures (as opposed to investing in such schemes) was shared by other Tory writers: Charles Hopkins' Prologue to his *Friendship Improv'd* suggests that, were a poet to write for the anti-theatrical "moneyed men" of the City, he might benefit materially:

> They'd fit you out, for *Ceylon*, or *Japan*,
> Teach you to Trade, and set you up a man;
> Make you grow Rich; - that's if a Poet can.
> What City-like Estates, might one procure at
> Those Golden Ports, or of *Bengale*, or *Surat*?
> None of our Tribe e're made the Voyage yet.[27]

He makes the very Tory assertion that the poet's natural alliance is with the Court, however, rather than those who grow rich by Indies voyaging: "Poets with the love of Courts are Curst." His remarks may have been aimed specifically at Peter Motteux, who would turn from dramatist and librettist to East Indies merchant but Hopkins's sense of the arts and colonial trade as antithetical activities had a broad cultural valence which seems to have crossed party lines. In the comedy, the East Indies merchant is sometimes a benevolist whose Providential appearance resolves questions of identity and provides unforeseen reserves of cash but he can also embody the fracture of civil identity and deculturation attendant on lengthy exposure to exotic, non-Western societies. Such figures not only are ludicrous but can appear threatening to the social and cultural relations of the metropolis, as the wealth they have acquired in their foreign adventures gives them the confidence to intervene in matters (like the drama) properly beyond their ken.[28]

One of the earliest examples of the East India merchant appears in John Caryll's *Sir Salomon: or, the Cautious Coxcomb* (1671), one of the many comedies inspired by Molière written in the early years of the Restoration. An adaptation of *L'Escolle des Femmes*, the play depicts a familial tyranny which has taken on the un-English color of despotism. Describing Sir Salomon's practices under the name of Evans, the young gallant Peregrine Woodland remarks that "Though I never saw the Man, yet the extravagant Economy of his Family, and his exotick way of training up this Lovely Creature sufficiently discovers to me the politick worme in his Pate."[29] Not only does Sir Salomon name and treat his servants as slaves, he attempts to bring up his ward in Oriental ignorance and enclosure. The situation is resolved by the return of her father, the East Indies merchant Barter, who removes her from Sir Salomon's authority, but the conclusion is actually stage-managed by the witty Peregrine, also newly returned home from travel on the Continent. The play closes with Wary's reminder to consider the fatigue of the travelers, underscoring the ambivalence towards travel implicit in the structure of the action. Although Peregrine tells Sir Salomon that he has returned home with a better "Relish" of his country than he had when he left it (ii, p. 26), a testimony to his judgment borne out by his skilled management of events, absences abroad like Barter's, and the adoption of "exotic" practices like Sir Salomon's, are shown to cause havoc in native domestic and social relations.

Crowne's *Sir Courtly Nice* provides a much fuller depiction, or rather caricature, of the Indies merchant, in Crack's magnificent impersonation of "Sir Thomas Calico," the supposed son of an East India Company President whose madness requires he be attended "like a great *Indian Mandarine*."[30] Like *Sir Salomon*, *Sir Courtly Nice* depicts a range of divergences from properly English manners. The crazed antics of the supposed Sir Calico are on a continuum of eccentricities which include Hothead's and Testimony's political and religious bigotry as well as Sir Courtly Nice's effeminized delicacy and Lord Bellguard's mania for female enclosure. The latter's thoroughly un-English desire to keep his sister and his future wife from enjoying the liberty habitual to ladies of their nation gives a specifically local cast to the Spanish plot on which the action is based, and Crack's use of an Orientalized disguise, which not only facilitates Leonora's escape but enables him to make caustic remarks about Bellguard's "polygamy," seems poetically apt, as the invocation of one fantastic form of the "exotic" drives out another.

Bellguard's enthusiasm for enclosure structures the plot, and provides the most serious, if not the most extreme, threat to habitual practices. As he himself acknowledges in act iv, in a proviso scene with an overtly political edge: "This I confess is the English dialect; and when I talk of Governing Women, I talk of a thing not understood by our Nation. I admire how it came about, that we who are of all Nations, the most wise and free in other respects, shou'd be the only Slaves and Fools to Women" (IV. 27–31). Violante responds to his proposals for wifely containment by picking up his reference to slavery and comparing the kind of relationship he suggests to indentured service in the American plantations:

Let no Woman marry a Man o' your humour, but she that for her Crimes is condemn'd to Transportation. The Slave that in *Virginia* toyls to plant her Lord Tobacco, is not more miserable, than she that in your bosome Labours to plant a good opinion; both drudge for smoke. I scorn the slavery, nor will marry a King to increase his Dominions, but to share 'em. (IV. 70–76)

This invocation of colonial servitude in the Western plantations serves as one geo-political marker of incivility and oppression while the world conjured up by Crack/Calico figures another. "Calico," who claims to have been bewitched by a "nauseous Indian baggage" (III, 479), is utterly averse to the sex and accuses Bellguard of keeping a harem like the King of Bantam or the Mogul (v. 39–44). His extreme misogyny, supposedly a function of Oriental enchantment, serves to suggest the delusory nature of Bellguard's own dream of female enclosure. Calico's disruptive presence, however, does more than underline the fantastic and exotic nature of Bellguard's oppression of women. Calico embodies all the psychological, social and cultural disruption potential in residence in the colonies. His distraction, he claims, was caused by magic but his conduct suggests he has been thoroughly "Indianized." He first appears "ridiculously drest, attended by Men in the Habits of *Siamites*, and *Bantammers*" (III. 454–55). His speech is affected, mimicking "oriental" forms of expression and misusing English words, with his acknowledging: "Pox on't I have been so long abroad, I have almost forgot my Mother tongue" (IV. 496–97). He compares Indies scenes and objects favorably to England's, identifying with the former (IV. 480–95), and the most potent forms of authority he recognizes are those of the Eastern rulers at whose pleasure the English merchants sat in their factories to trade: when Bellguard comes to search his rooms, he treats it as an invasion of capitulated territory: "How? the high and glorious Emperour o' *Siam* with all his guards? Thou most invincible *Paducco, Farucco, nelmocadin – bobbekin – bow – wow – wow –* why dost thou seek to destroy us *English,* seated on thy Dominions by thy own Letters Patent?" (v, 118–22). In creating Calico, Crack uses a compendium of Indianized markers of identity – costume, manners, language and acknowledgment of political authority – to create a model of the alienation potential in colonial adventuring.

"Calico" is exploded but the cultural anxieties and dreams of fantastic wealth he embodied were real. In *The Biter*, published some thirty years later, Nicholas Rowe created an East India Merchant, Sir Timothy Tallapoy, who is "a great affecter of Chinese customs."[31] By 1705, the East Indies trade had expanded exponentially, with tea, china and Chinese fabrics important elements of English domestic consumption and onward commerce. Chinoiserie first became voguish under William and Mary, who imported the Dutch enthusiasm for Chinese ware, while men of taste such as Sir William Temple created a fashion for Chinese landscape design. Temple was also involved in the active scholarly debate about the antiquity of Chinese culture. Sir Timothy is the focus of a comprehensive satire on the varied forms of Sinophilia, as well as exemplifying the dangers of deculturation. Having "got his Estate by the *China* Trade in the *East-Indies*" we are told, he "grew so fantastically fond of the Manners, Language, Habit and every thing that relates to those People, that he prefers 'em not only before those of his own Country, but all the World beside."[32] Tallapoy's enthusiasm mocks learned as well as modish Sinophiles: in conversation with Mariana, parodying Sir William Temple's conviction as to the age of the Chinese language, he tells her that "Arts began with them – It is thought the necessary Sciences of Eating and Drinking were discover'd some Ages among them, before they were known in *Europe* . . . The whole Oeconomy of the Beard was treated of Seven Thousand Years ago by a learned *Chinese* Philosopher, in Fifteen Volumes" (III, p. 59).

Tallapoy's affectations are amusing but the play also suggests they have grimmer implications. He is first depicted imprisoning another man's servant in his cellar for damaging his pagoda; running his household with the brutal absolutism of a Chinese potentate, he threatens the hapless Grumble with "Two Hundred and Seventy odd Blows on his Belly, Three Hundred on his Breech, and Four Hundred and Twenty-Nine on the Soles of his Feet" (II, p. 25). Later he puts Grumble's master Pinch in the cellar also. His treatment of his daughter is equally despotic and his plans for his own future are fantastic, as he plans to marry Mariana, and "engender a Male Off-Spring, who shall drink nothing but the

Divine Liquor Tea, and eat nothing but Oriental Rice, and be brought up after the Institutions of the most excellent *Confucius*" (II, p. 27–28). Tallapoy's cultural conversion to the authoritarian manners of the Chinese has not only brutalized his relations with his family, his servants and his peers but suggests madness. The play ends with his threatening to "take Post for the *East-Indies* and never converse with Man, Woman or Child again, on this side of the Cape of *Good-hope*" (III, p. 65). Like Malvolio's, his costume signals an alienation from his society which is also a kind of self-alienation, rendering all relations proper to his position impossible.

These plays suggest the Oriental mimicry of Englishmen long resident in the East Indies threatened to undermine national and civil identity to the point of madness. Representations of colonials in, from or intending to depart for the Western plantations are quite different: instead of adopting alien manners, such characters often embody the worst kinds of metropolitan vice. The plantations were presumed to allow dangerous moral and political tendencies to flourish relatively unchecked by traditional forms of authority.[33] This process is especially noticeable in the fullest comic depiction of plantation life, Behn's *The Widdow Ranter* (1689), which displays a topsy-turvy world where all proper social and sexual hierarchy has been disrupted, as the scum of Newgate assume judicial and political authority for which they are manifestly unfit. Almost without exception, Restoration plays imply the Western colonies are the last refuge of the scoundrel, bearing out the view of historian David Ogg that "In a sense, all the American colonies, other than New England, were penal settlements."[34] The misogynistic three ramblers of Durfey's *A Commonwealth of Women* all plan to "seek some other Countrey ... grow rich and plant a Colony" (1.ii) for the basest of reasons, as does *Sir Barnaby Whigg*'s blunt tarpaulin Captain Porpus, who intends to carry his jolly crew of whores to "Conquer some flourishing Island, where I will plant a Colony, live out my days merrily, and defie the Devil and Fortune."[35] Nahum Tate's adaptation of Jonson's *Eastward Ho* as *Cuckold's Haven* (1685) reiterates this logic, as the impecunious and cozening Sir Petronell Flash and the debauched servant Quicksilver seduce various city wives and set sail for America with their ill-gotten gains. Sir Charles Sedley's *Bellamira* shows Jamaican mores infecting London, as a gentlewoman, kidnapped, enslaved and sold on in the Caribbean and then brought back to England, is raped by her lover in the supposed security of her protectress's home.

Tate's *Cuckold's Haven* explores the dubious motivations of those involved in colonial adventuring. His would-be colonists are licentious, mercenary and incompetent, so the project, unsurprisingly, founders, with the Virginian party shipwrecked before they even clear the Thames. Even trade is treated skeptically in this play, not simply because its practitioners are low but because it is shown to be so risky, as Quicksilver's dismissal of ships as "tennis-balls for the Winds to play withal" is borne out by the failure of Petronell's expedition.[36] The farce is concerned with debunking apparently antithetical forms of fantasy about the possibility of creating new lives and identities, whether in the colonies or the counties. Sir Petronell, Quicksilver, Captain Seagull and the oppressed city-wives Mrs. Bramble and Mrs. Security all mistakenly imagine the Indies will render them wealthy and free, while Girtred, Alderman Touchstone's affected daughter, dreams that her marriage to Petronell will transport her to an elevated social sphere in the country far from her mercantile origins in the City. The utterly utopic nature of such beliefs is best expressed by Seagull's claim to his sailors that, in the Indies, there are "Vast endless mines: for so much red copper as I carry thither, I shall have thrice the weight in Gold. They hinge their doors with it, and barr their Windows" (II, p. 23). The play seasons its demonstration of the follies of believing a change of location will transform one's place in the world with the suggestion that internal or domestic reform is the only way of achieving satisfaction.

Tate's play represents the colonies as a focus for escapist fantasies by debauched and impecunious metropolitans; by contrast, Sedley's *Bellamira* dramatizes the socially disruptive and corrupting effects of the western plantations on England itself. Bellamira herself is an attractive, if rapacious, prostitute "well-known at *Jamaica*," come to London for yet more "Power and Plenty,"[37] who uses her lover Keepwell to accumulate a vast store of exotic commodities including Indian stuffs and hangings, china and slaves. Although his friend Merrymen deplores her domination of Keepwell, Bellamira's successful reinvention in, and exploitation of, the metropolis is not treated unsympathetically, primarily because she tries to protect and succour the innocent and virtuous gentlewoman Isabella, who was a slave in Jamaica in her mother's house before being sold on.

The contrasting female characters figure the antithetical identities for women being shaped in the colonies, neither of which is admirable. As Wycherley's Epistle Dedicatory to *The Plain Dealer* suggests, "our Plantations, are propagated by the least nice Women," convicted felons or slaves.[38] While Bellamira, often referred to with images of conquest and empire, is full of resource and energy, Isabella is depicted as melancholy and passive. The latter's story, a tragic tale of kidnapping, enslavement in Bellamira's mother's household, and sale by the latter's wicked uncle to Bellamira's lustful admirer Dangerfield, depicts the novel extension of female oppression created by colonial slavery. Despite her passivity, Isabella has shown a Clarissa-like fortitude in resisting Dangerfield's attempts at rape: "if at any time he offered to be rude, I held a Dagger to my Breast, and vow'd to kill myself" (III.i, p. 18), while, when the knife was taken from her, she successfully convinced him that she would starve herself to death. All Isabella's fortitude, however, is not proof against the violent advances of Lionel, her brother Eustace's best friend, who insinuates himself into Bellamira's house in the guise of eunuch, and rapes her. Isabella's ravishing, made not only possible but seemingly inevitable by her status as a slave, is "repaired" by her marriage to Lionel, which also allows her to resume her genteel status.

Despite her love for Lionel, the marriage, and the conclusion to the play, remain ambiguous: although Lionel compares Isabella to Lucrece, Bellamira herself tells Eustace that she is "asham'd to offer her thus stain'd and sulli'd" (v.i, p. 59). Meredith tells Bellamira that "in the matter of women, we are all in the State of Nature, every man's hand against every man" (III.i, p. 33) but the homosocial bonding between the men in the play is strong while female vulnerability to lawless male appetite is marked. In this context, Isabella's slavery does not so much exemplify as amplify masculine brutality. While the institution has stripped her of parents, country and the "honour" which comprised both status and virtue, Lionel, who has raped his own wife, has also been dishonored. Isabella's situation highlights the way the female slave's vulnerability functions repeatedly as a provocation to a violence which degrades the actor as well as the victim. The play thus dramatizes that mutual degradation of slave-owner and slave central to the institution and noted by Hume many years later:

The remains which are found of domestic slavery, in the American colonies, and among some European nations, would never surely create a desire of rendering it more universal. The little humanity, commonly observed in persons, accustomed, from their infancy, to exercise so great an authority over their fellow-creatures, and to trample upon human-nature, were sufficient alone to disgust us with that unbounded domination. Nor can a more probable reason be assigned to the severe, I might say barbarous, manners of ancient times, than the practice of domestic slavery; by which every man of rank was rendered a petty tyrant, and educated amidst the flattery, submission and low debasement of his slaves.[39]

Bellamira suggests the corrupting institution of slavery was a violence inflicted on England from without: that kidnappers raid the counties and export their human cargo to the Western colonies, from which slaves and slave-owners return to contaminate the social and sexual relations of the metropolis. This disavowal of the practice was hardly surprising, given that slavery was an institution utterly at odds with the one of the most fundamental tenets of British ideology, a belief in the unique degree of liberty enjoyed by all English subjects. The ambivalent tenor of the conclusion, however, is symptomatic of an uneasy sense that England's plantation-derived wealth was not without its corrupting consequences. It is unsurprising that Tory dramatists were particularly critical of the effects of colonial expansion, their patrons' enthusiastic investment in the trading companies notwithstanding. Colonial trade and settlement not only created wealth (and hence power) for those of dubious social provenance but also created societies in which radical political and commercial imperatives were presumed to threaten traditional forms of authority. The fullest depiction of such a society is found in Behn's tragi-comic *The Widdow Ranter*, first staged in 1689.[40]

Montague Summers suggests the only source of Behn's play is *Strange News from Virginia being a full and true account of the Life and Death of Nathanial Bacon esq.* (1677). As Janet Todd points out, however, there are a number of points of resemblance between the play and *The Beginning, Progress and Conclusion of Bacon's Rebellion in Virginia in the Years 1675 & 1676.*[41] The latter text features a notably timorous and unconsciously comic narrator unwillingly forced into public life, quite evidently as ill equipped for office as any of Behn's "Justices of the Peace, and very great Cowards":

Col. Spencer being my neighbour and intimate friend, and a prevalent member in the councill I pray'd him to intreat the govern'r we might be dissolved, for that was my first and shoud be my last going astray from my wonted sphere of merchandize and other my private concernments into the dark and slippery meanders of court embarrassments, he told me the govern'r had not (then) determined his intention, but he wou'd move his hono'r about itt, and in 2 or 3 dayes we were dissolved, which I was most heartily glad of, because of my getting loose againe from being hampered amongst those pernicious entanglem'ts in the labyrinths and snares of state ambiguities, and which untill then I had not seen the practice nor the dangers of.[42]

Moreover, while Summers claims that the Bacon–Semernia love plot is entirely Behn's invention, *Beginning, Progress and Conclusion* contains a lengthy description of an Indian Queen, ally to the British, who is reputed to have had a liaison with an English "Colonel":

Our comittee being sat, the Queen of *Pamunky* (descended from *Oppechankenough* a former Emperor of *Virginia*) was introduced, who en-tred the chamber with a comportment gracefull to admiration, ... thus with grave courtlike gestures and a majestick air in her face, she walk'd up our long room to the lower end of the table, where after a few intreaties she sat down; th'interpreter and her son standing by her on either side as they had walked up, our chairman asked her what men she woud lend us for guides in the wilderness and to assist us against our enemy Indians, she spake to th'interpreter to inform her what the chairman said, (tho' we believed she understood him) he told us she bid him ask her son to whom the *English* tongue was familiar, and who was reputed the son of an *English* colonel, yet neither woud he speak to or seem to understand the chairman but th'interpreter told us, he referred all to his mother, who being againe urged she after a little musing with an earnest passionate countenance as if tears were ready to gush out and a fervent sort of ex-pression made a harangue about a quarter of an hour often, interlacing (with a high shrill voice and vehement passion) these words "*Tatapatamoi Chepiack*, i.e. *Tatapatamoi* dead Coll. Hill being next me, shook his head, I ask'd him what was the matter, he told me all she said was too true to our shame, and that his father was generall in that battle, where diverse years before *Tatapatamoi* her husband had led a hundred of his *Indians* in help to th' *English* against our former enemy *Indians*, and was there slaine with most of his men; for which no compensation (at all) has been to that day rendered to her wherewith she now upbraided us.[43]

The majesty of her deportment and the lament for her people's betrayal are echoed in Behn's characterization of the Indian King and Queen. Finally, the appendix of this account links Bacon to

"a wealthy widow who kept a large house of publick entertainm't.
unto which resorted those of the best quality."[44] This is Hazard's
rather than the hero's fate in *The Widdow Ranter* but a common
element all the same.

Behn's reshaping of the source material is complex and best
understood in the context of a brief account of the historical
episode which she dramatized.[45] In 1674, the English colonists in
Maryland abandoned their traditional allies the Susquehannock
to make peace with the Sevesa. The Susquehannock were subse-
quently pushed back to the upper borders of Virginia, where over-
crowding produced attacks on colonists by Doeg Indians. Early in
1675 a planter was killed, and Governor Berkely ordered and then
cancelled a punitive expedition against the Doeg. This increased
the unpopularity of a Governor who was regarded as favoring a
small group of Council Members, leaving freemen and the county
magistracy discontented. In 1676 Bacon, himself a well-connected
and wealthy Council Member, led a vigilante group against the
friendly Pamunkey Indians. Berkely, who seems to have avoided
conflict with Indians where possible, was furious, but focused on
trying to win greater popular support by extending the franchise
to all freemen. Bacon's support continued to grow, however, and
in an extraordinary scene the rebel confronted the Governor, demanding a commission from the latter who suggested their conflict would be best resolved by hand-to-hand single combat. Bacon
refused the offer and got his commission but Berkely revoked it
almost immediately, whereupon Bacon, now in command of most
of Virginia, exacted oaths from his followers, and let them loose
to loot loyalists, massacre Pamunkeys and burn Jamestown, before
dying of a "Bloody Flux." The rebellion ended with his death, well
before the arrival of English troops and a new Governor in January
1677. The two crucial changes Behn makes to the source material are her inclusion of a comic subplot which has as its focus
the inversions of traditional class and gender hierarchies in colonial society and her representation of Bacon as a thoroughly heroic
figure whose nobility links him to the doomed but aristocratic Indians. The aggressive sexual energy of the Widow Ranter and the
cowardly connivings of the ineffectual council members and magistrates Timorous, Dunce and Dullard (set against the bravery of
Hazard, Daring and Friendly) are the focus of the comic plot, and
Bacon's love for and military conflict with the Indian King and
Queen form the substance of the high action.

Behn's rewriting of the history of the rebellion itself minimizes the tensions discussed in the pamphlets between the settler populace and an unpopular Governor whose grip on the fur trade was as widely resented as his failure to attack local Indian tribes, and his "forwardness avarice and French despotick methods,"[46] and emphasizes the venality of the Council members.[47] Virginia was in fact the most highly stratified colonial society in North America but Behn's satire on incompetent upstart officials reflected a widespread metropolitan contempt, especially strong in royalists, for the members of aggressively independent legislative assemblies.[48] Her heroicized account of Bacon, who stands in contrast to the "cowards," picks up on the Roman tropes consistently invoked by contemporary pamphleteers: C. H. Cotton for instance wrote in reply to his wife's account of "Our Late Troubles":

The same moment that saw *Ceaser* cheife Man in the senate, beheld him in a worss condition then the meanest slave in Rome; and in less than 6 howers *Phoebus* ey'd the *Marquis* of *Ancrey*, in the midst of his Rustling traine of servitures, not onely streameing out his blood, but spurn'd and drag'd up and down the dirtie streets of Paris, by the worst of mecanicks. It is but the tother day that I did see N. B. in the condition of a Tratour, to be tryed for his life; who but a few days before was judged the most accomplish'd Gen: man, in *Verginia* to serve his King and countrey, at the councell Table, or to put a stop to the insolencies of the Heathen, and the next day rais'd to his dignities againe.[49]

A poem lamenting Bacon's death compared him to Cato, and, in both panegyrics and excoriations, his relation to the Caesars, patriots or traitors, is constantly at issue. In Behn's dramatization, the hero compares himself to Hannibal: "Come, my good Poison, like that of *Hannibal*, Long I have born a noble Remedy for all the ills of life," a parallel whose moral he spells out himself, instructing his followers: "Now while you are Victors, make a peace with the *English* Council, and never let Ambition, – Love, – or Interest, make you forget, as I have done, your Duty and Allegiance."[50] Behn's attempts to recuperate the incompetent gubernatorial rule of Berkely and excoriate the upstart councillors are interestingly at odds with her exploitation of the heroicizing tropes which governed contemporary representations of Bacon: it seems curious that a play presumably written by a loyal royalist in 1688 should be so sympathetic to a rebel. However, if one sees her revision of Virginian history as inflected by a wishful attempt to justify the

"French despotick methods" of the deposed Stuart monarchs by pointing to the chaos engendered by their absence through an evocation of a society without a strong leader and governed by "loose vagrant people," then her celebration of the nobility personified by both the Indians and Bacon himself begins to make sense.

The Widdow Ranter does have a specifically metropolitan reference but its comic energy and the pathos of Bacon's relations with Semernia and Cavernio, the Queen and Indian King, are functions of its specifically colonial subject. Like Dryden's *Amboyna*, the text satirizes contemptible settlers and ennobles an indigenous aristocrat but, having a martial hero of genteel status rather than a passive company servant, the play's mixed mode is much more successful. The comic plot encompasses the quotidian desires and conflicts of genteel adventurers and upstart planters, framing, but only briefly impinging on, the tragic action which is mostly quite separate. In consequence, the doomed world of the Indians, entered only by Bacon, who is also marked for death, can be represented with an elegiac pathos informed also by Behn's nostalgia for the fading order of the Stuarts.

The "new world" of settlers we see in Virginia is a topsy-turvy society in which rogues and "transported criminals" have assumed an improper power, as Friendly makes clear to his newly arrived friend Hazard in the first scene: "This country wants nothing but to be peopled with a well-born race, to make it one of the best colonies in the world; but for want of a Governor we are ruled by a Council, some of whom have been perhaps transported criminals, who having acquired great Estates are now become your Honour and Right Worshipful, and possess all Places of Authority" (I.i). Despite the contempt for such upstarts, however, the Widow Ranter is presented with considerable sympathy, even though her name marks her out as potentially subversive, not only because widows, sexually knowledgeable and economically independent, represented a threat to the gender order but because "Ranter" suggests one of the most radical sects to emerge during the Civil War. Thus she literally embodies the metropolitan suspicion that colonies not only were places where those of ill repute could disguise their degenerate origins but were also rife with religious and political subversives.[51] The hard-drinking, tobacco-smoking, breeches-wearing, man-chasing Ranter, however, is eventually reintegrated into traditional structures through her marriage to the genteel

Daring. In the comic plot, the attraction of Virginian women (Ranter, Chrisante, Mrs. Surelove) to well-born English gentlemen (Hazard, Daring, Friendly) ensures that the colony's wealth and power passes to a "well-born race" rather than being concentrated in the hands of the upstart councilmen. However, while the play celebrates the restoration of social order in the colonies, the text also bears evidence of the cost involved to the native inhabitants of Virginia.

The description of the Pamunkey Queen cited above, with its emphasis on "comportment gracefull to admiration," "grave courtlike gestures" and "majestick air" mobilizes tropes of native nobility which also inform the representation of Cavernio and Semernia. The Latinized names of the King and Queen and the emphasis on the pagan quality of their Court rituals suggest that in Behn's text the native figures as an anachronism, a remnant of past glory: unlike Bacon the Indians are not simply compared to Roman figures, but instead are fully characterized as noble primitives. Behn may have known of the christening of two Wampanoag chiefs as Phillip and Alexander, after the martial but rough Macedonians, but her mythicization of the Indian goes beyond mere nomenclature. Imbued with aristocratic ideals which the sordid settler society manifestly lacks, preoccupied with mourning the loss of a golden world and engaged in a hopeless struggle against impossible odds, the heroicized representation of the Indians works to suggest that the Indians are already cut off from history, sutured from the quotidian moment, the present so forcefully evoked in the play's comic action. The comic plot settles the future of the colony while the tragedy laments its past: "For your part, Sir," says the Indian King to Bacon,

you've been so noble, that I repent the fatal Difference that makes us meet in Arms. Yet tho I'm young, I'm sensible of Injuries; and oft I've heard my Grandsire say, that we were Monarchs once of all this spacious world, till you, an unknown people, landing here, distress'd and min'd by destructive storms, abusing all our charitable hospitality, usurp'd our Right, and made your Friends your slaves. (II.i. 11–14)

While the comic action concludes in betrothals which secure the position of the gentlemen adventurers, the tragedy's romance plot ends in Bacon killing the thing he loves. Semernia's passion for Bacon implies the same surrender of territory and cultural integrity as Ysabinda's to Towerson in Dryden's *Amboyna*, or Cydaria's to

Cortez in *The Indian Emperor*: "Take all our Kingdoms – make our People Slaves, and let me fall beneath your conquering Sword: but never let me hear you talk again, or gaze upon your Eyes.–" (II.i.147–48). The single combat between Cavernio and Bacon which secures Virginia for the English similarly elides the land and the Queen: "You, Sir," says the King, "first taught me how to use a Sword, which heretofore has served me with Success: But no – 'tis for *Semernia* that it draws, a Prize more valued than my Kingdom, Sir" (IV.ii. 30–33). When Bacon orders a free passage for his rival, Daring's and Fearless's amazement expresses the conventional wisdom of pragmatic victors standing in contrast to Bacon's "Romantick" bond with the defeated Indians. The final turn of the plot, however, when the General accidentally kills Semernia, brings the logic of native destruction that governs the interaction between the two groups to a conclusion, as Bacon kills her "who would not hurt thee to regain my Kingdom–" (v.ii).

Behn's nostalgic evocation of the nobility of the native Americans is no proto-liberal representation of imperial excess: *The Widdow Ranter* also exploits the exoticism of its setting to the hilt, introducing a large Indian temple, strange rites and "Negroes" doing the Highland fling. The text clearly endorses the order imposed by Colonel Wellmen and the future which awaits the colony. The play does, however, bear traces of an awareness that just as the Stuarts were passing into history, so too certain modes of heroic representation, in which the colonizer and colonized figured in equally "Romantick" terms, as similar and assimilable human subjects, were becoming less and less viable as vehicles for figuring the interaction of Europeans and Indians. The ennobling classical tropologies would serve more and more to mark off the archaism of the "Indian" while the colonizer adopted and was figured in the prosaic terms of a Crusoe, a Cotton, a Hazard or a Timorous.

SEA-DOGS AND SOLDIERS

The primary means by which the English established, appropriated and defended their colonies and trade-routes was the navy: the army was seen as an essentially alien force of Stuart, Cromwellian, Williamite and Hanoverian construction.[52] The central political, economic and military role played by the senior service has been thoroughly documented but, as Jeremy Black has remarked, the navy's persistent mythicization in English and British culture has never been systematically examined.[53] Steven Pincus and others have shown that political actors of the Restoration and the late seventeenth century were in no doubt about its importance.[54] The Marquis of Halifax prefaced his contribution to yet another controversy over the "gentlemen and tarpalins," given urgency by the prospect of a French invasion, by a classic articulation of the reasons for the blue water policy to which a strong navy was vital: "I will make no other introduction to the following discourse, than the importance of our being strong at Sea, as it was ever very great, so in our present Circumstances it is grown to bee much greater; whereas formerly, our Force in Shipping contributed to our Trade, now it is become indispensibly necessary to our very Being."[55]

Evidence of the importance of the navy permeates representations of the monarchy: Howard Erskine-Hill has drawn attention to the special role of an entertainment outside East India House during Charles II's 1661 Royal Entry, which used Father Thames and three "sailors" to celebrate England's naval power, and Durfey praised William's victories in 1691 with a *Pindarick Ode on the Royal Navy*.[56] We have noted the importance of James's status as Lord High Admiral in Dryden's celebration of heroic virtue but the most obvious place to find representations of naval officers is the comic drama. There are a plethora of sailors in Restoration and Augustan comedy, most of them satiric butts. The seamen seen on the stage appear, for the most part, to exhibit the manners of "tarpaulins" rather than those of the gentlemanly officers. As J. D. Davies explains in his recent study, the Restoration navy was the scene of considerable controversy over the relative virtues of these two components of the officer cadre.[57] The navy inherited by Charles II was very much a Cromwellian creation, so there was a political motive to the later Stuarts' interest in replacing the tarpaulins with men of cavalier loyalties, especially if such appointments could help repay the financial losses incurred by royalists through sequestration. Nonetheless, the policy was criticized, even by such a loyal servant as Pepys, as it was widely believed those who served as "volunteers" with a King's Letter (rather than entering as cabin boys) were not only incompetent but licentious – hard drinkers, great swearers, whoremongers and effeminate dressers who corrupted the other officers.[58] Although Pepys's introduction of a Lieutenant's examination and the ability of the navy to hold its own in the Second and Third Dutch Wars, as well as winning a decisive victory against the French fleet in 1692, argued for naval competence, the issue of the relative capacities of gentlemen and "wapineers" remained charged well into the first decade of the eighteenth century.

The most complex dramatization of these tensions in the Restoration is Wycherley's *Plain Dealer*. Manly is clearly a gentleman: the tarpaulins were largely excluded from the lucrative convoy service and would have had difficulty in acquiring the kind of capital required for carrying valuable cargoes, as he does. His possession of a "volunteer" also argues his gentility, as such youths were themselves genteel, and the proliferation of boys serving as pages was an on-going scandal. Even more tellingly, one Captain O'Brien, who gained his commission as a result of his dancing prettily at Court, took a woman on board disguised as a volunteer, and kept her in his cabin by passing her off as a kinsman. As a cross-dressing volunteer, Fidelia Gray had antecedents other than Viola of *Twelfth Night* and *Cymbeline*'s Imogene/Fidele.[59]

Among literary historians Manly's characterization is generally agreed to emerge from the humors tradition, with a Theophrastian "Blunt Man" his ultimate origin, but critical opinion about his satiric role, morally, socially and politically has been much contested. Part of his resonance for a Restoration audience surely lay in his recognizability as a very specific type, the naval officer eager to make his fortune through "good voyages" to the Indies, obsessed with his own and his nation's honor. Manly, however, also embodied the wider social tensions which gave rise to and accompanied the rise of professionalism in governmental and military functions as English trade and territory expanded. Like all naval officers, whether gentlemen or tarpaulins, he is driven both by avarice and by ambition, qualities which, as we have seen, were generally viewed as contradictory. Naval service was potentially a proving ground of valor but the reality was that most who entered the service desperately needed to make money: almost by definition, naval officers lacked the capital to live as landed gentlemen, and only the most successful would make enough to purchase a country estate at the end of their career. To make such fortunes, in fact, the "gentlemen" (who engrossed the lucrative voyages) acted as merchants, carrying cargoes of dubious legality. So while the navy might seem to offer both fortune and fame, it turned warriors into traders in conditions of service which were seen as lowering:

The sea can never be a trade for a nobleman or courtier, because it is impossible for him to live so in it, but that his conversation and company and diet and clothes must all be common with the meanest seaman, and his greatest trust too, while his other companions of his own sort are but troubles to him and no use. Nor can he be neat and nice to make love in the fashion, when he comes among the ladies.[60]

Despite such views, however, aristocratic and genteel families continued to send uncapitalized sons into the navy. Gradually, while retaining the traditional claims to honor provided by military action, the modernized and professionalized service lost its "tarpaulin" character.[61] Emphasizing virtue rather than lucre, Halifax was to conclude that naval service was a needful way of repairing threatened gentility:

In plain English, Men of quality in their severall degrees must either restore themselves to a better opinion both for morality and diligence, or else *Quality* itselfe will bee in danger of being extinguished. The Originall Gentleman is almost lost. In strictnesse, when Posterity doth not still further adorne, by their own vertue, the Scutcheon their Ancestours first got for them by their Meritt, they deserve the penalty of being deprived of it.[62]

Wycherley's depiction of Manly's vicissitudes depicts the tensions surrounding the emergence of a professional military identity, in a context in which "honour" can be dismissed as obsolete and "civility" depends on inherited wealth and leisure. The Plain Dealer has made money through voyaging but he is manifestly lacking in "courtliness." Like a tarpaulin, he regards his bluntness as an emblem of virtue but, to observers, his voyaging has rendered him uncivil, fit only for the savage Indies to which he plans to decamp. Olivia's dismissal of him, aided by Novel and Plausible, invokes the whole gamut of sea-slurs. She complains she will "be pester'd again with his Sea-love, have my Alcove smell like a Cabin, my Chamber perfum'd with his Tarpaulin Brandenburgh, and hear volleys of Brandy sighs"[63] while Novel complains of the roughness of "sea-raillery" (II.i.543) and is contemptuous of his appearance – "'Gad, these Sea-Captains make nothing of dressing" (II.i.565), a theme Olivia develops: "Then, that noble, Lyon-like Mein of yours, that Soldier-like weather-beaten complexion, and that manly roughness of your voice, how can they otherwise than charm us Women, who hate Effeminacy!" (II.i.590–93). His sullenness, his rage and his

social position are all indicted (II.i.657–61) but the most interesting insults refer to his courage, a quality Olivia and her intimates
hold in utter contempt. Manly, Novel suggests, "has been these two
years pretending to a wooden Leg, which he wou'd take from Fortune as kindly as the Staff of a Marshall of *France*, and rather read
his name in a Gazette – ," "Than in the Entail of a good Estate"
(II.i.499–502), finishes Olivia – while being "ambitious of losing
their arms" and "Looking like a pair of compasses" (II.i.506–507)
is also mocked.

The hostility to honor and to "warrior" virtue, and the preference
for landed property and courtliness among Olivia's acquaintances,
could hardly be more marked. Manly views the denizens of such
a society as savages: "I rather choose to go where honest, downright Barbarity is professed; where men devour one another like
generous, hungry Lyons and Tygers, not like Crocodiles; where
they think the Devil white, of our complexion, and I am already so
far an *Indian*" (I.i.595–98), but it is hard to say that the play as a
whole endorses his view. Olivia, Vernish, Novel *et al.* are clearly corrupt but Manly's alternative, retirement to the Indies after making
money out of a convoy, is not only unsuccessful but voluntarily abandoned when Fidelia reconciles him to life in England. Marriage to
Fidelia brings Manly precisely the "good estate" to which Olivia
suggests he is indifferent, so that he ends by abandoning his naval
identity for that of a landed gentleman, while his belated recognition of Fidelia's value (which includes, of course, her property in
Yorkshire) suggests that his previous obsession with the Indies, to
which he hoped to transport Olivia, was as chimerical as his first
love. In keeping with other Restoration comic representations,
life in the Indies is only ever figured negatively, in terms of can-
nibalism, sati or polygamy (I.i.542–46), suggesting that Manly's
settlement there would signify a degree of alienation close to
madness, comparable perhaps to that suffered by the crazed Calico
and Tallapoy.

Wycherley's play may have been so persistently successful and
admired in the Restoration because its depiction of the tension
between "honour" and "courtliness," and the related conflict between the need for money and the desire to maintain genteel status, is elaborated by means of the concrete and detailed example
of professional life provided by naval service. Most other Restoration plays which include sea-captains elide the distinction between

gentlemen and tarpaulins, treating them as the latter: completely without sympathy for the new route to financial independence offered by professional careers in naval and colonial affairs, they submerge the man in his occupation. Without the money provided through inheritance or marriage, earning their living in the degrading proximity to sailors, the Sea-gulls and Porpuses lose any claim on genteel or civil identity. In many instances, they are even described as cannibals, the *ne plus ultra* of savagery. "What a damn'd Canibal-Rogue is this?" (III.iii, p. 32) asks Sir Walter Wiseacre of *Sir Barnaby Whigg*'s Captain Porpus.

After 1688, with the Nine Years War (1689–97) being followed by the War of the Spanish Succession (1702–12), the representation of the services alters, as the armed forces become both more prominent and more professional. Like Wycherley, who served against the Dutch, Farquhar was a military man, and *The Recruiting Officer* of 1706 echoes *The Plain Dealer*'s love-intrigue, both by using Plume's lover Silvia, disguised as a man, to pursue another woman and by using the romance to extricate the hero from a military career. These structural similarities aside, however, the dynamic and tone of the plays are very different. Although much of Plume's activity in recruiting involves chicanery, he delegates most such action to his Sergeant Kite, and attracts no odium for these activities. Content with the esteem in which he is held as a soldier but mindful of the advantages of a quiet life, in terms which echo Olivia's, he abandons the army for a good estate at the end of the play with no apparent regrets: "Why then, I have sav'd my Legs and Arms, and lost my Liberty; secure from Wounds, I'm prepar'd for the Gout; farewell Subsistence and welcome Taxes."[64] There is nothing of the financial and psychological intensity of *The Plain Dealer*: no dream of another, better world, or wish to evade one's own home counties. Accepted as a gentleman by the Shropshire natives, Plume exhibits none of the aggression which in Manly suggests a defensive projection of the contempt attracted by his "amphibious" status, half-genteel, half-tar.

In his two service plays, rather than representing officers in society, Charles Shadwell depicts the interior workings of the navy and the army respectively, as they undergo modernization. *The Fair Quaker of Deal*'s characterization of naval officers is especially interesting, as Shadwell presents a series of types ranging from Commodore Flipp, "a most illiterate Wapineer-Tar" who "hates the Gentlemen of the Navy, gets drunk with his Boat's Crew, and values himself upon [his] Brutal Management"; through Worthy and Sir Charles Pleasant, both gentlemen of the navy, and "gentleman of honour" and "man of quality" respectively; to Mizen, a "finical sea-Fop, a mighty Reformer of the Navy" who "keeps a visiting-Day, and is Flipp's opposite."[65] In *The Fair Quaker*, the anxieties about status, money and identity so prominent in *The Plain Dealer* are refigured and disavowed. The gentility of the "Gentlemen" of the navy, evident in their civil conduct, freedom from sea-cant and sexual success, is underscored by their friendship with characters like Rovewell, "a Gentleman of Fortune, and a true Lover of the Officers of the Navy"(1). Flipp's drunken brutality emphasizes their civility, while Mizen's effeminacy highlights their manliness. Mizen's mission, to render the navy "polite," is evidently unnecessary: with officers like Worthy and Pleasant, the navy is already substantially reformed. Flipp, picking up the references to lost limbs initiated by Olivia, mourns the old regime – "Oh! It was not so in the *Dutch* Wars, then we valu'd ourselves upon Wooden Legs, and Stumps of Arms, and fought as if Heaven and Earth were coming together" (I.i, p. 15) – but Mizen's aim, that "by the time I am made an Admiral, I doubt not of bringing every Sailor in the Navy to be more polite than most of our Country Gentlemen" (I.i, p. 19), suggests that the new cultural ideal may have its own limitations. The sea-fop is effeminate, modeling himself on women's scandal-mongering and luxurious consumption: "we imitate the ladies as near we can" in laughing at the Navy Board and the Victualling Office, while decorating his cabin with wainscoting, china, *India* and *Japan* and looking glass (I.i, p. 17). The caricature of "politeness" in Mizen is comparable to the many Restoration jibes at "courtliness" in characters like Dorimant/Cortage, Sir Courtly Nice and *The Plain Dealer*'s Lord Plausible. New ideals of "social personality" or manners were continually tested in the comedy against the continuing benchmarks provided by the manliness of officers and rakes.

The Fair Quaker suggests that the navy is as manly and as civil as need be, its survivals and its reformers notwithstanding. Shadwell's *The Humours of the Army* (1713), written after service in the Peninsular campaign, also shows a modern force with disparate and contending elements, successfully unified by a competent and honorable commander. In *The Humours of the Army*, however, internal dispute arises not from conflicts between different classes of soldiers but from the diversity of nationalities in the new "British" army. The commanding officer Brigadier Bloodmore is of course an Englishman, as is the hero, Captain Wildish, and his friends Hearty and Fox; regimental disunity arises from the incessant quarrels between Colonel Hyland, a North Briton, and Majors Cadwallader (a Welshman) and Outside (Irish). The Prologue underlines Shadwell's interest in dramatizing the effects of national differences within the forces:

> You see a Foreign Camp in Drury-Lane.
> His Characters of several Nations are
> Such, as when joyn'd, compose the Gross of War.
> The Varying Humours of the differing Breed,
> Display which *British* is, which *Irish* seed;
> Which sprung on this side, which beyond the *Tweed*.
> The Accent, Manner, Wit and Breeding shew,
> In what kind Clime the youthful Plant did grow;
> And though Transplanting can't affect the Root,
> The softer Earth improves, or Spoyls, the Fruit:
> Yet not so far, but to discerning Eyes;
> Some inbred Mark betrays its genial Rise
> For *Britain's* Sons, by their Fore-Fathers led,
> To neighbring Realms, in diff'ring Manners bred;
> Some tincture of the Foreign Soil they have,
> But still retain to be by Nation brave.
> Howe'er in private Contests they cabal,
> Shew 'em a Foe, you'll sing 'em *Britain's* all:
> All Toils, all Hazards, they'll united dare,
> They'll bravely conquer, and as bravely spare.[66]

The characterization of the three Celts extends to their accents but not much further: all three share an irritable national pride and all three are equally poverty-stricken and mercenary, seeing the army solely as a means of improving their miserable financial circumstances. The Englishmen consistently stand aside from or seal up the dissension but do not escape stricture entirely. Wildish's marriage to the heroine is nearly derailed by her parents' insistence that she marry Bisket, a Lisbon merchant who supplies the regiment. Their enthusiasm for the marriage arises from their fear that, as the regiment is a new one, it will be disbanded quickly with the coming peace, and Bloodmore's financial investment in the commission will not be recouped, leaving the family in poverty. By including the Bloodmores, Shadwell's satire on the monetary motivation of the new officer-corps appears to make no distinction between nationalities; except for the fact that Wildish and his friends are animated by ambition rather than avarice. The gallantry of Wildish, Hearty and Fox notwithstanding, the play's depiction of military greed and dissension stands rather at odds with the uplift of the Prologue, with the caustic assessment of Celtic participation in Britain's wars suggesting the glue holding the Union together was economic rather than patriotic. Here the satire on national manners joins a Patriot critique of mercenaries.

FROZEN LOVERS OF LUKE-WARM ENGLAND?

When Victoria Bloodmore agrees to marry Bisket and "bury myself in this monument of your own choosing" (III.ii, p. 30), she provides a vivid projection of the dismal life to come as the wife of a Lisbon merchant, in which she will: "Dine with my Book-Keeper, and *New-Foundland* chaplain; know how to buy a bargain of Stock-Fish; Go on board an *India-Man* and beg coffee and calicoes" and "Be pen'd up in all the sultry weather in a *Quinto* of my own; where none but the Worshipful Wretch my Husband, and a Portugese Gardiner must come near me" (III.ii, p. 30). Like almost all other female characters in Restoration and early eighteenth-century comedy, Victoria regards life as a London lady as the standard of civility, pleasure and liberty, compared to which rustic, provincial, foreign or colonial residence is more or less inferior. This conviction depended on and contributed to a growing belief both in the superiority of metropolitan existence and in the peculiar advantages of the position of Englishwomen. As plays set in Spain demonstrate, the English would concede the beauty, wit and amorousness of Latin women but they deplored their perceived oppression, the domestic and sexual or private correlate to the despotic political order of southern nations. In Dryden and Dennis, the traditional comic action in which young men release young women from the blocking agency of patriarchal power is reinflected in nationalist terms, as English heroes enter Spanish society as female liberators. Other dramatists used Spanish or Italian settings to explore even more extreme categories of sexual tyranny, with Francis Fane and Aphra Behn exploiting the traditional Venetian and Spanish conflict with the Turks to highlight the arbitrary nature of extant orderings of gender relations beyond Europe, while, after '88, Whiggish dramatists like Pix and Centlivre returned to the Peninsular locales popularized by war, to reiterate the virtues of British freedom in courtship and conjugality.

Fane's *Love in the Dark* (1675) presents a Venice inflected by various previous playwrights, with *Volpone*'s Sir Politick Wouldbe a model for Intriguo, a hint of *Othello* in the heroic outsider Sforza's pursuit of the Doge's daughter Parhelia, and a Portian strain in Trivultio's plea for mercy rather than strict judgment in the court-room scene of the final Act.[67] Fane, however, invests the secretive and arbitrary oligarchy depicted by earlier dramatists with more re-cent historical and political color by underlining the Venetian con-flicts with the Turks and the Spanish. As the play opens, the naval hero Sforza, a native of Milan, is being made a Gentleman of Venice for his "exemplary service last year, against the Turks in *Candia*; where he slew two *Bassas* with his own hands" (I, p. 2) – Bassas whom he later faces in ghostly form to test his constancy (III, pp. 51–52). Intriguo's servant Circumstantio habitually swears by his Grand-father's presence "at Lepanto" (V, p. 87), another famous naval battle; and in trying the eloping lovers for treason at the end of the play, the Senators are convulsed by fears of a Spanish plot, pursuant to the Emperor's plans for "Universal Monarchy" (V, p. 78).

The invocation of these long-standing military and political conflicts invites the viewer to see a parallel between the paranoid suspicion of state-treachery among the Venetian oligarchs and the domestic anxieties of Venice's jealous husbands and fathers. In public matters, xenophobia threatens justice and pushes the state towards arbitrary tyranny while, in individual households, the same irrational fear of outsiders and of domestic betrayal produces de-spotic conduct which mirrors that of the Venetians' enemies. Cor-nanti, "an old, jealous Senator," attempts to mimic the Ottoman practice of keeping his wife from all men except African eunuchs, by attempting to buy an African slave as guard. "My Husband fears no Devils but your White ones" says Bellinganna his wife to her gal-lant Trivultio, "therefore for the security of his Person, he has just now sent out his servant *Jacomo*, to buy a Negro Slave" (II, p. 17), a plan foiled by Bellinganna and another admirer, the incompa-rably incompetent Intriguo. Having been cured of jealousy, though, Cornanti revels in fantasies of amorous excess which shade into primitive polygamy, articulating precisely the rapacious appetite he so fears in others, and which fuels his desire to keep his wife captive: "I have a Project, that every one of these Women shall bear me two Male Children at a birth every year: so that about twenty years hence, I shall be able to bring every year a fresh Army of Sixteen hundred thousand fighting Men into the Field, out of my own Loyns, boy. The old Patrirchs were Asses to me: poor, inpotent broken-belly'd Fumblers" (IV, p. 66). Cornanti's dreams are ended appropriately, by imprisonment and Trivultio's judgment that he resume his former role as usurious senator, laying aside the gallant. The xenophobic prejudices of the Procurator Grimani are defeated by his daughter's betrothal to the Milanese Visconti while the latter is still disguised as an absurd Frenchman, and his countryman Sforza wins the Doge's daughter. "'Twas never a good World, since there were so many Blakamoors and *Frenchmen* in the Nation" (II, p. 35) Circumstantio complains, but the play suggests the Venetians will benefit from the increase in sociability and liberality conferred by exogamy. Trivultio, a rambling rake who regards marriage as imprisonment, criticizes the Venetian *penchant* for female enclosure:

> I hate to see our Mistresses at grates
> Look like the coop'd Chickens pining for their Meat,
> Or like poor Prisoners, begging for an Alms
> And Lovers in the street, like helpless friends,
> Who may uncharitably entertain 'em
> With a discourse of their miseries,
> But will not lend a farthing to their Purse.   (II, pp. 19–20)

The wrongful domestic imprisonment suffered by Bellinganna has its public counterpart in Intriguo's and Trivultio's later incarceration in prison, both examples of the arbitrary and excessive oppression of the over-suspicious Venetian state.

Although all ends well, *Love in the Dark* uses its Venetian setting to provide a negative exemplar of domestic and political tyranny against which the English (who recognized parallels with the Italian city-state's history of marine greatness and her struggle for autonomy) were implicitly defined as free and liberal, uncorrupted by Oriental excesses. In *The False Count*, Behn turns to Spain, another location associated with arbitrary government in home and nation, to castigate forced marriage and improper social aspiration. Like her own characters, however, Behn uses the traditional associations of Spain and Turkey with despotism and cruelty in sexual relations, strategically. The most oppressive *senex* in the play is the very

English, jumped-up cobbler Francisco, who has rather implausibly moved to the Peninsula because "in the Humour of Jealousy," he could "even [outdo] the *Spaniards*."[68] Francisco is a "Brute," who attempts to render his well-born wife equally degraded: "my Wife's my slave" (1.ii. 142), he emphasizes, "I scorn my wife should be Civil" (1.ii.125–26). Francisco finally surrenders control of Julia, whom he has kept, as she complains, "more like a Prisoner than a Wife" (1.ii.5–6) but only because he sees her as damaged goods, a "Chattel" which he is free to discard. Although Francisco is roundly humiliated, because Julia is handed over to her lover Don Carlos as a debauched married woman, the lovers' eventual union seems fraught and ambiguous.

Moreover, despite the contrasts in age, breeding and attractiveness between Francisco and Carlos, both men exploit national customs oppressive to women to get control of Julia. By pretending to be the Sultan, one of whose ships has supposedly taken the party prisoner, Carlos is able to imprison and then cuckold Francisco, with his own consent. The imposture plays on the merchant's ignorance, unable to distinguish between a country estate in Spain and the summer seraglio of the Sultan. Behn also uses Turkish tropes, to titillate and amuse, with Don Carlos the Sultan signalling his choice of partner by handkerchief, and "mutes" placing strings to Francisco's throat. While the ruse works a certain poetic justice on Francisco, it also forces Julia into Carlos's hands in a manner which leaves her little room to negotiate her own future. As with *The Rover*, the play eschews any easy implicit or explicit distinction between English and comparatively more severe gender regimes. Although the play acknowledges, and indeed exploits, distinctions between Ottoman, Spanish and English custom, the masculine impulse to dominate appears in each, modified only perhaps by civility, a quality which the well-bred of any nation may share. Behn's feminism thus allows her to cast a characteristically cold eye on English presumptions as to the superior gender order of her own country.

In Behn's plays, her hostility to the brutish impulse to domestic domination she thought particularly noticeable in ill-bred plebians and merchants overrides national distinctions in civility. Other dramatists, including Pix and Centlivre, were more nationalistic, using foreign locales, Oriental and continental mimics and boorish colonials to celebrate the free and liberal customs of the English, especially in courtship and marriage, vital indices of "political" freedom *per se*. This aggrandizement of English manners was informed, as we have seen, by external political and economic rivalries and conflicts as British commercial and colonial expansion came up against Spanish, Dutch, French, Ottoman and "Indies" power. As the "lubbardly" English expanded their navy, their trade, their territorial possessions and their ambitions, the comic drama, as well as serious plays, provided and tested new models of the peculiarly English civility, the moral and social forms of personality, which underwrote and justified the success of such projects. At the same time, however, the comedy recorded and processed the often disturbing rise of new men (and a few new women), perceived to be making their fortunes and reputations at the expense of landed proprietors, through military service and colonial trade. The occasional depiction of planters, or persons long resident in the Indies, confirmed suspicions that the new wealth generated by colonial trade and settlement was tainted, having savagified or crazed its possessors, and threatening to infect the metropolis itself. Whether courtly or polite, however valiant they have proved in naval or military service, the heroes of Restoration plays mostly still end by opting for Olivia's "good estate" at home. Although they were enthusiastic consumers of exotic commodities from sugar to china, and eager investors in colonial ventures, profound ambivalence towards trade remained among the social elite. As that enthusiastic propagandist of "Navigation and Commerce" John Evelyn expressed it, "the most illustrious Nations have esteem'd to gain by Traffick and Commerce incompatible with *Noblesse*" and the comic stage generally declined, in this period at least, to suggest otherwise.[69]

CHAPTER 8

Romans and Britons

Late seventeenth-century Englishmen regarded the Ottoman and the Spanish polities as the most immediate approximations of universal monarchy, although they feared the aspirations of the Dutch and the French to global mastery, whether through marine power and commerce in the first instance, or more traditional territorial and dynastic aggrandizement in the second. In depicting and analyzing these ambitious states, whether in philosophical discourse or in dramatic representation, English commentators and playwrights quite naturally drew on the pre-eminent European model of empire, that of the Romans, the pervasiveness of whose inheritance in the development of early modern imperial ideology in Spain, France and England has been described recently by Anthony Pagden. Other recent scholarship has drawn attention to the peculiarly modern dimensions of seventeenth-century conceptions of empire, with Steven Pincus in particular demonstrating the new awareness of the importance of sea-power and colonial commerce in the establishment of global dominance. Although the English defined themselves through the figure of litotes *against* such aspirations to *imperium* as defenders of liberty, their traditional blue water policies put them in a particularly good position to develop an oceanic empire, which they undertook with vigor and considerable success between 1660 and 1688. The Royalist ideology encoded in masques, Royal Entries and panegyric figured the Stuarts as the monarchs of the sea but there was sufficient broad-based investment in the expansion of trade after 1660 to render the expansion (and celebration) of naval and commercial power relatively uncontroversial, a rare context for the harmonization of usually jarring interests in the Restoration. Royalist and Tory writers did at times deplore the nation's mercantile expansionism as a degraded pursuit of avarice but articulations of imperial ambition were almost always either litotic, or identified with past marine triumphs.

In the years after 1688, however, many Englishmen became more conscious and more confident of their own potential as an imperial power. This awareness, and the literature it fostered, has long been recognized in the naming of the period as "Augustan" both by contemporaries and by modern literary historians. While Augustan parallels were traditionally a significant element in the English celebration of monarchy, as Howard Erskine-Hill has demonstrated, the broader elite identification with Roman greatness after 1688 is a crucial marker in the development of British imperial identity.[1] Identification with Rome was hardly novel: the legend of Aeneas's great-grandson Brutus's founding of the nation was an important strand in mediaeval and early modern myths of British origin, and Elizabethans such as Camden regarded the English as post-Conquest genetic descendants of the Romans.[2] Roman parallels were also central to seventeenth-century political discourse beyond the Court. As has been amply documented, the classical–republican analysis of the English struggle against the Stuarts depended on identifying the latter with the oppressive rule of the Kings from whose tyranny the Republic freed itself, as well as the despotic rule of the Emperors which threatened the balance of the constitution.[3] Both before and after the Glorious Revolution, it is not hard to find classical–republican argument dramatized.

The precise nature of the elite British perspective on the Romans after 1688 is, however, much contested. Howard Weinbrot's recent study, *Britannia's Issue* (1993), argues that from the seventeenth century on, anti-Roman sentiment critical of the empire's genocidal colonial aggression, hostility to trade, debauchery and paganism swelled, as the English began to define their own commercial, Christian *pax Britannica* against the bloody *pax Romana.*[4] Philip Ayres, however, stresses the way classical–republican ideas, shorn of their anti-monarchalism, were adopted by an oligarchy eager to defend the Revolution Settlement of '88; and that, while Rome under the Kings, or under the Emperors, might have attracted opprobrium, no-one attacked the early Republic. In his account, the nation's imperial expansion encouraged the identification in both positive and negative aspects, with the British increasingly confident that their empire would surpass the Roman while the decline and fall of the earlier state served as a continual rhetorical resource for those wishing to warn against complacency and corruption.[5] In part, the difference between these two perspectives turns on their sources and the groups whose views they articulate: Weinbrot's extensive citation of Defoe privileges a mercantilist perspective, while Ayres is primarily concerned with the ideology of the aristocratic oligarchy. The divergence in these accounts highlights the ideological differences of the early eighteenth-century participants in debates over the nation and its expansion.

Like political and economic writing, the theatre between 1660 and 1714 presents a variety of perspectives on the Roman Republic and Empire, from Tory celebrations of Augustan absolutism to classical–republican critiques of tyranny. In addition to the allegorical uses of parallels, however, Roman history offered an unsurpassed context in which to examine the process by which an imperial state emerged from a *civis*, expanded, grew mighty and fell into corruption and dissolution. The specifically theatrical attractions of Rome's frequently lurid history were not lessened because ancient historiography emphasized that crises and transformations in states were generally triggered or accompanied by sexual crimes: Restoration dramatists fully exploited the opportunities to display violence, especially sexual violence, provided by classical subjects.[6] After 1688 English playwrights continued to present Roman episodes, unsurprisingly focusing quite obsessively on the Lucretian themes which implicitly justified the nation's own recent deposition of a ruler regarded as tyrannous, and whose defeat was presumed (or hoped) to usher in a new era of civic virtue. William's wars, continued under Anne, also offered fruitful opportunities for increasingly self-confident identifications with expansionist Rome: as Dennis proclaimed in his Prologue to *Appius and Virginia*, to an audience increasingly habituated to such pronouncements, "Yes, all the *Roman Spirit* lives in you"; "While *Britain* fought like *Rome*, like *Scipio*, *Marlborough* led"; "And *British* Acts, these *Roman* Scenes inspir'd."[7] Dennis's *Liberty Asserted* also provided the first dramatic articulation of the doctrine of *patrocinium*, an understanding of empire not as *imperium*, or unified centralized rule, but as a federation of semi-autonomous states. As David Armitage has demonstrated, this originally Cromwellian adaptation of Roman imperial thought was to reappear in Whig defenses of empire at various points throughout the eighteenth century.[8]

After '88, however, dramatists also began, for the first time since the Restoration, to depict episodes drawn from the shared history of the Romans and Britons, along with scenes from the early English past. These plays, two of which focus on Boadicea, whose resistance to invasion is habitually ascribed to her fury at her daughters' rapes by Romans, mark a new stage in English self-confidence, as the nation's own historical relation to Rome is examined.[9] These texts present and negotiate the kind of tensions inherent in the affiliation with (and against) Rome noted above. The plays are loyal to the English conviction of their unique position as defenders of liberty, by showing the ancient Britons as victims of precisely the kind of sexual violence which traditionally licensed resistance to tyranny, but they also reveal a strong identification with the civilizing mission of the Romans.[10] The contradiction implied here is resolved through Boadicea's scapegoating, with her military failures blamed on her intemperate and unwomanly violence and lack of judgment. The plays thus re-enact a narrative familiar from other dramatic and philosophical contexts, in which a barbarous, because female-dominated, polity is "properly" reconstituted through masculine violence.[11] Following the Boadicean dramas of Romanization, in the years just before and after the unification with Scotland in 1707, plays appeared which focused on the early history of the British Isles, with the conversion of Saxon Kings a favored topic. The dramatization of early English history followed on from the late seventeenth-century scholarly investigations of Anglo-Saxon, which reflected a growing conviction in the cultural value of the indigenous past, as well as the long-standing political investment in the period which gave rise to the ancient constitution and England's famed "Liberty."[12] Thus George Powell's *Bonduca: or, the British Heroine* appeared in 1696, followed by Charles Hopkins's *Boadicea* a year later, while 1697 also saw the production of *Brutus of Alba; or, Augusta's Triumph*. In 1701, *Love's Victim: or, The Queen of Wales* appeared, followed in 1707 by Rowe's *The Royal Convert*, set in Kent about ten years after the Saxon invasion, and Aaron Hill's *Elfrid: or, the Fair Inconstant* (1710). Delariviere Manley returned to the conversion theme with *Lucius, the First Christian King of Britain* in 1717. Britain's origins, as well as her imperial exploits in the Western world, were being thoroughly canvassed to define, and celebrate, the reconstituted nation in her new incarnation of global greatness.

GLORIES INTERR'D

Between 1660 and 1688, theatrical depictions of triumphant episodes in English history were few and far between. Although articulated in 1692, Halifax's location of English greatness in her marine power and the eschewal of land-conquests still helps to explain the paucity of British themes in the Restoration: the Plantagenet campaigns in France were rather exceptions to the rule of English defiance against the encroaching Popish masters of the universe. The imperial iconography employed to legitimate later Stuart rule reflects this special emphasis on marine power, and includes an expansionist strain. Erskine-Hill argues that "What almost certainly established the Augustan parallel with Charles II in the imagination of educated Londoners was the series of ceremonial arches erected for the King's ceremonial passage from London to Westminster for his coronation in 1661."[13] Central to these events was an entertainment at East India House, before the second Naval Arch at Cornhill, which celebrated English naval and commercial power. Such panegyrics were widespread: Dryden's reiteration of this figuration of Carolean rule as an era of peace and wealth generated by naval supremacy in *Annus Mirabilis* is the best-known literary example and needs no rehearsal here. Evelyn's *Navigation and Commerce* (1674), written well into Charles's reign during the taxing period of the Third Dutch War, is another classic statement in a discursive mode. Evelyn argues the civilizing effects of navigation and commerce, emphasizing that their virtue lies in more than the production of wealth, as they allow men "to visit strange, and distant lands; to People, Cultivate, and Civilize, un-inhabited and Barbarous Regions." His praise of Charles's support reiterates the political and territorial as well as economic benefits of a blue water policy:

Our Glorious Monarch . . . by whose Influence alone . . . such a Trade has been Reviv'd, and Carried on, and such a Fleet, and Strength at Sea to protect it, as never this Nation had a greater, nor any other of past Ages approach'd: Witness, you three mighty Neighbours, at Once, taught to submit to him! For the blessings of Navigation, and visiting distant Climes, does not stop at Traffick only; but it enables us likewise with means to defend what our honest Industry has gotten; and if Necessity and Justice require; with inlarging our Domains too.[14]

Navigation was one arena in which even the most die-hard Ancient (such as Temple) would admit modern superiority, and, as a new form of heroism and learning in which the English could claim excellence, it served as a crucial prop in national and royal self-representation. Acutely conscious, as Evelyn puts it, that "the most illustrious Nations have esteem'd the gain by Traffick and Commerce incompatible with *Noblesse*: Not, for being Enemies to Trade, but because they esteemed it an ignoble way of Gain, *Quaestus Omnis indecorus Patribus* {Lib. I. Dec. 3} Saies Livy, and were all for Conquest and Sword," the modern superiority in voyaging was nonetheless used as a means of asserting superiority over the Romans.[15] Thus Ogilby began his translation of *An Embassy from the East-India Company of the United Provinces, to the ... Emperor of China* (1669) with a comparison of Roman and recent European travel much in favor of the latter:

Inclinations no less vigorous hath of late been observ'd in *Europe*, but with more success; when not being bounded by the *Herculean* bars, past so far through (till then) the unmeasured *Atlantick*, that they lighted upon a new World, a flourishing *Hesperides*, Regions where Sands were Gold, Earth Plate, and Rivers Silver, a Paradice extending to the *Arctick* and *Antartick* Circles, which several other Countries and Islands that reach almost the utmost latitude of either Poles, out-shining all the Fables of Antiquity, and boldest Tales of their Poetick dreams; so that the Ancients are not to stand in any Competition with our Modern Discoverers, who found out in less than one Century more than they in their many thousand years.[16]

It is unsurprising, therefore, that, when making one of the few attempts to produce a heroic play on an English theme, the (probably) unperformed *Edgar*, Rymer larded his love-intrigue with references to Edgar's fleet and English naval power. The play was dedicated to the King, and attempted, rather unusually, to establish the continuity of Anglo-Saxon and Stuart monarchy via their shared *imperium* over the seas:

> Great Sir, whose throne amidst the Waters set,
> O're all design'd by God and Nature Great,
> Here, in that fam'd, long-wish't, unheard-of Spot:
> Stedfast on which, planting your Royall Foot,
> You turn the Other World, you give it Law,
> You Arbitrate, and all its Motions awe.
> This Honour was to *England* early pay'd;
> And thus Your great *Fore-runner, Edgar* sway'd.[17]

Presumably inspired by Ravenscroft's *King Edgar and Alfreda* (1677), Rymer reworks the material to invest the play with the patriotism he thought sadly lacking in other serious plays: as the *Advertisement* announces, his "*Heroick Tragedy*" is so called, because he has in it "chiefly sought occasions to extoll the *English* monarchy." The occasions include the narrative of a tourney in which competing national champions, including Spanish, German and Moorish representatives ("There *Osmin* lay, his eye-balls roll'd in death; / And there *Almanzor* grinning for new breath; / Too late repenting, they from *Africk* came" [1, p. 3]), are all defeated by the English hero. Most of the extolling is, however, naval, and recalls earlier Stuart masque. The first Act sees Edgar appear in a Triumphant Barge rowed by eight other Kings (1, p. 10), and the fourth opens with a masque in which Neptune acknowledges the suzerainty of the English monarchs (IV, p. 38). In the barge scene, the eight Kings, clutching their gilded oars, salute Edgar and collectively articulate the Stuart claim to a universal monarchy of the sea:

> 1. KING. A Homage ever shall be paid by me
>   To him that rules and that defends the Sea.
> 2. KING. His part of Earth to every Prince is due;
>   Whilst on the Waters none is King but You.
> 3. KING. In narrow bounds are our Dominions pent.
>   The strongest Winds fall dead, their last breath spent,
>   E're they attain your Empire's vast extent.
> 4. KING. The spacious Heaven and Natur's care scarce
>   stretch
>   So far as your immense Dominions reach.   (1, p. 9)

Edgar was never a successful play but the way it attempted to fill a significant vacuum was telling. Edward Howard had attempted a non-dramatic heroic poem also extolling "the famous encounters of our Ancestors" (who for him, it appears, encompassed both Romans and Britons) in his *British Princes* (1669).[18] Although the poem was another of the era's many "failed epics" (in Staves's phrase), Howard's own prefatory remarks and those of a number of commendatory verses emphasize the poet's choice of a British subject as the crucial aspect of the patriotic impulse animating the composition. Orrery, who had also written the two early heroic dramas celebrating English continental triumphs, applauds the poetic recovery of past greatness which gilds the present:

> That Noble Poem, which thou giv'st us now,
> Does both oblige the Dead, and Living too:
> Till the old *Brittains* fame thou didst display,
> Their Glories were interr'd, as much as they.

Echoing Rymer's disgust at Davenant's heroes being "all foreigners," Orrery complains that "th'English, who Heroick Poems write / In praise of Foreigners, employ their Pen, / Though their own Country yields the bravest men." Denham also celebrates Howard's "raising up" Bonduca's "glories from the dust," as "to Old *England*, you that right have done, / To shew, no nobler story than her own," and Hobbes himself salutes the "piety" which the poem induces. Although the execution may have been feeble, it was not difficult for the poem's readers to applaud its motives. Dryden himself proposed writing an English epic on an Arthurian theme, and did in fact take up the subject in his operatic *King Arthur* but that work, though first composed in 1684, only appeared, along with the other "British" productions, after 1688. *Albion and Albanius* was his only serious work on a British theme to appear under the Stuarts. Despite the effusions of patriotic enthusiasm, the distant British past was too ideologically fraught with republican valences to serve readily as a subject, while the emergent Oceanic empire was difficult to map onto traditional models of empire, about whose contemporary forms, as we have seen, many in the political nation felt profound misgivings. In contrast to this native dearth, however, "Roman" plays which depicted critical moments in the emergence and decline of Republic and Empire crowded the stage. Dryden, Tate, Ravenscroft, Durfey and Sedley revised the Shakespearean treatments of Antony and Cleopatra, Titus Andronicus, Cymbeline and Coriolanus, and Lucretian narratives of virtuous chastity tested, such as *Lucius Junius Brutus* and *Tyranick Love*, abounded. The Shakespearean adaptations made their own contribution to the establishment of a national canon, but also adapted their classical subjects to immediate political circumstances.[19] Erskine-Hill has argued the adaptation of the habitual contrast of Augustan and Antonian modes of rule to Carolean circumstances shaped the Restoration dramatic treatments of kingship in *Antony and Cleopatra* and other plays and the invocation of republican ideology in the ancient historical scenes represented has been carefully analyzed.[20] More broadly, while the frequent depiction of Ottoman and Eastern empire allowed the English to define their social and political order against past and present Asian despotisms, the Romans were established as cultural and political (and even to some degree) genetic ancestors of the English. Their representation, particularly in terms which emphasized parallels with contemporary politics, served as an extremely powerful mode of cultural appropriation and identification, one which insisted, implicitly and, after 1688, explicitly, on the English inheritance of the *translatio imperii.*

Along with the obvious allegorical purposes of Roman subjects, however, it is important to note the other uses and pleasures of such themes. As with the plays which depicted Oriental and New World states, these appear to have included costume, exotic dances and settings, extraordinary supernatural effects, and excesses of sensuality and violence. Lee's early plays, though not without local political resonance, are good examples of such attractions.[21] His *Nero* (1675) depicts a ruler without parallel in the heroic drama; by the beginning of the second scene, his mother, whom he has raped, has suicided at his instructions; in the second Act, he offers Octavia the choice of killing her brother or being herself murdered; in the third Act, he debauches Poppaea, already married to Otho; in the fourth he dooms Rome to burn, and only in the last, surrounded by the dead, does he face a successful revolt. The play not only includes an unprecedented amount of violence enacted personally by the Emperor but depicts the delirium which threatened to accompany untrammeled authority. Nero's madness expresses itself not simply in appalling acts of violence but in delusions as to the extent of his power and imperial sway; he believes himself to be, quite literally, the master of the universe. His speeches to this effect bound the play, with his claim to divinity in Act I, scene ii:

> The World's eternal, and its Monarch, I:
> Then how is't possible for me to dye,
> Yet give my creature immortality?
> If, when I leave this world, men should debate
> The manner: Say, I did myself translate.[22]

He returns to the theme of his divine omnipotence at the close of the play, when he claims "My smile brings Life, and death attends my frown. / My Empire's bounds Nature alone does make" (v.iii.189–90).

Nero's is an extreme form of the psychological disturbance, not just corruption, which Lee appeared to identify with the heights of imperial power. In *Sophonisba* (1676), he explores another disturbance to personality caused by too rigid an adherence to Roman values. In this play, both the African warriors Hannibal and Massinissa, and the latter's warlike protégé Massina, are madly in love with their mistresses Rosalinda and Sophonisba. Scipio, by contrast, though tempted by Rosalinda, is a model of rigid virtue so resistant to passion that he drives Massinissa and Sophonisba to suicide, as well as refusing Hannibal's reasonable offers of peace. The play invests the familiar conflict of love and honor with unusual fervor and a certain cultural specificity. When Scipio refuses to yield to Massinissa' s pleas for Sophonisba's hand, he invests his decree with all his authority "as Rome's Consul and the Lord of power" (v.i, p. 261), to which Massinissa responds with a fierce denunciation: "Tyrannick Rome! Barbarous are all thy Laws" (v.i.267). Scipio reminds him "Kind Rome presents you an Imperial Crown" (v.i.287) but Massinissa, repenting his ambition and his loyalty, scorns the "glory" and "Roman pride." The Consul ends with political victory but personal abjection, repenting the human havoc his unbending adherence to imperial ends has caused, and resolving to retire to a secluded village.

Lee uses traditional tropes of vilification to describe plebian African women, with Massina describing the rural women of Numidia as "all black," with "rowling eyes, / Thick lips, flat noses, breasts of mighty size" (1.ii.192–93), although Massinissa tells him the ladies of "shining Courts" are "fair," "white Maids" (1.ii.193 and 200). This racialist distinction between different classes of Numidian women is the only obvious point at which cultural polarities between the passionate, amorous, valiant, loyal Africans and the calculating, chilly, rigid and ruthless Romans figures the former negatively. Lee's sympathies, so hostile in *The Rival Queens* to the abandonment of European virtue, are here engaged by the victims of Rome's relentless expansion. Scipio's final admission of the hollowness of his victory suggests that Lee regarded imperial aggrandizement as corrupting to the victors, as well as destructive of the victims.

In addition to the critique of empire, the drama gave Lee the chance to produce stupendous spectacular effects, often cited as benchmarks in the Restoration exploitation of the new theatrical machinery. Both the close of Act II, in which "The SCENE drawn, discovers a Heaven of blood, two Suns, Spirits in Battle, Arrows shot to and fro in the Air" (p. 102), and the scene of priestesses, apparitions and dancing spirits in the Temple of Bellona at the beginning of Act IV, must have contributed to the play's success.

Glorianna, the playwright's next swingeing attack on the Empire, this time by recasting Augustus, unusually, as a lustful sensualist rather than a chilly manipulator, lacks the spectacle but amplifies the critique of the tyranny consequent on imperial power. Here he prefigures the sexual aggression central to *Lucius Junius Brutus,* whose inflammatory retelling of the Lucrece narrative provoked the play's censorship.

Although the trials of virtuous virgins under cruel, pagan Romans could be dramatized by royalists like Dryden in *Tyrannick Love,* the efflorescence of plays with such themes after the Glorious Revolution bears an obviously republican political resonance, with the years after 1695 in particular displaying what Hughes calls "an open season" on rapist tyrants, many of them Roman.[23] The Punic wars also served through these years to figure the trials of internal dissension and external challenge, first in Crowne's *Regulus* (1692), and then in Southerne's *The Fate of Capua* (1700), while Addison's *Cato,* so fine a negotiation of apparently warring political ideals that both sides claimed it as their own, also returned to an African Roman setting.[24] Lucretian and Punic themes had Restoration analogues but the two "Bonduca" dramas, produced in 1696 and 1697 respectively, were novel. For the first time since Fletcher's philo-Roman *Bonduca,* these productions revisited the original colonial struggle with Rome, presenting the period in which the British themselves might be conceived of as entering history and receiving a legible identity. Although the productions, one operatic and the other tragic, have different perspectives on the eponymous heroine and her opponents, both attempt to articulate a powerful British patriotism, while conceding Roman greatness. Both texts record a tension between sympathy with the Britons' resistance and attachment to liberty, and qualified admiration for the Romans' successful expansionism. By closing his play with a Roman–British marriage, however, Hopkins resolves the tension in a manner consistent with the attempts of early Georgian aristocrats to figure themselves "as descendents of the British and Roman patriciate of ancient Britain."[25] The grounds for claiming such a cultural and genetic inheritance, soon to be animating activities such as nuministic and archeological research, were literalized on stage.

The adaptation of Fletcher's *Bonduca,* author unknown, presents a kindlier and more patriotic image of the British than the original.[26] The plot construction is still slanted to the Romans, in

that this treatment of the rebellion of AD 60 omits the grave provo-
cations to the Britons (notably the rapes suffered by Boadicea's
daughters), and implicitly conflates her campaign with the slightly
earlier resistance of Caractacus, represented here by Caratach.
Caratach's role is central to the opera, for, drawing on the positive accounts of Caractacus in the Roman historians, he embodies
a model of virtue recognized by Suetonius, the Roman General, as
thoroughly admirable. The other Britons and the solitary, "monstrous" Pict, the would-be rapist Comes, are all markedly less civil.
Caratach's virtue is confirmed in an extraordinary scene in which
he and Suetonius, arguing over a possible peace treaty, discover
each other to be kindred souls, fired by an identical patriotism and
ambition for glory. The Briton will not accept "one Eagle wav'd in
British air" and the Roman will not resign his conquests: "I ne'er
march't but to encrease our Empire."[27] The stubbornness each
shows bonds them:

> Now by that blood that warms thee,
> By that true rigid Temper that has forg'd
> Our tempers so alike: I swear, O Roman,
> Thou fir'd my Soul to Arms.   (II, p. 15)

"O more than Britain!" replies Suetonius, as Caratach tells him
he is equal "To the great Spirits that inform'd Old Rome" and
claims "Sure Nature means us friends." This orgy of homosocial
bonding reaches its climax when they embrace, rivetted "like the
first furious Clasps / Of Lovers in the heat of stoln Delight" (II,
p. 15). Unlike the historical Caractacus, who turned his humiliation
in a Roman Triumph to his own glory, Caratach will be hunted down
and die with the knowledge of failure but his moral stature, like
his namesake's, is unquestioned.

Bonduca, by contrast, is a figure whose boastfulness, cruelty,
poor judgment and, most of all, femininity, signals her unfitness
for leadership and lack of virtue. In judgments confirmed by the
action, Caratach blames the failings caused by her gender for the
Britons' military defeats, indicting the native gender order which
made female rule possible. Her reign is the most significant index of the barbarousness of the British polity, an incivility also
figured by the Druidic sacrifices. Caratach's "unnatural" subordination to Bonduca suggests that her defeat is necessary to create a
civil society in Britain; although Suetonius and Caratach's mutual

recognition suggests British manhood is fully equal to Roman, it is only when the inverted gender order which allows female rule has been overthrown that Romans and Britons will be able to function as equals.

The text emphasizes Bonduca's warlike demeanor: she and her daughters enter dressed like Amazons, a Captain calls her "the War-like Bonduca, / That greatly Towers above the humble Sex" (I, p. 1) and she first appears vaunting her success: "A Woman beat 'em, Caratach, a weak Woman, / A Woman beat these Romans!" (I. p. 2). Caratach's characteristically misogynistic response is to tell her "A Man woud blush to talk so," criticism she acknowledges by blaming her "Woman's Frailty" (I, p. 3). After thus upbraiding her, however, Caratach expatiates on his own exploits in considerable detail, implicitly claiming credit for the British success. Later, prior to the crucial battle, Comes the monstrous Pict reiterates this masculine suspicion of female leadership, saying "When Women Rule, and Boys Command in War, / We've askt the Gods what they will never grant us" (III, p. 23), a judgment borne out by the subsequent defeat, when Caratach blames the disaster on Bonduca, telling her not to "meddle in Men's Affairs" and "Go home and spin" (IV, p. 34). The climax of her unnaturalness only comes in the last Act, however, when, ignoring Suetonius's assurances that Rome will protect her position, she not only suicides but, ignoring the Romans' cries of "Woman! Woman! Unnatural Woman!" (V, p. 48), forces her unwilling daughter Bonvica to do likewise. To her destruction of what Caratach calls "the sad millions" of Britons, she adds infanticide.

Bonduca is not the only bloodthirsty and barbaric Briton: Nennius opens the play by boasting that "Our British Fields fatten with Roman slaughter" (I, p. 1), and Comes, the "object Pict" and would-be ravisher of Claudia, Bonduca's warlike daughter, is described as monstrous in both mind and body. The play places the weight of barbarism most distinctly on the British side but Caratach's role, along with Bonduca's continual articulation of resistance to tyranny, suggests that British virtue has not simply been extinguished by the Roman triumph. In a final, powerful image of British–Roman unity which figures the identification beloved of early eighteenth-century Englishmen, Bonduca tells Suetonius that "If you will keep your Laws and Empire whole, / Place in your *Romans* Flesh, a *British* soul" (V, p. 48).

A year later Charles Hopkins revisited the Bonduca story in a version considerably more sympathetic to the British. Here Boadicea is a critic of Roman expansionism whose complaints that "The Lust of Power has set proud *Rome* on flame, / And Universal Empire is her aim" would resonate with an audience hoping to see a successful conclusion to the nine-year struggle with France.[28] The British Queen stresses her nation's peculiar adherence to liberty – "Let Earth submit to her Tyrannick Sway, / No *Briton* born, can servilely obey" (I, p. 3) – and the conduct of the rapist Decius, who ravishes Boadicea's daughter Camilla, provides evidence of the Romans' abuse of "sway." As was the case in Dryden's *The Indian Emperor*, however, the play carefully divides the invaders into the virtuous (Paulinus and Fabian), and the vicious (Decius and Caska). Paulinus bears the values of civilization: not only gallant in love and war, explicitly rejecting Decius's sexual exploitation of military victory, he is also humane and politic, attempting to prevent the royal suicides and transform the conquered Britons into allies. Decius embodies the brutality of conquest shorn of civility, telling Camilla before dragging her off to be violated that he regards sexual predation as his right:

> In all my former Wars when Towns were won,
> And prostrate Beauties crouded up my way,
> My boundless Rage forbore to rifle none,
> Seizing on whom I pleas'd as lawful Prey
> Scorn'd when enjoy'd and cheaply cast away   (III, p. 20)

Decius reiterates his understanding of the sexual privilege of conquest by telling Paulinus that "Britain is made to feel the *Roman* Powers, / And both her Beauteous Heiresses are ours" (III, p. 28), but the latter decides to release his beloved Venutia so that she feels free to acknowledge her love without external restraint. Before he can effect this, however, Boadicea appears to upbraid both the Roman Generals for Camilla's rape. In an interesting reappropriation of the high moral ground, Paulinus takes over from the chorus of British women to become the most voluble denouncer of Decius:

> PAUL: Thou Fiend!
> VEN: Thou Monster
> CAM: [recovering] Ravisher.
> PAUL: Barbarian.
> BO: Roman.

PAUL: ...
>   In all our Annals, thou shalt stand accurst,
>   A second *Tarquin*, blacker than the first.   (III, p. 32)

The rape provokes two forms of vengeance by the British. The first
is barbaric: echoing the historical record, Boadicea orders a ghastly
slaughter of Roman soldiers as sacrifices to the Druidic gods, telling
her men to "Tear them with Racks, ply them with Sword and Fire"
(IV, p. 43) before "horrid scenes" appear, discovering "several Prisoners put to death by several sorts of Tortures" (IV, p. 43). The
second punishment serves as a proper act of manly justice, as Cas-
sibelan, Camilla's betrothed, executes Decius. The resolution of
the Roman–British conflict, figured here in terms of courtship and
sexual crime, is finally resolved by the betrothal of Paulinus and
Venutia, which provides another emblem of the genetic dimension
of Britain's Roman inheritance. Paulinus's words close the play, in
an apparently even-handed account of the action:

> *Rome* triumph'd still o'er *Britain* in distress:
> *Britain*, when prosp'rous, show'd her Mercy less.
> So high the Cruelty of both were driv'n,
> That both are punish'd by offended Heav'n.   (V, p. 56)

As the scene of Decius's denunciation suggests, however, the interpretation of events, and its moral evaluation, appears to be as
much a prerogative of victory as sexual violence. Although the text
concurs with Paulinus's assessment of the Britons as more cruel
than the Romans, by virtue of the massacre Boadicea ordered,
and her later attempt to stab Venutia, the power of Camilla's and
Boadicea's rhetoric casts doubt on Paulinus's supposedly judicial
assessment. The terms in which Camilla urges her mother on to
suicide echo the high words of resistance to invasive power in the
first Act – "Drink, Mother, and defie Barbarian Power, / *Rome* has
prevail'd, and *Britain* is no more" (V, p. 53) – but they also echo
Massinissa's inversion of the usual association of Rome with civility:
for Camilla, Elysium will be pre-Roman Britain, "Where never Impious Ravisher has been, / And never Barbarous *Roman* enter'd in"
(V, p. 53).

   Boadicea implicitly concurs with *Bonduca*'s much more overt identification of ancient British barbarity in the cruelty and misjudg-
ment associated with female rule but Hopkins is considerably more

skeptical about the Roman claims to civility than his predecessor. Both these texts rework the Lucretian narrative of tyrannical sexual crime legible in the Boadicea narrative to accommodate and legitimate Britain's ancient incorporation by an overweening empire, valorizing the tenacity of a fundamental British resistance to tyranny but also claiming a direct and legitimate Roman inheritance. Boadicea herself is both the occasion for this theme and its main problem: unlike Lucretia, who relied on her complaints and her male relations to avenge her, and who turned the violence acted upon her inward by suiciding, the historical and dramatic Boadicea actively pursued vengeance for the crimes against her daughters. While the comic drama enthusiastically celebrated the agency of British women, serious plays had not only tended to present European Christian women as mild contrasts to ancient and Oriental viragos, but were becoming even more hostile to depictions of politically powerful women.[29] Boadicea's energy and courage were a source of pride to the English but also deeply disturbing to a culture increasingly invested in a domestic and maternal understanding of femininity. The implicit or explicit identification of Boadicea's female barbarity with British defeat in the late seventeenth-century dramatic depictions enabled playwrights to re-present an apparent national defeat as a triumph of civilization and order, as the establishment of a Roman-British polity, ancestor of a revived "Great Britain" with her own expansionist agenda, embraced civilization and masculine rule.

In 1701, Gildon returned to an early British theme in *Love's Victim: Or, The Queen of Wales*. The Prologue, written for the playwright by Betterton, celebrates the patriotic nature of the subject by providing a not-unfamiliar critique of the past failure of the English stage to praise national heroes:

> So ill our Poets have the Patriot shown,
> That they have sung all Countries but their own.
> Old and new *Greece, France, Italy* and *Spain*;
> Nay, distant *China*, and remote *Japan*.
> In sooty *Afric* too, they've Hero's found;
> *Afric* for other Monsters still renown'd
> Our Bards, with Heroes too have made abound.
> Each barbarous Corner of the Earth they've sought
> And from each barbarous Corner Heroes brought.

From *India* tawny Braves, and Blacks from *Guinny*;
Secure with forraign Baubles still to win ye.
Our Vent'rous Poet makes a bold Essay
To show Domestic Virtue here to day,
And draw a generous Nation in a Play.
. . .

The World of old has of her heroes rung
Nor shou'd you slight the Race from whence you sprung.
For Virtue sure we need not flie to *Rome*,
Or *Greece* for Beauty, who have more at home.[30]

Betterton's verses echo much earlier Restoration complaints about the English failure to heroicize themselves on stage but also display a shrewd understanding of the way dramas set in exotic locales served as commodities – "forraign Baubles" – which turned concise but spectacular evocations of other cultures into occasions for pleasurable consumption. In praising Gildon's rehearsal of "Domestic Virtue," the actor also reveals more assurance than Rymer or Orrery or Hobbes: as England prepared to meet again the might of France, the nation had the confidence provided by nine years of not unsuccessful warfare against the greatest modern continental power. Modern self-confidence suffuses the play text also; although Rome is the dominant political force in the world presented in *Love's Victim*, the empire is marginal to the battle between the ancient Britons and Gauls. Rome provides the context, as it were, either politically, in the ancient struggle, or culturally, in the modern conflict, but the real contention is between Williamite England and Louis's France.

Love's Victim depicts the trials of the Welsh Queen Guinoenda, kidnapped by a Hibernian King, shipwrecked with her two children on the coast of Bayonne, the last kingdom to resist the invading Romans. Guinoenda has attracted the unwelcome addresses of the Bayonne King, married to the fierce daughter of Dumnacus, recently and resentfully driven out of his Andean kingdom by the Romans. Guinoenda, aided by a sage and virtuous Druid, shelters in the Druid Temple of Hermes and holds off the King's advances and the Queen's murderous jealousy long enough to be reunited with her husband, Rhesus of Wales, who has also been shipwrecked on the Bayonne shore while pursuing her. Rhesus and Guinoenda are planning to escape by faking a marine burial for the supposedly dead Rhesus, when the sudden appearance of two Welsh Princes exposes the plan. The King plans to sacrifice the Welsh men to Neptune while the Queen is dispatched back to the Druidic Temple. The arrival of the British fleet frees the Welsh Princes and sees the perfidious Dumnacus killed but Guinoenda is tricked into drinking poison, supposedly to save her husband's life, by the wicked Bayonne Queen, who has fallen in love with Rhesus. The play ends with a heartrending deathbed scene between Guinoenda and her two children.

The play is susceptible to allegorical reading: as a resentful ruler exiled in France, Dumnacus suggests a hostile depiction of James. The play's action, however, is primarily shaped to contrast the manly virtue of the British men, and the beauty and wifely and maternal qualities of British women, against the sexual rapacity, deviousness, cruelty and failures in honor of the Gauls. In this text, the cruelty associated with Druidic religion, believed to encourage human sacrifice, is dissociated from the priesthood and identified with the King and Queen of Bayonne's intentions to sacrifice Rhesus, Guinoenda and their siblings and children to various pagan gods.[31] The British, though not Christian, are possessed of all proper virtues; Guinoenda, in particular, is a model "Matron," who draws a clear distinction between her own wifely obedience and the Bayonne Queen's aggression, telling the latter that if she wishes to regain her husband's affection, "you must teach your tongue / The humble Arts of a fond, tender wife" (I, p. 8). The contrast between the two nations is encapsulated in the respective royal marriages. Not only are the Bayonne couple both in love with other people but their relationship is structured by oppression, for, as the Queen complains, "the Gallic Laws / Give Men o'er Wives a Pow'r Unjust" (IV, p. 29). Guinoenda, however, willingly prepares to sacrifice herself, first for her children and then for her husband, displaying the kind of self-sacrifice previously identified only with the Indian and Colchian wives of *Aureng-Zebe* and *The Royal Mischief*. In contrast to Boadicea's wrathful suicide, undertaken like Cleopatra's and Sophonisba's to prevent her humiliation at Roman hands, Guinoenda embodies an ancient British female virtue of a conjugal and maternal kind. In contrast to "the most Wicked" of women who killed her, she was, her distraught son proclaims, "the best of mothers" (V, p. 52).

In 1707, Nicholas Rowe turned to early English history with *The Royal Convert*, set in the Saxon kingdom of Kent. Douglas Canfield reads the play in hagiographic terms, as part of Rowe's celebration of Christian heroism, but does acknowledge the importance of the play's depiction of the establishment of national unity in the year of the Union with Scotland.[32] Rowe's interest in conversion was not simply personal but was conditioned by wider post-1688 attempts at moral reform. The representation of Britain's own Christianization, however, was also an obvious step in slow composite dramatization of her national origins and destiny. The Restoration depictions of the establishment of earlier European empires showed their struggles with infidelity and paganism; once the Romanization of Britain had been staged, showing the originally barbarous, feminine and Druidic polity reduced to political order, the nation's adoption of true religion was the next obvious step. In *The Royal Convert*, the love-plot ties Christianization and British unity closely together, with the unlawful love and ambition of the invasive Saxons Rodogune and Hengist emerging as a threat to the concord offered by the marriage between Christian Saxon Aribert and British Ethelinda.

Like Gildon, Rowe exploits the spectacular and bloody possibilities presented by the ancient practice of human sacrifice; Hengist's savagery is confirmed by his willingness to make his own brother a holy offering. The Scene in which Aribert faces death shows "a Temple adorn'd according to the Superstition of the Ancient *Saxons*," in the middle of which "are plac'd their three principal Idols, *Thor*, *Woden*, and *Freya*," suggesting an indigenous version of those exotic temples of horrid sacrifice so frequently depicted in earlier heroic plays.[33] The language with which Aribert describes the Temple's scenes is, however, novel in this context, being markedly gothic. The "bloody Priests, a dreadful Band," "Delight in reeking streams of human Gore," "And now, as if with sudden Madness struck, / With Screamings shrill they shook the vaulted Roof, / And vex'd the still, the silent solemn Midnight" (IV.i, p. 54). Rowe is not the first to exploit dramatically the paganism of Britain's early inhabitants but the emphasis he places on the constitutive effect of idolatry on English barbarism is novel. He binds the prior critique of female rule in the Boadicea plays to the question of paganism by casting Rodogune, the fierce and ambitious Saxon lover of Aribert, against the gentle and Christian Ethelinda. By means of this contrast, an improperly aggressive and ambitious femininity is again set against a properly domestic form of womanhood. The latter's

amatory success signals the emergence of a polity in which valiant
but civil Christian men govern with the aid of modest women, and
Rowe concludes with Ethelinda's vision, a panegyric to England's
current "nursing mother":

> Of *Royal* Race a *British* Queen shall rise,
> Great, Gracious, Pious, Fortunate and Wise;
> To distant Lands she shall extend her Fame,
> And leave to latter Times a mighty Name;
>   . . .
> But chief this happy Land her Care shall prove,
> And find from her a more than Mother's Love.
> From Hostile Rage she shall preserve it free,
> Safe in the compass of her ambient Sea;
> Tho' fam'd her Arms in many a cruel Fight,
> Yet most in peaceful arts she shall delight,
> And her chief Glory shall be to UNITE.
> *Picts, Saxons, Angles,* shall no more be known,
> But *Britain* be the noble Name alone.   (v.iii, p. 84)

Rowe's celebration of modern Britain's recapitulation of her own
ancient origins of religious and political order is a powerful articulation of English national confidence. Not all dramatists were so
sanguine: in *Elfrid: Or, The Fair Inconstant,* Aaron Hill revisited the
material treated by Rymer in *Edgar.* Hill's depiction of Edgar omits
all Rymer's naval flourishes to provide a thorough, if belated in-
dictment of "courtly" conduct, presented here as sexual predation.
Like Rowe, Hill embellishes his drama with gothic flourishes, in the
form of a haunting account of Athelwold's ghostly father but here
the effects are rhetorical rather than symbolic of the savagery of
pre-Christian England. The British past appears here, rather unusually for these years, simply as a context for depicting the nature
of relations between sovereign and subject.

It is hardly surprising the ancient history of Rome and Britain
would continue to provide material for dramatists intent on analyzing contemporary political conflicts well into the eighteenth
century. Such conflicts were now frequently external as well as
internal: England had become Britain, and Britain had an empire which the British could compare, with increasing plausibil-
ity, to that of Rome. Although reservations about the nation's expansion beyond her newly reconstituted borders continued, the

existence of her colonial possessions, and ambitions, was a fact. Litotic theatricalizations of past and present empires were no longer adequate in such circumstances, so it is unsurprising that, from 1688, the English stage began to dramatize the nation's own heroic age, and her original struggle with Europe's then dominant power, with increasing frequency. The ideological emergence of the first Empire is legible in the often ambivalent fashion in which English playwrights defined their nation's ancient accession to civil society, true religion and domestic propriety.

Conclusion

The study of the relations between literature and empire has recently entered a new phase, as historians have attempted to rein in what David Armitage has described as the anachronistic projection of post-colonial categories onto early modern texts. Attacking the recent tendency of critics to identify "the 'imperial' experiences of racial difference, irreducible 'otherness,' assertions of hierarchy, and national self-determination" in sixteenth- and early seventeenth-century writing, Armitage stresses instead that the anti-imperialism "at the heart of the classical curriculum," in this period at least, helped prevent writers using a despised vernacular from imagining an expanding empire for Britain.[1] This reminder of the importance of humanist skepticism in regard to colonialism is certainly salient in the context of the theatrical representations of empire after 1660. I hope to have shown, however, that vernacular writers, notably Dryden, did in fact display a distinctly elevated sense of their role as celebrants of heroic greatness, despite contemporary mockery and their own interest in depicting the corruption and weakness of earlier and rival empires. The most vigorous debates over what we call literature in the period from 1660 to 1714 were precisely concerned with elevating the status of the vernacular or Modern writers against the Ancient, contesting the propriety of current poetic and dramatic practice, and claiming both national and imperial greatness for writing in English. A key word here is "debates" – like the emergent maritime empire which poets and pamphleteers both hymned and condemned, what Dryden called "the Empire of Wit" was also much disputed. Nonetheless, the connection between greatness and art is a consistent thread from Dryden's *Essay of Dramatick Poesie*, famously set during the Battle of Lowestoft, to Dennis's arguments against Collier, composed during the campaigns against "Gallick Ambition" on two continents.

The disputants of wit did not confine themselves to identifying and praising a national tradition or setting out poetic projects: even Rymer wrote his *Edgar*. Restoration and early eighteenth-century serious drama presents a remarkably comprehensive and varied treatment of the kinds of concerns incident to "empire," often in a heroic form understood to parallel epic. On the one hand, the drama rehearses the history of the rise, decline and, in some instances, collapse of almost all the significant imperial states known to Europeans, from Egypt and Persia to Turkey, Spain, France and newly constituted Britain itself. As a whole, this corpus dramatized the *translatio imperii*, heading westwards on Providentialist wings to the liberty-loving sons and daughters of Neptune. The theatre did not, however, minimize the perils attendant on imperial destiny. The sources of serious plays included Scripture, classical historians both republican and Augustan, recorders of the triumphs and horrors of the Ottomans and diplomatic anecdotes. While reflecting on domestic political problems, whether those of usurpation, rebellion or succession, dramatists chose episodes in which imperial states faced crises brought on by over-expansion, luxury or the predatory invasion of hardy foreigners. Imperial aspiration itself, whether motivated by Ambition or Avarice, was both celebrated and condemned.

In a context in which English historiography was contentious, and English colonialism an oceanic, commercial and settler experiment, the depiction of classical, Catholic and Oriental states provided the means of defining a novel maritime empire against the plethora of predecessors and rivals. Resistance to the suppression of liberty that was widely believed to accompany the establishment of universal monarchies fueled suspicion of Cromwellian and Stuart aspirations to empire, but the creation of a mercantile *imperium* driven by material interest rather than a civilizing or conversion mission also aroused antipathy. The dramatic representation of empire includes this range of perspectives but also finally begins to include heroic depictions of Britain's origins in her early struggles with Rome and the Norsemen, as William's and Anne's wars provided evidence of English and British military prowess across the globe. Still chary of representing commercial activity, the form of empire celebrated by Rowe and Dennis stresses the value of religious and customary tolerance, the rule of law and the relative autonomy of the *patrocinium*, in imperial states construed as federations rather than centralized oppressors. The broad cultural appeal of this vision of a *Pax Britannica* is reflected in the fact that Rowe's *Tamerlane* was almost always played on William's birthday until 1815.

In addition to providing a theatre in which imperial aspirations and anxieties could be played out, the stage pleasured its audience with visions of the exotic domains which provided the popular new commodities of tea, coffee and sugar, muslis, calicoes and silks. However generalized these scenes appear now, it is obvious that dramatists not only emphasized the attracting wealth of such locales but took pains to signal their significant differences from, and inferiority to, European political and gender orders, religion and customs. Gradually, coincident with the rise of the slave-trade, the expansion of plantation colonies and wars against Native Americans, the terms in which non-Europeans were presented on stage began to change. Gildon protested Rymer's racist denunciation of *Othello*'s supposedly indecorous pairing of an African and a Venetian but dramatic practice altered to emphasize ethnic difference in cruder and more contemptuous terms. Miscegenation, a means of underwriting Christian conquest in *The Indian Emperour*, becomes a cause of tragedy in *Don Sebastian* and *The Mourning Bride*.

It would be wrong, however, to presume that the ambivalence which accompanied colonial expansion in the Restoration was simply resolved into an enthusiastic consensus during the first decade of the eighteenth century. Comedy continued to mock the new social types thrown up by the empire in the form of East Indies merchants, Jamaican prostitutes, sea-captains and indentured servants made good. The colonies were regarded as breeding grounds of metropolitan riff-raff, populated by fanatics or men of a brutality to rival pirates. As anxiety about the possible despotism of an imperial monarch faded, fears of luxury and of the socially disturbing consequences of the effects of colonial wealth intensified.[2]

I want to close with a brief inspection of two serious plays whose depictions of the new British empire reveal the on-going tensions surrounding its development. Despite some generic overlap, these texts articulate very different perspectives on the emergent empire. Dennis's *Liberty Asserted* invites reading as a thoroughgoing defence of a Whig *patrocinium* while Southerne's *Oroonoko* is informed by a disgust for mercantile colonialism similar to that of the Tory Behn and Jacobite Dryden. Neither play has received much recent critical attention, an omission symptomatic of the lack of interest in dramatic, as opposed to novelistic, depictions of the First Empire. This is surprising given that the theatrical version(s) of *Oroonoko* would have reached a much more significant contemporary audience than the novella, as Southerne himself implies in the Dedicatory Epistle to the Duke of Devonshire: "She had a great command of the stage and I have often wondered that she would bury her favorite hero in a novel when she might have revived him in the scene. She thought either no actor could represent him, or she could not bear him represented. And I believe the last when I remember what I have heard from a friend of hers, that she always told his story more feelingly than she writ it."[3] In a gesture familiar from other Dedications, Southerne attributes Oroonoko's rebirth and fame to his dedicatee: "Whatever happened to him at Surinam, he has mended his condition in England. He was born here under your Grace's influence, and that has carried his fortune farther into the world than all the poetical stars that I could have solicited for his success" (lines 25–28).[4]

Recent commentators have assessed Oroonoko's theatrical reappearance under this markedly aristocratic and patriarchal aegis negatively, with Suvir Kaul arguing particularly persuasively that Southerne's redaction represses the novella's disturbing triangulation of inter-racial desire, erases the unassimilable black Amazonian Imoinda and occludes the full horror of the protagonist's ghastly, and specifically colonial, torture and execution.[5] Certainly Southerne's text reorders Behn's expansive narrative but the translation to the tragi-comic stage does not simply diminish the critique of colonial commerce and society. Southerne was consistently hostile to the commodification of persons and relations.[6] Although some critics resist this conclusion, as Maximillian Novak and David Rodes point out, the tragi-comedy's plot division underscores the parallel between women and slaves implicit in Behn's narrative, extending the social criticism from Surinam to the metropolis, the latter as governed by materialist and potentially violent misogyny as the colony.[7] Imoinda's whitening is similarly ambiguous in regard to the play's critique of colonialism. As a genre, the heroic drama featured many non-European *femmes fortes*, ranging from the Indian Queen Zempoalla, to the Empress of Morocco, *Aureng-Zebe*'s Nourmahal and Manley's Royal Mischief. These figures were usually set in implicit or explicit contrast with gentle models of

Christian womanhood. There were also white Amazons, such as
Rowe's fierce Saxon Rodogune and the murderous Druidic Queen
of Bayonne, whose barbarism was identified with their paganism.
Southerne's recasting of Imoinda as a docile European certainly
represses the threat embodied in the genre's celebrated Amazons
but it also renders the presumably subversive cross-racial desire of
the novella unambiguous. By recasting Oroonoko in terms recalling Othello, Southerne supports Gildon's call for a drama which
ignores "accidents of complexion" in order "to do justice to nations as well as to persons," and deliberately flouts Rymer's contemporaneous call for a racist drama purified of miscegenation
and "blackamoor" heroes.

Finally, Southerne's staging of Oroonoko's torture has a more
complex relation to the heroic tradition than has been recently
allowed, arguably gaining in effect through an invocation of a notorious precedent probably very obvious to the play's early spectators but less visible to contemporary critics. The scene in which
Blanford, Stanmore, the Widow Lackit and the Welldon sisters enter to find Oroonoko stretched on the rack occurs at a similar
point in the action to Cortez's discovery that Montezuma is being racked by Pizarro in *The Indian Emperor.* In Dryden's text, I
have argued, this indecorous irregularity not only bears witness
to the playwright's horrified fascination with the violence embedded in his sources but is symptomatic of the brutality of the imperial processes thematized but often repressed in the heroic drama.
In the case of *The Indian Emperor,* however disturbing the scene,
the torture could be disavowed by an English audience convinced
of their superiority to the cruel Catholic conquerors of America.
By mirroring Montezuma's racking in Oroonoko's (by means of
identical timing, means of torture, and discovery by well-meaning
Europeans), Southerne leaves little room for an English audience's
comfortable presumption that such barbarities were a peculiarity of Spanish *conquistadores.* The scene demonstrates with the utmost clarity that the English had taken to drinking from poisoned
chalices.

The central role of slavery in much colonial discourse analysis of eighteenth-century texts at least ensures that the dramatic
Oroonoko should generate more commentary in the future.[8] By
contrast, Dennis's *Liberty Asserted,* set in North America during the
Anglo-French conflicts which accompanied the European wars, is
largely invisible in critical terms. This is partly because the play at

first sight resists interpretation as an "anti-conquest" narrative, to borrow Mary-Louise Pratt's phrase: it is a triumphalist celebration of English expansion conceived of as a civilizing mission to secure the liberty of indigenes threatened by the tyrannic ambitions of France. Perhaps because such triumphalism is axiomatic to critics of literature and empire, it has not seemed useful to determine its precise contours.[9] The second reason for the lack of attention to such a text may in fact result from the very centrality of slavery in post-colonial critiques, which has perhaps deflected attention away from the violent, at points genocidal, process by which the American colonies were wrested from their first inhabitants. As with slavery, there now exists a rich revisionist historical literature of "the cant of conquest" which accompanied the European invasion, but there is relatively little critical writing on the English and British literature that represented that process to metropolitan spectators, with Behn's *The Widdow Ranter* being a notable exception.[10] Even Joseph Roach's fascinating account of the inter-cultural performances which accompanied the famous visit to London of five Iroquois leaders in 1710, makes no mention of Dennis's dramatization of Indian–English military co-operation although the latter was the aim of the visitors' presence some six years later.[11]

Dennis's play was received by contemporaries as a thoroughly partisan attack on the French. The party argument reflects Whig enthusiasm for the War of the Spanish Succession, disliked by Tories hostile to Marlborough's continental campaigns, and preferring a blue water policy.[12] In the best recent reading of the play, Richard Braverman argues that Dennis uses the Canadian setting to figure the state of nature, where native, code for "country," values are threatened by the over-refined and arbitrary French. By locating the conflict in a wilderness, Braverman suggests, the play "literalizes the state of nature in order to transform Whig myth into national myth."[13] While this account is certainly consonant with Dennis's continuing contributions to Whig revisionism, the Republican sentiments of which Dennis was accused had implications beyond a defense of the Revolution. In the Dedication to Henley, Dennis stresses the generosity of English principles, and his desire to inspire men with the "love of Liberty" which would enable them "to unite against the common Foe of *Europe*."[14] In the Preface he emphasized that "this was an *English* and not a Party Play," that it was "not a Whig but an *English* Play." The attempt here may well be to elevate party myth to national myth as Braverman proposes but it also suggests that the text requires reading in terms of inter-state rivalry; as, precisely, a depiction of specifically English values and conduct versus those of the French. If we follow Dennis's suggestion to bracket an allegorical or party reading in order to interpret the text as indeed, an "English play," the ideological contours of *Liberty Asserted* take on a new appearance.

The action is set in a region of Canada called Angie and centers on the competing claims of the French and the English to Angian, or Iroquois, loyalty. By 1675, the Iroquois dominated the frontier of English settlement in the North and they remained allied to the English through the duration of King William's War in the 1690s, although some defected to the French, who were led by the Comte de Frontenac, a central figure in *Liberty Asserted.* Dennis's play draws on contemporaneous developments in the three-sided relationship. In the first decade of the eighteenth century, the Iroquois remained friendly with the English but entered into agreements with the French to stay neutral in future wars.[15] The hero of *Liberty Asserted*, Ulumar, is general of the Iroquois federation, and is eventually revealed to be Frontenac's son, although he has been educated by a gallant Englishman, Beaufort. Ulumar is pressured by his mother Saskia to make peace with the Hurons, allies of the French, a policy which Beaufort naturally opposes. Ulumar refuses a "union" with the French but agrees to a peace-making treaty of commerce. Feeling betrayed, Beaufort leaves the Angian camp; shortly afterwards, the French attack the Iroquois. Only the arrival of the English, with Iroquoian allies, saves Ulumar from death, as he resists French offers of absolute sway over the Angians in return for accepting French sovereignty.

The play's treatment of the conflict is remarkably revealing about the various ways in which what one historian has called "the war within" was conducted.[16] As was the case in seventeenth-century North America, religious beliefs, political convictions, education into European customs and manners and sexual exchange all figure as points of contestation between the English and the French in their attempts to secure indigenous alliances, conversion and assimilation. Saskia's pro-Huron, pro-French sympathies rise from her original dalliance with a European, and have persuaded her Ulumar should honor his father's wish that he marry a Christian. The strength of her personality, matched by that of the fierce "child of war" Zelmura, may reflect the central role of women in Iroquois political life. Beaufort's gentle tutelage has inclined both Saskia and Ulumar "T'embrace the Christian faith" (i.iii, p. 13) although she was originally deterred from it by the bigotry of the Jesuits, for "those haughty Priests," "unless I would embrace their Faith / Forbad all nuptial League twixt me and *Miramont*" (i.iii, p. 13). Beaufort believes his educative process has been successful, and that "Ulumar seems sent express from Heaven / To civilize this rugged Indian clime" (i.ii, p. 8) but after his *protégé* makes the treaty with the French, he denounces him as corrupted by them. In the central scene of negotiation, the competing European claims to superior "manners" are highlighted. Ulumar, suspicious of French designs, believes the Governor wishes to enslave the tribes but the Second Ambassador assures him that he is mistaken: "He sees and pities the Barbarity / In which so brave a Nation now has plung'd / And he would civilize your rugged ways" (iii.iii, p. 33), teaching the Iroquois "Those pleasing Manners, which the World admires / And which the wisest Nations have embrac'd" (iii.iii, p. 33). Tellingly, both Beaufort and Ulumar respond to this invitation with a keen sense of the political implications consequent on abandoning one's native ways. The Englishman laments that Europe's leaders have "suffer'd poor unthinking Sots, to unlearn / Their Native Customs, and their Native Tongues / To speak your Jargon, and assume your Ways," while Ulumar asks "What have you you taught the Nations after all? / What have you taught them but inglorious Arts; / To emasculate their Minds?" (iii.iii, p. 33).

Resistant to French religion and manners, the Iroquois cannot long be kept from a settlement with their natural allies, the English. The action is structured to highlight French–Indian contact, figuring the English presence as minimal, embodied for most of the play only by Beaumont, who lives among the Angians. This focus on French designs underscores the invasiveness of the French presence in North America, while downplaying English settlement, actually much more extensive. The contest of imperial ideology, however, is rendered entirely explicit in the words, as well as implied in the shape of the action. Trying to persuade Frontenac to abandon his expansionist ambitions, Ulumar begs him "To bring the Nations round to happy Freedom, / And make attonement to our *Indian* World, / For all the Woes thou curst Ambition caus'd" (v.i, p. 55). The haughty and tyrannical ambition of the French is set in continual contrast to the English, whom Ulumar describes as a "generous Nation / That never basely yet resigned their Liberty" (IV.i, p. 38). The conclusion to the treaty-making process sought by Ulumar is the establishment of a confederation of free nations under the patronage of Britain strongly suggesting the republican imperial ideal of the *patrocinium*. Ulumar hymns the impulse which informs this empire:

> For every brave Man's Country is the Universe,
> His Countrymen Mankind, but chiefly those
> Who wish the Happiness of all the rest,
> And who are friends to all their Fellow Creatures:
> And such are the brave *Iroquoian* Tribes,
> Such th'unconquer'd *English*, free themselves,
> And loving all who actually are free.   (II.ii, p. 16)

Whereas the French, eager seekers after universal monarchy, are "Damn'd to eternal Slavery themselves" (II.ii, p. 16), the play closes by celebrating the English as global guarantors of liberty: "O Great *Britannia* thro' the World renown'd / For propping falling Liberty, / Supporting sinking Nations!" (V.v, p. 67).

The presence of Beaumont and the English forces notwithstanding, Dennis's play shares with most of the other texts we have examined a strong tendency to figure English colonial activity indirectly and in the context of a comparison by which another European empire suffers. If *The Indian Emperor* provided the canonical rehearsal of the black legend of Spanish conquest in Latin America, *Liberty Asserted* presents a dark myth of Gallic Ambition in the North. This repeated pattern of disavowal in the representation of colonization is symptomatic of the ambivalence, indeed contradictions, which continued to riddle English imperial ideology. As in the plays set in Roman Britain, where the British figures embody both a noble resistance to tyranny and a savagery which justifies the civilizing Roman conquest, Dennis's Iroquois are defenders of the most notable English virtue but also require tutelage and conversion. The process is one by which the negative sides of conquest – violence, territorial appropriation, the attempted erasure of "native custom," political subordination – are, again as in Dryden's play, identified solely with a non-British continental power. Resistance to foreign invasion, loyalty to one's own traditions and a willingness to enter into mutually beneficial relations of exchange, backed up by military prowess, are all associated with both the Iroquois and the English.

However obvious the contradictions in Dennis's cant of anti-Gallic conquest might appear to modern readers, the power of the ideology he articulated in *Liberty Asserted* should not be underestimated. Far from being anachronistic, defending the military invasion of states riddled by "ancient tribal hatreds" in the name of freedom is still a most familiar rhetorical gesture in the Anglophone states created during the First Empire. The critiques of other heroic dramatists, whether focused on the internally corrupting or externally oppressive effects of authoritarian universal monarchies and globalized empires of trade, are also not without contemporary pertinence. In reflecting on what Ulumar calls the "European insolence" depicted in the extensive dramatic representation of empire in the period 1660–1714, modern critics are less likely, in my view, to project erroneous identifications than disavow continuities.

Notes

1 NEW HABITS ON THE STAGE

1. John Evelyn, *The Diary of John Evelyn*, ed. E. S. deBeer, 6 vols. (Oxford: Oxford University Press, 1955), vol. III, pp. 464–65.
2. John Evelyn, *Tyrannus, or the Mode: A Discourse of Sumptuary Laws* (London: prtd. by G. Bedel, T. Collins and J. Crook, 1661), p. 4.
3. Nathaniel Lee, *The Rival Queens*, ed. P. F. Vernon (Lincoln, NE: University of Nebraska Press, 1970), 4.1.1–6. Quotations from this play will be taken from this edition, and act, scene and line numbers cited in the text.
4. Samuel C. Chew, *The Crescent and the Rose: Islam and England During the Renaissance* (New York: Oxford University Press, 1937), pp. 452–59.
5. See Steven Mullaney, *The Place of the Stage: License, Play and Power in Renaissance England* (Chicago: University of Chicago Press, 1988), pp. 62–87. Mullaney's study is only one of a burgeoning number of "new historicist" accounts of Renaissance literature as colonialist discourse: a few prominent examples include Stephen Orgel's "Shakespeare and the Cannibals" in *Cannibals, Witches and Divorce: Estranging the Renaissance*, ed. Marjorie Garber (Baltimore and London: The Johns Hopkins University Press, 1987), pp. 40–67, and Stephen Greenblatt's *Learning to Curse: Essays in Early Modern Culture* (New York: Routledge, 1990).
6. Nancy Klein Maguire, *Regicide and Restoration: English Tragicomedy, 1660–1671* (Cambridge: Cambridge University Press, 1992), pp. 1–12.
7. Anne T. Barbeau, *The Intellectual Design of John Dryden's Plays* (New Haven and London: Yale University Press, 1970), p. 7; and John Loftis, *The Spanish Plays of Neo-Classical England* (New Haven and London: Yale University Press, 1973), p. 180.
8. David Bruce Kramer, *The Imperial Dryden: The Poetics of Appropriation in Seventeenth-Century England* (Athens, GA, and London: University of Georgia Press, 1994).
9. See especially J. R. Jones, *Britain and the World 1649–1815* (Brighton:

Harvester Press, 1980), pp. 12–13, and Ronald Hutton, *The Restoration: A Political and Religious History of England and Wales, 1658–1667* (Oxford: Clarendon Press, 1985). In a recent survey of Restoration historiography, Tim Harris seems to confirm this tendency, arguing that the three central questions for Restoration scholars have been, and are still, the nature of the Restoration settlement and the legacy of the civil war; the causes, nature and resolution of the Exclusion Crisis (and the related issue of whether party politics emerged during that crisis); and the causes, nature and achievement of the Glorious Revolution. See p. 189 in "What's New About the Restoration?" *Albion* 29.2 (Summer 1997), pp. 188–222.

10. See John Miller, *Popery and Politics in England, 1660–1688* (Cambridge: Cambridge University Press, 1973), ch. 4 (pp. 67–90) especially.

11. Jonathan Scott, "England's Troubles: Exhuming the Popish Plot" in *The Politics of Religion in Restoration England*, ed. Tim Harris, Paul Seaward and Mark Goldie (Oxford: Basil Blackwell, 1990), pp. 107–32. See also Scott's *Algernon Sidney and the Restoration Crisis, 1677–1683* (Cambridge: Cambridge University Press, 1991) for a fuller development of this claim, in the context of his controversial argument that the political developments of the later seventeenth century are "xerox copies" of the first half (p. 6).

12. Gary S. De Krey, *A Fractured Society: The Politics of London in the First Age of Party 1688–1715* (Oxford: Clarendon Press, 1985), p. 27. See, especially, "The Spoils of Trade," pp. 22–9; and "Dissent and Trade," pp. 101–5.

13. Paul Seaward, *The Restoration, 1660–1688* (New York: St. Martin's Press, 1991), ch. 4, pp. 70–100.

14. Steven C. A. Pincus, *Protestantism and Patriotism: Ideologies and the Making of English Foreign Policy, 1650–1668* (Cambridge: Cambridge University Press, 1996).

15. Pincus, *Protestantistism and Patriotism*, pp. 451–52.

16. Despite the recent expansion in perspective, most recent Restoration historians, unlike scholars of European history, continue to ignore the very real anxiety engendered both by Ottoman territorial gains and by their effect on inter-state politics. It would also be helpful to see some analysis of the insistent use of comparisons and distinctions between absolutism and (Ottoman) despotism in political dispute. Perhaps this is a more complicated matter than the frequent Republican and Whig identification of the supposed absolutism of the Crown with despotism; or the more general English view of Louis XIV as grand seigneurial. If Tim Harris is correct in asserting that Toryism "owed as much to conservative legal-constitutionalism as it did to absolutism" (*Politics under the Later Stuarts: Party Conflict in a Divided Society* [London and New York: Longman, 1993], p. 37), a position holding that the King was himself limited by law,

contemporary accounts of the Ottomans and Mogols (which stressed the rulers' freedom from legal restraint) presumably contributed more than tropes to Anglican Cavalier, Anglican royalist and Tory, as well as Whig, political discourse.

17. As Anthony Pagden points out, "empire" is a word with a variety of meanings in the early modern period, including "rule", "state" and the meaning with which we are more familiar: a "political, and cultural, unity created out of a diversity of different states widely separated in space." See *Lords of all the World: Ideologies of Empire in Spain, Britain and France c. 1500–c. 1800* (New Haven and London: Yale University Press, 1995), pp. 11–14. Pagden suggests that the modern meaning of the term was acquired in the early eighteenth century; my view is that the heroic plays contributed to that shift in definition.

18. See especially Michael McKeon, *Politics and Poetry in Restoration England: The Case of Dryden's* Annus Mirabilis (Cambridge, MA: Harvard University Press, 1975); M. Thale, "The Framework of 'An Essay of Dramatick Poesie'" *Papers in Language and Literature* 12.2 (1976), pp. 363–69. The commentary on parts of Behn's *oeuvre* and colonialism is much more extensive but tends not to be carefully contextualized. For an exception, see Laura Brown, "The Romance of Empire: *Oroonoko* and the Trade in Slaves" in *The New Eighteenth Century: Theory, Politics, English Literature*, ed. Felicity Nussbaum and Laura Brown (New York and London: Methuen, 1987), pp. 41–61. For two recent essays on *The Widow Ranter*, see Margaret Ferguson, "Whose Dominion, or News from the New World: Aphra Behn's Representation of Miscegenous Romance in *Oroonoko* and *The Widow Ranter*" in *The Production of English Renaissance Culture*, ed. David Lee Miller, Sharon O'Dair and Harold Weber (Ithaca, NY: Cornell University Press, 1994) and Margo Hendricks, "Civility, Barbarism and Aphra Behn's *The Widow Ranter*" in *Women, "Race" and Writing in the Early Modern Period*, ed. Margo Hendricks and Patricia Parker (New York and London: Routledge, 1994), pp. 225–42.

19. *An Essay of Dramatick Poesie*, in *The Works of John Dryden*, ed. H. T. Swedenberg Jr. *et al.*, 19 vols. (Los Angeles and Berkeley: University of California Press, 1956–), vol. 17, p. 8. Where possible, quotations from Dryden's works follow this edition: poems are cited by line number, prose by volume and page from *Works*.

20. *The Critical Works of John Dennis*, ed. Edward Niles Hooker, 2 vols. (Baltimore: The Johns Hopkins University Press, 1939–43), vol. 1, p. 203. Quotations from Dennis's critical works follow this edition; volume and page number are cited in the text.

21. *The Critical Works of Thomas Rymer*, ed. Curt A. Zimansky (New Haven and London: Yale University Press, 1956), p. 119. All quotations from Rymer's works will follow this edition; page numbers will be cited in the text.

22. See Lois G. Schwoerer, *"No Standing Armies!": The Anti-Army Ideology in Seventeenth-Century England* (Baltimore: The Johns Hopkins University Press, 1974), chs. 5–9.

23. Pincus, *Protestantism and Patriotism*, p. 259.

24. John Evelyn, *Navigation and Commerce, Their Original and Progress* (London: Benj. Tooke, 1674), p. 16.

25. Charles Davenant, *Essays upon the Balance of Power, The Right of Making War, Peace and Alliances, and Universal Monarchy* (London: James Knapton, 1701), p. 7.

26. David Armitage, "The Cromwellian Protectorate and the Languages of Empire," *Historical Journal* 35 (1992), pp. 531–55.

27. *Andrew Fletcher: Political Works*, ed. John Robertson (Cambridge: Cambridge University Press, 1997), pp. 208–209.

28. For recent assessments see Jeremy Black, *A System of Ambition? British Foreign Policy 1660–1793* (London and New York: Longman, 1991), pp. 20–8; and Geoffrey Holmes, *The Making of a Great Power: Late Stuart and Early Georgian Britain 1660–1722* (London and New York: Longman, 1993), pp. 93–105. Paul Seaward stresses Charles's early ambition and belligerence (*The Restoration*, p. 73) rather than his laziness but regards him as enfeebled externally as well as internally by 1678 (p. 100). Jonathan Israel, however, stresses that continental rulers regarded an expansionist England warily throughout the later half of the seventeenth century. See "The Emerging Empire: The Continental Perspective, 1650–1713" in *The Oxford History of the British Empire*, vol. 1, *The Origins of Empire: British Overseas Enterprise to the Close of the Seventeenth Century*, ed. Nicholas Canny and Aline Low (Oxford and New York: Oxford University Press, 1998), pp. 423–44.

29. See Holmes, *Making of a Great Power*, pp. 58–68.

30. For the latter, see Oscar Theodore Barck and Hugh Talmadge Lefler, *Colonial America* (London: Macmillan, 1968), p. 146; and Seaward, *The Restoration*, pp. 90–4, for discussion of colonial affairs.

31. For a detailed account of Charles's involvement in foreign policy and the prosecution of war, see Ronald Hutton, *Charles the Second: King of England, Scotland and Ireland* (Oxford: Clarendon Press, 1989), chs. 9, 11 and 12.

32. This is not to suggest that both Charles and James did not have significant conflicts with their colonial subjects in North America and the Caribbean, nor to downplay the pressure both among the political elites and "out-of-doors" on issues of trade and war: rather that the management of foreign policy and external trade was less provocative of challenges to royal authority than policy regarding religion and domestic governance.

33. "Lives, Liberties and Estates: Rhetorics of Liberty in the Reign of Charles II" in Harris *et al.*, *The Politics of Religion in Restoration England*, pp. 217–241.

34. My use of "heroic drama" is more extended than that of Maguire, who restricts it to the rhymed tragicomedies produced between 1660 and 1671. Here I follow Robert Hume in *The Development of English Drama in the Late Seventeenth Century* (Oxford: Clarendon Press, 1976) who identifies instances of the heroic mode up to 1710 (pp. 432–94) and, more recently, Derek Hughes in *English Drama 1660–1700* (Oxford: Clarendon Press, 1996) who refers to the serious drama throughout the period as tragedy but also notes "heroic" elements consistently.

35. See Rene Wellek, *The Rise of English Literary History* (1944; New York: McGraw-Hill Book Co., 1960), pp. 15–44. Rose A. Zimbardo's *A Mirror to Nature: Transformations in Drama and Aesthetics 1660–1732* (Lexington, KY: University Press of Kentucky, 1986) argues that part of the difficulty modern readers experience in interpreting Restoration texts springs from the Platonic epistemology and psychology which shape their idealist and "fabulist" aesthetics. She suggests that the emergence of Lockean empiricism helped shape drama more concerned with the "particular and experiential," with a more pronounced "locatedness in time and space" from the 1690s on (pp. 2–27). My own view is that "scene," or location, is always a significant element, even in the earlier "idealist" drama, but the means of conveying place or locatedness may elude modern readers.

36. Evelyn, *Tyrannus*, p. 6.

37. Jean Chardin, *A New and Accurate Description of Persia*, trans. Edmond Lloyd, 2 vols. (1686; London, A. Bettesworth and J. Batley, 1724), vol. II, p. 130.

38. Peter Heylyn, *Cosmographie in Four Bookes, Contayning the Chorographie & Historie of the Whole World* (3rd. edn.: London, prtd. for Anne Seile, 1665), p. 138.

39. Evelyn, *Tyrannus*, pp. 16–18.

40. James A. Boon, *Other Tribes, Other Scribes: Symbolic Anthropology in the Comparative Study of Cultures, Histories, Religions and Texts* (Cambridge: Cambridge University Press, 1982), p. 31.

41. Winthrop D. Jordan, *White Over Black: American Attitudes Toward the Negro, 1550–1812* (Chapel Hill, NC: University of North Carolina Press, 1968), p. 32.

42. Michael Ryan, "Assimilating New Worlds in the Sixteenth and Seventeenth Centuries" *Comparative Studies in Society and History* 23.4 (1981), pp. 519–38.

43. See the introductory chapter in George W. Stocking, *Victorian Anthropology* (New York: Free Press, 1987), and Margaret T. Hodgen, *Early Anthropology in the Sixteenth and Seventeenth Centuries* (Philadelphia: University of Pennsylvania Press, 1964), ch. 8.

44. Anthony Pagden, *The Fall of Natural Man: The American Indian and the Origins of Comparative Ethnography* (Cambridge: Cambridge University Press, 1986), p. 5.

45. Boon, *Other Tribes*, pp. 28–9.
46. Boon, *Other Tribes*, p. 154.
47. Boon, *Other Tribes*, p. 176.
48. Evelyn, *Diary*, vol. IV, pp. 265–66.
49. Evelyn, *Diary*, vol. IV, pp. 267–68.
50. Evelyn, *Diary*, vol. IV, pp. 268–69.
51. François Bernier, *The History of the Late Revolution of the Empire of the Great Mogol* (London: Moses Pitt, Simon Miller, John Starkey, 1671), pp. 31–32. Quotations from this work will be from this edition and cited by page number in the text.
52. Boon, *Other Tribes*, p. 156.
53. See Thomas Docherty, *On Modern Authority: The Theory and Condition of Writing: 1500 to the Present Day* (Brighton, and New York: The Harvester Press, 1987), pp. 218–19; and Christopher Pye, "The Sovereign, the Theatre and the Kingdome of Darknesse: Hobbes and the Spectacle of Power," *Representations* 8 (1984), p. 91.
54. This position is becoming more widely accepted: see, for example, Louis Montrose's recent "The Work of Gender in the Discourse of Colonialism," *Representations* 33 (1991), pp. 1–41. Montrose suggests here that "race" is an inappropriate term to use in a seventeenth-century context.
55. Anthony G. Barthelemy, *Black Face, Maligned Race: The Representation of Blacks in English Drama from Shakespeare to Southerne* (Baton Rouge and London: Louisiana State University Press, 1987).
56. Barthelemy, *Black Face*, p. 198.
57. There is very little evidence to indicate customary practice in these matters. However, as no engravings from contemporary play texts I have seen include figures in black-face, aside from masquers, it seems unlikely that make-up was used to indicate a distinctive "complexion" in the main characters.
58. For a recent authoritative survey of the intellectual and material processes involved, see Robin Blackburn, *The Making of New World Slavery: From the Baroque to the Modern Period* (London and New York: Verso, 1997), Part I, chs. 1 and 6 especially.
59. Hodgen, *Early Anthropology*, p. 412.
60. Morgan Godwyn, *The Negro's and Indians Advocate, suing for their Admission into the Church: or a Persuasive to the Instructing and Baptizing of the "Negros" and Indians in our Plantations* ... (London: prtd. for the author by J. D., 1680), p. 3.
61. Godwyn, *The Negro's and Indians Advocate*, p. 13.
62. David Brion Davis, *The Problem of Slavery in Western Culture* (1966; Oxford: Oxford University Press, 1988), p. 268.
63. Godwyn, *The Negro's and Indians Advocate*, p. 34.
64. See Stocking, *Victorian Anthropology*, pp. 8–45, and Anthony J. Barker, *The African Link: British Attitudes to the Negro in the 17th and 18th Centuries* (London: Frank Cass, 1978), p. 199.

65. See Hodgen, *Early Anthropology*, chs. 5 and 6, and Harry Bracken, "Essence, Accident and Race" *Hermathena* 116 (1973), pp. 81–96.

66. Godwyn, *The Negro's and Indians Advocate*, p. 20.

67. See Michel Foucault, *The Order of Things: An Archaeology of the Human Sciences*, trans. Alan Sheridan-Smith (New York: Random House, 1973), chs. 2 and 3.

68. Godwyn, *The Negro's and Indians Advocate*, p. 36.

69. Rymer, "Short View" in *Critical Works* ed. Zimansky, pp. 167 and 171.

70. See Rymer, *Critical Works*, pp. 258–65, for an account of responses to Rymer by Dennis, Dryden, Pope, Theobald and Warburton.

71. Lewis Theobald, ed., *The Works of Shakespeare*, 7 vols. (London: A. Betterworth, C. Hitch, J. Tonson, F. Clay, W. Feales, R. Wellington, 1733), vol. VII, pp. 371–72.

72. Theobald, *Works*, vol. VII, pp. 371–2.

73. Charles Gildon, *Miscellaneous Letters and Essays on Several Subjects, Philosophical, Moral, Historical, Critical, Amorous &c. By Several Gentlemen and Ladies* (London: Benjamin Bragg, 1694), p. 96.

74. Gildon, *Miscellaneous Letters*, p. 95.

75. Gildon, *Miscellaneous Letters*, pp. 97–98.

76. Gildon, *Miscellaneous Letters*, p. 99.

77. Gildon, *Miscellaneous Letters*, p. 100.

78. Nicholas Rowe, ed., *The Works of William Shakespeare*, 9 vols. (London: J. Tonson, E. Curll, J. Pemberton, K. Sanger, 1714), vol. I, pp. xxxiv–xxxv.

79. Rowe, *Works*, p. 97.

80. John Dennis, *Liberty Asserted* (London: George Strahan and Bernard Lintott, 1704). All quotations are from this edition and will be cited in the text by page number.

81. See especially Nicholas Thomas, *Colonialism's Cultures: Anthropology, Travel, Government* (Cambridge: Polity Press, 1994).

82. See Homi Bhabha's "Signs Taken for Wonders: Questions of Ambivalence and Authority Under a Tree Outside Delhi, May 1817" *Critical Inquiry* 12 (1985), pp. 144–65.

83. See, for example, Benita Parry, "Problems in Current Theories of Colonial Discourse" *Oxford Literary Review* 9 (1987), pp. 27–58.

84. Steven Pincus's work, discussed above, is extremely important in the Restoration context and John Brewer's *The Sinews of Power*, and Linda Colley's *Britons: Forging the Nation, 1707–1837* (New Haven and London: Yale University Press, 1992) have been very influential in eighteenth-century studies.

2 ENLARGING THE POET'S EMPIRE: POETICS, POLITICS AND
HEROIC PLAYS 1660–1714

1. See Wellek, *The Rise of English Literary History*, pp. 14–44; and Robert Hume, *Dryden's Criticism* (Ithaca, NY: Cornell University Press, 1970).

2. *The English Writings of Abraham Cowley,* ed. A. R. Waller, 4 vols. (Cambridge: Cambridge University Press, 1905), vol. I, p. 188.

3. For the relation between the *civitas* and empire, see Pagden, *Lords of All the World,* p. 18.

4. *The Poems of Edmund Waller,* ed. G. Thorn Drury, 2 vols. (London and New York: A. H. Bullen and Charles Scribner's Sons, 1901), vol. II, pp. 87–88. Quotations from Waller will be from this edition and cited by line number in the text.

5. William Davenant, *Preface to Gondibert* (1650), in *Critical Essays of the Seventeenth Century,* ed. Joel Elias Spingarn, 3 vols. (Oxford: Clarendon Press, 1908–1909), vol. II, p. 36.

6. Dryden, *Works,* vol. XVII, p. 63.

7. Richard Flecknoe, "On the Death of Sir William Davenant" and "Of his Playes" in *Epigrams of all Sorts, made at Diverse Times and on Different Occasions* (London: 1670; New York: Garland, 1975), pp. 53–54.

8. *Dramatic Essays, John Dryden,* ed. William Henry Hudson (1912; London: Dent, 1931), pp. 88–89.

9. Richard Leigh, *The Censure of the Rota. On Mr Dryden's Conquest of Granada* (Oxford: 1673; New York: Garland, 1974), p. 13.

10. *The Plays of Thomas Shadwell,* ed. Montague Summers, 5 vols. (London: The Fortune Press, 1927), vol. II, p. 18.

11. The phrase is George Granville's, from "An Essay Upon Unnatural Flights in Poetry" (1701) in Spingarn's *Critical Essays,* vol. III, p. 294.

12. For the first, see Laura Brown, *English Dramatic Form, 1660–1700: An Essay in Generic History* (New Haven and London: Yale University Press, 1981).

13. William Davenant, *Preface to Gondibert,* in Spingarn, *Critical Essays,* p. 36.

14. For a full literary genealogy of this figure, see Eugene M. Waith, *The Herculean Hero in Marlowe, Chapman, Shakespeare and Dryden* (London: Chatto and Windus, 1962).

15. See, for example, Dryden's "A Defence of an Essay of Dramatick Poesie, being an Answer to the Preface of *The Great Favorite, or the Duke of Guise*" in *Works,* vol. X, p. 15.

16. Quoted by Richard Flecknoe, in "A Letter to a Gentleman" (1668), in *Drydeniana* (New York: Garland, 1974), vol. I, pp. 13–14.

17. Elkanah Settle, *A Farther Defence of Dramatick Poetry* (London: Eliz. Whitlock, 1698), pp. 28–29.

18. Rymer, "A Short View of Tragedy," *Critical Works,* pp. 90–91.

19. Sir William Temple, "An Essay on the Ancient and Modern Learning" in Spingarn, *Critical Essays,* vol. III, p. 69.

20. Temple, "An Essay on the Ancient and Modern Learning" in Spingarn, *Critical Essays,* p. 58.

21. See John Sekora, *Luxury: The Concept in Western Thought, Eden to Smollett* (Baltimore and London: The Johns Hopkins University Press, 1977) and, for an analysis of the feminization of luxurious consumption,

Laura Brown, *Ends of Empire: Women and Ideology in Early Eighteenth-Century English Literature* (Ithaca and London: Cornell University Press, 1993), pp. 103–34.

22. Sir William Temple, "Of Poetry," in Spingarn, *Critical Essays*, vol. III, p. 104.

23. John Dennis, "The Essay on the Opera's," in *Critical Works*, vol. I, p. 390.

24. Dennis, "The Usefulness of the Stage," *Critical Works*, vol. I, p. 167.

25. Dennis, "The Advancement and Reformation of Poetry," *Critical Works*, vol. I, p. 206.

26. See Seaward, *The Restoration*, p. 73, on Charles's ambition. Their experience in exile exposed both Stuart brothers (and members of their entourage) to the Spanish and, especially, the French models of drama, which Charles in particular encouraged. For an extended account of the Spanish influence, see John Loftis, *The Spanish Plays of Neo-Classical England*.

27. In *Epic and Empire: Politics and Generic Form from Virgil to Milton* (Princeton: Princeton University Press, 1993), David Quint argues that Virgilian epic is the genre of choice for imperial victors, while Lucan's *Pharsalia* serves as the origin of a counter-tradition of romance deployed by the defeated; further arguing that the increasing marginalization of the nobility in seventeenth-century Europe (as power was absorbed by the absolutist monarchs above, and the wealthy bourgeois below) was fatal for the form. In this account, the warrior class Joseph Schumpter regarded as necessary for expansion is alienated from the wars of the monarch, and the epic, which had previously represented the successful alliance of royal and aristocratic power, declines into nostalgic romance. The heroic plays of the Restoration and beyond do not fit entirely neatly into this account. They drew both on epic and on romance sources, and while their articulation of conflict within and between imperial states depended quite markedly on the political predilections of particular playwrights, arguing "republican," oligarchical or monarchical positions variously, their representation of Christian expansionism and pagan despotism also made a supra-partisan, national and European appeal.

28. Dryden, "Of Heroic Plays," *Dramatic Essays*, p. 89. The presumption that heroic plays were generically akin to epic was hardly peculiar to Dryden. In his *Remarks on Mr Rowe's Tragedy of the Lady Jane Gray, and All His Other Plays* (1715), Charles Gildon attacked Rowe's presumption in identifying himself with Virgil and for confusing his heroic drama with epic. Rowe figures here as Dryden's heir, being called the younger "Mr Bays," and is rebuked because in his Prologue to *Tamerlane,* he "takes care to inform us, that as *Virgil* sung *Aeneas,* so he designs to sing *Tamberlane.*" Amplifying this criticism, the next participant in the dialogue remarks: "That is, he writing a Dramatic

Poem, imitates *Virgil*, who writ an Epic one, extremely judicious I profess. Now I had been such a Sot to imagine there was a very material difference between the *Epic* and *Dramatic* Poems. *Aristotle* and all the Critics had misled me, but Mr *Bays* has rectified my judgement." To which his interlocutor replies, tellingly, "In this indeed, Mr *Bays*, has a great Number of our Moderns, who have sinn'd with him": *Remarks*, ed. Arthur Freeman (New York and London: Garland, 1974), p. 50.

29. Rymer, "Preface to Rapin," *Critical Works*, pp. 5–6.

30. Rymer, "Short View," *Critical Works*, p. 90.

31. Rymer, "Short View," *Critical Works*, p. 91.

32. The hostility to standing armies came from a wide variety of groups. While the Cromwellian force was obviously a focus of cavalier and royalist suspicion, James's expansion of the militia frightened Tories as well as Whigs, and William's and Anne's forces were also criticized by Tories, who generally preferred a blue-water policy, especially after 1688. See Schwoerer, "*No Standing Armies!*" chs. 5–9. The tyranny associated with the army could be assigned to absolutist monarchs or oppressive usurpers but the navy, its strength under Cromwell notwithstanding, continued to be seen as the quintessentially English means of resisting foreign threats and protecting commerce and colonies.

33. It was sufficiently unusual to have a serious play with an English theme for the fact to be noted in the Prologue to Orrery's *Henry the Fifth*.

34. "A Rough Draft of a New Modell at Sea," in *The Works of George Savile, Marquis of Halifax*, ed. Mark K. Brown, 3 vols. (Oxford: Clarendon Press, 1989), vol. I, pp. 294–95.

35. The *locus classicus* for an account of the historiography is J. G. A. Pocock, *The Ancient Constitution and the Feudal Law: A Study of English Historical Thought in the Seventeenth Century* (Cambridge: Cambridge University Press, 1957).

36. These include Crowne's *The Misery of Civil War* (1679/80) and his *Henry the Sixth, The First Part* (1681); Tate's *The History of King Lear* (1680/1) and his *History of King Richard the Second* (1680); John Banks's *The Unhappy Favorite; or, The Earl of Essex* and *Vertue Betray'd; or, Anne Bullen* (1682); and Thomas Durfey's *The Injured Princess* (1682). It seems likely that Banks's *The Innocent Usurper; or, The Death of Lady Jane Grey* and his *The Island Queens; or, The Death of Mary, Queen of Scotland* were also written in the early 1680s.

37. For the connection between Davenant's interludes and the Western design, see William S. Maltby, *The Black Legend in England: The Development of Anti-Spanish Sentiment, 1558–1660* (Durham, NC: Durham University Press, 1975).

38. Dryden, *Works*, vol. IX, p. 25.

39. Elkanah Settle, The Epistle Dedicatory to Anne, Duchess of Bucclugh and Monmouth, in *Cambyses, King of Persia. A Tragedy*

(London: William Cademan, 1671). All quotations will be from this edition and will be cited in the text by act, scene and page number.

40. See, for example, Quintus Curtius Rufus, *The Life and Death of Alexander the Great*, trans. Roger Codrington (London: prtd. by E. Alsop and Robert Wood, 1661), p. 32.

41. See Seaward, *The Restoration*, pp. 90–92.

42. Charles Davenant, *Essay Upon Universal Monarchy*, p. 234.

43. Holmes, *Making of a Great Power*, pp. 98–99.

44. Elkanah Settle, *Distress'd Innocence* (London: prtd. by E. J. for Abel Roper, 1691).

45. *The Dramatic Works of Roger Boyle, Earl of Orrery*, ed. William Smith Clark, 2 vols. (Cambridge, MA: Harvard University Press, 1937), vol. i: I. i. 23–26. Subsequent references to *Mustapha* will be to this edition and will be cited in the text.

46. The presentation of Amazonian, if often criminally heroic, women in these plays introduces those *femmes fortes*, beloved of the French *précieuses*, who proved so inspiring to women writers later in the period. For a discussion of their French antecedents and English influence, see Carol Barash, *English Women's Poetry 1649–1714: Politics, Community and Linguistic Authority* (Oxford: Clarendon Press, 1996), pp. 32–40. She cites an interesting suggestion in an unpublished paper by Margaret Doody that these Amazonian figures served as the female equivalent of the heroic drama's "Herculean heroes."

47. Bernier, *History*, pp. 31–32.

48. *The Dramatic Works of John Dryden*, ed. Sir Walter Scott and George Saintsbury, 8 vols. (Edinburgh: William Patterson, 1882), vol. ii, p. 318.

49. See George Parfitt, "The Exotic in Restoration Drama" in *All Before Them, 1660–1780*, ed. John McVeagh (London and Atlantic Highlands, NJ: The Ashfield Press, 1990), pp. 81–96.

50. Dryden, *Works*, vol. xvii, p. 188. Dryden refers here to the needs of contemporary audiences but a certain cultural relativism informs his remarks.

51. Edward Filmer, *A Defence of Plays, or, The Stage Vindicated . . .* (London: Joseph Tonson, 1707), pp. 3off.

52. *The Ancient and Modern Stages Survey'd . . .* (London: Abel Roper, 1699), pp. 208–209.

53. Settle, *Farther Defence*, pp. 42–43.

54. Charles Gildon, *A Comparison between the Two Stages* (London: no pub., 1702), p. 191.

55. Gildon, *Comparison*, p. 193.

56. Gildon, *Comparison*, p. 194.

57. Edward Phillips, Preface to *Theatrum* in Spingarn, *Critical Essays*, vol. ii, p. 269.

58. For a recent discussion, see Maguire, *Regicide and Restoration*, pp. 85–86.

59. For discussion of the ideological role of the Stuart masque, including its celebration of British marine power, see Roy Strong and Stephen Orgel, *Inigo Jones: The Theatre of the Stuart Court*, 2 vols. (London and Berkeley: Sotheby Parke Bernet and University of California Press, 1973), vol. I, p. 72.
60. Richard Southern, *Changeable Scenery: Its Origin and Development in the British Theatre* (London: Faber and Faber, 1952), pp. 109–23.
61. Peter Holland, *The Ornament of Action: Text and Performance in Restoration Comedy* (Cambridge: Cambridge University Press, 1979), pp. 28–32.
62. Holland, *Ornament of Action*, p. 40.
63. John Loftis provides an explanation of this term in his commentary on *The Conquest of Granada* in Dryden, *Works*, vol. XI, p. 421.
64. For discussion of this process in the context of travel writing, see Mary-Louise Pratt, *Imperial Eyes: Travel Writing and Transculturation* (London and New York: Routledge, 1992), and Stephen Greenblatt, *Marvellous Possessions: The Wonder of the New World* (Chicago and Oxford: The University of Chicago Press, 1991), pp. 7–25.
65. Richard Knolles, *The Turkish History*, ed. Paul Rycaut, 2 vols. (6th. edn.: London: Tho. Basset, 1686), vol. I, p. 406.
66. Knolles and Rycaut, *Turkish History*, vol. I, p. 401. The source of Webb's engravings in Artus is discussed in the Introduction to *The Siege of Rhodes: A Critical Edition*, ed. Ann-Mari Hedback (Uppsala: Universitatis Upsaliensis, 1973). All further quotations from *The Siege* are from this edition and will be included in the text.
67. See Holland, *Ornament of Action*, p. 36.
68. Mary-Louise Pratt, "Conventions of Representation: Where Discourse and Ideology Meet" in *The Taming of the Text*, ed. W. van Peer (New York and London: Routledge, 1988), p. 16.
69. Comparisons of illustrations in Knolles–Rycaut and the figures in Stuart masques suggest a close degree of overlap. See Strong and Orgel's *Inigo Jones*, pp. 588 and 699 for illustrations of a noble Persian and Turk respectively, and compare with the many illustrations of Turkish dress in Rycaut's *The History of the Present State of the Ottoman Empire* 5th edn.: (London: prtd. by T. N. for Joanna Brome, 1687). Rycaut is interestingly emphatic about the importance of national costume and identity, pointing out that the universal propensity to follow fashion, especially among those of a "vain and gay humour," leads many living under the Ottomans to be "catched and enrapt with the fancy and enticement of the *Turkish* Mode, and be contented to despoil themselves of the Garment of Christian Vertues" (Bk.1, pp. 152–53). Rycaut claims that such converts to Islam are recognizable by their white turbans (illustrated in Bk. 1, p. 83). His conclusion about the political implications of the desire to adopt the customs of one's imperial masters (signified by costume) is similar to Evelyn's in the latter's

Tyrannus: "the *Britains*, and other Nations, after conquered by the *Romans*, began to delight themselves in their Language and Habit, their Banquets and Buildings, which they accounted to the Humanity and refinement of their Manners; but *Tacitus* sayeth, *Pars servitutis erat*, a signal symptom of their subjection" (Rycaut, *Present State*, Bk. 1, p. 153).

70. *The Diary of Samuel Pepys*, ed. Robert Latham and William Mathews, 11 vols. (London: G. Bell and Sons Ltd., 1970–83), vol. v, pp. 78–79. Jocelyn Powell, in *Restoration Theatre Production* (London and Boston: Routledge and Kegan Paul, 1984), is skeptical about the effect of such costuming but Maguire argues that spectacle was a considerable lure to audiences (see *Regicide and Restoration*, pp. 108–111). Powell argues that the exactness of garb would still have been adapted to prevailing baroque conventions, which used details in costume to emphasize the "idea" of a character, often with an eye to establishing parallels with modern conditions (*Restoration Theatre*, p. 60). My own emphasis would be towards underlining the frequently articulated concern to avoid anachronism and observe scenic decorum, along with the evident delight in the spectacular displays of wealth, luxury and violence with which exotic locales were presented. Without a modern concern with verisimilitude, or "realism," cultural difference could still be highlighted. This view is not, I believe, at odds with Powell's emphasis on the "baroque" or, in Zimbardo's and Rothstein's terms, the idealist and fabulist aesthetic of the drama.

71. See Thomas Jordan, "London's Glory, or the Lord Mayor's Show" (1680) in *The Lord Mayor's Pageants of the Merchant Taylors' Company in the 15th, 16th and 17th Centuries*, ed. Robert T. D. Sayle (London: The Eastern Press Ltd., 1931), pp. 6–8.

72. Jordan, "London's Glory," p. 6.

73. Jordan, "London's Glory," p. 9.

74. Hume, *Development*, esp. pp. 280–99.

75. Settle, Prologue to *Ibrahim*. All quotations will be from this edition and will be cited in the text by act, scene and page number.

76. Epilogue to *Ibrahim*.

77. See Hume, *Development of English Drama*, p. 213.

78. *Elkanah Settle's The Empress of Morocco et al.* Intro. Maximillian E. Novak (Los Angeles: William Andrews Clark Memorial Library, University of California at Los Angeles, 1968), v. ii, p. 70. Subsequent references to *The Empress* will be to this edition and will be cited in the text by act, scene and page number.

79. *The Conquest of China*, v, p. 57. All quotations are from this edition and will be cited in the text by act and page number.

80. Richard Morton, "'Roman Drops from British Eyes': Latin History on the Restoration Stage" in *The Stage in the Eighteenth Century*, ed. J. D. Browning and Joseph Donohue (New York: Garland, 1981), p. 110.

81. Evelyn, *Diary*, vol. III, p. 73.

82. See Hume, *Development of English Drama*, p. 247.
83. Pepys, *Diary*, vol. v, p. 230.
84. Sourel quoted by Southern, *Changeable Scenery*, p. 122.
85. Dryden, *Works*, vol. xii, p. 5.

3 THE GREAT TURKS: THE OTTOMANS ON STAGE, 1660–1714

1. See J. E. Svilpis, "Orientalism, Kinship and Will in Restoration Drama" in *Studies on Voltaire and the Eighteenth Century* 303 (1992), pp. 435–39, and Nandini Bhattacharya, "Ethnopolitical Dynamics and the Language of Gendering in Dryden's *Aureng-Zebe*" *Cultural Critique* 25 (Fall 1993), pp. 153–76.
2. For a full account of these conflicts, see Kenneth M. Setten, *Venice, Austria and the Turks in the Seventeenth Century* (Philadelphia: The American Philosophical Society, 1993). See also Geoffrey Treave, *The Making of Modern Europe 1648–1780* (London and New York: Methuen, 1985), pp. 603–12; Paul Coles, *The Ottoman Impact on Europe* (London: Harcourt, Brace and World, 1969); and Justin McCarthy, *The Ottoman Turks* (New York and London: Longman, 1997).
3. See De Krey, *A Fractured Society*, p. 142.
4. De Krey, p. 142.
5. See, for example, "The Third Part of Advice to the Painter" in *Poems on Affairs of State: Augustan Satirical Verse, 1660–1714*, ed. Howard H. Schless, vol. iii (New Haven and London: Yale University Press, 1968), pp. 555–60. For Bodin's views, see Coles, *Ottoman Impact*, p. 151.
6. For a survey of attitudes to the Ottomans in travel writing, see Beck H. Brandon, *From the Rising of the Sun: English Images of the Ottoman Empire to 1715* (New York: P. Lang, 1987); and for literary images, see Byron Porter Smith, *Islam in English Literature*, ed. S. B. Bushrui and Anahid Melikian, foreword Omar A. Farrukh (1937; 2nd. edn.: Delmar, NY: Caravan Books, 1977). There is also a rich summary account of European attitudes to Islamic states in Norman Daniel's *Islam, Europe and Empire* (Edinburgh: University of Edinburgh Press, 1966). Nabil Matar's recent account, *Islam in Britain, 1558–1685* (Cambridge: Cambridge University Press, 1998), provides a useful corrective to the view that Christian Europe regarded the Turks in particular with complacent superiority, emphasizing English vulnerability to Barbary slavers, the lure of Islamic learning, and the constant volume of Christian conversions to Islam. His chapter on theatre, however, focuses rather narrowly on representations of renegades (pp. 50–72) and ignores the plethora of plays located in Islamic states.
7. John Marsh, *A New Survey of the Turkish Empire and Government . . .* (London: Henry Marsh, 1663).
8. Marsh, *New Survey*, p. 36.
9. *Europae Modernae Speculum; or, A View of the Empires, Kingdoms,*

Principalities, Signieuries, and Commonwealths of Europe (London: prtd. by T. Leach for Tho. Johnson, 1665), p. 235.

10. *Europae Modernae*, p. 235.

11. Paul Rycaut, "The Epistle to the Reader" in *The Present State of the Ottoman Empire* (3rd. edn.: London: prtd. for John Starkey and Henry Brome to be sold by Robert Boulter, 1670).

12. Rycaut, *Present State*, p. 7.

13. Rycaut, *Present State*, p. 7.

14. Rycaut, *Present State*, p. 8.

15. Tim Harris, *Politics Under the Later Stuarts*, p. 37.

16. Rycaut, *Present State*, p. 67.

17. Rycaut, *Present State*, p. 74.

18. Sue Wiseman, "History Digested: Opera and Colonialism in the 1650s" in *Literature and the Civil War*, ed. Thomas Healey and Jonathan Sawday (Cambridge: Cambridge University Press, 1990), pp. 189–204.

19. Rycaut, *Present State*, p. 216.

20. Richard Knolles, *The Turkish Historie from the Original of that Nation to the Growth of the Ottoman Empire . . .* , ed. Paul Rycaut, 2 vols. (6th edn.: London, prtd. for Tho. Basset, 1687), vol. 1, 512–513.

21. Heylyn, *Cosmographie*, p. 795. Heylyn goes on to specify the murders committed by various Ottomans: "The first amonst the *Turks* that began this barbarous cruelty, was *Bajazet* the First, on his brother *Jacup*; whom immediately after his Father's death he strangled with a Bow-string; this being the only Instrument of their *Fratricide*, because none of the blood-royal of *Ottoman* is spilt to the ground. After him, *Mahomet* the *Great* caused his young brother, then at nurse, to die the death; and was not without much ado perswaded from being the executioner himself. *Amurath* the third, caused his five brethren to be at once strangled before his face: and *Mahomet*, his Son, no fewer than nineteen in one day" (p. 795).

22. Knolles, *The Turkish Historie*, vol. 1, p. 240.

23. Hughes, *English Drama*, p. 43.

24. Anon. *Irena. A Tragedy* (London: prtd. by Robert White for Octavian Pulleyn Jr., 1664), III.ii, pp. 40–41. All quotations are from this edition and will be cited by act, scene and page number in the text.

25. Henry Neville Payne, *The Siege of Constantinople; A Tragedy* (London: prtd. for Thos. Dring, 1675), I.i, p. 2. All quotations will be from this edition and will be cited in the text by act, scene and page number.

26. Charles Saunders, *Tamerlane the Great. A Tragedy* (London: prtd. for Richard Bentley and M. Magnes, 1681), III, p. 34. All quotations will be from this edition and act number and page will be cited in the text.

27. Hume, *Development*, p. 475. Jacqueline Pearson makes a similar observation in "Blacker than Hell Creates: Pix rewrites *Othello*" in

Katherine M. Quinsey, ed., *Broken Boundaries: Women and Feminism in Restoration Drama* (Lexington, KY: University of Kentucky Press, 1996), pp. 13–30. Pearson argues that women ransacked the pre-1660 canon for plays depicting ethnic otherness to a much greater degree than male dramatists because of the "sympathetic identification" such texts allowed between women and other cultural outsiders. There are, however, many more plays with exotic subjects by male Restoration dramatists than female playwrights, including those written in the period 1688–1714; and female dramatists seem broadly to share, rather than dissent from, prevailing views of Turks, Persians, Arabs, Indians and Africans, although their interest in the different gender orders of non-European societies is arguably distinct.

28. See Moira Ferguson, *Subject to Others: British Women Writers and Colonial Slavery, 1670–1834* (New York and London: Routledge, 1992), ch. 1.

29. See Melinda Alliker Rabb, "Angry Beauties: (Wo)Manley Satire and the Stage" in *Cutting Edges: Postmodern Critical Essays on Eighteenth-Century Satire*, ed. James E. Gill (Knoxville: University of Tennessee Press, 1995), pp. 127–58.

30. For a detailed discussion of the consequences of Anne's failed attempts to employ a maternal symbology to strengthen her rule, see Toni Bowers, *The Politics of Motherhood: British Writing and Culture, 1680–1760* (Cambridge: Cambridge University Press, 1996), pp. 37–69. Carole Pateman's *The Sexual Contract* (Cambridge: Polity Press, 1988) contains a useful critique of the erasure of the maternal body in both Filmerian patriarchalist and Lockean contract theory, pp. 92–96.

31. Catherine Belsey, *The Subject of Tragedy: Identity and Difference in Renaissance Drama* (New York and London: Methuen, 1985), pp. 192–93.

32. Charlotte Lennox's *The Female Quixote* (1748) is the *locus classicus* of such satire. See Laurie Langbauer's *Women and Romance: The Consolations of Gender in the English Novel* (Ithaca, NY: Cornell University Press, 1990), pp. 62–92, for a feminist analysis of this development.

33. Mary Pix, *Ibrahim the Thirteenth Emperor of the Turks* (London: prtd. for John Harding and Richard Wilkin, 1696), I, p. 1. All quotations will be from this edition and will be cited by act and page number in the text.

34. Joseph Trapp, *Abra-mule* (1708; London: Jacob Tonson, 1735), II, p. 35. All quotations will be from this edition and will be quoted by act and page number in the text.

35. Nicholas Rowe, *Tamerlane. A Tragedy* (1701; 5th. edn.: London: prtd. for J. T. and sold by T. Jauncey, 1720). All quotations will be from this edition and will be cited in the text by act, scene and page number.

36. Charles Davenant, *Essay Upon the Ballance of Power*, pp. 28–29.

37. John Loftis's discussion in his *The Politics of Drama in Augustan England* (Oxford: Clarendon Press, 1963), pp. 31–34, emphasizes the play's

role as a "chief vehicle" for the dissemination of Lockean ideas on constitutional theory and religious toleration, an account of Rowe's work developed recently by Richard Braverman in *Plots and Counterplots: Sexual Politics and the Body Politic in English Literature, 1660–1730* (Cambridge: Cambridge University Press, 1993), pp. 239–42.

38. In *Nicholas Rowe and Christian Tragedy* (Gainsville, FL: University Presses of Florida, 1977), pp. 47–49, J. Douglas Canfield reads Rowe's adaptation of Knolles as a theodicy, emphasizing Tamerlane's role as instrument of Providence. While the Providentialist dimension of *Tamerlane*'s action is important, it is not at odds with the play's interest in contrasting forms of imperial power, which are culturally and religiously inflected.

39. In *The Turkish History*, Knolles characterizes Tamberlane's religious views as follows: "God in essence one, and in himself immutable, without change or diversity; yet for the Manifesting of his Omnipotency and Power, as he had created in the World sundry kinds of People, much differing both in Nature, Manners and Condition, yet all framed to the Image of himself; so was he also contented to be of them diversely served, according to the diversity of their Nature and Manners; so that they worshipped no other Strange Gods, but him alone, the Maker and Creator of all things; which was the cause he suffered the use of all Religions within the Countries subject to his Obedience, were they not mere Atheists, Idolaters, or worshippers of strange and vain gods" (vol. 1, p. 146).

40. The common identification of the Turk, the Pope and Louis XIV is announced in the titles of popular performances in markets and fairs. One such example is *King William's Happy Deliverance and Glorious Triumph over his Enemies; or, the Consultation of The Pope, Devil, French King and the Great Turk* ... performed at Miller's Loyal Association Booth, May Fair, 1696.

41. Charles Goring, *Irene; or, the Fair Greek. A Tragedy* (London: J. Bayley, 1708), v.ii, p. 60.

42. Davenant, *Essay Upon Universal Monarchy*, p. 268.

43. Andrew Fletcher, "A Discourse Concerning the Affairs of Spain" in *Political Works*, pp. 83–117.

44. See vol. 1 in *The Complete Letters of Lady Mary Wortley Montagu*, ed. R. Halsband (Oxford: The Clarendon Press, 1965).

45. Justin McCarthy, *The Ottoman Turks*, p. 151.

4 THE MOST FAMOUS MONARCHS OF THE EAST

1. The problem of finding a suitably epic mode in which to celebrate deeds of national greatness in sea-borne, commercial empires was first encountered by the Portuguese and then by the English. For a discussion of the origins of this problem, see Richard Helgerson,

Forms of Nationhood: The Elizabethan Writing of England (Chicago and London: University of Chicago Press, 1992).

2. Samuel Pufendorf, *Of the Law of Nature and Nations,* trans. Basil Kennet (1660; 3rd. edn.: London: prtd. for R. Sare, R. Bonwicke, T. Godwyn, etc., 1717), p. 167.

3. See James Walvin, *Fruits of Empire: Exotic Produce and British Taste 1660–1800* (London: Macmillan, 1997), for a discussion of the trade in Asian and New World products.

4. Edward Said's account of the role of Greek antipathy to the Persians in the development of Orientalism can be found in his groundbreaking *Orientalism* (London: Routledge and Kegan Paul, 1979), p. 21.

5. Derek Hughes (*English Drama*, p. 95) has provided a much more suggestive account recently, seeing the Moroccan court as exemplary of a "dark and brutal chaos at the heart of the family and state," which prefigures the concerns of Lee and Otway.

6. Sari Hornstein, "Tangier, English Naval Power, and Exclusion" in *Restoration, Ideology, and Revolution: Proceedings of the Folger Institute Centre for the History of British Political Thought,* vol. IV (Washington, DC: The Folger Institute, 1990), pp. 327–84.

7. Hornstein, "Tangier," p. 328.

8. J. S. Corbett, cited by Hornstein, "Tangier," p. 328.

9. *The London Stage 1660–1800,* ed. William Van Lennep, 5 vols. (Carbondale, IL: Southern Illinois University Press, 1965), Vol. I, p. 304.

10. Van Lennep, *The London Stage,* Vol. I, p. 310.

11. Lancelot Addison, *West Barbary, or a Short Narrative of the Revolutions of the Kingdoms of Fez and Morocco* (Oxford: prtd. at the Theatre and to be sold by John Wilmot, 1671). Settle seems to have used Addison's account as a starting point, unifying a narrative of unresolved strife which continued through several generations. The names of his characters (Muly Labas, Muly Hamet, Crimalhaz and Laula) recall Addison's Muly Hamet Sheck, Muly Labesh and the upstart Cidi Kirum and adulterous Laella, while his later *Heir of Morocco* is based on Gaylan, sometime ally of the English at Tangiers. Interestingly, Addison includes several letters from Barbary rulers, including one from Gaylan to the Lieutenant-Governor of Tangier, Col. Henry Norwood, in his narrative, thus emphasizing the interpenetration of English and Moroccan affairs. See *West Barbary,* p. 56.

12. Settle, *"Notes and Observations on* The Empress of Morocco *Revised"* (1674), in *The Empress of Morocco,* ed. Novak, p. 62.

13. Dryden, Shadwell and Crowne, *Notes and Observations on* The Empress of Morocco (1674) in *The Empress of Morocco,* p. 13, p. 49 and p. 65.

14. Settle, *"Notes and Observations,* p. 4 and p. 7.

15. Settle, *Notes and Observations,* p. 32.

16. Novak, Introduction to *The Empress of Morocco et al.,* p. 7.

17. Hornstein, "Tangier," p. 328.

18. Heylyn, *Cosmographie*, p. 933.
19. Addison, *West Barbary*, p. 18.
20. Dryden *et al.*, *Notes and Observations on* The Empress of Morocco in *The Empress of Morocco*, p. 63.
21. Addison, who regarded the Barbary states as bereft of their former excellence in learning, also viewed them as corrupt politically: "As for the Ancient Model of the Moresco Polite, it is so miserably convuls'd and shaken through manifold alterations caus'd by prevailing Interests, that not many of its first Maxims, nor much of its old Constitution, are visible in the present state" (*West Barbary*, p. 74).
22. Elkanah Settle, *The Heir of Morocco, with the Death of Gayland* (1682; London: prtd. for Thomas Chapman, 1694), I.i. All quotations will be from this edition and will be cited in the text by act and scene number.
23. Addison's critical assessment of Gayland's perfidy to the English can be found in *West Barbary*, p. 71.
24. See P. J. Marshall and Glyndwr Williams, *The Great Map of Mankind: British Perceptions of the World in the Age of Enlightenment* (London: J. Dent and Sons, 1982), p. 23.
25. Heylyn, *Cosmographie*, p. 856.
26. Heylyn, *Cosmographie*, p. 849.
27. Heylyn, *Cosmographie*, p. 846.
28. Heylyn, *Cosmographie*, p. 846.
29. See Holden Furber, *Rival Empires of Trade in the Orient, 1600–1800* (Minneapolis: University of Minnesota Press, 1976), pp. 126–27.
30. Hughes, *English Drama*, p. 98.
31. Hughes, *English Drama*, p. 100.
32. For a recent survey of seventeenth-century accounts of this conflict, see Donald F. Lach and Edwin J. Van Kley, *Asia in the Making of Europe*, 3 vols. (Chicago: The University of Chicago Press, 1965–96), vol. III, Book 4: *East Asia* (1993), chs. 20 and 21.
33. For a full genealogy of this theory, see Clarence J. Glacken's *Traces on the Rhodian Shore: Nature and Culture in Western Thought from Ancient Times to the End of the Eighteenth Century* (Berkeley and Los Angeles, CA: University of California Press, 1967), esp. pp. 429–60.
34. Settle, *The Conquest of China*, I.i, p. 1. All quotations will be from this edition, with act, scene and page number, and will be cited in the text.
35. Martin Martinius, *Bellum Tartaricum, or the Conquest of the Great and most Renowned Empire of China by the Invasion of the Tartars . . .* (London: prtd. for John Crook, 1655), p. 261. Heylyn also discusses the Chinese Amazon who "went to the aid of the Emperor *Vanley* against the *Tartars, Anno* 1618. She took with her a small Army of 3,000 women,

performing Actions not unworthy the bravest Men" (*Cosmographie*, p. 853).

36. F. Alvarez Semedo, *The History of the Great and Renowned Monarchy of China* (London: prtd. by E. Tyler for John Crook, 1655), p. 120.

37. Martinius, *Bellum Tartaricum*, p. 274.

38. Martinius, *Bellum Tartaricum*, pp. 266–67.

39. See James Anderson Winn, *John Dryden and his World* (New Haven and London: Yale University Press, 1987), pp. 492 and 499 for details. The manuscript, if it exists, has never been found.

40. Dryden, *Works*, vol. XII, p. 383.

41. Furber, *Rival Empires*, p. 92.

42. See especially Michael W. Alssid, "The Design of Dryden's *Aureng-Zebe*" *Journal of English and Germanic Philology* 64 (1965), pp. 45–69.

43. Arthur C. Kirsch, "The Importance of Dryden's *Aureng-Zebe*," *English Literary History* 29 (1962), pp. 160–74.

44. Samuel Johnson, "Dryden" in *The Lives of the English Poets*, in *The Works of Samuel Johnson, LL.D*, ed. George Birkbeck, 3 vols. (Oxford: Clarendon Press, 1905), vol. I, p. 360.

45. Bernier, *History*, p. 59.

46. Bernier, *History*, p. 61.

47. *Aureng-Zebe*, in *Works*, vol. XII, ed. Vincent A. Dearing, III.i.304–309. All subsequent references will be taken from this edition and cited in the text by act, scene and line number.

48. Bernier, *History*, pp. 31–32. This assumption was shared by a number of commentators on Asian courts. Thomas Herbert, whose *A Relation of Some Years Travaille into Afrique and the Great Asia* (London: prtd. by William Stansby and Jacob Blome, 1634) was republished in the Restoration, believed that the discontentment caused by enclosure and polygamy produced dangerous intrigue: "Eight or ten lustfull Women, by the law subjected to one (and he perhaps an impotent one), their only Libertie is to haunt the Gardens, which being spacious, receive many, where they parly at Pleasure, but not free from Eunuchs, their jealous *Argoes*, whose sole care is, from out of the Women's abundent luscious talk, to screw out some thing that may be gratefull to the King, touching the Nobles, (anatomized by these Women) by which many great ones are come to unexpected Destruction" (p. 148).

49. Bernier, *History*, p. 157.

50. Pufendorf, *Law of Nature*, p. 77.

51. Lata Mani, "The Production of an Official Discourse in Sati in Early Nineteenth Century Bengal" in *Europe and its Others*, ed. Francis Barker *et al.*, vol. I (Colchester: Essex University Press, 1985), pp. 107–27.

52. Bernier, *History*, pp. 89–91.

53. John-Baptiste Tavernier, *The Six Voyages by John Baptista Tavernier . . .*

through Turkey into Persia and the East Indies ... (London: prtd. for R. L. and M. P., 1678), Part 2, Book 2, p. 169.

54. John Fryer, *A New Account of East India and Persia in Eight Letters* (London: prtd. for R. R. for R. Chiswell, 1698), p. 327.

55. Tavernier, *Six Voyages*, p. 169.

56. John Dryden, "Dedication to the Earl of Mulgrave," *Works*, XII: lines 34–36, 21–24.

57. John Ogilby, *Asia, the First Part. Being an Accurate Description of Persia* (London: prtd. by the author, 1673), pp. 49, 48.

58. For a recent overview of Persian–European relations in this period, see Roger Savory, *Iran under the Safavids* (Cambridge: Cambridge University Press, 1980).

59. Samuel Pufendorf, *An Introduction to the History of the Principal Kingdoms and States of Europe* (London: prtd. for M. Gilliflower and T. Newborough, 1690), p. 5. All quotations will be from this edition and cited in the text by page number.

60. *Travels of Sir John Chardin into Persia and the East Indies through the Black Sea and the Country of Colchis* (London: Moses Pitt, 1686). All quotations will be from this edition and will be cited by page number in the text. In Marshall and Williams's discussion of late seventeenth- and early eighteenth-century views of Asian societies, this perception of Oriental stasis is discussed extensively (*Great Map*, pp. 128–38).

61. Hughes, *English Drama*, p. 87.

62. Samuel Clarke, *The Life and Death of Cyrus the Great* (London: William Miller, 1664), p. 47.

63. Clarke, *Cyrus*, p. 47.

64. Nathaniel Lee, *The Rival Queens*, ed. P. F. Vernon (1677; Lincoln, NE: University of Nebraska Press, 1970), pp. xx–xxi. All quotations will be from this edition and will be cited by act, scene and line number in the text.

65. Curtius Rufus, *Alexander the Great*, p. 92.

66. Pufendorf, *Law of Nature*, p. 90.

67. John Crowne, *Darius, King of Persia. A Tragedy* (London: prtd. for R. Bentley, 1688) I, p. 5. All quotations will be from this edition and will be cited in the text by act and page number.

68. *The Life of Alexander the Great written in Latin by Quintus Curtius Rufus and translated into English by Several Gentlemen in the University of Cambridge* (London: prtd. for Francis Saunders, 1690), p. 32.

69. Curtius, *Life* (1690), pp. 27–28.

70. John Banks, *Cyrus the Great: or, the Tragedy of Love* (London: prtd. for Richard Bentley, 1696) I.i, p. 2. All quotations will be from this edition and will be cited by act, scene and page number in the text.

71. *Xerses. A Tragedy. The Dramatick Works of Colley Cibber*, 5 vols. (London: prtd. for W. Feales, 1736), vol. IV: I, p. 13. All quotations will be

from this edition and will be cited by act and page number in the text.

72. Nicholas Rowe, *The Ambitious Step-Mother. A Tragedy* in *Works* (3rd edn.: London: prtd. by J. Darby for M. Wellington, sold by A. Bettersworth and F. Clay, 1720), vol. IV, p. vii. All quotations will be from this edition and will be cited by act, scene and page number in the text.

73. Elkanah Settle, *The Ambitious Slave: or, A Generous Revenge* (London: prtd. for A. Roper and E. Wilkinson, 1694), II.ii, p. 21. All quotations will be from this edition and will be cited in the text by act, scene and page number.

74. Rowe, *The Ambitious Step-Mother*, III.ii, p. 47.

75. Chardin, *Travels*, p. 134.

76. Chardin, *Travels*, p. 133.

77. Chardin, *Travels*, p. 133.

78. Heylyn, *Cosmographie*, p. 785.

79. See Rebecca Merrens, "Unmanned with Thy Words: Regendering Tragedy in Manley and Trotter" in *Broken Boundaries: Women and Feminism in Restoration Drama*, ed. Katherine M. Quinsey (Lexington, KY: University of Kentucky Press, 1996), pp. 31–53. See, also, Rabb, "Angry Beauties," pp. 127–58. Derek Hughes's recent discussion also emphasizes the play's identification of justice with "the exercise of male sexual aggression" but sees the drama as a depiction of the dangerous incoherence of familial and political relationships in civilization generally (*English Drama*, pp. 447–48).

80. Lewis Theobald, *The Persian Princess: or, the Royal Villain. A Tragedy* (London: prtd. for Jonas Browne, 1717) I.i, p. 1.

81. Fryer, *New Account*, pp. 346 and 348. Ogilby's account concurs, stressing that "the Government of this Countrey is an absolute Monarchy, for the King being the Chief, hath all things in his own Power, to do whatsoe'er he pleases, being able to make or break Lawes without any contradiction, nay, to take away any one's Estate or Life, though he be the greatest Lord in the Countrey; in short, his Will is a Law in all things to his People" (*Asia*, p. 74).

82. Fryer, *New Account*, p. 348.

83. Fryer, *New Account*, p. 347.

84. For details of this development, see Lawrence E. Klein, *Shaftesbury and the Culture of Politeness: Moral Discourse and Cultural Politics in Early Eighteenth-Century England* (Cambridge: Cambridge University Press, 1994), p. 207.

85. Daniel, *Islam*, pp. 8–10.

86. The feminist dimension of the text has been mentioned briefly by Nancy Cotton, *Women Playwrights in England ca. 1363–1750* (Lewisburg, PA: Bucknell University Press, 1980), p. 99.

87. Delariviere Manley, *Almyna; or, The Arabian Vow* (London: prtd. for

William Turner and Egbert Sanger, 1707), III.ii, p. 9. All quotations will be from this edition and will be cited in the text by act, scene and page number.
88. Quoted in Daniel, *Islam*, p. 19.

5 SPAIN'S GRAND PROJECT OF A UNIVERSAL EMPIRE

1. *Europae Modernae Speculum*, p. 163.
2. For exemplary contemporary views, see Heylyn's *Cosmographie*; Pufendorf's *Introduction*, pp. 27–75; and *Europae Modernae Speculum*, pp. 99–113. For more recent analysis, see Pincus's *Protestantism and Patriotism*, pp. 256–57 and pp. 267–68.
3. Loftis, *The Politics of Drama*, p. 39.
4. John Loftis, *The Spanish Plays of Neo-Classical England*, p. 256.
5. Kramer, *The Imperial Dryden*, pp. 63–115.
6. Seaward, *The Restoration*, p. 76.
7. Helgerson, *Forms of Nationhood*, p. 181.
8. Helgerson, *Forms of Nationhood*, p. 11.
9. Helgerson, *Forms of Nationhood*, p. 181.
10. For a recent discussion of the association of romance with aristocratic ideology, see Michael McKeon, *The Origins of the English Novel, 1600–1740* (Baltimore: The Johns Hopkins University Press, 1987), chs. 4 and 5, and for the heroic plays' contribution to a celebration of Stuart kingship, Maguire, *Regicide and Restoration*, pp. 13–42 and 190–214.
11. *Europae Modernae Speculum*, p. 99.
12. Heylyn, *Cosmographie*, p. 142. Felicity Nussbaum's *Torrid Zones: Maternity, Sexuality and Empire in Eighteenth-Century English Narratives* (Baltimore and London: The Johns Hopkins University Press, 1995) discusses the effects of such environmentalist thinking in fiction of the next century. Novelistic examples such as Defoe's Roxana clearly draw on images already circulating in dramatic texts.
13. Here I differ from Jaqueline Pearson, who claims that ethnic differences in plays by female dramatists created alternative worlds in which various kinds of alienation and difference could be happily reconciled. See "Blacker than Hell Creates," pp. 21–22.
14. Pufendorf, *Introduction*, p. 87.
15. Pufendorf, *Introduction*, p. 40. Heylyn comments in *Cosmographie* that "They are a mixt People, descending from the Gothes, Moores, Jews and the antient Spaniards. From the Jews they borrow Superstition, from the Moores Melancholy, Pride from the Gothes, and from the old Spaniards, the desire of Liberty" (p. 142).
16. Pufendorf, *Introduction*, p. 40.
17. See Maltby, *Black Legend*; and for a more recent discussion, Armitage, "The Cromwellian Protectorate."

18. William Davenant, "The Cruelty of the Spaniards in Peru," *The Playhouse to be Let* in *The Dramatic Works of William Davenant*, ed. James Maidment and W. H. Logan, 5 vols. (Edinburgh and London: W. Patterson, 1872–74), vol. IV: p. 88.

19. See Kramer, *The Imperial Dryden*, pp. 70–71, for a useful discussion of national characterization along these lines in the poem. McKeon's *Politics and Poetry* provides an important account of the context of the poem's production by emphasizing the economic interests of courtiers in fomenting war with the Dutch, and the consequent mobilization of economic rhetoric, legible in *Annus Mirabilis*, in garnering support.

20. Clarendon, cited in Pincus, *Protestantism and Patriotism*, p. 262.

21. William Morris, cited in Pincus, *Protestantism and Patriotism*, p. 262.

22. Dryden was not, of course, alone in viewing colonial trade and, especially, colonial settlement, with suspicion. Critics feared the effects of luxury on the metropolis, documented by Sekora in *Luxury*, pp. 63–80. There were also widespread anxieties about the degeneration in populations far from the centres of civility; doubts about the legality of the slave-trade, and settlement on indigenous territory; and anxieties about colonies draining resources from the metropolis. See Klaus E. Knorr, *British Colonial Theories, 1550–1750* (Toronto: University of Toronto Press, 1944), pp. 105–22.

23. Dryden, *The Indian Queen* in *Works*, vol. XII: 1.i.61. Other quotations will be cited in the text by act, scene and line number.

24. Samuel Purchas, *Hakluytus Posthumus, or Purchas his Pilgrimes*, 20 vols. (1625; Glasgow: James MacLehose and Sons, 1905), vol. v, p. 871.

25. Purchas, *Hakluytus Posthumus*, vol. 5, p. 868.

26. See Laura Brown, "The Romance of Empire: *Oroonoko* and the Trade in Slaves" in *The New Eighteenth Century: Theory, Politics, English Literature*, ed. Felicity Nussbaum and Laura Brown (New York and London: Methuen, 1987), pp. 41–61.

27. See Hughes, *English Drama*, p. 47, and Maguire, *Regicide and Restoration*, pp. 69–71, for analyses of the play's treatment of usurpation and restoration.

28. Maguire provides a reading determined entirely by local political events and argument (*Regicide and Restoration*, pp. 196–99), focusing on the anxieties over absolute monarchy, the perceived collapse of Caroline honor and the destructive effect of factionalism in the context of impending invasion. While all these concerns are legible in the text, such a reading ignores both Dryden's own account of his intentions in writing the play and its reception.

29. Pagden, *Lords of All the World*, pp. 34–36.

30. Loftis, Commentary, in Dryden, *Works*, vol. 9, p. 318.

31. Max Harris has revisited the question of Dryden's blindness to (or erasure of) cultural difference in *The Indian Emperor* to suggest that

the play's treatment of cultural conflict is more dialogic than it may first appear: "Aztec Maidens in Satin Gowns: Alterity and Dialogue in Dryden's *The Indian Emperor* and Hogarth's *The Indian Emperor*," *Restoration: Studies in English Literary Culture, 1660–1700* 15.2 (Fall 1991), pp. 59–70.

32. Pagden, *Lords of All the World*, p. 51.

33. See Pufendorf, *Introduction*, p. 65.

34. Loftis, *The Spanish Plays of Neo-Classical England*, p. 13.

35. See Pagden, *Lords of All the World*, pp. 63–125.

36. *A Description of the Academy of the Athenian Virtuosi* (Oxford: prtd. for Maurice Atkins, 1673), p. 13.

37. Dryden, *Amboyna* in *Works*, vol. XII: Dedication, 31–32. All other quotations will be cited in the text by act, scene and line number.

38. Dryden, *The Conquest of Granada, Parts I & II* in *Works*, Dedication, p. 4, lines 28–35 – p. 5, lines 1–2. All other quotations will be cited in the text by act, scene and line number.

39. Eugene M. Waith, *Ideas of Greatness: Heroic Drama in England* (London: Routledge and Kegan Paul, 1971), esp. pp. 203–34.

40. James Thompson, "Dryden's *Conquest of Granada* and the Dutch Wars," *The Eighteenth Century: Theory and Interpretation* 31.3 (1990), pp. 211–26.

41. Purchas, *Hakluytus Posthumus*, vol. I, p. 5.

42. See Pincus, *Protestantism and Patriotism*, pp. 448–49.

43. See Pagden, *Lords of All the World*, p. 74.

44. My account here is similar to Maguire's explanation of the Yorkist parallel in terms which suggest an equivalence between Dryden's mythologization of James and his father's apotheosis by earlier masquemakers (*Regicide and Restoration*, p. 207).

45. See Hughes, *English Drama*, pp. 79–84, and Braverman, *Plots and Counterplots*, pp. 117–25, for recent discussions.

46. Pagden, *Lords of All the World*, p. 61.

47. William Davenant, *Preface to Gondibert* in Spingarn, *Critical Essays*, vol. I, p. 36.

48. Hughes, *English Drama*, p. 80.

49. See Settle's *Notes and Observations on* The Empress of Morocco *Revised* in *The Empress of Morocco*, p. 92. Arguing that Almahide's gift of a scarf to Almanzor violates Islamic proprieties, Settle remarks that Dryden "remembered a *jealousie* occasioned by a *Handkercher* in the *Moor of Venice*; and so enlarg'd upon that foundation."

50. Loftis registers this important dimension of the play in his *Spanish Plays of Neo-Classical England*, p. 181: "In North Africa, the historical process responsible for the expansion of Christianity had reached its limit."

51. Pufendorf, *Introduction*, p. 85.

52. Dryden, *Don Sebastian* in *Works*, vol. XV: IV.iii.365–68. All quotations

will be from this edition and will be cited by act, scene and line number.

53. See William Spencer, *Algiers in the Age of the Corsairs* (Norman, OK: University of Oklahoma Press, 1976); Stephen Clissold, *The Barbary Slaves* (London: Paul Elek, 1977), and Nabil Matar's *Islam in Britain, 1558–1685*. Matar's documentation of the fear generated by slave-raids into England (pp. 5–10) provides a useful corrective to the view that such anxieties were merely projections of English guilt (Ferguson, *Subject to Others*, p. 5).

54. Norman Daniel, *Islam and the West* (Edinburgh: University of Edinburgh Press, 1958), p. 32. Matar also emphasizes that some categories of renegades were drawn by the attractions that conversion offered to Christians: see *Islam in England*, p. 38 and p. 40.

55. References to African monstrosity, an ancient trope discussed by Earl Miner in the Notes (*Works* 428) also occur at II.i.458, III.i.179 and v.i.551.

56. The obvious reason for such a change is England's participation in the slave-trade after 1660, a commercial venture which was not yet very profitable but highly valued. See E. E. Rich, "The Slave Trade and National Rivalries" in E. E. Rich and C. H. Wilson, eds., *The Cambridge Economic History of Europe*, 7 vols., vol. IV (2nd. edn.: Cambridge: Cambridge University Press, 1967), pp. 323–38. For a recent, strong claim of the importance of the slave-trade in producing modern racism, see Blackburn, *The Making of Modern Slavery*, pp. 1–30.

57. See Jane Spencer, *The Rise of the Woman Novelist: From Aphra Behn to Jane Austen* (Oxford and New York: Basil Blackwell, 1986). In "Looks that Kill: Violence and Representation in Aphra Behn's *Oroonoko*" in *The Discourse of Slavery: Aphra Behn to Toni Morrison*, ed. Cal Plasa and Betty J. Ring (London and New York: Routledge, 1994), pp. 1–17, Anne Fogarty reviews the decade of criticism which has seen feminist treatment of this text shift from the assumption of Behn's sympathy for African victimage to the analysis of her imbrication in colonial power relations. It seems peculiar that contributors to this debate have neglected to compare the novella to Behn's other representations of European–African relations.

58. Aphra Behn, *Abdelazer, or the Moor's Revenge. A Tragedy* (London: prtd. for J. Magnes and R. Bentley [etc.], 1677), I.i, p. 5. All quotations will be from this edition and will be cited by act, scene and page number in the text.

59. Andrew Fletcher's *A Discourse concerning the Affairs of Spain* (1698) analyzed the causes of Spanish decline (the neglect of trade, agriculture and industry, population loss through religious intolerance) and argued possible means of resuscitating the empire in an ironic pamphlet intended to provide a warning of the danger presented by

the looming crisis of the Spanish succession. Fletcher, *Political Works*, pp. 83–117.

60. Charles Davenant, *Essay Upon Universal Monarchy*, p. 282.

61. Charles Davenant, *Essay Upon Universal Monarchy*, p. 237.

62. Charles Davenant, *Essay Upon Universal Monarchy*, p. 288.

63. Charles Davenant, *Essay Upon Universal Monarchy*, p. 284 and p. 234.

64. See Braverman, *Plots and Counterplots*, p. 201; and Merrens, "Unmanned," p. 37. I also tend to agree with Derek Hughes's suggestion that Congreve's treatment of tyranny in his tragedy is congruent with his attacks on patriarchal oppression in his comedies, and, hence, scarcely misogynistic (*English Drama*, pp. 427–28).

65. See Dryden's translation of the Fourth Book of the *Aeneid*, *Works*, vol. 5, p. 469, lines 537–41.

66. Martin Wechselblatt, "Gender and Race in Yarico's Epistles to Inkle: Voicing the Feminine/Slave," *Studies in Eighteenth-Century Culture* 19 (1989), pp. 197–223.

67. Mary Pix, *The False Friend; or, The Fate of Disobedience* (London: prtd. for Richard Basset, 1699), I.i, p. 20. All quotations will be from this edition and will be cited in the text by act, scene and page number.

68. Pix had adapted Rowley's *All's Lost by Lust* (1616–19), but the story was well known: Pufendorf includes an abbreviated version in the section on Spain in his *Introduction*, pp. 27–28.

69. Mary Pix, *The Conquest of Spain. A Tragedy* (London: prtd. for Richard Wellington, 1705), II.ii, p. 13. All quotations will be from this edition and will be cited in the text by act, scene and page number.

70. *Europae Modernae Speculum*, p. 115.

71. See Furber, *Rival Empires*, pp. 86–87, for details.

72. See Lach and Van Kley, *Asia in the Making of Europe*, Vol. III, Pt. 3, pp. 1397–408, for an account of European records of these developments. George Walton Williams suggests that Fletcher's source for the play was *Conquista de las Islas Malucas* (1609) by Bartoleme Leonardo de Argensola, which he may have read in De Bellan's French novel based on this account, *Histoire memorable de Dias espagnol, et de Quixaire princesse des Moluques* (1614). See Fredson Bowers, ed. *The Dramatic Works in the Beaumont and Fletcher Canon*, 10 vols., (Cambridge: Cambridge University Press, 1966–96), vol. V, p. 543, for details.

73. Apart from a more pervasive hostility on the part of the Portuguese towards the Ternateans, Tate's most significant departures from Fletcher's text include Quisara being the King's sister, rather than daughter. Both Ruidias and Quisara are depicted more favorably: in the original version, Ruidias planned to revenge himself on Armusia and was encouraged in this underhand scheme by Quisara, who also gave initial encouragement to the "Moor-Priest."

74. Nahum Tate, *The Island Princess: Revived with Alterations* (London: prtd.

for W. Canning, 1687), ii.ii, p. 25. All quotations will be from this edition and will be cited in the text by act, scene and page number.

75. Peter Motteux, *The Island Princess, or The Generous Portuguese* (London: prtd. for Richard Wellington, 1699), i.i 1. All quotations will be from this edition and will be included in the text with act, scene and page number.

6 BRAVE NEW WORLDS: UTOPIAN PLAYS OF THE RESTORATION

1. See Dryden, *Works*, Commentary, pp. 321–23, for an account of the stage history.

2. Nancy Klein Maguire does discuss Weston's *The Amazon Queen* but without reference to the way its Amazon characterizations inflect the treatment of sexual relations. See *Regicide and Restoration*, pp. 96–97. There is a brief discussion of Howard's plays as feminist satire in Derek Hughes's *English Drama*, pp.165–66, but even more illuminating is Hughes's discussion of Durfey's consistent feminism (although his commentary on the latter's *Commonwealth of Women* [p. 319] is brief).

3. For masculine prose utopias, see J. C. Davis, *Utopia and the Ideal Society: A Study of English Utopian Writing 1516–1700* (Cambridge: Cambridge University Press, 1981), and David Faussett, *Writing the New World: Imaginary Voyages and Utopias of the Great Southern Land* (Syracuse: Syracuse University Press, 1993); for Cavendish and Astell, see Amy Boesky, *Founding Fictions: Utopias in Early Modern England* (Athens, GA: University of Georgia Press, 1996). Jeffrey Knapp's *An Empire Nowhere: England, America and Literature from* Utopia *to* The Tempest (Berkeley: University of California Press, 1992) analyzes connections between colonial and utopian literary texts prior to the Restoration. There is discussion of Amazonian figures in Simon Shepherd's *Amazons and Warrior Women: Varieties of Feminism in Seventeenth-Century Drama* (Brighton: The Harvester Press, 1981) but not of Restoration plays.

4. See "Blazing Worlds: Seventeenth Century Women's Utopian Writing" in *Women, Texts and Histories, 1575–1760*, ed. Clare Brant and Diane Purkiss (London and New York: Routledge, 1992), pp. 102–33.

5. David Faussett, *Images of the Antipodes in the Eighteenth Century: A Study in Stereotyping* (Amsterdam: Rodopi, 1995), pp. 1–6.

6. For a discussion of Restoration examples, see Roger Thompson, *Unfit for Modest Ears: A Study of Pornographic, Obscene, and Bawdy Works Written or Published in England in the Second Half of the Seventeenth Century* (Totowa, NJ: Rowman and Littlefield, 1979).

7. Recent feminist criticism has been attentive to the novel possibilities for the exploration and exploitation of female subjectivity and sexuality created by the advent of actresses on the Restoration stage but such accounts tend to focus on the hostile or expropriative effects

of female players. See Elin Diamond, "*Gestus* and Signature in Aphra Behn's *The Rover*," *English Literary History* 56 (1989), pp. 519–41; and Jean I. Marsden, "Rape, Voyeurism and the Restoration Stage" (185–200), and Laura J. Rosenthal, "Reading Masks: The Actress and the Spectatrix in Restoration Shakespeare," in *Broken Boundaries*, ed. Quinsey, pp. 201–18. For a full study of the role of the actress in the Restoration theatre, see Elizabeth Howe, *The First English Actresses: Women and Drama 1660–1700* (Cambridge: Cambridge University Press, 1992). Susan Staves is skeptical about the importance of the theatre *per se* in contributing to the emergence of feminist discourse in the seventeenth century, arguing the concern with the status of women and familial relations was an effect of Protestantism, as well as Hobbes's and Locke's detachment of domestic authority from Scriptural and natural law roots. See *Players' Sceptres: Fictions of Authority in the Restoration* (Lincoln, NE, and London: University of Nebraska Press, 1979), pp. 111–89. The first argument sets Staves in an interesting conjunction with Julia Kristeva, who argues in "Women's Time" that feminism emerged in North-Western Europe to compensate for the loss of a powerful symbolization of the feminine, in its maternal dimension, provided by the Roman Catholic cult of Mary. See "Women's Time" in *The Kristeva Reader*, ed. Toril Moi (Oxford: Basil Blackwell, reprint 1987), pp. 187–213.

8. See G. J. Barker-Benfield, *The Culture of Sensibility: Sex and Society in Eighteenth-Century Britain* (Chicago: University of Chicago Press, 1992).

9. See Ros Ballaster, *Seductive Forms: Women's Amatory Fiction from 1684–1740: with Particular Reference to Aphra Behn, Delariviere Manley and Eliza Haywood* (Oxford: Clarendon Press, 1992).

10. See Pagden, *Lord of All the World*, pp. 63–102, for a discussion of the legal problems associated with settlement.

11. For a survey of degenerationist thinking in this period, see Hodgen, *Early Anthropology*, pp. 254–94. For the process of "savagification," see Jonathan Lamb, "Eye-witnessing in the South Seas," *The Eighteenth Century: Theory and Interpretation* 38 (1997), pp. 201–12.

12. For a discussion of the role of Descartes in early English feminism, see Hilda L. Smith, *Reason's Disciples: Seventeenth-Century English Feminists* (Urbana: University of Illinois Press, 1982).

13. Sir Robert Filmer, Preface to "Observations upon Aristotle's *Politiques*" in *Patriarchia and Other Writings*, ed. Johoun P. Summerville (Cambridge: Cambridge University Press, 1991).

14. Seventeenth-century geographers such as Heylyn treated the existence of the Amazons as historical fact: see Heylyn's *Cosmographie*, p. 645: "In this part of *Pontus* . . . the *Amazons*, a sort of warlike women, are said to dwell; so called . . . either because they used to cut off their right Pappes, that they might not be an impediment to their

shooting ... or because they used not to live together." For a recent survey of early modern representations of Amazons, see Page DuBois, *Centaurs and Amazons: Women and the Pre-History of the Great Chain of Being* (Ann Arbor: University of Michigan Press, 1982).

15. My account here is more limited than Laura Brown's exploration of the way the Amazon functioned as a common denominator of difference in mercantile capitalist ideology in "Amazons and Africans: Daniel Defoe" in her *Ends of Empire*, pp. 135–69; or that of Dianne Dugaw, whose *Warrior Women and Popular Balladry 1650–1850* (Cambridge: Cambridge University Press, 1989) surveys the myriad popular representations of female fighters, arguing that female heroism expressed male anxieties about valor in a period of near-continuous warfare (pp. 213–15).

16. John Weston, *The Amazon Queen: or, The Amours of Thalestris to Alexander the Great* (London: prtd. for Hen. Herringman, 1667). All quotations will be from this edition and will be cited in the text by act, scene and page number.

17. Earl Miner, "The Wild Man Through the Looking Glass" in *The Wild Man Within: An Image in Western Thought from the Renaissance to Romanticism*, ed. E. Dudley and M. E. Novak (Pittsburgh: University of Pennsylvania Press, 1972), pp. 87–114.

18. Katherine Eisaman Maus, "Arcadia Lost: Politics and Revision in the Restoration *Tempest*," *Renaissance Drama* 13 (1982), pp. 189–209.

19. See David Ogg, "The Plantations and Dependencies" in *England in the Reign of Charles II*, 2 vols. (2nd. edn.: Oxford: Clarendon Press, 1955), vol. II, pp. 657–91, for an overview of the legal and administrative problems raised by the informal expansion of empire in this period.

20. Emeriche de Vattel, "Introduction," *Le Droit des Gens, ou Principes de la Loi Naturelle, appliqués à la Conduite et aux Affaires des Nations et des Souverains*, trans. by C. G. Fenwick (Washington: Carnegie Institute, 1916), 3.

21. Paul McHugh, "Constitutional Theory and Maori Claims" in *Waitangi: Maori and Pakeha Perspectives of the Treaty of Waitangi*, ed. I. H. Kawharu (Auckland: Oxford University Press, 1989), pp. 29–31.

22. McHugh, "Constitutional Theory," p. 30. This is not a view universally accepted. In *The Invasion of America: Indians, Colonization, and the Cant of Conquest* (Chapel Hill: University of North Carolina Press, 1975), Francis Jennings is thoroughly skeptical of Stuart treaty-making practices. Robert A. Williams, in *The American Indian in Western Legal Thought: The Discourses of Conquest* (New York and Oxford: Oxford University Press, 1990), stresses the harmful effects of *res nullius*.

23. See W. Franklin, *Discoverers, Explorers, Settlers: The Diligent Writers of Early America* (Chicago and London: The University of Chicago Press, 1979), and Bernard W. Sheehan, *Savagism and Civility: Indians and Englishmen in Colonial Virginia* (Cambridge: Cambridge University

Press, 1980), for accounts of the language of savagery developed by colonial Englishmen.

24. See Thomas Hobbes, *Philosophical Rudiments Concerning Government and Society* in *The English Works of Thomas Hobbes of Malmesbury*, ed. Sir William Molesworth, 11 vols. (1839–1845; repr. edn. Aalen: Scientin Verlag, 1962), vol. II, p. 116. Staves also discusses Hobbes's account of female sovereignty in *Players' Sceptres: Fictions of Authority in the Restoration*, (Lincoln, NE: University of Nebraska Press, 1979), p. 141.

25. Edward Howard, *The Six Days Adventure, or the New Utopia* (London: prtd. for Tho. Dring, 1671), preface. All quotations will be from this edition and will be cited in the text by act and page number.

26. The poem appears before Howard's text in the 1671 edition.

27. Edward Howard, *The Womens Conquest. A Tragi-comedy* (London: prtd. by J. M. for H. Herringman, 1670). All quotations will be from this edition and will be cited in the text by act, scene and page number.

28. Thomas Durfey, *A Commonwealth of Women* (prtd. for R. Bentley and J. Hindmarsh, 1686). All quotations will be from this edition and will be cited in the text by act and page number.

29. Barash, *English Women's Poetry*, pp. 231–53.

30. Peter Motteux, *Thomyris, Queen of Scythia* (London: prtd. for Jacob Tonson, 1707). All quotations will be from this edition and will be cited in the text by act and page number.

31. For a brief discussion of militarism and femininity in Hopkins's plays, see Hughes, *English Drama*, pp. 433–34.

32. See Pateman, *The Sexual Contract.*

33. See Barash, *English Women's Poetry*, p. 226.

34. See Staves, *Players' Sceptres*, p. 186.

35. See Hughes, *English Drama*, p. 430, for remarks on "rapist tyrants" in the mid–late 1690s.

36. For accounts of the historiographic and literary relationship between rape as a marker of change in legal and in political systems, see Ettore Pais, *Ancient Legends of Roman History* (1905), trans. Mario Constanza (Freeport, NY: Books for Libraries Press, 1971), and Stephanie H. Jed, *Chaste Thinking: The Rape of Lucretia and the Birth of Humanism* (Bloomington and Indianapolis: Indiana University Press, 1989), pp. 1–17. For the development of the "she-tragedy" see Catherine Belsey, *The Subject of Tragedy: Identity and Difference in Renaissance Drama* (New York and London: Methuen, 1985) and Laura Brown, "Staging Sexuality: Violence and Pleasure in the Domestic She-Tragedy" in *Ends of Empire*, pp. 64–102.

37. For context, see the excellent brief introduction by Joel H. Baer in Charles Johnson, *The Life and Adventures of Captain John Avery* [1709?] *and The Successful Pyrate* [1713] (Los Angeles: The Augustan Reprint Society, William Clark Memorial Library, 1980), pp. iii–xiii.

All quotations from *The Successful Pyrate* will be from this edition and will be cited in the text by act and page number.

38. John Esquemeling and Daniel Defoe quoted in Baer, "Introduction" in Charles Johnson, *Life and Adventures*, p. vii.

39. "Libertalia: The Pirate's Utopia" in *Pirates: Terror on the High Seas from the Caribbean to the South China Sea* (Atlanta, GA: Turner Publishing Inc., 1996), pp. 124–39.

40. Rediker, "Libertalia," pp. 126–27.

41. One of the most notorious violations of natural law by the buccaneers was, of course, their predilection for sodomy, hinted at by Johnson in his choice of the matrimonial issue as the provocation to rebellion. See the classic study by B. R. Burg, *Sodomy and the Pirate Tradition: English Sea Rovers in the Seventeenth-Century Caribbean* (New York and London: New York University Press, 1984).

42. Angus Calder records a series of extraordinary episodes in the disorderly Leewards. These include a *de facto* ruler called Norton bullying the governor of Anguilla into signing indentures and then working him semi-naked in the fields as a slave under the whip; and the assassination of an unpopular governor in Antigua by rioting planters, who were rumored to have dragged his maimed body along a road before leaving him to die in the sun. The conduct Calder recounts is reminiscent of the excesses recorded of pirates. See the latter's *Revolutionary Empire: The Rise of the English-Speaking Empires from the Fifteenth Century to the 1780s* (New York: E. P. Dutton, 1981), pp. 413–14.

43. See Baer, "Introduction," in Charles Johnson, *Life and Adventures*, p. vii.

44. Daniel Defoe *The General History of the Pyrates*, ed. Manuel Schonhorn (1724; London: J. M. Dent and Sons, 1972), pp. 587–88. All quotations will be from this edition and will be cited by page number in the text.

45. Quoted by Baer, "Introduction," in Charles Johnson, *Life and Adventures*, p. x.

7 THE CUSTOMS OF THE COUNTRY: COLONIALISM AND COMEDY

1. Maximillian Novak in Dryden, *Works*, vol. x, pp. 450–51. All quotations from *An Evening's Love* will be from this edition and will be cited by act, scene and line number in the text.

2. See Hughes, *English Drama*, pp. 71–73, and Kramer, *The Imperial Dryden*, pp. 88–95.

3. See Glacken, *Traces on the Rhodian Shore*, pp. 429–60.

4. Henry Peacham, *The Compleat Gentleman* (London: Frances Constable, 1622), p. 66.

5. Defending himself against charges of plagiarism in respect to *An Evening's Love*, Dryden remarks in the Preface: "'Tis true, that where ever I have lik'd any story in a Romance, Novel, or forreign Play, I have

made no difficulty, nor ever shall, to take the foundation of it and build it up, to make it proper for the *English* Stage. And I will be so vain to say it has lost nothing in my hands: But it alwayes cost me so much trouble to heighten it for our Theatre (which is incomparably more curious in all the ornaments of Dramatick Poesie, than the *French* or *Spanish*) that when I had finish'd my Play, it was like the Hulk of *Sir Francis Drake*, so strangely alter'd, that there scarce remain'd any Plank of the Timber which first built it" (Preface to *An Evening's Love*, pp. 210–11). For an even more nationalist view, see the Earl of Roscommon's *Essay on Translated Verse* (1684), in Spingarn, *Critical Essays*, pp. 297–309, esp. p. 298 lines 15–32.

6. See Settle's *Farther Defence of Dramatick Poetry*, pp. 28–29.

7. Temple, "Of Poetry" in Spingarn, *Critical Essays*, p. 104.

8. See John Wilcox, *The Relation of Molière to Restoration Comedy* (New York: Columbia University Press, 1938), and Loftis, *Spanish Plays*, p. 106.

9. See Peter Stallybrass and Allon White, *The Politics and Poetics of Transgression* (London: Methuen, 1986). J. Douglas Canfield's recent *Tricksters and Estates: On the Ideology of Restoration Comedy* (Lexington, KY: University of Kentucky Press, 1997) is alert to the class implications of spatial distinctions within the metropolis but unconcerned with national differences.

10. See Dagney Boebel, "In the Carnival World of Adam's Garden: Roving and Rape in Behn's *Rover*" and Pearson, "Blacker than Hell Creates" in Quinsey, *Broken Boundaries*, pp. 54–70 and pp. 13–30; and Hughes, *English Drama*, pp. 30–77, pp. 307–30.

11. Recent criticism concerned with construction and policing of gendered identities in Restoration comedy includes Harold Weber, *The Restoration Rake-Hero: Transformations in Sexual Understanding in Seventeenth-Century England* (Madison, WI: The University of Wisconsin Press, 1986); Pat Gill, *Interpreting Ladies: Women, Wit and Morality in the Restoration Comedy of Manners* (Athens, GA, and London: University of Georgia Press, 1994); and Quinsey, *Broken Boundaries*. J. Douglas Canfield's *Tricksters and Estates* provides an account of comic genre, governed by (or resistant to) Stuart ideology, which distinguishes between social comedy, subversive comedy and comic satire in terms of the dramatic affirmation or critique of dominant assumptions. None of these critics is concerned with the definition of specifically English forms of identity or inter-cultural conflicts.

12. For a recent discussion see Robert E. Glass, "The Image of the Sea Officer in English Literature, 1660–1714," *Albion* 26.4 (Winter 1994), pp. 583–99.

13. In making this claim, literary historians have tended to cite J. G. A. Pocock, especially *Virtue, Commerce, and History: Essays on Political Thought, Chiefly in the Eighteenth Century* (Cambridge: Cambridge University Press, 1985), pp. 37–50 and pp. 103–24. For an important

recent extrapolation, see Klein, *Shaftesbury and the Culture of Politeness*, pp. 175–212. Susan Staves makes a similar, if less nuanced claim about the displacement of the warrior by the private gentleman in her *Players' Sceptres*, p. 189, citing the historical influence of Lawrence Stone's formulations of shifts in sexual and familial roles in this period in *The Family, Sex and Marriage in England, 1500–1800* (New York: Harper and Row, 1977).

14. Pocock, *Virtue, Commerce and History*, p. 110.
15. Klein, *Shaftesbury and the Culture of Politeness*, pp. 175–212.
16. Holmes discusses the quite wide-ranging antagonism to the expansion of the services and the military accretion of power and money in his *Augustan England: Professions, State and Society, 1680–1730* (London: George Allen and Unwin, 1982), pp. 262–64.
17. See Nussbaum, *Torrid Zones.*
18. See Peacham, *Compleat Gentleman*, p. 200, p. 202.
19. Pagden, *Lords of All the World*, p. 61.
20. The play conforms to what Loftis defines as a "Spanish plot" consisting of the Peninsular setting, the inclusion of characters with a rigid code of conduct, elaborate intrigue and at least one high-spirited female character. See Loftis, *Spanish Plays*, p. 99.
21. The characterization of the Englishmen in *The Rover* seems to adhere to a stereotypical representation consistent from Evelyn's *Character of England* (1659) through John Arbuthnot's *The History of John Bull* (1712). In Arbuthnot's words, Bull "was an honest plain dealing Fellow, Cholerick, Bold, and of a very unconstant Temper": fickle, bibulous and open-handed, John Arbuthnot, *John Bull*, ed. Alan W. Bower and Robert A. Erickson (Oxford: Clarendon Press, 1976), p. lviii.
22. John Dennis, *Gibraltar: or, the Spanish Adventure* (London: prtd. for Wm. Turner, 1705) I, p. 2. All quotations are from this edition and will be cited in the text by act and page number.
23. Evelyn, *Tyrannus*, p. 4.
24. Seaward points out that English anti-Gallicism was fueled by the large trade deficit. See *The Restoration*, p. 76.
25. *The Man of Mode, or Sir Fopling Flutter* in *The Plays of Sir George Etherege*, ed. Michael Cordner (Cambridge: Cambridge University Press, 1982), iii.ii. 246–47, and 250–58. All quotations will be from this edition and will be cited in the text by act, scene and line number.
26. See Laura Brown, *Ends of Empire*, pp. 114–21, for a discussion of the way the trope of dressing locates the motive force of capitalism in the female consumer, rather than the masculine profiteer.
27. Charles Hopkins, *Friendship Improv'd: or, the Female Warrior* (London: prtd. for Jacob Tonson, 1700). All quotations are from this edition.
28. Charlotte Bradford Hughes points out that the *indiano*, or colonist returned from America, often incredibly wealthy and intolerably complacent, was a stock satiric type in seventeenth-century Spanish drama.

See *John Crowne's* Sir Courtly Nice*: A Critical Edition* (The Hague and Paris: Mouton and Co., 1966), p. 51.

29. John Caryll, *Sir Salomon: or, the Cautious Coxcomb* (London: prtd. for H. Herringman, 1671), II, p. 28. All quotations will be from this edition and will be cited in the text by act and page number.

30. III. l. 448. All quotations will be from Hughes's edition and will be cited in the text by act and line number.

31. For a summary account of the rise of *chinoiserie* in England during this period, see William A. Appleton, *A Cycle of Cathay: The Chinese Vogue in England during the Seventeenth and Eighteenth Centuries* (New York: Columbia University Press, 1951). Appleton includes a brief account of Rowe's *Biter* (p. 73).

32. Nicholas Rowe, *The Biter* (London: prtd. for J. T. and sold by T. Jauncey, 1720), I, p. 19. All quotations will be from this edition and will be cited in the text by act and page number.

33. See Ogg, "The Plantations and Dependencies" in *England in the Reign of Charles II*, pp. 682–85, on the rebelliousness of the inhabitants of Massachussetts in particular.

34. Ogg, "The Plantations and Dependencies," *England in the Reign of Charles II*, p. 686.

35. Thomas Durfey, *Sir Barnaby Whigg: or, No Wit Like a Woman's* (London: prtd. by A. G. and J. P. for Joseph Hindmarsh, 1681), v, p. 62. All quotations will be from this edition and will be cited in the text by act and page number.

36. Nahum Tate, *Cuckold's Haven: or, An Alderman No Conjurer* (London: prtd. for J. H. to be sold by Edward Poole, 1685), I, p. 7. All quotations will be from this edition and will be cited by act and page number in the text.

37. Charles Sedley, *Bellamira: or The Mistress* (London: prtd. for L. C. and Timothy Goodwin, 1687), I.i, p. 7 and I.i, p. 11. All other quotations are from this edition and will be cited in the text by act, scene and page number.

38. Dedication to *The Plain Dealer*, lines 92–93, p. 366 in *The Plays of William Wycherley*, ed. Arthur Friedmann (Oxford: Clarendon Press, 1979). All quotations will be from this edition and will be cited in the text by act, scene and line number.

39. David Hume, *Essays, Moral, Political and Literary*, 2 vols. (1753; London: T. Cadell, 1784), vol.I, p. 402.

40. Criticism of this long-neglected play has finally begun to appear. For readings which intersect with my own, see Margaret Ferguson, "Whose Dominion, or News from the New World: Aphra Behn's Representation of Miscegenous Romance in *Oroonoko* and *The Widow Ranter*" in *The Production of English Renaissance Cultures*, ed. David Lee Miller, Sharon O'Dair and Harold Weber (Ithaca and London: Cornell University Press, 1994), and Margo Hendricks, "Civility, Barbarism and Aphra Behn's *The Widow Ranter*" in *Women, "Race" and*

Writing in the Early Modern Period, ed. Margo Hendricks and Patricia Parker (New York and London: Routledge, 1994), pp. 225–42.

41. *The Beginning, Progress and Conclusion of Bacon's Rebellion in Virginia in the Years 1675 & 1676* is included with other documents in *Tracts and Other Papers, Relating Principally to the Colonies in North America*, ed. P. Force (Washington: pubd. by the author, 1836), vol. I, p. 19. For Todd's comments see her edition, *The Works of Aphra Behn* (Columbus, OH: Ohio State University Press, 1992–98), vol. VII, p. 289.

42. *Beginning, Progress and Conclusion*, p. 19.

43. *Beginning, Progress and Conclusion*, p. 14.

44. *Beginning, Progress and Conclusion*, p. 25.

45. The following account is drawn from Calder, *Revolutionary Empire*, pp. 309–13.

46. *Beginning, Progress and Conclusion*, p. 25.

47. Calder, *Revolutionary Empire*, p. 312.

48. Calder, *Revolutionary Empire*, p. 311.

49. C. H. Cotton, *To his Wife, A. L. at Q. Creek*, in *Tracts and Other Papers*, ed. Force, vol. I, p. 11.

50. *The Works of Aphra Behn*, ed. Janet Todd, v.iv. Subsequent references are from this edition and will be included in the text.

51. Knorr, *British Colonial Theories*, p. 106.

52. See Jeremy Black and Phillip Woodfine, eds. *The British Navy and the Use of Naval Power in the Eighteenth Century* (Leicester: Leicester University Press, 1988), p. 3.

53. Black and Woodfine, eds. *British Navy*, p. 3.

54. Pincus, *Protestantism and Patriotism*, pp. 246–49.

55. "A Rough Draft" in Savile, *Works*, vol. I, pp. 294–95.

56. See Howard Erskine-Hill, *The Augustan Idea in English Literature* (London: Edward Arnold, 1983), pp. 214–18.

57. J. D. Davies, *Gentlemen and Tarpaulins: The Officers and Men of the Restoration Navy* (Oxford: Clarendon Press, 1992). Davies's account is in part designed to contest the Pepysian view, generally confirmed by historians, that the navy needed to be rescued from the debilitating effects of the incompetent and licentious "gentlemen" put in under the Stuarts to replace the rough but ready "tarps."

58. See Davies, *Gentlemen and Tarpaulins*, ch. 3, for details of this dispute.

59. See Davies, *Gentlemen and Tarpaulins*, on lucrative voyages, p. 51; on pages, p. 31; on O'Brien's commission, p. 26; on his mistress, p. 92. The ruse was discovered when he tried to get her paid by the Navy Board.

60. *The Tangier Papers of Samuel Pepys*, ed. Edwin Chappell (London: Publications of Navy Records Society, 1935), vol. LXXIII, p. 166.

61. For officers' hyper-sensitivity to "honour," see Davies, *Gentlemen and Tarpaulins*, pp. 31–33.

62. "A Rough Draft" in Savile, *Works*, vol. I, p. 306.

63. *The Plain Dealer* (II. i.517–20) in Wycherley, *Plays*. All quotations will

be from this edition and will be cited in the text by Act, scene and line number.

64. George Farquhar, *The Recruiting Officer* (v.vii. 90–93) in *The Works of George Farquhar*, ed. Shirley Strum Kenny, 2 vols. (Oxford: Clarendon Press, 1988). All quotations will be from this edition and will be cited in the text by act, scene and line numbers.

65. Charles Shadwell, *The Fair Quaker of Deal; or, The Humours of the Navy* in *The English Theatre*, 8 vols. (London: prtd. for T. Lowndes, 1765), vol. III. All quotations will be from this edition and will be cited in the text by act, scene and page number.

66. Charles Shadwell, *The Humours of the Army* (London: prtd. by James Knapton, 1713). All quotations will be from this edition and will be cited in the text by act, scene and page number.

67. Sir Francis Fane, *Love in the Dark; or, The Man of Business* (London: prtd. for Hen. Herringman, 1675). All quotations will be from this edition and will be cited in the text by act and page number.

68. Aphra Behn, *The False Count; or, A New Way to Play an Old Game* in *Works*, vol. VI (1996), I.i. 59–60. All quotations will be from this edition and will be cited in the text by act, scene and line number.

69. Evelyn, *Navigation and Commerce*, p. 11.

8 ROMANS AND BRITONS

1. Erskine-Hill, *The Augustan Idea*, ch. 8 esp.

2. For the Brutus legend, see Hugh A. MacDougall, *Racial Myth in English History: Trojans, Teutons and Anglo-Saxons* (Montreal: Harvest House, 1982). Philip Ayres documents Camden's belief in the "mutual engrafting" of Romans and Britons in the latter's *Britannia* (1586) in his *Classical Culture and the Idea of Rome in Eighteenth-Century England* (Cambridge: Cambridge University Press, 1997), pp. 85–86. Although a rich account of cultural and political discourses and practices from architecture and archeology through to literature, this study does not discuss "Roman" plays in any depth.

3. See Zera S. Fink, *The Classical Republicans* (Evanston, IL: Northwestern University Press, 1946; 2nd. edn.: 1962); Caroline Robbins, *The Eighteenth-Century Commonwealths Man* (Cambridge, MA: Harvard University Press, 1959); and J. G. A. Pocock, *The Machiavellian Moment: Florentine Political Thought and the Atlantic Republican Tradition* (Princeton: Princeton University Press, 1975).

4. Howard D. Weinbrot, *Britannia's Issue: the Rise of British Literature from Dryden to Ossian* (Cambridge: Cambridge University Press, 1993). See, especially, ch. 7, "The 'Pax Romana' and the 'Pax Britannica': The Ethics of War and the Ethics of Trade." For a review of evidence contesting Weinbrot's claims that the Augustan Age (of Rome) was generally deplored in the late seventeenth and eighteenth centuries, see Erskine-Hill, *The Augustan Idea*, p. 236.

5. Ayres, *Classical Culture*, ch. 1.
6. Stephanie Jed remarks in *Chaste Thinking*: "From the earliest histori-ographic records, some erotic offence . . . is always required in order to justify the overthrow of tyrants. Aristotle abstracts from this nar-rative pattern a political formula: one of the primary reasons tyrants are ruined is that they offend the honour of their male subjects by raping and violating their wives and breaking up their marriages" (p. 3).
7. John Dennis, Prologue from *Appius and Virginia. A Tragedy* (London: Bernard Lintott, 1707). All quotations will be from this edition and will be cited in the text by act and page number.
8. Armitage, "The Cromwellian Protectorate," pp. 531–55.
9. See Graham Webster, *Boudica: the British Revolt against Rome, AD 60* (London: B. T. Batsford, 1978). Webster cites as the three main causes of the Revolt: "the appropriation of lands and brutal behaviour of the colonists towards the Trinovantes; the building of the (Claudian) Temple; and, the final straw, the seizure of the royal properties of the Iceni, and the violence and shameful acts against Boudica and her daughters" (p. 89).
10. For a comprehensive recent account of the role of ancient ethni-city in theological and constitutional components of identity in the period 1600–1800, see Colin Kidd, *British Identities Before Nationalism: Ethnicity and Nationhood in the Atlantic World, 1600–1800* (Cambridge: Cambridge University Press, 1999), chs. 4 and 5 especially.
11. *The Empress of Morocco* is a good example of this process in the heroic genre. See also the discussion of Dryden and Davenant's *Tempest* above.
12. For the latter, see Pocock, *The Ancient Constitution*.
13. Erskine-Hill, *The Augustan Idea*, p. 216.
14. Evelyn, *Navigation and Commerce*, p. 14.
15. Evelyn, *Navigation and Commerce*, p. 11.
16. *An Embassy from the East-India Company of the United Provinces, to the Great Tartar Cham, Emperor of China*, Englished by John Ogilby (London: prtd. by John Macock, 1669), p. 3.
17. Thomas Rymer, *Edgar, or The English Monarch* (London: prtd. for Richard Tonson, 1677). All quotations will be from this edition and will be cited by act and page number in the text.
18. Edward Howard, *The British Princes* (London: prtd. by T. N. for H. Herringman, 1669). All quotations will be from this edition and will be cited in the text.
19. See Michael Dobson, *The Making of the National Poet: Shakespeare, Adap-tation and Authorship 1660–1769* (Oxford: Clarendon Press, 1992).
20. Erskine-Hill, *The Augustan Idea*, pp. 224–225: see also George McFadden, *Dryden: The Public Writer, 1660–1685* (Princeton: Prince-ton University Press, 1978) for the Charles/Antony parallels. For dis-cussions of Whig and republican critique see J. Douglas Canfield,

"Royalism's Last Dramatic Stand: English Political Tragedy, 1679–1689," *Studies in Philology* 82 (1985), 234–63, and *"Regulus* and *Cleomenes* and 1688: From Royalism to Self-Reliance," *Eighteenth-Century Life* 12 (1988), pp. 67–75; Barbara A. Murray, "The Butt of Otway's Political Moral in *The History and Fall of Caius Marius* (1680)," *Notes and Queries* 234 (1989), pp. 48–50; Susan Jane Owen, "'Partial tyrants' and 'Freeborn People' in *Lucius Junius Brutus*," *Studies in English Literature* 31 (1991), pp. 463–82, and "Interpreting the Politics of Restoration Drama," *Seventeenth Century* 8 (1993), pp. 67–97.

21. For commentary on allegorical purposes, see David Scott Kastan, *"Nero* and the Politics of Nathaniel Lee," *Papers on Language and Literature* 13 (1977), pp. 125–135.

22. *The Tragedy of Nero, Emperor of Rome* in *The Works of Nathaniel Lee*, ed. Thomas B. Strup and Arthur L. Cooke, 2 vols. (Metuchen, NJ: Scarecrow Reprint Corp., 1968), vol. I, I.ii. 60–64. All quotations from Lee's works will be from this edition and will be cited by vol., act, scene and line number in the text.

23. Hughes, *English Drama*, p. 430.

24. For important recent analysis of *Cato*'s treatment of specifically imperial themes, notably in relation to race, see Julie Ellison, "Cato's Tears," *English Literary History* 63.2 (Spring 1996), pp. 571–601, and Srinivas Aravamudan, *Tropicopolitans: Colonialism and Agency, 1688–1804* (Durham and London: Duke University Press, 1999), pp. 113–27.

25. Ayres, *Classical Culture*, p. 86.

26. See Curtis A. Price, *Henry Purcell and the London Stage* (Cambridge: Cambridge University Press, 1984), pp. 117–25.

27. *Bonduca, or, The British Heroine* (London: prtd. for Richard Bentley, 1696), II, p. 15. All quotations will be from this edition and will be cited in the text by act and page number.

28. Charles Hopkins, *Boadicea, Queen of Britain. A Tragedy*. (London: prtd. for Jacob Tonson, 1696), I, p. 3. All quotations will be from this edition and will be cited in the text by act and page number.

29. See above, ch. 6, for discussion of this issue. For a discussion of the broad socio-cultural reasons for the rise of the pathetic heroines of she-tragedy, see Laura Brown, *Ends of Empire*, pp. 64–102.

30. The Prologue to Charles Gildon's *Love's Victim: Or, The Queen of Wales. A Tragedy* (London: prtd. by M. Bennet for Richard Parker and George Strahan, 1701). All quotations will be from this edition and will be cited in the text by act and page number.

31. It seems possible the kindly treatment of the Druid reflects dramatists' caution at bringing the wrath of Collierites on their heads after the debate over Dryden's supposedly irreverent treatment of priests in *Don Sebastian*.

32. See J. Douglas Canfield, *Nicholas Rowe*.

33. *The Royal Convert* from *The Dramatick Works of Nicholas Rowe* (London:

prtd. by T. Jauncey, 1720), vol. 2, IV.i., p. 54. All quotations will be from this edition and will be cited in the text by act, scene and page number.

CONCLUSION

1. David Armitage, "Literature and Empire" in *The Origins of Empire: British Overseas Enterprise to the Close of the Seventeenth Century*, ed. Nicholas Canny (Oxford and New York: Oxford University Press, 1998), pp. 98–123.
2. See Laura Brown, *Ends of Empire*, for an extended analysis.
3. Thomas Southerne, *Oroonoko*, ed. Maximillian E. Novak and David Stuart Rodes (Lincoln, NE: University of Nebraska Press, 1976), lines 16–24. All quotations will be from this edition and will be cited by act, scene and line number in the text.
4. Mary Vermillion argues that these remarks are governed by Southerne's hostility to Behn's status as a female author, and that he deliberately disrupts her identification with Oroonoko to parody her assertions of literary authority. See "Buried Heroism: Critiques of Female Authorship in Southerne's Adaptation of Behn's *Oroonoko*," *Restoration: Studies in English Literary Culture, 1660–1700* 16.1 (Spring 1992), pp. 28–37. Given Southerne's sympathetic treatment of female characters in other plays, I find this reading somewhat implausible.
5. Suvir Kaul, "Reading Literary Symptoms: Colonial Pathologies and the *Oroonoko* Fictions of Behn, Southerne and Hawkesworth," *Eighteenth-Century Life* 18.3 (November 1994), pp. 80–96.
6. See Hughes, *English Drama*, pp. 344–45 for an overview of this theme in Southerne.
7. See the Introduction to Novak's and Rodes's edition of the text. For the opposing view, see Vermillion's "Buried Heroism," p. 29; and Julia A. Rich, "Heroic Tragedy in Southerne's *Oroonoko* (1695): An Approach to a Splitplot Tragicomedy," *Philological Quarterly* 62 (1983), pp. 187–200.
8. See Laura Brown, *Ends of Empire*, p. 172.
9. Pratt, *Imperial Eyes*. Pratt argues that apparently sympathetic accounts of colonized peoples serve to establish a fantasy of fellow-feeling between a few select colonists and a few deserving colonial subjects, in a process which eases a disavowal of the full horrors of the colonial process.
10. See for example, Francis Jennings, *The Invasion of America: Indians, Colonization and the Cant of Conquest* (Chapel Hill: University of North Carolina Press, 1975); Robert A. Williams, *The American Indian in Western Legal Thought: The Discourses of Conquest* (New York and Oxford: Oxford University Press, 1990); and David K. Richter, *The Ordeal of the Long-House: The Peoples of the Iroquois League in the Era of*

European Colonization (Chapel Hill: University of North Carolina Press, 1992).

11. "Feathered Peoples" in *Cities of the Dead: Circum-Atlantic Performance* (New York: Columbia University Press, 1996), pp. 119–77.

12. See Loftis, *The Politics of Drama.*

13. Braverman, *Plots and Counter-plots*, pp. 242–43.

14. Dennis, *Liberty Asserted.* All subsequent quotations from this edition will be cited in the text by act, scene and page number.

15. I draw here on Angus Calder's account in *Revolutionary Empire*, p. 191.

16. See James Axtell, *The Invasion Within: The Contest of Cultures in Colonial North America* (New York: Oxford University Press, 1985).

Works Cited

I. PRIMARY SOURCES

MODERN EDITIONS

Arbuthnot, John. *The History of John Bull.* Ed. Alan W. Bower and Robert A. Erickson. Oxford: Clarendon Press, 1976.

Aubrey, John. *Aubrey's Brief Lives.* Ed. Oliver Lawson Dick. 1949; Harmondsworth: Penguin, 1982.

Behn, Aphra. *The Works of Aphra Behn.* Ed. Janet Todd. 7 vols. Columbus, OH: Ohio State University Press, 1992–96.

Bowers, Fredson, ed. *Beaumont and Fletcher: Dramatic Works.* Cambridge: Cambridge University Press, 1966–96.

Boyle, Roger. *The Dramatic Works of Roger Boyle, Earl of Orrery.* Ed. William Smith Clark. 2 vols. Cambridge, MA: Harvard University Press, 1937.

Congreve, William. *The Complete Plays of William Congreve.* Ed. Herbert Davis. Chicago: Chicago University Press, 1967.

Cowley, Abraham. *The English Writings of Abraham Cowley.* Ed. A. R. Waller. 4 vols. Cambridge: Cambridge University Press, 1905.

Crowne, John. *John Crowne's Sir Courtly Nice: A Critical Edition.* Ed. C.B. Hughes. The Hague and Paris: Mouton and Co., 1966.

Davenant, William. *The Dramatic Works of William Davenant.* Ed. James Maidment and W. H. Logan. 5 vols. Edinburgh and London: W. Patterson, 1872–74.

The Siege of Rhodes: A Critical Edition. Ed. Ann-Mari Hedback. Uppsala: Universitatis Upsaliensis, 1973.

Defoe, Daniel. *The General History of the Pyrates.* Ed. Manuel Schonhorn. 1724; London: J. M. Dent and Sons, 1972.

Dennis, John. *The Critical Works of John Dennis.* Ed. Edward Niles Hooker. 2 vols. Baltimore: Johns Hopkins University Press, 1939–43.

De Scudery, Madeleine. *Prefaces to Fiction.* Intro. B. Boyce. Los Angeles: Augustan Reprint Society, Publ. No. 32, 1952.

De Vattel, Emeriche. *Le Droit des Gens, ou Principes de la Loi Naturelle, appliqués à la Conduite et aux Affaires des Nations et des Souverains.* Trans. C. G. Fenwick. Washington, DC: Carnegie Institute, 1916.

Doyle, Anne T., ed. *Elkanah Settle's* The Empress of Morocco *and the Controversy Surrounding It: A Critical Edition.* New York and London: Garland, 1987.

Dryden, John. *Dramatic Essays, John Dryden.* Ed. William Henry Hudson. 1912; London: Dent, 1931.

The Dramatic Works of John Dryden. Ed. Sir Walter Scott and George Saintsbury. 8 vols. Edinburgh: William Patterson, 1882.

The Letters of John Dryden. Ed. Charles E. Ward. Durham, NC: University of North Carolina Press, 1942.

The Works of John Dryden. Ed. H. T. Swedenberg Jr. *et al.* 19 vols. Los Angeles and Berkeley, CA: University of California Press, 1956–.

Etherege, George. *The Plays of George Etherege.* Ed. Michael Cordner. Cambridge: Cambridge University Press, 1982.

Evelyn, John. *The Diary of John Evelyn.* Ed. E. S. de Beer. 6 vols. Oxford: Oxford University Press, 1959.

Farquhar, George. *The Works of George Farquhar.* Ed. Shirley Stren Kerry. 2 vols. Oxford: Clarendon Press, 1988.

Filmer, Sir Robert. *Patriarcha and Other Writings.* Ed. Johoun P. Summerville. Cambridge: Cambridge University Press, 1991.

Flecknoe, Richard. *Epigrams of all Sorts, made at Diverse Times and on Different Occasions.* London: 1670; New York: Garland, 1975.

Fletcher, Andrew. *Andrew Fletcher: Political Works.* Ed. John Robertson. Cambridge: Cambridge University Press, 1997.

Gildon, Charles. *Remarks on Mr. Rowe's Tragedy of the Lady Jane Gray, and All His Other Plays.* Ed. Arthur Freeman. 1715; New York and London: Garland, 1974.

Hobbes, Thomas. *The English Works of Thomas Hobbes of Malmesbury.* Ed. Sir William Molesworth. 11 vols. 1839–45; repr. edn. Aalen: Scientin Verlag, 1962.

Hopkins, Charles. *The Successful Pyrate* (1713) in *The Life and Adventures of Captain John Avery (1709) and The Successful Pyrate (1713).* Ed. Joel H. Baer. Los Angeles: The Augustan Reprint Society and William Clark Memorial Library, 1980.

Johnson, Samuel. *The Works of Samuel Johnson, LL.D.* Ed. George Birkbeck. 3 vols. Oxford: Clarendon Press, 1905.

Jordan, Thomas. "London's Glory, or the Lord Mayor's Show" (1680) in *The Lord Mayor's Pageants of the Merchant Taylors' Company in the 15th, 16th and 17th Centuries.* Ed. Robert T. D. Sayle. London: The Eastern Press Ltd., 1931.

Lee, Nathaniel. *The Rival Queens.* Ed. P. F. Vernon. 1677; Lincoln, NE: University of Nebraska Press, 1970.

The Works of Nathaniel Lee. Ed. Thomas B. Strup and Arthur L. Cooke 2 vols. Metuchen, NJ: Scarecrow Reprint Corp., 1968.

Leigh, Richard. *The Censure of the Rota. On Mr. Dryden's Conquest of Granada.* Oxford, 1673; New York: Garland, 1974.

Locke, John. *The Two Treatises of Government.* Ed. Peter Laslett. 2nd. edn. Cambridge: Cambridge University Press, 1963.

Magalotti, Lorenzo. *Lorenzo Magalotti at the Court of Charles II: His "Relazione a'Inghilterra" of 1688.* Ed. and trans. W. E. Knowles Middleton. Waterloo: Wilfred Laurier University Press, 1980.

Montagu, Lady Mary Wortley. *The Complete Letters of Lady Mary Wortley Montagu.* Ed. R. Haisband. Oxford: The Clarendon Press, 1965.

Pepys, Samuel. *The Diary of Samuel Pepys.* Ed. Robert Latham and William Mathews. 11 vols. London: G. Bell and Sons Ltd., 1970–83.

The Tangier Papers of Samuel Pepys. Ed. Edwin Chappell. London: Publications of the Navy Records Society, 1935.

Pix, Mary, and Catherine Trotter. *The Plays of Mary Pix and Catherine Trotter.* Ed. and intro. Edna L. Stevens. New York and London: Garland, 1982.

Purchas, Samuel. *Hakluytus Posthumus, or Purchas His Pilgrimes.* 20 vols. 1625; Glasgow: James MacLehose and Sons, 1905.

Rymer, Thomas. *The Critical Works of Thomas Rymer.* Ed. Curt A. Zimansky. New Haven and London: Yale University Press, 1956.

Savile, George. *The Works of George Savile, Marquis of Halifax.* Ed. Mark K. Brown. 3 vols. Oxford: Clarendon Press, 1989.

Schless, Howard H., ed. *Poems on Affairs of State: Augustan Satirical Verse, 1660–1714.* Vol. III. New Haven and London: Yale University Press, 1968.

Settle, Elkanah. *Elkanah Settle's* The Empress of Morocco *et al.* Intro. Maximillian E. Novak. Los Angeles: William Andrews Clark Memorial Library, University of California at Los Angeles, 1968.

Shadwell, Thomas. *The Plays of Thomas Shadwell.* Ed. Montague Summers. 5 vols. London: The Fortune Press, 1927.

Southerne, Thomas. *Oroonoko.* Ed. Maximillian E. Novak and David Stuart Rodes. Lincoln, NE: University of Nebraska Press, 1976.

The Works of Thomas Southerne. Ed. Robert Jordan and Harold Love. 2 vols. Oxford: Clarendon Press, 1988.

Spingarn, J. E. ed. *Critical Essays of the Seventeenth Century.* 3 vols. Oxford: Clarendon Press, 1908–1909.

Tracts and Other Papers, Relating Principally to the Colonies in North America. Ed. P. Force. 4 vols. Washington, DC: published by the author, 1836–46.

Waller, Edmund. *The Poems of Edmund Waller.* Ed. G. Thorn Drury. 2 vols. London and New York: A. H. Bullen and Charles Scribner's Sons, 1901.

Wycherley, William. *The Plays of William Wycherley.* Ed. Arthur Friedmann. Oxford: Clarendon Press, 1979.

FIRST LONDON EDITIONS

A Description of the Academy of the Athenian Virtuosi. Oxford: prtd. for Maurice Atkins, 1673.

Addison, Lancelot. *West Barbary, or a Short Narrative of the Revolutions of the Kingdoms of Fez and Morocco.* Oxford: prtd. at the Theatre, 1671.

The Ancient and Modern Stages Survey'd . . . London: Abel Roper, 1699.

Astell, Mary. *A Serious Proposal to the Ladies For the Advancement of their True and Greatest Interest.* Ed. Patricia Springborg. 1694; Brookfield, VT: Pickering and Chatto, 1996.

  Some Reflections Upon Marriage. 1700; New York: Source Book Press, 1970.

Banks, John. *Cyrus the Great; or, the Tragedy of Love.* London: prtd. for Richard Bentley, 1696.

Behn, Aphra. *Abdelezar, or the Moor's Revenge. A Tragedy.* London: prtd. for J. Magnes and R. Bentley (etc.), 1677.

Bernier, François. *The History of the Late Revolution of the Empire of the Great Mogol.* London: Moses Pitt, Simon Miller, John Starkey, 1671.

Bonduca, or, The British Heroine. London: prtd. for Richard Bentley, 1696.

Caryll, John. *Sir Salomon; or, the Cautious Coxcomb.* London: prtd. for H. Herringman, 1671.

Chardin, Jean. *A New and Accurate Description of Persia.* Trans. Edmond Lloyd. 2 vols. 1686; London: A. Bettesworth and J. Batley, 1724.

  The Present State of Persia. London, 1686.

  Travels of Sir John Chardin into Persia and the East Indies through the Black Sea and the Country of Colchis. London: Moses Pitt, 1686.

Cibber, Colley. *Xerses. A Tragedy. The Dramatick Works of Colley Cibber.* 5 vols. Vol. IV. London: prtd. for W. Feales, 1736.

Clarke, Samuel. *The Life and Death of Cyrus the Great.* London: William Miller, 1664.

Crowne, John. *Darius, King of Persia. A Tragedy.* London: prtd. for R. Bentley, 1688.

Curtius Rufus, Quintus. *The Life and Death of Alexander the Great.* Trans. Roger Codrington. London: prtd. by E. Alsop and Robert Wood, 1661.

  The Life of Alexander the Great written in Latin by Quintus Curtius Rufus and translated into English by Several Gentlemen in the University of Cambridge. London: prtd. for Francis Saunders, 1690.

Davenant, Charles. *Essays upon the Balance of Power, The Right of Making War, Peace and Alliances, and Universal Monarchy.* London: James Knapton, 1701.

Dennis, John. *Appius and Virginia. A Tragedy.* London: Bernard Lintott, 1707.

  Gibraltar; or, the Spanish Adventure. London: prtd. for Wm. Turner, 1705.

  Liberty Asserted. London: George Strahan and Bernard Lintott, 1704.

Durfey, Thomas. *A Commonwealth of Women.* London: prtd. for R. Bentley and J. Hindmarsh, 1686.

   Sir Barnaby Whigg: or, No Wit Like a Woman's. London: prtd. by A. G. and J. P. for Joseph Hindmarsh, 1681.

Elstob, Elizabeth. *An English-Saxon Homily on the Birthday of Saint Gregory: Anciently used in the English-Saxon Church* . . . London: prtd. by W. Bowyer, 1709.

An Embassy from the East-India Company of the United Provinces to the Great Tartar Cham, Emperor of China. Englished by John Ogilby. London: prtd. by John Macock, 1669.

The Emblem of Ingratitude, A True Relation of the Unjust, Uncivill and Barbarous Proceedings Against the English at Amboyna in the East Indies, by the Neatherlandish Governor and Counsel There. 1624; London, 1672.

Europae Modernae Speculum; or, A View of the Empires, Kingdoms, Principalities, Signieuries, and Commonwealths of Europe. London: prtd. by T. Leach for Tho. Johnson, 1665.

Evelyn, John. *Navigation and Commerce, Their Original and Progress.* London: Benj. Tooke, 1674.

   Tyrannus, or the Mode: A Discourse of Sumptuary Laws. London: prtd. by G. Bedel, T. Collins and J. Crook, 1661.

Fane, Sir Francis. *Love in the Dark; or, The Man of Business.* London: prtd. for Hen. Herringman, 1675.

Filmer, Edward. *A Defence of Plays, or, The Stage Vindicated* . . . London: Joseph Tonson, 1707.

Flecknoe, Richard. *A Short Discourse of the English Stage.* London, 1664.

Fryer, John. *A New Account of East India and Persia in Eight Letters.* London: R. Chiswell, 1698.

Gildon, Charles. *A comparison between the Two Stages.* London, 1702.

   Love's Victim: Or, The Queen of Wales. A Tragedy. London: prtd. by M. Bennet for Richard Parker and George Strahan, 1701.

   Miscellaneous Letters and Essays on Several Subjects, Philosophical, Moral, Historical, Critical, Amorous &c. By Several Gentlemen and Ladies. London: Benjamin Bragg, 1694.

Godwyn, Morgan. *The Negro's and Indians Advocate, suing for their Admission into the Church: or a Persuasive to the Instructing and Baptizing of the "Negros" and Indians in our Plantations* . . . London: prtd. for the author by J. D. 1680.

Goring, Charles. *Irene; or, the Fair Greek. A Tragedy.* London: J. Bayley, 1708.

Herbert, Thomas. *A Relation of Some Years Travaille into Afrique and the Great Asia.* London: prtd. by William Stansby and Jacob Blome, 1634.

Heylyn, Peter. *Cosmographie in Four Bookes, Contayning the Chorographie & Historie of the Whole World.* 3rd. edn. London: prtd. for Anne Seile, 1665.

Hoadley, Benjamin. *The Humble Reply to the Right Reverent the Lord Bishop of Exeter's Answer.* 2nd. edn. London, 1709.

Hopkins, Charles. *Boadicea, Queen of Britain. A Tragedy.* London: prtd. for Jacob Tonson, 1696.

Friendship Improv'd; or, the Female Warriour. London: prtd. for Jacob Tonson, 1700.

Howard, Edward. *The British Princess.* London: prtd. by T. N. for H. Herringman, 1669.

The Six Days Adventure, or the New Utopia. London: prtd. for Tho. Dring, 1671.

The Womens Conquest. A Tragi-comedy. London: prtd. by J. M. for H. Herringman, 1670.

Hume, David. *Essays, Moral, Political and Literary.* 2 vols. 1753; London: T. Cadell, 1784.

Irena, A Tragedy. London: prtd. by Robert White for Octavian Pulleyn Jr., 1664.

"King William's Happy Deliverance and Glorious Triumph over his Enemies; or, the Consultation of the Pope, Devil, French King and the Great Turk . . . " Performed at Miller's Loyal Association Booth, May Fair, 1696.

Knolles, Richard. *The Turkish Historie.* Ed. Paul Rycaut. 6th. edn. London, 1687.

Manley, Mary Delariviere. *Almyna; or, the Arabian Vow.* London: prtd. for William Turner and Egbert Sanger, 1707.

Marsh, John. *A New Survey of the Turkish Empire and Government . . .* London: Henry Marsh, 1663.

Martinius, Martin. *Bellum Tartaricum, or the Conquest of the Great and most Renowned Empire of China by the Invasion of the Tartars . . .* London: prtd. for John Crook, 1655.

Motteux, Peter. *The Island Princess, or The Generous Portuguese.* London: prtd. for Richard Wellington, 1699.

Thomyris, Queen of Scythia. London: prtd. for Jacob Tonson, 1707.

Ogilby, John. *Asia, the First Part. Being an Accurate Description of Persia.* London: prtd. by the author, 1673.

Payne, Henry Neville. *The Siege of Constantinople; A Tragedy.* London: prtd. for Thos. Dring, 1675.

Peacham, Henry. *The Compleat Gentleman.* London: Frances Constable, 1622.

Pix, Mary. *The Conquest of Spain. A Tragedy.* London: prtd. for Richard Wellington, 1705.

The False Friend; or, The Fate of Disobedience. London: prtd. for Richard Basset, 1699.

Ibrahim the Thirteenth Emperor of the Turks. London: prtd. for John Harding and Richard Wilkin, 1696.

Pufendorf, Samuel. *An Introduction to the History of the Principal Kingdoms and States of Europe.* London: prtd. for M. Gilliflower and T. Newborough, 1690.

    Of the Law of Nature and Nations. Trans. Basil Kennet. 1660; 3rd. edn. London: prtd. for R. Sare, R. Bonwicke, T. Godwyn, etc., 1717.

Puttenham, Richard. *The Arte of English Poesie, Contrived into Three Bookes: the First of Poets and Poesie, the Second of Proportion, the Third of Ornament.* London: R. Field, 1589.

Rowe, Nicholas. *The Ambitious Step-Mother. A Tragedy.* 1700; 3rd. edn. London: prtd. by J. Darby for M. Wellington, sold by A. Bettersworth and F. Clay, 1720.

    The Biter. London: prtd. for J. T. and sold by T. Jauncey, 1720.

    The Royal Convert. In *The Dramatick Works of Nicholas Rowe.* London: prtd. by T. Jauncey, 1720.

    Tamerlane. A Tragedy. 1701; 5th. edn. London: prtd. for J. T., 1720.

Rowe, Nicholas, ed. *The Works of William Shakespeare.* 9 vols. London: J. Tonson, E. Curll, J. Pemberton, K. Sanger, 1714.

Rycaut, Paul. *The Present State of the Ottoman Empire.* 3rd. edn. London: prtd. for John Starkey and Henry Brome, 1670.

Rymer, Thomas. *Edgar, or The English Monarch.* London: prtd. for Richard Tonson, 1677.

Saunders, Charles. *Tamerlane the Great. A Tragedy.* London: prtd. for Richard Bentley and M. Magnes, 1681.

Sedley, Charles. *Bellamira; or the Mistress.* London: prtd. for L. C. and Timothy Goodwin, 1687.

Semedo, F. Alvarez. *The History of the Great and Renowned Monarchy of China.* London: prtd. by E. Tyles for John Crook, 1655.

Settle, Elkanah. *The Ambitious Slave; or, A Generous Revenge.* London: prtd. for A. Roper and E. Wilkinson, 1694.

    Cambyses, King of Persia. A Tragedy. London: William Cademan, 1671.

    The Conquest of China, by the Tartars. A Tragedy. London: prtd. by T. M. for William Cademan, 1676.

    Distress'd Innocence. London: prtd. by E.J. for Abel Roper, 1691.

    A Farther Defence of Dramatick Poetry. London: Eliz. Whitlock, 1698.

    The Heir of Morocco, with the Death of Gayland. 1682; London: prtd. for Thomas Chapman, 1694.

    Ibrahim the Illustrious Bassa. London: prtd. by T. M. for William Cademan, 1676.

Shadwell, Charles. *The Fair Quaker of Deal; or, The Humours of the Navy.* Vol. III. *The English Theatre.* 8 vols. London: prtd. for T. Lowndes, 1765.

    The Humours of the Army. London: prtd. by James Knapton, 1713.

Tate, Nahum. *Cuckold's Haven: or, An Alderman No Conjurer.* London: prtd. for J. H. to be sold by Edward Poole, 1685.

The Island Princess: Revived with Alterations. London: prtd for W. Canning, 1687.

Tavernier, Jean-Baptiste. *The Six Voyages by John Baptista Tavernier... through Turkey into Persia and the East Indies...* London: prtd. for R. L. and M. P., 1678.

Theobald, Lewis. *The Persian Princess; or, the Royal Villain. A Tragedy.* London: prtd. for Jonas Browne, 1717.

Theobald, Lewis, ed. *The Works of Shakespeare.* 7 vols. London: A. Betterworth, C. Hitch, J. Tonson, F. Clay, W. Feales, R. Wellington, 1733.

Trapp, Joseph. *Abra-mule.* 1708; London: Jacob Tonson, 1735.

Weston, John. *The Amazon Queen; or, The Amours of Thalestris to Alexander the Great.* London: prtd. for Hen. Herringman, 1667.

II. SECONDARY SOURCES

Adams, Percy G. *Travel Literature and the Evolution of the Novel.* Lexington: University Press of Kentucky, 1983.

Alssid, Michael W. "The Design of Dryden's *Aurung-Zebe.*" *Journal of English and Germanic Philology* 64 (1965): 45–69.

Anderson, Sonia P. *An English Consul in Smyrna: Paul Rycaut at Smyrna, 1667–1678.* Oxford: Clarendon Press, 1989.

Appleton, William A. *A Cycle of Cathay: The Chinese Vogue in England during the Seventeenth and Eighteenth Centuries.* New York: Columbia University Press, 1951.

Aravamudan, Srinivas. *Tropicopolitans: Colonialism and Agency, 1688–1804.* Durham and London: Duke University Press, 1999.

Armitage, David. "The Cromwellian Protectorate and the Languages of Empire." *Historical Journal* 35 (1992): 531–55.

"Literature and Empire" in *The Origins of Empire: British Overseas Enterprise to the Close of the Seventeenth Century.* Ed. Nicolas Canny. Oxford and New York: Oxford University Press, 1998. 98–123.

Armstrong, Isobel, ed. *New Feminist Discourses: Critical Essays on Theories and Texts.* London and New York: Routledge, 1992.

Axtell, James. *The Invasion Within: The Contest of Cultures in Colonial North America.* New York: Oxford University Press, 1985.

Ayres, Philip. *Classical Culture and the Idea of Rome in Eighteenth-Century England.* Cambridge: Cambridge University Press, 1997.

Backsheider, Paula R. *Spectacular Politics: Theatrical Power and Mass Culture in Early Modern England.* Baltimore and London: The Johns Hopkins University Press, 1993.

Ballaster, Ros. *Seductive Forms: Women's Amatory Fiction from 1684–1740; with Particular Reference to Aphra Behn, Delariviere Manley and Eliza Haywood.* Oxford: Clarendon Press, 1992.

Barash, Carol. "The Character of Difference: The Creole Woman as Cultural Mediator in Narratives about Jamaica." *Eighteenth Century Studies* 23:4 (1990): 407–28.

English Women's Poetry 1649–1714: Politics, Community and Linguistic Authority. Oxford: Clarendon Press, 1996.

Barbeau, Anne T. *The Intellectual Design of John Dryden's Plays.* New Haven and London: Yale University Press, 1970.

Barck, Oscar Theodore, and Hugh Talmadge Lefler. *Colonial America.* London: Macmillan, 1968.

Barker, Anthony J. *The African Link: British Attitudes to the Negro in the 17th and 18th Centuries.* London: Frank Cass, 1978.

Barker, Francis, *et al.*, eds. *Europe and Its Others.* 2 vols. Colchester: University of Essex Press, 1985.

Barker-Benfield, G. J. *The Culture of Sensibility: Sex and Society in Eighteenth Century Britain.* Chicago: University of Chicago Press, 1992.

Barthelemy, Anthony G. *Black Face, Maligned Race: The Representation of Blacks in English Drama from Shakespeare to Southerne.* Baton Rouge and London: Louisiana State University Press, 1987.

Belsey, Catherine. *The Subject of Tragedy: Identity and Difference in Renaissance Drama.* New York and London: Methuen, 1985.

Bernheimer, Richard. *Wild Men in the Middle Ages: A Study in Art, Sentiment and Demonology.* Cambridge: Harvard University Press, 1959.

Bhabha, Homi. *The Location of Culture.* London and New York: Routledge, 1994.

"Signs Taken for Wonders: Questions of Ambivalence and Authority Under a Tree Outside Delhi, May 1817." *Critical Inquiry* 12 (1985): 144–65.

Bhabha, Homi, ed. *Nations and Narration.* London and New York: Routledge, 1990.

Bhattacharya, Nandini. "Ethnopolitical Dynamics and the Language of Gendering in Dryden's *Aureng-Zebe.*" *Cultural Critique* 25 (Fall 1993): 153–76.

Black, Jeremy. *A System of Ambition? British Foreign Policy 1660–1793.* London and New York: Longman, 1991.

Black, Jeremy, and Phillip Woodfine, eds. *The British Navy and the Use of Naval Power in the Eighteenth Century.* Leicester: Leicester University Press, 1988.

Blackburn, Robin. *The Making of New World Slavery: From the Baroque to the Modern Period, 1492–1800.* London and New York: Verro, 1997.

Blunt, Wilfrid. *Black Sunrise: An Account of the Life and Times of Mulai Ismail, Emperor of Morocco, 1646–1727.* London: Methuen and Co., 1951.

Boebel, Dagney. "In the Carnival World of Adam's Garden: Roving and Rope in Behr's *Rover*" in Quinsey, *Broken Boundaries.* 54–70.

Boesky, Amy. *Founding Fictions: Utopias in Early Modern England.* Athens, GA: University of Georgia Press, 1996.

Boon, James A. *Other Tribes, Other Scribes: Symbolic Anthropology in the Comparative Study of Cultures, Histories, Religions and Texts.* Cambridge: Cambridge University Press, 1982.

Bowers, Toni. *The Politics of Motherhood: British Writing and Culture, 1680–1760*. Cambridge: Cambridge University Press, 1996.

Bracken, Harry. "Essence, Accident and Race." *Hermathena* 116 (1973): 81–96.

Brandon, Beck H. *From the Rising of the Sun: English Images of the Ottoman Empire to 1715*. New York: P. Lang, 1987.

Brant, Clare, and Diane Purkiss, eds. *Women, Texts and Histories, 1575–1760*. London and New York: Routledge, 1992.

Braverman, Richard. *Plots and Counterplots: Sexual Politics and the Body Politic in English Literature, 1660–1730*. Cambridge: Cambridge University Press, 1993.

Bredvold, Louis I. *The Intellectual Milieu of John Dryden*. Ann Arbor: University of Michigan Press, 1934.

Brewer, John. *The Sinews of Power: War, Money, and the English State, 1688–1783*. London: Century Hutchinson, 1988.

Brown, Kathleen. "Native Americans and Early Modern Concepts of Race" in *Empire and Others: British Encounters with Indigenous Peoples, 1660–1850*. Ed. Martin Daunton and Rick Halpern. Philadelphia: University of Pennsylvania Press, 1999. 79–100.

Brown, Laura. *Ends of Empire: Women and Ideology in Early Eighteenth-Century English Literature*. Ithaca and London: Cornell University Press, 1993.

    English Dramatic Form, 1660–1700: An Essay in Generic History. New Haven and London: Yale University Press, 1981.

    "The Romance of Empire: *Oroonoko* and the Trade in Slaves" in *The New Eighteenth Century: Theory, Politics, English Literature*. Ed. Felicity Nussbaum and Laura Brown. New York and London: Methuen, 1987. 41–61.

Brown, Paul. "'This thing of darkness I acknowledge mine.' *The Tempest* and the Discourse of Colonialism" in *Political Shakespeare: New Essays in Cultural Materialism*. Ed. Jonathan Dollimore and Alan Sinfield. Manchester: Manchester University Press, 1985. 48–71.

Burg, B. R. *Sodomy and the Pirate Tradition: English Sea Rovers in the Seventeenth Century Caribbean*. New York and London: New York University Press, 1984.

Burstein, Isaac. "The Moor in the Text: Metaphor, Emblem, and Silence" in *"Race," Writing and Difference*. Ed. Henry Louis Gates Jr. Chicago and London: University of Chicago Press, 1986. 117–38.

Calder, Angus. *Revolutionary Empire: The Rise of the English-Speaking Empires from the Fifteenth Century to the 1780s*. New York: E. P. Dutton, 1981.

Canfield, J. Douglas. *Nicholas Rowe and Christian Tragedy*. Gainsville, FL: University Presses of Florida, 1977.

    "Regulus and *Cleomenes* and 1688: From Royalism to Self-Reliance." *Eighteenth-Century Life* 12 (1988): 67–75.

    "Royalism's Last Dramatic Stand: English Political Tragedy, 1679–1689." *Studies in Philology* 82 (1985): 234–63.

Tricksters and Estates: On the Ideology of Restoration Comedy. Lexington, KY: University of Kentucky Press, 1997.

Chew, Samuel C. *The Crescent and the Rose: Islam and England During the Renaissance.* New York: Oxford University Press, 1937.

Clark, Constance. *Three Augustan Women Playwrights.* New York, Berne and Frankfurt: Peter Lang, 1986.

Clark, J. C. D. *English Society 1688–1832: Ideology, Social Structure and Political Practice during the Ancien Regime.* Cambridge: Cambridge University Press, 1985.

   Revolution and Rebellion: State and Society in England in the Seventeenth and Eighteenth Centuries. Cambridge: Cambridge University Press, 1986.

Clifford, James, and George E. Marcus, eds. *Writing Culture: The Poetics and Politics of Ethnography.* Berkeley: University of California Press, 1986.

Clissold, Stephen. *The Barbary Slaves.* London: Paul Elek, 1977.

Coles, Paul. *The Ottoman Impact on Europe.* London: Harcourt, Brace and World, 1969.

Colley, Linda. *Britons: Forging the Nation, 1707–1837.* New Haven and London: Yale University Press, 1992.

Cotton, Nancy. *Women Playwrights in England ca 1363–1750.* Lewisburg, PA: Bucknell University Press, 1980.

Coward, Rosalind. *Patriarchal Precedents: Sexuality and Social Relations.* London: Routledge and Kegan Paul Ltd., 1983.

Dabydeen, David, ed. *The Black Presence in English Literature.* Manchester: Manchester University Press, 1985.

D'Amico, Jack. *The Moor in English Renaissance Drama.* Tampa: University of South Florida Press, 1991.

Daniel, Norman. *Islam and the West.* Edinburgh: University of Edinburgh Press, 1958.

   Islam, Europe and Empire. Edinburgh: University of Edinburgh Press, 1966.

Davies, J. D. *Gentlemen and Tarpaulins: The Officers and Men of the Restoration Navy.* Oxford: Clarendon Press, 1992.

Davis, David Brion. *The Problem of Slavery in Western Culture.* 1966; Oxford: Oxford University Press, 1988.

Davis, J. C. *Utopia and the Ideal Society: A Study of English Utopian Writing 1516–1700.* Cambridge: Cambridge University Press, 1981.

Davis, Lennard G. "The Fact of Events and the Event of Facts: New World Explorers and the Early Novel." *Eighteenth-Century Studies* 32 (1991): 246–55.

Day, Robert Adams. "Aphra Behn and the Works of the Intellect" in *Fetter'd or Free? British Women Novelists 1670–1815.* Ed. Mary Anne Schofield and Cecilia Macheski. Athens: Ohio University Press, 1986.

Deane, Cecil Victor. *Dramatic Theory and the Rhymed Heroic Play.* London: Oxford University Press, 1931.

De Krey, Gary S. *A Fractured Society: The Politics of London in the First Age of Party.* Oxford: Clarendon Press, 1985.

Diamond, Elin. "*Gestus* and Signature in Aphra Benn's *The Rover.*" *English Literary History* 56 (1989): 519–41.

Dobrée, Bonamy. *Restoration Tragedy 1660–1720.* Oxford: Clarendon Press, 1929.

Dobson, Michael. *The Making of the National Poet: Shakespeare, Adaptation and Authorship 1660–1769.* Oxford: Clarendon Press, 1992.

Docherty, Thomas. *On Modern Authority: The Theory and Condition of Writing: 1500 to the Present Day.* Brighton and New York: The Harvester Press, 1987.

Dollimore, Jonathan, and Alan Sinfield, eds. *Political Shakespeare: New Essays in Cultural Materialism.* Manchester: Manchester University Press, 1985.

Donaldson, Ian. *The Rapes of Lucretia: A Myth and its Transformations.* Oxford: Clarendon Press, 1982.

DuBois, Page. *Centaurs and Amazons: Women and the Pre-History of the Great Chain of Being.* Ann Arbor: The University of Michigan Press, 1982.

Duffy, Maureen. *The Passionate Shepherdess: Aphra Behn 1640–89.* London: Jonathan Cape, 1977.

Dugaw, Dianne. *Warrior Women and Popular Balladry 1650–1850.* Cambridge: Cambridge University Press, 1989.

Elliot, J. H. *Imperial Spain 1496–1716.* London: Edward Arnold, 1963.
The Old World and the New 1492–1650. Cambridge: Cambridge University Press, 1970.

Ellison, Julie. "Cato's Tears." *English Literary History* 63:2 (Fall 1996): 571–601.

Erskine-Hill, Howard. *The Augustan Idea in English Literature.* London: Edward Arnold, 1983.

Fabian, Johannes. *Time and the Other: How Anthropology Makes its Object.* New York: Columbia University Press, 1962.

Fanon, Frantz. *Black Skins, White Masks.* Trans. Charles Lam Markmann. London and Sydney: Pluto Press, 1986.

Faussett, David. *Images of the Antipodes in the Eighteenth Century: a Study in Stereotyping.* Amsterdam: Rodopi, 1995.
Writing the New World: Imaginary Voyages and Utopias of the Great Southern Land. Syracuse: Syracuse University Press, 1993.

Ferguson, Margaret. "Whose Dominion, or News from the New World: Aphra Behn's Representation of Miscegenous Romance in *Oroonoko* and *The Widow Ranster*" in *The Production of English Renaissance Culture.* Ed. David Lee Miller, Sharon O'Dair and Harold Weber. Ithaca, NY: Cornell University Press, 1994.

Ferguson, Moira. *Subject to Others: British Women Writers and Colonial Slavery, 1670–1834.* New York and London: Routledge, 1992.

Fink, Zera S. *The Classical Republicans.* Evanston, IL: Northwestern University Press, 1946.

Foucault, Michel. *The Archaeology of Knowledge.* Trans. Alan Sheridan-Smith. New York: Random House, 1972.

 The Order of Things: An Archaeology of the Human Sciences. Trans. Alan Sheridan-Smith. New York: Random House, 1973.

Foxon, David. *Libertine Literature in England 1660–1745.* New York: University Books, 1965.

Franklin, W. *Discoverers, Explorers, Settlers: The Diligent Writers of Early America.* Chicago and London: University of Chicago Press, 1979.

Furber, Holden. *Rival Empires of Trade in the Orient, 1600–1800.* Minneapolis: University of Minnesota Press, 1976.

Gallagher, Catherine. "Who was that Masked Woman? The Prostitute and the Playwright in the Comedies of Aphra Behn." *Women's Studies* 17 (1988): 23–42.

Gardiner, Judith Kegan. "Aphra Behn: Sexuality and Self-Respect." *Women's Studies* 7.2 (1980): 67–78.

Gill, Pat. *Interpreting Ladies: Women, Wit and Morality in the Restoration Comedy of Manners.* Athens, GA, and London: University of Georgia Press, 1994.

Glacken, Clarence J. *Traces on the Rhodian Shore: Nature and Culture in Western Thought from Ancient Times to the End of the Eighteenth Century.* Berkeley and Los Angeles, CA: University of California Press, 1967.

Glass, Robert E. "The Image of the Sea Officer in English Literature, 1660–1714." *Albion* 26.4 (Winter 1994): 583–99.

Goreau, Angeline. *Reconstructing Aphra: A Social Biography of Aphra Behn.* New York: Dial Press, 1980.

Greenblatt, Stephen. *Learning to Curse: Essays in Early Modern Culture.* New York: Routledge, 1990.

 Marvellous Possessions: The Wonder of the New World. Chicago and Oxford: University of Chicago Press, 1991.

 Renaissance Self-Fashioning: From More to Shakespeare. Chicago and London: University of Chicago Press, 1980.

Grundy, Isobel, and Susan Wiseman, eds. *Women, Writing, History 1640–1740.* Athens, GA: University of Georgia Press, 1992.

Harris, Max. "Aztec Maidens in Satin Gowns: Alterity and Dialogue in Dryden's *The Indian Emperor* and Hogarth's *The Indian Emperor.*" *Restoration: Studies in English Literary Culture, 1660–1700* 15.2 (Fall 1991): 59–70.

Harris, Tim. *Politics Under the Later Stuarts: Party Conflict in a Divided Society 1660–1715.* London and New York: Longman, 1993.

 "What's New About the Restoration?" *Albion* 29.2 (Summer 1997): 187–222.

Harris, Tim, Seaward, Paul, and Mark Goldie, eds. *The Politics of Religion in Restoration England.* Oxford: Basil Blackwell, 1990.

Harth, Philip. *Contexts of Dryden's Thought.* Chicago: University of Chicago Press, 1968.

Helgerson, Richard. *Forms of Nationhood: The Elizabethan Writing of England.* Chicago and London: University of Chicago Press, 1992.

Hendricks, Margo and Patricia Parker, eds. *Women, "Race," and Writing in the Early Modern Period.* London and New York: Routledge, 1994.

Hill, Christopher. *The Century of Revolution 1603–1714.* Edinburgh: Thomas Nelson and Sons, 1961.

Hobby, Elaine. *Virtue of Necessity.* London: Virago, 1988.

Hodgen, Margaret T. *Early Anthropology in the Sixteenth and Seventeenth Centuries.* Philadelphia: University of Pennsylvania Press, 1964.

Holland, Peter. *The Ornament of Action: Text and Performance in Restoration Comedy.* Cambridge: Cambridge University Press, 1979.

Holmes, Geoffrey. *Augustan England: Professions, State and Society, 1680–1730.* London: George Allen and Unwin, 1982.

  The Making of a Great Power: Late Stuart and Early Georgian Britain 1660–1722. London and New York: Longman, 1993.

Hornstein, Sari. "Tangier, English Naval Power, and Exclusion" in *Restoration, Ideology, and Revolution: Proceedings of the Folger Institute Centre for the History of British Political Thought.* Vol. IV. Washington, DC: The Folger Institute, 1990. 327–84.

Howe, Elizabeth. *The First English Actresses: Women and Drama 1660–1700.* Cambridge: Cambridge University Press, 1992.

Hughes, Derek. *Dryden's Heroic Plays.* Lincoln, NE: Nebraska University Press, 1981.

  English Drama 1660–1700. Oxford: Clarendon Press, 1996.

Hulme, Peter. *Colonial Encounters: Europe and the Native Caribbean 1492–1797.* London and New York: Methuen, 1986.

Hume, Robert D. *The Development of English Drama in the Late Seventeenth Century.* Oxford: Clarendon Press, 1976.

  Dryden's Criticism. Ithaca, NY: Cornell University Press, 1970.

Hutton, Ronald. *Charles the Second King of England, Scotland and Ireland.* Oxford: Clarendon Press, 1989.

  The Restoration: A Political and Religious History of England and Wales, 1658–1667. Oxford: Clarendon Press, 1985.

Israel, Jonathan. "The Emerging Empire: The Continental Perspective, 1650–1713" in *The Oxford History of the British Empire,* vol. I, *The Origins of Empire: British Overseas Enterprise to the Close of the Seventeenth Century.* Ed. Nicholas Canny and Aline Low. Oxford and New York: Oxford University Press, 1998. 423–44.

JanMohamed, Abdul. "Humanism and Minority Literature: Towards a Definition of a Counter-Hegemonic Discourse." *Boundary* 2.13:1 (1984): 281–300.

Jed, Stephanie H. *Chaste Thinking: The Rape of Lucretia and the Birth of*

Humanism. Bloomington and Indianapolis: Indiana University Press, 1989.

Jennings, Francis. *The Invasion of America: Indians, Colonization and the Cant of Conquest.* Chapel Hill: University of North Carolina Press, 1975.

Jones, J. R. *Britain and the World 1649–1815.* Brighton: Harvester Press, 1980.

Jordan, Winthrop D. *White Over Black: American Attitudes Toward the Negro, 1550–1812.* Chapel Hill: University of North Carolina Press, 1968.

Kastan, David Scott. "*Nero* and the Politics of Nathaniel Lee." *Papers on Language and Literature* 13 (1977): 125–35.

Kaul, Suvir. "Reading Literary Symptoms: Colonial Pathologies and the *Oroonoko* Fictions of Behn, Southerne and Hawkesworth." *Eighteenth-Century Life* 18.3 (November 1994): 80–96.

Kidd, Colin. *British Identities Before Nationalism: Ethnicity and Nationhood in the Atlantic World, 1600–1800.* Cambridge: Cambridge University Press, 1999.

King, Bruce. *Dryden's Major Plays.* London: Oliver and Boyd, 1966.

Kirsch, Arthur C. *Dryden's Heroic Drama.* Princeton: Princeton University Press, 1965.

"The Importance of Dryden's *Aureng-Zebe.*" *English Literary History* 29 (1962): 160–74.

Klein, Lawrence. *Shaftesbury and the Culture of Politeness: Moral Discourse and Cultural Politics in Early Eighteenth-Century England.* Cambridge: Cambridge University Press, 1994.

Knapp, Jeffrey. *An Empire Nowhere: England, America and Literature from Utopia to* The Tempest. Berkeley, CA: University of California Press, 1992.

Knorr, Klaus E. *British Colonial Theories, 1550–1750.* Toronto: University of Toronto Press, 1944.

Kramer, David Bruce. *The Imperial Dryden: The Poetics of Appropriation in Seventeenth-Century England.* Athens, GA, and London: University of Georgia Press, 1994.

Kristeva, Julia. "Women's Time" in *The Kristeva Reader.* Ed. Toril Moi. Oxford: Basil Blackwell, rpt. (1987). 187–213.

Lach, Donald F. *Asia in the Making of Europe.* 3 vols. Chicago: University of Chicago Press, 1965–96.

Lamb, Jonathan, "Eye-witnessing in the South Seas." *The Eighteenth Century: Theory and Interpretation* 38 (1997): 201–12.

Levine, Joseph M. *The Battle of the Books: History and Literature in the Augustan Age.* Ithaca and London: Cornell University Press, 1991.

Lilley, Kate. "Blazing Worlds: Seventeenth Century Women's Utopian Writing" in Brant and Purkiss, *Women, Texts and Histories.* 102–33.

Loftis, John. *The Politics of Drama in Augustan England.* Oxford: Clarendon Press, 1963.

———. *The Spanish Plays of Neo-Classical England.* New Haven and London: Yale University Press, 1973.

Lowe, Lisa. *Critical Terrains: French and British Orientalisms.* Ithaca and London: Cornell University Press, 1991.

McCarthy, Justin. *The Ottoman Turks.* New York and London: Longman, 1997.

MacDougall, Hugh A. *Racial Myth in English History: Trojans, Teutons and Anglo-Saxons.* Montreal: Harvest House, 1982.

McFadden, George. *Dryden: The Public Writer, 1660–1685.* Princeton: Princeton University Press, 1978.

McHugh, Paul. "Constitutional Theory and Maori Claims" in *Waitangi: Maori and Pakeha Perspectives of the Treaty of Waitangi.* Ed. I. H. Kawharu. Auckland: Oxford University Press, 1989. 29–31.

McKeon, Michael. *The Origins of the English Novel, 1600–1740.* Baltimore: The Johns Hopkins University Press, 1987.

———. *Politics and Poetry in Restoration England: The Case of Dryden's "Annus Mirabilis."* Cambridge, MA: Harvard University Press, 1975.

MacLean, Gerald, ed. *Culture and Society in the Stuart Restoration: Literature, Drama, History.* Cambridge: Cambridge University Press, 1995.

Maguire, Nancy Klein. *Regicide and Restoration: English Tragicomedy, 1660–1671.* Cambridge: Cambridge University Press, 1992.

Maltby, William S. *The Black Legend in England: The Development of Anti-Spanish Sentiment, 1558–1660.* Durham, NC: Durham University Press, 1975.

Mani, Lata. "The Production of an Official Discourse in Sati in Early Nineteenth Century Bengal" in *Europe and its Others.* Ed. Francis Barker *et al.* 2 vols. Colchester: University of Essex Press, 1985. 107–27.

Markley, Robert. *Two-Edg'd Weapons: Style and Ideology in the Comedies of Etheredge, Wycherley and Congreve.* Oxford: Clarendon Press, 1988.

Marsden, Jean I. "Rape, Voyeurism and the Restoration Stage" in Quinsey, *Broken Boundaries.* 185–200.

Marshall, P. J., and Glyndwr Williams. *The Great Map of Mankind: British Perceptions of the World in the Age of Enlightenment.* London: J. Dent and Sons, 1982.

Matar, Nabil. *Islam in Britain, 1558–1685.* Cambridge: Cambridge University Press, 1998.

Maus, Katherine Eisaman. "Arcadia Lost: Politics and Revision in the Restoration *Tempest*." *Renaissance Drama* 13 (1982): 189–209.

Merrens, Rebecca. "Unmanned with Thy Words: Regendering Tragedy in Manley and Trotter" in Quinsey, *Broken Boundaries.* 31–53.

Miller, Christopher. *Blank Darkness.* Chicago and London: University of Chicago Press, 1985.

Miller, John. *Popery and Politics in England, 1660–1688.* Cambridge: Cambridge University Press, 1973.

Miner, Earl. "The Wild Man Through the Looking Glass" in *The Wild Man Within: An Image in Western Thought from the Renaissance to Romanticism.* Ed. E. Dudley and M. E. Novak. Pittsburgh: University of Pennsylvania Press, 1972. 87–114.

Montrose, Louis. "The Purpose of Playing: Reflections on a Shakespearian Anthropology." *Helios* 7 (1980): 51–74.

"Renaissance Literary Studies and the Subject of History." *English Literary Renaissance* 16.1 (1986): 5–12.

"The Work of Gender in the Discourse of Colonialism." *Representations* 33 (1991): 1–41.

Morgan, Fidelis. *The Female Wits: Women Playwrights of the Restoration.* London: Virago, 1981.

Morton, Richard. "'Roman Drops from British Eyes': Latin History on the Restoration Stage" in *The Stage in the Eighteenth Century.* Ed. J. D. Browning and Joseph Donohue. New York: Garland, 1981. 109–32.

Mullaney, Steven. *The Place of the Stage: License, Play and Power in Renaissance England.* Chicago: University of Chicago Press, 1988.

Murray, Barbara A. "The Butt of Otway's Political Moral in *The History and Fall of Caius Marius* (1680)." *Notes and Queries* 234 (1989): 48–50.

Nicol, Allardyce. *A History of English Drama, 1660–1900.* 6 vols. Cambridge: Cambridge University Press, 1931.

Nussbaum, Felicity. *The Brink of All We Hate: English Satires on Women 1660–1750.* Lexington: University Press of Kentucky, 1984.

Torrid Zones: Maternity, Sexuality and Empire in Eighteenth-Century English Narratives. Baltimore and London: The Johns Hopkins University Press, 1995.

Ogg, David. *England in the Reign of Charles II.* 2nd edn. Oxford: Clarendon Press, 1955.

Orgel, Stephen. "Shakespeare and the Cannibals" in *Cannibals, Witches and Divorce: Estranging the Renaissance.* Ed. Marjorie Garber. Baltimore and London: The Johns Hopkins University Press, 1987. 40–67.

Orkin, Martin. "Othello and the 'Plain Face' of Racism." *Shakespeare Quarterly* 2 (1987): 166–88.

Owen, Susan Jane. "Interpreting the Politics of Restoration Drama." *Seventeenth Century* 8 (1993): 67–97.

"'Partial tyrants' and 'Free-born People' in *Lucius Junius Brutus.*" *Studies in English Literature* 31 (1991): 463–82.

Pagden, Anthony. *European Encounters with the New World.* New Haven and London: Yale University Press, 1993.

The Fall of Natural Man: The American Indian and the Origins of Comparative Ethnography. Cambridge: Cambridge University Press, 1982.

Lords of All the World: Ideologies of Empire in Spain, Britain and France c. 1500–c. 1800. New Haven and London: Yale University Press, 1995.

Pais, Ettore. *Ancient Legends of Roman History.* 1905; trans. Mario Constanza, Freeport, NY: Books for Libraries Press, 1971.

Parfitt, George. "The Exotic in Restoration Drama" in *All Before Them, 1660–1780*. Ed. John McVeagh. London and Atlantic Highlands, NJ.: The Ashfield Press, 1990. 81–96.

Parker, Patricia. *Literary Fat Ladies: Rhetoric, Gender, Property*. London: Methuen, 1987.

Parry, Benita. "Problems in Current Theories of Colonial Discourse." *Oxford Literary Review* 9 (1987): 27–58.

Pateman, Carole. *The Sexual Contract*. Cambridge: Polity Press, 1988.

Pearson, Jaqueline. "Blacker than Hell Creates" in Quinsey, *Broken Boundaries*. 13–30.

   The Prostituted Muse: Images of Women and Women Dramatists 1642–1737. Hemel Hempstead: Harvester Wheatsheaf, 1988.

Pendlebury, B. J. *Dryden's Heroic Plays: A Study of the Origins*. London: Selwyn and Blount, 1923.

Perry, Ruth. *The Celebrated Mary Astell*. Chicago: University of Chicago Press, 1986.

   "Colonizing the Breast: Sexuality and Maternity in Eighteenth Century England." *Eighteenth Century Life* 16 (1992): 192–213.

Pincus, Steven C. A. *Protestantism and Patriotism: Ideologies and the Making of English Foreign Policy, 1650–1668*. Cambridge: Cambridge University Press, 1996.

Plasa, Cal, and Betty J. Ring, eds. *The Discourse of Slavery: Aphra Behn to Toni Morrison*. London and New York: Routledge, 1994.

Pocock, J. G. A. *The Ancient Constitution and the Feudal Law: A Study of English Historical Thought in the Seventeenth Century*. Cambridge: Cambridge University Press, 1957.

   The Machiavellian Moment: Florentine Political Thought and the Atlantic Republican Tradition. Princeton: Princeton University Press, 1975.

   Virtue, Commerce and History: Essays on Political Thought, Chiefly in the Eighteenth Century. Cambridge: Cambridge University Press, 1985.

Powell, Jocelyn. *Restoration Theatre Production*. London and Boston: Routledge and Kegan Paul, 1984.

Pratt, Mary-Louise. "Conventions of Representation: Where Discourse and Ideology Meet" in *The Taming of the Text*. Ed. W. van Peer. New York and London: Routledge, 1988. 14–34.

   Imperial Eyes: Travel Writing and Transculturation. London and New York: Routledge, 1992.

   "Scratches on the Face of the Country: or, What Mr. Barrow Saw in the Hand of the Bushman." *Critical Inquiry* 12 (1985): 119–43.

Price, Curtis A. *Henry Purcell and the London Stage*. Cambridge: Cambridge University Press, 1984.

Pye, Christopher. "The Sovereign, the Theatre and the Kingdome of Darknesse: Hobbes and the Spectacle of Power." *Representations* 8 (1984): 85–106.

Quinsey, Katherine M., ed. *Broken Boundaries: Women and Feminism in Restoration Drama.* Lexington, KY: University of Kentucky Press, 1996.

Quint, David. *Epic and Empire: Politics and Generic Form from Virgil to Milton.* Princeton: Princeton University Press, 1993.

Rabb, Melinda Alliker. "Angry Beauties: (Wo)Manley Satire and the Stage" in *Cutting Edges: Postmodern Critical Essays on Eighteenth-Century Satire.* Ed. James E. Gill. Knoxville: University of Tennessee Press, 1995. 127–58.

Ray, Ajit Kumar. *Widows are not for Burning.* New Delhi: ABC Publishing House, 1985.

Rediker, Marcus. "Libertalia: The Pirates' Utopia" in *Pirates: Terror on the High Seas from the Caribbean to the South China Sea.* Atlanta, GA: Turner Publishing Inc., 1996. 124–39.

Rich, A. Julia. "Heroic Tragedy in Southerne's *Oroonoko* (1695): An Approach to a Splitplot Tragicomedy." *Philological Quarterly* 62 (1983): 187–200.

Rich, E. E., and C. H. Wilson, eds. *The Cambridge Economic History of Europe.* 7 vols. Cambridge: Cambridge University Press, 1967.

Ricter, David K. *The Ordeal of the Long-House: The Peoples of the Iroquois League in the Era of European Colonization.* Chapel Hill: University of North Carolina Press, 1992.

Roach, Joseph. *Cities of the Dead: Circum-Atlantic Performance.* New York: Columbia University Press, 1996.

Robbins, Caroline. *The Eighteenth-Century Commonwealths Man.* Cambridge, MA: Harvard University Press, 1959.

Rosenthal, Laura J. "Reading Masks: The Actress and the Spectatrix in Restoration Shakespear" in Quinsey, *Broken Boundaries.* 201–18.

Rothstein, Eric. *Restoration Tragedy: Form and the Process of Change.* Madison: University of Wisconsin Press, 1967.

Ryan, Michael. "Assimilating New Worlds in the Sixteenth and Seventeenth Centuries." *Comparative Studies in Society and History* 23.4 (1981): 519–38.

Said, Edward. *Culture and Imperialism.* London: Vintage, 1994.

    Orientalism. London: Routedge and Kegan Paul, 1979.

Savory, Roger. *Iran under the Safavids.* Cambridge: Cambridge University Press, 1980.

Schochet, Gordon J. *Patriarchalism in Political Thought: The Authoritarian Family and Political Speculation and Attitudes, Especially in Seventeenth Century England.* Oxford: Basil Blackwell, 1975.

Schwoerer, Lois G. *"No Standing Armies!": The Anti-Army Ideology in Seventeenth-Century England.* Baltimore: The Johns Hopkins University Press, 1974.

Scott, Jonathan. *Algernon Sidney and the Restoration Crisis, 1677–1683.* Cambridge: Cambridge University Press, 1991.

    "England's Troubles: Exhuming the Popish Plot" in *The Politics of*

Religion in Restoration England. Ed. Tim Haris, Paul Seaward and Mark Goldie. Oxford: Basil Blackwell, 1990. 107–32.

Scouten, Arthur H., ed. *Restoration and Eighteenth Century Drama.* New York: St. Martin's Press, 1980.

Seaward, Paul. *The Restoration, 1660–1688.* New York: St. Martin's Press, 1991.

Sekora, John. *Luxury: The Concept in Western Thought, Eden to Smollett.* Baltimore and London: The Johns Hopkins University Press, 1977.

Setten, Kenneth M. *Venice, Austria and the Turks in the Seventeenth Century.* Philadelphia: The American Philosophical Society, 1993.

Sheehan, Bernard W. *Savagism and Civility: Indians and Englishmen in Colonial Virginia.* Cambridge: Cambridge University Press, 1980.

Shepherd, Simon. *Amazons and Warrior Women: Varieties of Feminism in Seventeenth-Century Drama.* Brighton: Harvester Press, 1981.

Smith, Byron Porter. *Islam in English Literature.* Ed. S. B. Bushrui and Anahid Melikian. Foreword Omar A. Farrukh. 1937; 2nd. edn. Delmar, NY: Caravan Books, 1977.

Smith, Hilda L. *Reason's Disciples: Seventeenth Century English Feminists.* Urbana: University of Illinois Press, 1982.

Southern, Richard. *Changeable Scenery: Its Origin and Development in the British Theatre.* London: Faber and Faber, 1952.

Spencer, Jane. *The Rise of the Woman Novelist: From Aphra Behn to Jane Austien.* Oxford and New York: Basil Blackwell, 1986.

Spencer, William. *Algiers in the Age of the Corsairs.* Norman, OK: University of Oklahoma Press, 1976.

Spivak, Gayatri Chakravorty. *In Other Worlds: Essays in Cultural Politics.* New York and London: Methuen, 1987.

Spurr, John. *The Restoration Church of England, 1646–1689.* New Haven and London: Yale University Press, 1991.

Stallybrass, Peter. "Patriarchal Territories: The Body Enclosed" in *Rewriting the Renaissance.* Ed. Margaret Quilligan and Nancy J. Vickers. Chicago: University of Chicago Press, 1986. 123–42.

Stallybrass, Peter, and Allon White. *The Politics and Poetics of Transgression.* London: Methuen, 1986.

Staves, Susan. *Players' Sceptres: Fictions of Authority in the Restoration.* Lincoln, NE: University of Nebraska Press, 1979.

Stocking, George W. *Victorian Anthropology.* New York: Free Press, 1987.

Stone, Lawrence. *The Family, Sex and Marriage in England, 1500–1800.* Abridged edn. 1979: New York: Harper and Row, 1978.

Strong, Roy, and Stephen Orgel. *Inigo Jones: The Theatre of the Stuart Court.* 2 vols. London and Berkeley, CA: Sotheby Parke Bernet and University of California Press, 1973.

Summers, Montague. *The Playhouse of Pepys.* London: Kegan Paul, 1935.

Svilpis, J. E. "Orientalism, Kinship, and Will in Restoration Drama." *Studies on Voltaire and the Eighteenth Century* 303 (1992): 435–39.

Sypher, Wylie. *Guinea's Captive Kings: British Anti-Slavery Literature of the XVIII Century*. Chapel Hill: University of North Carolina Press, 1942.

Tennenhouse, Leonard. *Power on Display*. London: Methuen, 1986.

Thale, M. "The Framework of 'An Essay of Dramatick Poesie.'" *Papers in Language and Literature* 12.2 (1976): 363–69.

Thiong'o, Ngugi War. *Decolonizing the Mind*. London: Methuen, 1985.

Thomas, Nicholas. *Colonialism's Cultures: Anthropology, Travel, Government*. Cambridge: Polity Press, 1994.

Thompson, James. "Dryden's *Conquest of Granada* and the Dutch Wars." *The Eighteenth Century: Theory and Interpretation* 31.3 (1990): 211–26.

Thompson, Roger. *Unfit for Modest Ears. A Study of Pornographic, Obscene and Bawdy Works Written or Published in England in the Second Half of the Seventeenth Century*. Totowa, NJ: Rowman and Littlefield, 1979.

Todd, Janet. *The Sign of Angellica: Women, Writing and Fiction, 1660–1800*. London: Virago, 1989.

Todd, Janet, ed. *Aphra Behn Studies*. Cambridge: Cambridge University Press, 1996.

Todorov, Tzvetan. *The Conquest of America*. Trans. Richard Howard. New York: Harper and Row, 1984.

Treave, Geoffrey. *The Making of Modern Europe 1648–1780*. London and New York: Methuen, 1985.

Van Lennep, William, ed. *The London Stage 1660–1800*. 5 vols. Carbondale, IL: Southern Illinois University Press, 1965.

Vermillion, Mary. "Buried Heroism: Critiques of Female Authorship in Southerne's Adaptation of Behn's *Oroonoko*." *Restoration: Studies in English Literary Culture, 1660–1700* 16.1 (1992): 28–37.

Visser, Colin. "John Dryden's *Amboyna* at Lincoln's Inn Field, 1673." *Restoration and Eighteenth Century Theatre Research* 15 (1976): 1–11.

Waith, Eugene M. *The Herculean Hero in Marlowe, Chapman, Shakespeare and Dryden*. London: Chatto and Windus, 1962.

   Ideas of Greatness: Heroic Drama in England. London: Routledge and Kegan Paul, 1971.

Walvin, James. *Fruits of Empire: Exotic Produce and British Taste 1660–1800*. London: Macmillan, 1997.

Weber, Harold. *The Restoration Rake-Hero: Transformations in Sexual Understanding in Seventeenth-Century England*. Madison, WI: University of Wisconson Press, 1986.

Webster, Graham. *Boudica: the British Revolt against Rome, AD 60*. London: B. T. Batsford, 1978.

Wechselblatt, Martin. "Gender and Race in Yarico's Epistles to Inkle: Voicing the Feminine/Slave." *Studies in Eighteenth-Century Culture* 19 (1989): 197–223.

Weinbrot, Howard D. *Britannia's Issue: the Rise of British Literature from Dryden to Ossian*. Cambridge: Cambridge University Press, 1993.

Works Cited

Wellek, Rene. *The Rise of English Literary History*. 1944; New York: McGraw-Hill Book Co., 1960.

Wilcox, John. *The Relation of Molière to Restoration Comedy*. New York: Columbia University Press, 1938.

Williams, Robert A. *The American Indian in Western Legal Thought: The Discourses of Conquest*. New York and Oxford: Oxford University Press, 1990.

Winn, James A. *John Dryden and his World*. New Haven and London: Yale University Press, 1987.

Wiseman, Sue. "History Digested: Opera and Colonialism in the 1650s" in *Literature and the Civil War*. Ed. Thomas Healy and Jonathan Sawday. Cambridge: Cambridge University Press, 1990. 189–204.

Wolf, Eric R. *Europe and the People Without History*. Berkeley and Los Angeles, CA: University of California Press, 1982.

Zimbardo, Rose A. *A Mirror to Nature: Transformations in Drama and Aesthetics 1660–1732*. Lexington, KY: University Press of Kentucky, 1986.

Zwicker, Steven N. *Lines of Authority: Politics and English Literary Culture, 1649–1689*. Ithaca and London: Cornell University Press, 1993.

Index

345